h.com

ld Wide Web site for
r direct source to dozens

find out about supple-
and student resources.
ny of our authors and pre-
ng new technologies.

ns®

Statistics for Evidence-Based Practice and Evaluation

Allen Rubin

University of Texas at Austin

THOMSON
™
BROOKS/COLE

Australia • Brazil • Canada • Mexico • Singapore • Spain • United Kingdom • United States

THOMSON

TM

BROOKS/COLE

Statistics for Evidence-Based Practice and Evaluation
Allen Rubin

Executive Editor: Lisa Gebo
Assistant Editor: Alma Dea Michelena
Editorial Assistant: Sheila Walsh
Technology Project Manager: Inna Fedoseyeva
Executive Marketing Manager: Caroline Concilla
Marketing Assistant: Rebecca Weisman
Senior Marketing Communications Manager: Tami Strang
Project Manager, Editorial Production: Christine Sosa
Creative Director: Rob Hugel
Art Director: Vernon Boes
Print Buyer: Barbara Britton

Permissions Editor: Kiely Sisk
Production Service: Matrix Productions Inc./Interactive
    Composition Corporation
Copy Editor: Janet Tilden
Illustrator: Interactive Composition Corporation
Cover Designer: Roger Knox
Cover Image: © Joseph Sohm; ChromoSohm Inc./CORBIS
Cover Printer: Thomson West
Compositor: Interactive Composition Corporation
Printer: Thomson West

Printed in the United States of America
1 2 3 4 5 6 7 09 08 07 06 05

ExamView® and ExamView Pro® are registered trademarks
of FSCreations, Inc. Windows is a registered trademark of
the Microsoft Corporation used herein under license.
Macintosh and Power Macintosh are registered trademarks
of Apple Computer, Inc. Used herein under license.

Library of Congress Control Number: 2005932839

ISBN: 0-495-00583-5

Thomson Higher Education
10 Davis Drive
Belmont, CA 94002-3098
USA

For more information about our products, contact us at:
Thomson Learning Academic Resource Center
1-800-423-0563

For permission to use material from this text or product,
submit a request online at **http://www.thomsonrights.com.**
Any additional questions about permissions can be
submitted by e-mail to **thomsonrights@thomson.com.**

Dedication

To evidence-based colleagues and students whose
compassion spurs them to study, utilize or teach
a challenging topic so that we can improve our
effectiveness in helping people in distress

Contents

Preface

This book aims to introduce statistics to undergraduate and graduate students in the helping professions in a way that demonstrates the value of understanding and utilizing statistics as an inescapable part of evidence-based practice. It also aims to explain the conceptual basis and applications of key statistical ideas and procedures so that readers can utilize statistics appropriately in their practice.

How the readers of this book utilize statistics will vary, depending on the way their careers unfold. Most will find that what they learn in this book will help them better understand the findings of research and evaluation reports and thus be better prepared to critically appraise the evidence in those reports as a potential guide for their practice. Some—including current practitioners—will find that this book not only helps them as critical consumers of research and evaluation, but also as informed participants or collaborators in research and evaluation studies. For example, they may be evaluating a program they are administering and seek consultation from a statistician. This book will help them better communicate with their consultant and comprehend the basis for the advice they receive, as well as the meanings and implications of the eventual findings of the evaluation.

Other careers will unfold in ways that lead readers to apply some of the statistical procedures covered in this book independently in their own research and evaluation efforts. For example, some will use single-case designs to evaluate their own practice, and this book will help them analyze and interpret the data they collect. Others will find that what they learn in this book will enable them—without the aid of a consultant—to analyze and interpret the data they collect in some group design evaluations or surveys of community needs or consumer satisfaction. Still others will be inspired to go beyond the introductory level and learn more about statistics by reading more advanced texts,

taking advanced courses, or perhaps pursuing a Ph.D. and becoming career researchers. They may find in studying the more advanced material that the emphasis is on the mathematics and calculations involved in the procedures rather than on the meaning and applicability of those procedures or when to use one procedure versus another. Having read this book, however, they may be prepared to study the advanced material without being puzzled about such things.

As you might surmise, writing an introductory statistics text that will achieve the above aims can be quite a challenge. The hardest dilemma is one faced by many statistics instructors. On the one hand, there is the urge to avoid formulas and calculations and to focus exclusively on meanings and applications, so as not to lose those students who have difficulty with the more mathematical material. This urge also stems from the recognition that most students will at best be consumers of research, not producers of it, and the recognition that computers can perform all the calculations for us. On the other hand, instructors recognize that examining some formulas and calculations can help students better comprehend the meanings and applications of various statistics, and that examining such material may be advisable even if students never go beyond the role of research consumers in their future practice. Consequently, instructors need to incorporate the formulas and calculations but to do so in a way that will not intimidate students who have trouble with math. This book attempts to achieve that objective in two ways. First, it separates most of the more mathematical material from the narrative, putting it into boxes, tables, and figures. Second, the narrative is written in a style that is geared to students who could get overwhelmed by the mathematical material. I suspect that there is no perfect solution to this dilemma, and instructors may vary in the extent to which they'd like to expose their students to formulas and calculations. In using this book, therefore, some instructors might encourage all students to master the formulas and calculations while others might encourage them to engage that material only as long as it does not overwhelm them.

A related dilemma involves computer applications. I see this as a two-pronged dilemma. One prong is that some instructors whose prime objective is teaching students to be critical consumers of research, not producers of it, may not want to involve students in utilizing computer software to analyze data. The other prong is recognizing that a variety of software packages are available for data analysis and the one I focus on in this book may not be the one that some students will have access to in their schools or that some instructors use in their courses. Because SPSS seems to be the most widely used statistical software package, I chose to cover it in this text. But in light of the considerations mentioned above, I've separated almost all of the SPSS material from the text narrative and put it in an appendix that appears at the end of this book. Appendix G provides a guide to the basics of using SPSS for most of the statistics covered in this book, together with SPSS exercises for each chapter. The SPSS procedures and exercises in that appendix are cross-referenced to the chapters that discuss the corresponding statistical concepts. That way, instructors can decide whether or not to assign the appendix on SPSS without having that decision interfere with the flow or clarity of the narrative.

Another dilemma in teaching statistics involves making decisions about the type and variety of illustrations to use. Some instructors like to use different practice applications for different statistical procedures. For example, they might discuss evaluating a clinical intervention in a small agency to illustrate the use of a *t*-Test and evaluating a national social policy to illustrate the use of regression analysis. Other instructors might prefer showing how the different procedures can be applied across different sorts of studies within the same practice setting. For example, they might show how the same evaluation in the same setting might use a *t*-Test, ANOVA, chi-square, or regression analysis depending upon the number of variables and their operational definitions, how many groups are being compared, and so on.

This book uses both approaches. It brings many different types of practice illustrations into the narrative and the exercises at the end of each chapter. At the same time, in most chapters it applies a simulated data set that I've concocted for an evaluation in an imaginary residential treatment center. Some instructors understandably might prefer using real data collected from a real study. The downside to that approach, however, is that such real data sets can overwhelm students who are new to this material and that those data sets rarely produce findings that consistently and clearly illustrate issues and nuances in the various statistical concepts we are trying to teach. For example, the simulated data set I've devised is practice-relevant and illustrates things like how the mean can be influenced by extreme values, the importance of assessing dispersion, how different statistical procedures can be used in the same evaluation depending upon decisions made in the evaluation design, and so on.

So as not to overwhelm students, the data set contains only 14 variables. Also, I've limited the sample size to 50 cases—for three reasons. One is so that students can manually enter the data easily into a SPSS data file (or a data file for alternative statistical software that instructors might assign). A second reason is so that students can see what the entire raw data set looks like. A third reason is to keep it at a size that permits some manual calculations. For example, the set includes an experimental group and a control group of 25 cases each. By juxtaposing a list of 25 values for a particular variable for each group, as I've done in some chapters, students can manually calculate descriptive statistics such as means, medians, modes, frequency distributions and so forth and visualize how the two distributions vary and the implications of those differences. If instructors would prefer using a data set with more than 50 cases, they can instruct students to copy and paste the data for the 50 cases as many times as needed to reach the sample size they desire, or they can ask students to download from our Book Companion Website at <http://humanservices.wadsworth.com/rubin_statistics> a data set of 500 cases in which I've already done the cutting and pasting. That website, described below, also makes accessible for downloading data from the National Opinion Research Center's General Social Survey, thus offering students a variety of data gathered from 1000 respondents around the United States in

1980 and 1990. Instructors also may want to assign students to examine the following additional features found on that website:

- Frequently Asked Questions About Statistics
- Assessing Clinical Significance Statistically

ORGANIZATION

The first part of this book provides an introductory chapter and a chapter on preparing data for analysis. Chapter 1 discusses the value of studying statistics and their use in evidence-based practice. Then it reviews levels of measurement, because references to the different levels pervade the text. Chapter 1 also alerts readers to the first two appendices of the text, which they may want to review before proceeding to the next chapter or whenever they encounter research concepts or basic math operations they have forgotten or never learned. Appendix A covers basic research methods terms that are necessary to understand when studying statistics. Appendix B covers some math basics that are most pertinent to the material in this text and which, based on my experience, students have the most difficulty with—such as how to calculate a percentage, what happens to the minus sign when you square a negative number, and so on.

Chapter 2 covers preparing data for analysis, with a focus on coding and data entry and cleaning. After that, in Part 2, the next six chapters cover the reduction, presentation, and analysis of data for descriptive purposes. The remaining 10 chapters, in Part 3, deal with inferential data analysis, beginning with three chapters (9 to 11) that introduce overarching inferential concepts such as probability, sampling error, theoretical sampling distributions, the null hypothesis, Type I and Type II errors, and so on. Chapters 12 through 16 then focus on different inferential statistical procedures, such as *t*-Tests, ANOVA, chi-square, and correlation, with an emphasis at the bivariate level. Some multivariate material also is covered from the standpoint of understanding how and when to utilize and apply it in connection with ANOVA, without getting into the formulas and calculations. Chapter 16 then returns to some overarching inferential concepts pertaining to interpreting the strength and substantive significance of relationships assessed across the gamut of significance tests. Chapter 17 is the longest and most challenging chapter in this text in that it moves from testing for significance to the use of bivariate and multiple regression for the purpose of prediction. I believe this chapter handles the multivariate material in a manner that students can understand and use (by focusing on meanings and applications and minimizing formulas and calculations). Some instructors may opt to assign this entire chapter. Others might opt to assign only the bivariate regression section.

The final chapter of the text applies material found throughout many of the earlier chapters to the analysis of data in single-system evaluations. In addition, it will introduce some concepts and procedures that are unique to that form of evaluation.

Seven appendices follow. The first two review basic research terminology and math operations, as discussed above. The next, Appendix C, lists and defines some basic statistical symbols that appear in this text and commonly appear in research and evaluation reports. Readers can refer to this appendix whenever they encounter such symbols and don't recall what they mean.

Appendix D offers a conceptually oriented glimpse into several prominent forms of multivariate analysis that weren't covered earlier in the text, but which are being used and reported more and more these days in published studies that evidence-based practitioners should read and understand. It does so without delving into their formulas and calculations, but with a focus on understanding the meaning and practical applications of such findings that others are reporting.

Appendix E provides an overview of some nonparametric statistics that were not covered in the main part of this text and when to use each. Appendix F provides the codebook and data set for the imaginary study that I mentioned above and which I refer to in most of the chapters of this text. It also can be used in the SPSS exercises that follow in Appendix G, which covers instructions for using SPSS. As I mentioned earlier, the SPSS procedures and exercises in Appendix G are cross-referenced to the chapters that discuss the corresponding statistical concepts.

Each chapter is followed by a summary list of the main points covered in that chapter and some review questions and exercises that do not involve SPSS and are highly applicable to evidence-based practice.

[The answers to most of those review questions (excluding several in essay format) can be found at the back of the book in a section called Answers to Selected Review Questions. Preceding that section is a Glossary that defines each term introduced in bold font throughout the text.] Also at the end of each chapter are InfoTrac exercises. These exercises involve published research articles that illustrate key concepts. Readers can retrieve the articles electronically from the InfoTrac College Edition website.

I hope this text will be of value to instructors and students at the undergraduate and graduate levels, either as the sole text in statistics courses or as a companion text with a research methods text in research methods courses. I also hope practitioners will be helped by it as they try to understand the statistical findings in studies they read to guide their practice or as they engage in practice evaluation efforts that are a necessary part of evidence-based practice and increasingly are required by funding sources. I'd like to hear from readers as to what they like about this book as well as suggestions they might have for improving it. Please write to me in care of Thomson Brooks/Cole, 60 Garden Court, Suite 205, Monterey, CA 93940, or e-mail me at arubin@mail.utexas.edu.

ACKNOWLEDGMENTS

Many people have made this book possible, including the students who have taken my research and statistics courses over so many years and have asked questions that helped me improve the way I teach and write about statistics. Three exceptional doctoral students at the University of Texas at Austin deserve special recognition for their assistance in preparing the manuscript and suggesting improvements: Kelly Gober, Danielle Parrish, and Stephanie Rivaux.

Very special thanks go to my colleagues who reviewed preliminary rough drafts of selected chapters and suggested significant improvements for the revised manuscript:

Brent Benda, University of Arkansas, Little Rock

Gary Koeske, University of Pittsburgh

Safiya Omari, Jackson State University

Ellen Whipple, Michigan State University

Adele Crudden, Mississippi State University

Paul R. Raffoul, University of Houston

Evaon Won-Kim, California State University, Hayward

Virginia Rondero Hernandez, California State University, Fresno

David B. Miller, Case Western Reserve University

Lisa Gebo, Executive Editor at Thomson Brooks/Cole, Thomson Higher Education's imprint for social work, also deserves special acknowledgment for being so helpful throughout the entire process, from urging me to write this text through its publication. I also appreciate the efforts of her colleagues, Sheila Walsh, Editorial Assistant, and Christine Sosa, Production Project Manager.

Allen Rubin

Introduction and Data Management

The first two chapters of this text introduce you to the value of studying statistics and to the basics of managing data. Chapter 1 emphasizes the importance of understanding statistics as part of evidence-based practice and then reviews some basic research concepts that influence our choice of statistical procedures. Chapter 2 examines how we prepare data for statistical analysis.

Why Study Statistics?

INTRODUCTION

Why must students who are studying to become clinical or administrative practitioners take a course in statistics? What does *that* subject have to do with becoming more skillful in helping people? Such questions may be on your mind as you begin reading this book. Moreover, your skepticism about the relevance of statistics to your professional practice might be coupled with a sense of dread about studying a topic that many students experience as boring and intimidating. Many feel they don't have the aptitude to handle this math-laden subject (Gustavsson & MacEachron, 2001; Royse, 2000; Irwin, 1995). Many believe that statistics is something people manipulate to deceive others, having heard the famous quote attributed to Benjamin Disraeli: "There are three kinds of lies: lies, damned lies, and statistics." Let's begin this book, then, by examining how learning about statistics is relevant to practice and how it can help you to avoid being misled.

STATISTICS IN EVIDENCE-BASED PRACTICE

The most important reason to learn about statistics is that it can make you more effective in helping people. Helping people means providing services or advocating policies that effectively address what people need. But various studies have shown that while some interventions are effective, many are not. Simply earning your professional degree will not assure that your efforts to help people will be effective. Some interventions employed by helping professionals, in fact, have been found to be harmful (Rubin & Babbie, 2005).

Recognition of this unfortunate situation led to the emergence of the **evidence-based practice**[*] movement. Today, although many helping professionals continue to employ some interventions that may be ineffective, various studies are supplying evidence supporting the effectiveness of various other interventions. Among these evidence-based interventions are the following:

- psychoeducational and support group interventions for family caregivers of family members with debilitating mental or physical disorders;

- cognitive and interpersonal therapies for depression;

- cognitive-behavioral exposure therapies for victims of trauma or for individuals with phobias or anxiety disorders;

- emotion-focused marital therapy; . . .

- assertive community treatment for chronic mental illnesses;

- the job-finding club approach to unemployment;

- the community reinforcement approach to reducing alcoholism and substance abuse;

- the teaching-family model for treating troubled adolescents;

- multisystemic therapy for juvenile delinquency, among others.

(Rubin & Babbie, 2005, p. 6)

According to the National Association of Social Workers Code of Ethics (NASW, 1999), social workers will not be *ethical* unless they keep current with and critically appraise practice-related studies and base their practice on evidence-based knowledge. The Code states, "Social workers should monitor and evaluate policies, the implementation of programs, and practice interventions." (sec. 5.02) To do so, they will need to understand basic statistics. The same applies to other practitioners in the helping professions.

Suppose your practice focuses on treating victims of domestic violence or sexual abuse. Your colleague recently underwent some expensive training in a new therapy that is being touted as a "miracle breakthrough" in the treatment of trauma symptoms for those victims. She is convinced that the new intervention really is every bit as effective as its proponents claim, and she tries to convince you to get the training so you can emphasize it in your practice.

Hearing the dramatic claims of a new "miracle" therapy might make you feel both hopeful and skeptical. On the one hand, you want to believe these claims, yet on the other hand they may sound too good to be true. You ask your colleague about the evidence supporting these claims, and she cites a study that found that after only one treatment session with the new therapy, clients experienced on

---

[*]Words in boldface are defined in the Glossary at the end of the book.

average a one-fifth (20%) reduction in distress connected to their memories of the trauma.

Had you taken a research course, you'd probably have quite a few questions about the validity of the research design and the possibility of biased measurement in the two studies. Having read this book, you'd also have questions about the statistics your colleague cited.

At first, the one-fifth reduction in symptoms after only one treatment session might seem very impressive. But upon inquiring about those statistics, suppose you found that out of the five clients in the study, the entire decrease was attributed to only one client. That client's decrease in symptoms accounted for a 20% drop in the overall number of symptoms for the entire sample, even though none of the other four clients had any improvement in their symptoms whatsoever. How could this happen, you may wonder. To keep the math simple, suppose all five clients started out with 2 symptoms. Thus, multiplying 2 times 5, there were a total of 10 symptoms before treatment. A reduction of two symptoms in the only client who improved brought the total down to 8 after treatment. Thus, a reduction of 2 symptoms is a one-fifth (20%) decrease from the 10 before-treatment symptoms. If your familiarity with statistics causes you to inquire about the above figures, you can avoid being misled. You would be less impressed with the one-fifth reduction after finding out that only one client improved and the other four did not improve at all.

Understanding statistics, you might also wonder whether the symptom reduction in the one client could have occurred by chance alone. Maybe clients like that one have frequent fluctuations in their distress levels without treatment, and had the study assessed similar clients who did not receive the new "miracle" treatment it would have found similar changes in some of the untreated clients. What you'll learn in this text will help you ask these questions and keep you from being misled by the answers you receive.

Suppose your colleague cites another study. This one found that one-third (33%) of the clients who received only one treatment session with the new therapy no longer were diagnosed with posttraumatic stress disorder (PTSD), as compared with none of the clients who received one session of routine treatment. Inquiring about these statistics, you learn that only six clients participated in the study: 3 who received the new therapy and 3 who received the routine treatment. Thus, the 33% figure is based on only one client's recovery from PTSD. If the study assigned clients randomly—such as by a coin toss—to the new therapy or the routine treatment, then the difference in recovery rates between the two groups very easily could have more to do with a coin coming up heads or tails than with the effectiveness of the new therapy. In other words, the one client who recovered could just as easily have been assigned to the routine treatment, and that would have reversed the study's results! Again, what you learn in this text will help you ask the right questions and prevent you from being misled by the misuse of statistics.

The above two examples are more relevant to students interested in clinical practice than in other levels of practice, such as in administration and planning or in community organization or social action regarding social policy. Here is a policy example. Suppose you are concerned about the impact that a proposed cut in the federal income tax is going to have on funding for social welfare programs. You may be concerned for either or both of two reasons: (1) you may want to campaign against the tax cuts in order to protect funding for social welfare; or (2) you simply may be wondering whom to vote for.

Let's suppose further that the main argument being expressed by proponents of the tax cut is that the average American taxpayer will save $1000 in taxes each year. We'll assume they based that statement on a calculation of the **arithmetic mean**. The mean is *the sum of all values divided by the number of values being summed*. To keep the math simple, let's further assume that there are only 10 taxpayers in the economy and that each taxpayer will save the amount indicated in the list below. To calculate the mean of that list (as in any list of numbers), we simply add up all the numbers and then divide by the number of numbers we've added. Since there are 10 numbers in the list, we get the mean by dividing the sum of those 10 numbers by 10.

The list shows how misleading it would be to argue that the average American taxpayer would save $1,000. That figure is based solely on a calculation of the mean. Although the mean really is $1,000, 90% of the taxpayers (9 out of 10) would save only $50. The only reason that the mean is $1000 is because one out of the ten people would be saving almost $10,000. This illustrates that

Taxpayer 1	$9,550
Taxpayer 2	$50
Taxpayer 3	$50
Taxpayer 4	$50
Taxpayer 5	$50
Taxpayer 6	$50
Taxpayer 7	$50
Taxpayer 8	$50
Taxpayer 9	$50
Taxpayer 10	$50
SUM	$10,000

Mean = $10,000/10 = $1,000

although statistics don't lie, people can lie, or at least mislead, with statistics. (In this case, they would be doing that by disregarding the large degree of *dispersion* of values away from the mean. We'll return to the concept of *dispersion* later in this text.) Although the foregoing is just a hypothetical example for the purpose of simplifying the math, similar arguments—based on the arithmetic mean and disregarding dispersion—have been made by some politicians who favor tax cuts.

Let's consider one more illustration of the value of understanding statistics, this time from the standpoint of administration and planning. As mentioned earlier, helping people means providing services or advocating policies that effectively address what people need. Administrators and planners often conduct needs assessment surveys of their community or target population as a basis for deciding what services are needed the most and will be most utilized. These surveys typically will produce a mass of data representing the characteristics and needs of hundreds or perhaps thousands of people. Statistics allow us to summarize the gist of all that information and make it comprehensible.

Imagine eyeballing a list describing the gender, age, ethnicity, needs, and other attributes of hundreds or even thousands of people. Without statistics summarizing averages or the proportion of people in certain categories, you would be overwhelmed and unable to do anything with the information. With statistics, however, not only might you learn how many people have what attributes

and need what services, you might also find that what people need varies according to certain personal attributes. For example, certain kinds of statistics and statistical tables can make it easy to detect whether ethnic minorities are more or less likely to participate in a caregiver support group or some other service.

The antidote to being misled by statistics is not to avoid them but to learn about them. Learning some of the basics—which, as the above examples illustrate, need not panic you—will not only protect you from being misled, it can make you a more effective advocate for social policies. You can be more effective by being able to marshal statistics in support of your position (in an ethical manner that does not mislead) and by being able to see through the misleading uses of statistics by your adversaries and to show others how their use of those statistics is misleading.

In addition to learning how to avoid being misled by statistics, being an evidenced-based (and thus ethical) practitioner requires that you learn some of the basics needed to understand and critically appraise the findings of studies that evaluate practice effectiveness. Most of those studies will present their findings in the form of statistics.

Becoming familiar with statistical concepts will also help you to critically appraise policy studies. For example, some propagandistic policy studies might manipulate statistics in a misleading way, as illustrated in the hypothetical tax savings example, in an attempt to persuade readers to endorse a particular policy. As a professional who wants to help people, you should be able to see through such attempts and to differentiate studies that manipulate statistics from those that do not. This ability in turn will help you better assess and support those policies that really do have credible evidence as to their effects on the people you care about. It also will help you to better advocate against policies that lack credible evidence. By trying to understand statistics, then, you become a more compassionate practitioner—one who is willing to learn and apply a subject that may at first seem dull and intimidating so that you can be more helpful to people in need.

Being able to understand and critically appraise the findings of research studies, however, is not the only way that learning statistics will make you more compassionate and effective. Another way is that you probably will conduct some research yourself as part of your professional practice, and if you do, you'll probably need to handle some basic statistics in presenting and interpreting your findings. For example, you may survey your agency's clients to find out why so many terminate treatment prematurely or to assess how satisfied they are with your agency's services. And if you are truly devoted to making sure that the services you are providing to your clients are really helping them, you will want to use research methods to evaluate your practice.

Evaluating your practice effectiveness is a vital part of being an **evidence-based practitioner.** You can do this by conducting or participating in program evaluations that are likely to involve many clients and various practitioners in the evaluations. You also can do this by using single-system designs to evaluate how effective you are in delivering particular interventions to particular clients.

You might, for example, ask a client to self-monitor how many times he engages in desired or undesired behaviors for each of 10 days before you apply an intervention, and how often he does that each day after you introduce the intervention. To assess your effectiveness with that intervention for that particular client, you could graph and statistically analyze the data to ascertain whether significant improvement occurs after you begin the intervention. By understanding basic statistics, you will not only be prepared to interpret your data appropriately, but you will be able to communicate your findings to others in a clear and credible manner. [You can examine research texts, such as Rubin and Babbie (2005), to learn how to conduct single-system and other practice evaluation studies.] In Chapter 18 you will learn how to apply the statistical concepts covered throughout this text to the analysis of single-system design data.

PLAN OF THIS BOOK

As you may already have surmised, this book will be distinguished by two emphases: (1) a minimization of mathematical complexities; and (2) an emphasis on using statistics as part of evidence-based practice and evaluation. In my teaching experience I have learned that while some students enjoy math and have been well educated in it, many others do not have a strong aptitude for mathematical formulae.

Many have at least some math anxiety and are more interested in learning what statistics mean from a practical standpoint and how to use them to guide or evaluate their practice than in learning their mathematical bases or how to perform complicated calculations.

Examining some mathematical formulae and calculations, however, is unavoidable in trying to understand what statistics mean and how to use them to guide or evaluate practice. Most of those formulae and calculations—especially the more complex ones—will be put in boxes that are separate from this text's narrative. My hope is that readers will be able to understand the meaning of all of the statistics covered in this text without becoming overwhelmed with the math. At the same time, however, I recognize that not all students have an aversion to math and statistics. You may have had good prior schooling in these topics and even enjoy them. I have tried to present and organize the material in this book in a fashion that will appeal to both groups of students. You can be guided by your own idiosyncratic learning style in deciding whether and when to examine the formulae and calculations in any particular box. Your instructor also might offer guidance in this area, and different instructors may have different instructional approaches regarding the formulae and calculations.

Various statistical software packages can do virtually all the necessary calculations for the statistics discussed in this book. One of the most user-friendly and popular packages is SPSS (Statistical Package for the Social Sciences). Because many college and university campuses provide access to SPSS, Appendix G of this text will provide user-friendly examples illustrating how to use SPSS to handle most of the statistical procedures discussed throughout the text. That appendix will be organized according to the text chapters and will indicate which chapter pertains to the SPSS procedure being addressed. The appendix will also list some guides for alternative software in case you do not have access to SPSS.

Even if you use SPSS or some alternative statistical software package, however, I encourage you to examine the formulae and calculations presented in this text's boxes. Although you can grasp what most of the statistics mean without examining their calculations, you'll have an even better grasp if you understand their calculations and formulae.

If you have already taken a research methods course before reading this book, you are probably familiar with many of the non-statistical research methods terms and ideas used throughout this book. I refer here to terms like *hypothesis, variable, reliability, validity, random sample, experimental and control groups,* and so on. One cannot study statistics without encountering these terms, because statistics are generated from studies that involve these terms. It is impossible to provide illustrations of various statistics or discuss the conditions under which certain statistics are and are not appropriate without mentioning related research methods terms. Consequently, if you are not yet familiar with these terms, I encourage you to read Appendix A of this text before proceeding to Chapter 2. In fact, even if you have already learned about these terms, you may want to examine Appendix A just to brush up on some key terms and concepts. Also, if you encounter any unfamiliar research methods terms as you read this book, you may want to turn to Appendix A and read up on them.

If you encounter any mathematical operations that you never learned well or have learned so long ago that you have forgotten, you might also want to read Appendix B. That appendix covers some math basics that are most pertinent to the material in this text, paying particular attention to procedures that tend to give students the most difficulty. For example, it shows how to calculate a percentage, what happens to the minus sign when you square a negative number, and things of that sort.

There is one area of research terminology, however, that is necessary to review in this chapter, regardless of your prior learning of research methods. That area involves *levels of measurement,* a topic that influences what kinds of statistical procedures can and cannot be used. The importance and ubiquity of that topic in statistics calls for reviewing it now, regardless of your prior exposure to it.

LEVELS OF MEASUREMENT

The things measured in research studies are called *variables.* **Variables** are *concepts* that are expected to vary in a research study. **Concepts** are mental images that symbolize ideas, objects, events, behaviors, people, and so on. For example, the concepts *gender, level of client satisfaction,* and *number of*

arrests all can vary and serve as variables in research studies. Gender can vary if we are interested in comparing men and women. Level of client satisfaction can vary according to whether various clients are more or less satisfied or dissatisfied with the services they've received. Number of arrests can vary according to an actual number, from zero on up.

Although the three foregoing concepts—gender, level of client satisfaction, and number of arrests—all can serve as variables in a research study, each is at a different **level of measurement** and consequently requires a different way of quantifying. Let's examine each of the four levels of measurement: *nominal, ordinal, interval,* and *ratio.*

Nominal Measures

Variables that can be measured only in terms of **frequencies**—such as gender—are at the **nominal level of measurement.** It doesn't make much sense, for example, to depict the "average" gender of an agency's caseload. Clients are either male or female; they are not at different levels of male or female. Consequently, we can measure gender only in terms of the number of men and women or the proportion of men and women—in other words, in terms of head counts. The statistical term for head counts or proportions of people in different categories is *frequencies.* Thus, we can say the *frequency distribution* of gender is 50% men and 50% women. A **frequency,** then, is simply a count of how many cases there are in a particular category of a particular variable.

Nominal-level variables vary only in categories that are qualitative in nature. If we want to examine our caseload to find out how many clients were born in the United States versus another country, our nominal level variable would be *country of origin.* It would make no sense to say, "The average country of origin is 3.64." Likewise, it would make no sense to say, "The average country of origin is '*moderately* United States' or '*very* Mexico.'" All we can do is report *how many* or *what proportion* were born in what country. In other words, we would only be able to report *frequencies.* If we listed the frequency for each country in a table, that table would be called a **frequency distribution.** (We'll examine frequency distributions in depth in Chapter 3.)

Ordinal Measures

At the next level of measurement are **ordinal-level variables.** The **ordinal level of measurement** applies to variables whose categories can be rank-ordered according to degree. That is, they can be ranked according to how much of that variable they are. Thus, with the variable *level of client satisfaction,* we can measure the degree (or level) of a client's satisfaction. If client A is very satisfied and client B is only slightly satisfied, then we know that client A is more satisfied than client B. But while variables at the ordinal level of measurement can be rank ordered in that different attributes of those variables represent relatively more or less of the concept being measured, the differences between the amounts are not precise.

At the ordinal level, we know only whether one case has more or less of something than another case, but we don't know precisely *how much* more. We can't, for example, say that client A is twice as satisfied as client B, 1.5 times as satisfied, and so on. Likewise, we have an ordinal measure if we know that the horse Seabiscuit won a race and the talking TV horse Mr. Ed came in second, but we don't know by how much. An ordinal level variable of great relevance to students is *grade point average* (GPA). A student who gets straight A's has a better GPA (4.0) than one who gets all C's (2.0), but that doesn't mean that the 4.0 student performed twice as well or learned twice as much as the 2.0 student. (Perhaps the A student's average grade on tests and papers is 91% and the C student's average grade is 76%. Although the GPA of 4.0 is twice the GPA of 2.0, it does not mean that the percentage scores were twice as high. Ninety-one percent is not twice as much as 76%, for example.)

Interval Measures

When we are working with variables at the **interval level of measurement,** differences between different levels have the same meanings. Thus, the difference between an IQ score of 95 and 100 is considered to be of the same magnitude as the difference between 100 and 105. Standardized scales that have had norms developed based on very large samples are about the only type of interval measures encountered by practitioners. Some scales that technically are at the ordinal level of measurement are

commonly treated statistically as if they were at the interval level. For example, in scales that ask how strongly respondents agree or disagree with a set of statements (known as *Likert scaling*), each item is at the ordinal level because we do not know the precise quantitative difference in degree of agreement between responses like *disagree, agree, strongly disagree,* and so on. Each response category gets a score; for example, *strongly agree* might get a 5, *agree* a 4, *undecided* a 3, *disagree* a 2, and *strongly disagree* a 1. The scores for the responses to each statement are added together, and the total score then usually is treated statistically with procedures that assume interval data.

Ratio Measures

Variables at the **ratio level of measurement** have the same attribute as interval measures, but in addition have a true zero point. Consider the variable *number of arrests.* A person can have no arrests, one arrest, two arrests, and so on. Because there is a true zero point, we know that the person with 4 arrests has been arrested exactly twice as many times as the person with 2 arrests. Thus, if we are examining the precise number of arrests different people have had, number of arrests would be a ratio-level variable. (This is in contrast to interval variables that lack a true zero point. We wouldn't consider a person who scored zero on an intelligence test, for example, to have zero intelligence.)

To review the four levels of measurement, Figure 1.1 presents a graphic illustration of each.

Altering a Variable's Level of Measurement

Sometimes research reports collect data at a higher level of measurement but then analyze or report the data at a lower level. For example, a report might list a ratio level variable like number of arrests in *grouped* categories. Thus, they might say that 20 clients had less than 3 arrests, 30 clients had 3 to 5 arrests, and so on. In this case, number of arrests will have been reduced to an *ordinal level variable* because we could only say that the 30 clients in the 3-to-5 group had more arrests than the 20 clients in the less-than-3 group. We could not, for example, say they had twice as many arrests based only on this grouped information. Some clients in

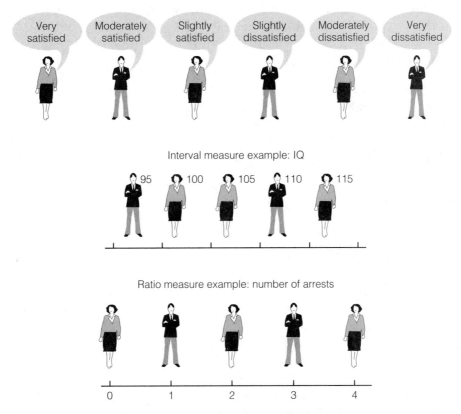

Figure 1-1   A Graphic Illustration of Four Levels of Measurement

the 3-to-5 group may have had 5 arrests and thus had 5 times as many arrests as those who had 1 arrest in the less-than-3 group. Other clients in the 3-to-5 group may have had 3 arrests and thus had one and a half times as many arrests as those who had 2 arrests in the less-than-3 group.

Sometimes a ratio-level variable can be reported in dichotomous grouped categories. For example, the variable *number of arrests* can be reduced to a *yes or no* variable such as whether or not a person has ever been arrested. You may collect ratio-level data on number of arrests, but then decide in

analyzing your data that you are less interested in how many arrests than in whether or not someone was ever arrested. In Chapter 2, when we discuss *coding,* we'll see how you can create a new variable from your ratio-level data and change all your zero arrests to a code for "no, never arrested" and all the higher numbers (1 and up) to a code for "yes, previously arrested."

When you reduce a ratio-level variable into dichotomous categories, you have reduced it into either the ordinal or nominal level of measurement. For example, since the category "yes, previously arrested" reflects more arrests than the category, "no, never arrested," we could say that even though we are dealing with a yes-or-no variable, it is still ordinal.

Suppose, however, we asked new clients entering a substance abuse treatment program, "How often have you used each of the following drugs?" Suppose the drug used most often for some clients is heroin, for others it is cocaine, and still others it is marijuana. If we analyze the data *not* in terms of *how often* they used each drug, but rather in terms of whether the drug used most often was either an opiate or a hallucinogenic *type* of drug, we would be analyzing a nominal-level variable.

Before we reduced *how often* to *type,* it was not clear whether we had an ordinal or ratio-level variable. If the question *how often* was followed by imprecise categories like *very often,* or *more than twice a week,* we would have had ordinal-level data. If, however, respondents could answer with the precise number of times they used the drug on average each week or in a specified time period, we would have ratio-level data. In either case, we could reduce the data down to nominal-level categories.

Although we can reduce ratio-level data down to ordinal or nominal categories, and ordinal-level data down to nominal categories, we cannot change levels of measurement in the other direction. We cannot, for example, change nominal-level variables like gender or country of origin into ordinal-level variables because we have no information about level or degree or rank order to begin with. Moreover, thinking of such variables in terms of *more of* or *less of* makes no sense to begin with. Likewise, we cannot change an ordinal-level variable into a ratio-level variable if we don't have precise quantities to begin with. If all we know is that Client A is very satisfied and Client B is moderately satisfied, there is no way to turn this rank-ordered information into precise quantities.

A variable's level of measurement will imply what kind of statistical procedures can be used to depict it. As already noted, nominal-level variables can be depicted in terms of frequencies only. Frequencies can also be used when reporting variables at the other levels of measurement. For example, we can report how many clients are very satisfied, very dissatisfied, and so on. And we can report how many clients had no prior arrests, one prior arrest,

two prior arrests, and so on. But unlike nominal-level variables, frequencies are not the only option for reporting variables at other levels of measurement. For example, even though ordinal-level variables do not indicate precise amounts, things like grade point *averages* can be used as a rough summary indicator of how high one's grades are. Likewise, we can talk about the *average* number of arrests clients have had after receiving alternative forms of intervention.

Throughout this book you'll encounter various alternative statistical procedures. As you'll see, which alternative is the most appropriate to choose will be influenced at least in part by the level of measurement of the variables to be analyzed. So the term *level of measurement* is one that you're likely to be comfortable with after you finish reading this book. Having covered that term, let's move on to Chapter 2, which explains how to prepare data for analysis. But first, you may want to read Appendix A to brush up on some key terms and concepts regarding research methods—especially if you have not yet taken a research methods course.

Main Points

• The most important reason to learn about statistics is that it will make you better able to help people.

• By trying to understand statistics, you become a more compassionate practitioner—one who is willing to learn and apply a subject that may at first seem dull and intimidating so that you can be more helpful to people in need.

• You will not be an *ethical* practitioner unless you keep current with and critically appraise practice-related studies and base your practice on evidence-based knowledge.

• Learning statistics will help you use evidence about the effectiveness of interventions to guide your practice and thus make sure your practice is evidence-based.

• Learning about statistics is useful at all levels of practice, including clinical practice, administration and planning, community organization, social action, policy analysis, and other areas.

• Learning about statistics will help you avoid being misled by those who misuse statistics as a way to propagandize their political agenda.

• Learning about statistics will help you be more effective in marshalling data in support of your position (in an ethical manner that does not mislead) and to be able to see through the misleading uses of statistics by your adversaries and to show others how their use of those statistics is misleading.

• Learning about statistics will help you evaluate the effectiveness of your own direct practice.

• Variables are *concepts* that are expected to vary in a research study.

• There are four levels of measurement: nominal, ordinal, interval, and ratio.

• Nominal-level variables, such as gender or country of origin, can vary only in categories that are qualitative in nature and thus can be measured only in terms of head counts.

• The statistical term for head counts or proportions of people in different categories is *frequencies*.

• Variables at the ordinal level of measurement, such as client satisfaction level, can be rank ordered according to degree, but the differences between the amounts are not precise.

• At the interval level of measurement, differences between different levels have the same meanings, but there is no true zero point. Thus, the difference between IQ scores of 95 and 100 is considered to be of the same magnitude as the difference between 100 and 105, but nobody has zero intelligence.

• Variables at the ratio level of measurement, such as number of arrests, have the same attribute as interval measures, but in addition have a true zero point.

• Variables at the ratio or interval level of measurement can be collapsed down to the ordinal or nominal level, and variables at the ordinal level can be collapsed down to the nominal level, but variables cannot be changed in the other direction. That is, nominal-level data cannot be transformed into any other level, and ordinal-level data cannot be transformed into the interval or ratio level.

Review Questions and Exercises

1. Suppose a colleague told you that your community has relatively little need for services for poor people, since the average income per household in the community is $5,000 above the poverty line. How might what you read in Chapter 1 influence your reply?

2. Find someone who disagrees with you about the value of studying statistics for students preparing to become clinical or administrative practitioners. Ask the person to debate you on the issue, with the two of you switching positions in the debate. That is, you would each argue the opposite position of what you initially believed. After the debate, write a brief paragraph summarizing whether, how, and why your view on this issue did or did not change or intensify as a result of the debate.

3. Suppose you want to evaluate the effectiveness of two alternative interventions aimed at motivating teenage substance abusers to seek treatment. The variable pertaining to which intervention they receive can be called *type of intervention*. Suppose you will assess the effectiveness of each intervention according to two variables. One of the two variables will be the *precise number of substance abuse treatment sessions each teen attends*. The other variable will be their *level of motivation to change*, as determined by a clinical interview. The interviewer will assign each teen to one of the following motivation levels:

Level 1: Very little or no motivation to change.

Level 2: Desire to stop substance abuse, but no commitment to take the actions necessary to accomplish change in the immediate future.

Level 3: Commitment to take the actions necessary to accomplish change in the immediate future.

a. At what level of measurement is each of your three variables? Explain why.
b. Describe how the variable *precise number of substance abuse treatment sessions each teen attends* could be transformed to another level of measurement.

4. Using InfoTrac College Edition, find a research study relevant to your practice interests. Identify the level of measurement of each of its variables. Explain your reasoning.

5. Using an Internet search engine (such as Google), search for sites offering free statistical calculations. For example, you might enter the keyword term *statistical calculations*. Write down how many sites you find that offer free statistical calculations. Also write down the site addresses; they may come in handy soon!

InfoTrac Exercises

1. Type in the keyword phrase "evidence-based practice." Find an article that discusses issues in evidence-based practice regarding an area of professional practice that interests you. Summarize the main points of that article.

2. Read the following article and notice how it treats the summated scores of its ordinal-level scale items as if they were interval level (by calculating mean scores):

Walsh, J., Green, R., Matthews, J., & Bonucelli-Puerto, B. (2005). Social workers' views of the etiology of mental disorders: Results of a national study. *Social Work, 50*(1), 43–52.

3. In the article below, examine Figure 2 and the associated narrative. Then explain why the variable in Figure 2 is at the ordinal level instead of the interval level.

McHugh, M. L. (2003). Descriptive statistics, Part I: Level of measurement. (Scientific Inquiry). *Journal for Specialists in Pediatric Nursing, 8*(1), 35–37.

Preparing Data for Analysis

INTRODUCTION

As mentioned in Chapter 1, today statistical software programs such as SPSS can perform almost all the statistical calculations we desire. But to do so, these programs require that we convert our data to a machine-readable format. This conversion process involves **coding**. Suppose, for example, we surveyed clients who prematurely terminated treatment and we asked them why they dropped out. Suppose one client said, "I couldn't afford the childcare needed for me to make the treatment sessions." Suppose a second client said, "The babysitter was too expensive." Imagine how much more cumbersome it would be to enter all their words into the computer instead of simply giving each client the same numerical code (such as a 1 or a 2, etc.) representing all responses referring to the affordability of childcare. Likewise, suppose a third client said, "I moved and am no longer near the bus line," and a fourth client said, "My car broke down, and I couldn't afford to get it repaired." Both of these clients could receive the same numerical code (perhaps a 2 or a 3, etc.) representing all responses referring to transportation difficulties. Assigning such codes simplifies our task in entering data into the computer, enables the computer to perform statistical calculations, and makes it easier for us to comprehend our computer output.

Similarly, if we are comparing two treatment groups, we could code our treatment group variable as either a "1" or a "2." Clients in the experimental group receiving the treatment being evaluated could receive one of the codes—let's say a "1"—and clients in the other group would receive another code—in this case, a "2." Likewise, female clients could receive a "1" for the variable *gender,* and males would then receive a "2."

The nature of your coding scheme will vary depending upon the statistical software you use and the level of measurement of your variables. For example, if you use SPSS, you could just enter the words male and female (or the letters *m* and *f*) instead of numbers for the nominal-level variable *gender.* Whether you entered numbers or letters for nominal variables would not affect your data analysis because nominal variables are not analyzed in terms of averages, such as average gender or average country of origin. With ordinal-level variables, however, if you entered a word or a letter you would not be able to obtain mathematical calculations.

For example, if you entered students' letter grades in each course they take (A, B, C, D, or F) instead of a numerical code (4, 3, 2, 1, 0), you would not be able to calculate the students' grade point averages.

Even if you can enter words for nominal-level variables instead of numbers, doing so may be inefficient. For example, it takes less time to enter a 1 for *experimental group* than to enter the words. Let's begin this chapter by exploring how to code with different levels of measurement.

CODING WITH DIFFERENT LEVELS OF MEASUREMENT

With nominal-level variables, it doesn't matter what code number we assign to each category, as long as we assign the codes consistently and keep a record of what category each code signifies. For example, we could assign the code 1 to men and 2 to women, 1 to women and 2 to men, or even assign them different numbers, such as 0 and 1. And as indicated above, we may just want to assign a letter, such as *m* for male and *f* for female.

With ordinal-level or ratio-level variables, on the other hand, the numbers we assign *will* matter. For example, suppose we asked parents how often their child exhibited various behavior problems, using the following four response categories: never, rarely, occasionally, and often. It would get pretty confusing if we assigned a code of 1 to occasionally, 2 to never, 3 to often, and 4 to rarely. Assigning the codes in order of frequency of each problem would be more logical and would avoid turning data analysis into a nightmare.

But even with ordinal data, we could choose to assign ascending or descending code numbers as the rank order increases or decreases. For example, each of the following four coding schemes would make sense for the ordinal information about frequency of behavioral problems:

SCHEME 1	SCHEME 2	SCHEME 3	SCHEME 4
0-Never	1-Never	4-Never	3-Never
1-Rarely	2-Rarely	3-Rarely	2-Rarely
2-Occasionally	3-Occasionally	2-Occasionally	1-Occasionally
3-Often	4-Often	1-Often	0-Often

In schemes 1 and 2, a higher score would signify a more serious behavioral disorder. In schemes 3 and 4, a lower score would do so. In schemes 3 and 4, a higher score would signify a more desirable condition; in schemes 1 and 2 a higher score would be less desirable. Suppose we were using these data to evaluate the effectiveness of our treatment program. We might want to use scheme 3 or 4 so that an increase in scores signified improvement. However, we still could use scheme 1 or 2, as long as we remembered that a decrease in scores signified improvement. As long as we know the directional meaning of our coding scheme, and as long as the direction maintains logical consistency, it doesn't matter which direction we choose to code the ordinal data.

With ratio-level data, however, the direction probably will matter. Because ratio-level data are inherently numerical, we can just enter the actual raw number, without having to code it. Thus, if a client is 32 years old and has two children, we would enter *32* for the variable *age* and *2* for the variable *number of children*. It wouldn't make much sense—and it certainly would be more time consuming—to give lower numbers for more children or older ages and higher numbers to fewer children or younger ages.

But you may recall from Chapter 1 that ratio-level data can be collapsed down to ordinal or nominal levels. Suppose we had ratio-level data on the exact annual income earned, and decided to collapse that variable down to ordinal categories of socioeconomic status. Suppose we used three ordinal categories: upper income, middle income, and lower income. We could opt to assign a 1 to upper income or a 3 to it, while assigning a 3 or a 1 to lower income. To be logical, middle income would receive the middle code regardless of the direction of our coding scheme.

But even if we want to collapse ratio-level data down to ordinal grouped categories, it's usually best to first enter the raw (ungrouped) number. We can instruct our software program, such as SPSS, to recode the data after we enter the actual number. For example, we could recode age as $1 = $ less than 20, $2 = 20 - 29$, $3 = 30 - 39$, and so on. Moreover, we could create a new (ordinal-level) variable with the recoded data, while maintaining our original ratio-level variable. (We'll examine how to do that using

SPSS later in this text.) By entering the actual number, and recoding later, we have the option of analyzing ratio- or interval-level variables at their original level of measurement or at the ordinal level.

However, in some studies variables such as age or income are collected from respondents in ordinal grouped categories only. For example, we may have reason to expect reluctance by respondents to enter their exact income and therefore only request them to check a grouped category on a questionnaire (such as less than $10,000, $10,000- $19,999, and so on). In that case we would have no alternative to entering a code for the ordinal level instead of the actual amount.

CODING OPEN-ENDED DATA

Open-ended data can be harder to code. Open-ended data typically are associated with qualitative research (as discussed in Appendix A), but quantitative studies sometimes ask open-ended questions as well. Answers to open-ended questions often produce a wide variety of idiosyncratic items of information that cannot be anticipated in advance, and which must be reduced to a smaller number of coded categories after the data are collected. Suppose, for example, that we conduct a survey of 200 former clients who prematurely stopped using our agency's services and ask them to identify the main reason why they stopped. We might get a wide variety of answers. Below is a very incomplete, partial list of how 20 former clients might reply:

Respondent 1: The service costs too much.

Respondent 2: I can't afford the fees.

Respondent 3: Parking is too expensive.

Respondent 4: I can't afford the parking costs.

Respondent 5: The service wasn't helping me.

Respondent 6: The service was ineffective.

Respondent 7: My therapist was not nice.

Respondent 8: I did not like my therapist.

Respondent 9: Receptionists are unfriendly.

Respondent 10: Receptionists were rude and condescending.

Respondent 11: I couldn't find childcare that I could afford.

Respondent 12: No childcare services were provided.

Respondent 13: I moved out of town.

Respondent 14: It takes too long to get to the agency from my new residence.

Respondent 15: My work schedule changed from evenings to days.

Respondent 16: No evening or weekend hours.

Respondent 17: I have trouble speaking English, and none of the staff spoke my language.

Respondent 18: No bilingual staff.

Respondent 19: Habla Español (I speak Spanish).

Respondent 20: An astrologist advised me to seek new avenues of fulfillment.

Although it would be possible to assign each respondent's answer a separate numerical code, that procedure would not group similar answers and would result in an unwieldy number of codes for our 200 respondents. Consequently, we would have to come up with a coding scheme that reduced the number of categories by grouping answers that had commonalities. For example, the following list indicates one way to combine some answers with some commonalities.

CODE 1—FINANCIAL CONCERNS

Respondent 1: The service costs too much.

Respondent 2: I can't afford the fees.

Respondent 3: Parking is too expensive.

Respondent 4: I can't afford the parking costs.

CODE 2—DISSATISFACTION WITH SERVICES

Respondent 5: The service wasn't helping me.

Respondent 6: The service was ineffective.

Respondent 7: My social worker was not nice.

Respondent 8: I did not like my social worker.

Respondent 9: Receptionists are unfriendly.

Respondent 10: Receptionists were rude and condescending.

CODE 3—INCONVENIENCE OF APPOINTMENTS

Respondent 11: I couldn't find childcare that I could afford.

Respondent 12: No childcare services were provided.

Respondent 13: I moved out of town.

Respondent 14: It takes too long to get to the agency from my new residence.

Respondent 15: My work schedule changed from evenings to days.

Respondent 16: No evening or weekend hours.

CODE 4—LANGUAGE PROBLEMS

Respondent 17: I have trouble speaking English, and none of the staff spoke my language.

Respondent 18: No bilingual staff.

Respondent 19: Habla Español (I speak Spanish).

CODE 5—OTHER

Respondent 20: An astrologist advised me to seek new avenues of fulfillment.

While the above list simplifies the number of codes we'd have to analyze, it goes overboard by lumping too many different kinds of answers together under one gross coded category and thereby loses some distinctions that might be important in guiding agency administration and planning. For example, consider the answers of respondents 3 and 4. Just knowing how many clients prematurely terminate services due to financial concerns won't tell us how many we could retain if we expanded our free parking area or perhaps offered a shuttle service. Therefore, a separate code pertaining to parking problems might be in order.

Likewise, consider the important distinctions among the answers of respondents 5 through 10. These answers might merit three separate codes instead of one gross dissatisfaction code. Three codes that would give more useful guidance for the ways in which dissatisfaction with services might be reduced are as follows:

Ineffective services

Problems in practitioner-client relationship

Insensitive support staff

Important distinctions also can be detected in the answers of respondents 11 through 16. For example, the code *inconvenience of appointments* does not tell us how many clients could be retained if we offered a childcare service for clients during their appointment times. Also, that code would not tell us how many clients could be retained if we offered evening or weekend appointments. Therefore, instead of one code for those six respondents, we might need three, as follows:

No childcare

Client moved

No evening or weekend appointments

Another problem with the above coding scheme is that some answers might fit more than one code category. For example, some coders might assign code 1 (financial concerns) to Respondent 11's answer, "I couldn't find childcare that I could afford." Thus, rather than our original five-code scheme, we might get more useful findings from the following scheme (with the pertinent respondent answers listed under each code).

CODE 1—SERVICE FEES TOO EXPENSIVE

Respondent 1: The service costs too much.

Respondent 2: I can't afford the fees.

CODE 2—PARKING PROBLEMS

Respondent 3: Parking is too expensive.

Respondent 4: I can't afford the parking costs.

CODE 3—INEFFECTIVE SERVICES

Respondent 5: The service wasn't helping me.

Respondent 6: The service was ineffective.

CODE 4—PROBLEMS IN PRACTITIONER-CLIENT RELATIONSHIP

Respondent 7: My therapist was not nice.

Respondent 8: I did not like my therapist.

CODE 5—INSENSITIVE SUPPORT STAFF

Respondent 9: Receptionists are unfriendly.

Respondent 10: Receptionists were rude and condescending.

CODE 6—NO CHILDCARE

Respondent 11: I couldn't find childcare that I could afford.

Respondent 12: No childcare services were provided.

CODE 7—CLIENT MOVED

Respondent 13: I moved out of town.

Respondent 14: It takes too long to get to the agency from my new residence.

CODE 8—NO EVENING OR WEEKEND APPOINTMENTS

Respondent 15: My work schedule changed from evenings to days.

Respondent 16: No evening or weekend hours.

CODE 9—LANGUAGE PROBLEMS

Respondent 17: I have trouble speaking English, and none of the staff spoke my language.

Respondent 18: No bilingual staff.

Respondent 19: Habla Español (I speak Spanish).

CODE 10—OTHER

Respondent 20: An astrologist advised me to seek new avenues of fulfillment.

There are various possible schemes for coding a set of open-ended data. The scheme you develop should fit your research purposes as well as the logic in your data. You may need to modify the code categories as the coding process proceeds. Whenever you do, however, be sure to review the data you already coded to see whether they need to be changed, too.

The list of code categories should be exhaustive and mutually exclusive. That means that there should be a code category for each response, and each response should fit into one category only. If you have assistance with coding, your coders need to be trained to understand the definitions and proper use of your code categories. This involves not only explaining your definitions to them and giving them examples of responses for each code category, but also giving them some cases to code as part of the training to compare their codes with the codes you gave to those cases. If there are discrepancies between your codes and theirs, more training may be needed. Rubin and Babbie (2005) offer the following additional suggestions:

> If you're not fortunate enough to have assistance in coding, you should still obtain some verification of your own reliability as a coder. Nobody's perfect, especially a researcher hot on the trail of a finding. Suppose that you're coding the reasons given by runaway adolescents as to why they ran away. Suppose your hunch is that most have run away because they were abused at home. The danger is that you might unconsciously bias your coding to fit your hunch. For example, you might code as *abuse* responses that merely referred to parents being too harsh in their discipline. You might not consider that some adolescents might deem things like being grounded as harsh discipline. If at all possible, then, get someone else to code some of your cases to see whether that person makes the same assignments you made. Ideally, that person should not have the same predilection you have and should not be aware of the hypothesis you are hoping to support.
>
> (RUBIN & BABBIE, 2005, pp. 554–555)

CODEBOOK CONSTRUCTION

To ensure that you'll remember your code categories for each variable in your data file, you should develop a codebook. A **data file** (or *data set*) is a spreadsheet matrix of rows and columns, with each row representing a particular case (such as a particular respondent in a survey) and each column listing the coded data for that case. A **codebook** is a document that identifies the location of each variable in the data file and the codes that apply to each attribute for each variable.

Codebooks are used in two ways. One is to guide coders in how to code each variable for each case. The other is to guide you in your data analysis. Your codebook will help you locate variables in your data file and will remind you of what each code represents. For example, suppose you have surveyed 200 former clients to assess why they prematurely terminated treatment. You may want to see whether some types of clients gave different reasons from others. Therefore, in addition to your column for the variable pertaining to their main reason for dropping out, you may have columns for other variables such as gender, ethnicity, age, country of origin, practitioner degree, and so on. Also, you would have 200 rows of coded data across the columns. If you wanted to see whether certain ethnic groups tended to give different reasons from others, your codebook would help you find the column for ethnicity and would remind you of what codes you assigned to each of your categories of ethnicity.

Figure 2.1 illustrates what part of your codebook might look like for this study and how that would guide you in locating items in your data file. If you examine the data file at the bottom of Figure 2.1, for example, you will notice that each column is headed by a number and a label. It is not always possible to enter the entire variable label atop the column for each variable, especially when variables have lengthy labels, such as "reason for dropping out." Your codebook can remind you of the column number for each variable and any abbreviated labels you assigned to each. Thus, with the data in Figure 2.1, your codebook would tell you that the client with case number 001 has the following attributes: female, white, aged 34, born in USA, assigned to a BSW practitioner, and dropped out because service fees are too expensive.

Likewise, you would know that client 002 is an African American male, age 26, born in USA, assigned to a MSW practitioner, and dropped out because he thought services were ineffective. Continuing on to client 003, the codes indicate a White Hispanic female, age 47, born in another country, assigned to a practitioner with a non-social work master's degree, and dropped out because of language problems. The last of the 200 rows in our

CODEBOOK

Column	Variable	SPSS Variable Name	Codes-Categories
1	Case Number	ID	Enter actual number atop questionnaire
2	Gender	gender	1 = Female
			2 = Male
3	Ethnicity	ethn	1 = White, not Hispanic
			2 = White Hispanic
			3 = Hispanic, not White
			4 = African American
			5 = Asian American
			6 = Native American
			7 = Other
			9 = Not answered
4	Age	age	Enter actual age (raw number)
			0 = Not answered
5	Country of origin	cofo	1 = USA
			2 = Elsewhere
			9 = Not answered
6	Practitioner degree	degree	1 = BSW
			2 = Other undergraduate degree
			3 = MSW
			4 = Other master's degree
			5 = Social Work Doctorate
			6 = Other doctorate
			7 = Other
			9 = No answer
7	Main reason for dropping out	reason	1 = Service fees too expensive
			2 = Parking problems
			3 = Ineffective services
			4 = Problems in practitioner-client relationship
			5 = Insensitive support staff
			6 = No childcare
			7 = Client moved
			8 = No evening or weekend appointments
			9 = Language problems
			10 = Other
			99 = No answer

DATA FILE

1	2	3	4	5	6	7
ID	gender	ethn	age	cofo	degree	reason
001	1	1	34	1	1	1
002	2	4	26	1	3	3
003	1	2	47	2	4	9
.						
.						
.						
200	2	6	14	1	2	4

Figure 2.1 An Illustrative Partial Codebook and Data File

data file would be for client 200, who is male, Native American, age 14, born in the USA, assigned to a practitioner with a non-social work undergraduate degree, and dropped out because of problems in the practitioner-client relationship.

DATA ENTRY

At the start of this chapter we noted that the purpose of coding is to convert your data into a machine-readable format. After you have developed your coding scheme, you'll have various options for entering your data into your computer software program for analysis. The options you have will depend on the original form of your data and the computer software you use. For example, with SPSS, you have the option of entering your data into an SPSS data spreadsheet or importing data in another spreadsheet, such as Excel. (Appendix G will show you how to use either option.)

Some studies use data collection procedures that spare you the work of manually entering the data yourself using your keyboard. For example, optical scan sheets can be scanned directly into a data analysis program. However, these sheets usually are limited to closed-ended data and research participants who are comfortable with them. Some (typically well-funded) studies use computer-assisted telephone interviewing, in which an interviewer enters interview responses directly into the computer. Likewise, online surveys typically enable respondent answers to be entered directly into an accumulating data file.

DATA CLEANING

Data entry errors can occur regardless of the data entry procedure used. Errors can occur in various ways, including in coding, in misreading written codes, and in optical scanning malfunctions. The process of correcting these errors is called *data cleaning*. There are different ways to clean data; the important thing is to be sure to use at least one of them.

One option is to have two people independently code and enter data. Software can be used to check for discrepancies between them. Those discrepancies can then be examined and corrected. Another option is called *possible-code cleaning*. Consider the variable *gender,* for example. Typically there are only three possible codes for this variable, such as 1 for female, 2 for male, and 0 or 9 for no answer. If you find in your preliminary examination of head counts for each code category that you have 95 ones, 95 twos, 5 nines (or zeros) and 5 sevens, then you know that the cases that got the code seven for gender need to be cleaned for that variable. Likewise, if you find that some cases are more than 200 years old, you know that they need to be cleaned for the *age* variable.

Some software programs can check for impossible codes as the data are entered. For example, they might refuse to enter a code 7 for gender or 236 for age. Other software programs can test for impossible codes after data entry. If you do not have access to such software, you can obtain a frequency distribution showing how many responses you have for each code in each variable in your data file. (Frequency distributions will be discussed in the next chapter.) You will know an error needs to be corrected for every response that is not one of your codes (such as 7 for *gender*) or that is an impossible raw number (such as 2 for *age* in a survey of nursing home residents or staff.)

Each error you discover can be corrected by retrieving the original document in which the data were first provided. For example, in a mailed survey of former clients, that document would be the questionnaire they completed and returned. The questionnaire from the respondent who received a code 7 for gender will indicate how to correct that code in your data file for that respondent. Referring back to Figure 2.1, notice that the first column in the data file is for case number (or ID). By providing a case number for each element in our sample—and its corresponding original document—we are able to locate the documents with errors and then make the proper corrections.

Main Points

• Coding is the process of converting data to a machine-readable format.

• The nature of your coding scheme will vary depending upon the statistical software you use and the level of measurement of your variables.

• Number or letter codes can be used with nominal variables because nominal-level variables are not analyzed in terms of averages. With ordinal-level variables, however, if you entered a word or a letter you would not be able do obtain mathematical calculations.

• With nominal-level variables, it doesn't matter what code number we assign to each category, as long as we assign the codes consistently and keep a record of what category each code signifies.

- With ordinal data we could assign ascending or descending code numbers as the rank order increases or decreases.

- Because ratio-level data are inherently numerical, we can just enter the actual raw number without having to code it.

- If we want to collapse ratio-level data down to ordinal grouped categories, it's usually best to first enter the raw (ungrouped) number. We can instruct our software program to recode the data after we enter the actual number.

- Answers to open-ended questions often produce a wide variety of idiosyncratic items of information that cannot be anticipated in advance and must be reduced to a smaller number of coded categories after the data are collected.

- There are various possible schemes for coding a set of open-ended data. The scheme you develop should fit your research purposes as well as the logic in your data. You may need to modify the code categories as the coding process proceeds. Whenever you do, however, be sure to review the data you already coded to see whether they need to be changed, too.

- The list of code categories should be exhaustive and mutually exclusive.

- A data file (or *data set*) is a spreadsheet matrix of rows and columns, with each row representing a particular case (such as a particular respondent in a survey) and each column listing the coded data for that case.

- A codebook is a document that identifies the location of each variable in the data file and the codes that apply to each attribute for each variable.

- There are various options for entering your data into your computer software program for analysis. The options available to you will depend on the original form of your data and the computer software you use.

- Some studies use data collection procedures that spare you the work of manually entering the data yourself using your keyboard.

- Data entry errors can occur regardless of the data entry procedure used. Errors can occur in various ways, including in coding, in misreading written codes, and in optical scanning malfunctions. The process of correcting these errors is called *data cleaning*. There are different ways to clean data; the important thing is to be sure to use at least one of them.

Review Questions and Exercises

1. Suppose you are evaluating the effectiveness of a child abuse prevention program for high-risk parents. Create a codebook for your data, using the following variables:

Treatment Group (experimental or control)

Gender

Age

Number of Children

SES—Socioeconomic Status (high, medium, low)

Abuse? (yes/no)

2. Construct a data file for the first four cases in the above study, assuming that those four cases have the following attributes:

Case 1: Control group, male, aged 28, 3 children, medium SES, abused his children during the study period

Case 2: Experimental group, female, aged 24, 2 children, low SES, did not abuse

Case 3: Control group, female, no answer for age, 2 children, low SES, abused her children during the study period

Case 4: Experimental group, male, aged 27, 4 children, medium SES, did not abuse

3. Identify one impossible code for each variable in the above study. Describe the process you would use to identify a data entry error using that code and how you would correct it.

4. Explain how your options differ in the above study for coding the variables *treatment group* versus *SES*.

5. Develop a coding scheme for the following answers given by 10 surveyed students in response to an open-ended question regarding their attitude about statistics:

Boring!

Irrelevant to clinical practice.

Too difficult.

Scary.

Not useful.

Why do I have to study something I'll never use?

Math formulas are too complicated.

Yawn!!!!

Can help us provide more effective services.

More useful than most students think!

InfoTrac Exercise

1. Discuss the alternative techniques for cleaning data discussed in this article:

O'Rourke, T. W. (2000). Techniques for screening and cleaning data for analysis. *American Journal of Health Studies, 16*(4), 205–207.

Descriptive Statistics

Most practice-related research studies, whether they are surveys with very large samples or agency evaluations with smaller samples, produce a mass of data that cannot be interpreted just by eyeballing the data file or spreadsheet. Consequently, we must transform the data from a mass of unmanageable details into manageable summaries. The various statistics used to organize, summarize, and display a set of data—without testing hypotheses about possible relationships among variables—are called **descriptive statistics.** The six chapters in this section examine various descriptive statistics most relevant to evidence-based practitioners.

Frequency Distributions

INTRODUCTION

The first step in descriptive analysis involves transforming a mass of data into a manageable format. That data reduction process begins by producing a frequency distribution. As mentioned in Chapter 1, *frequency* is the statistical term pertaining to a count of how many cases there are in a particular category of a particular variable, and a *frequency distribution* is a list of the frequencies for each category of a variable. By telling us the number and percentage of (i.e., *frequency* of) cases that are in each value category of each variable in our study, frequency distributions help us get a beginning sense of the overall nature of our data, and sometimes display useful findings in their own right. Knowing how our data are distributed across the categories of each of our variables will help us choose the appropriate additional statistical analyses to perform later and will help us interpret those analyses.

Recall the example in Chapter 1 that illustrated how the arithmetic mean can be misleading if a small percentage of cases with extreme values makes the mean much larger than the value for the majority of cases. Examining your frequency distribution can enable you to see whether such a phenomenon is likely to occur in your analyses. And, as mentioned in Chapter 2, by examining your frequency distribution you also can spot coding and data entry errors that need to be cleaned.

To illustrate how frequency distributions can transform a mass of unmanageable details into manageable summaries, suppose we are comparing the effectiveness of two treatment approaches for alleviating or preventing behavioral problems in a residential treatment center for children and adolescents who have been traumatized. Half the cases will receive the center's routine array of treatments, and the other half will receive a new treatment. Let's assume that part of our evaluation data include the raw data displayed in Table 3.1.

Our study might include more cases and variables than are listed in Table 3.1, but let's just consider that partial list at this point to make things more manageable visually. Notice how hard it is to interpret our findings just by looking at the raw data file. Imagine how much harder it would be if there were many more cases—say, 100 or more—in the file.

Suppose you tried to describe the listed data in narrative form. You might write the following paragraph in your report.

Of the 50 youths in our study, 25 were male and 25 were female. Twenty youths were Caucasian, 15 were African American, 13 were Hispanic, and two had other ethnicities. Twenty-five youths received the new treatment, and 25 received the routine treatment. Two youths were 7 years old, three were 8, eight were 9, eleven were 10, nine were 11, five were 12, seven were 13, three were 14, and two were 15. Six youths had no serious behavioral incidents, four had 1 serious behavioral incident, another four had 2 serious behavioral incidents, six had 3 serious behavioral incidents, four had 4 serious behavioral incidents, nine had 5 serious behavioral incidents, six had 6 serious behavioral incidents, three had 7 serious behavioral incidents, two had 8 serious behavioral incidents, one had 11 serious behavioral incidents, one had 18 serious behavioral incidents, one had 19 serious behavioral incidents, one had 20 serious behavioral incidents, one had 21 serious behavioral incidents, and one had 22 serious behavioral incidents.

Notice how easy it is to get overwhelmed by the details in the above paragraph. Frequency distributions transform those unmanageable details into tables that are visually manageable. Let's look now at how they do this.

TYPES OF FREQUENCY DISTRIBUTIONS

Frequencies can be displayed in three ways: as *absolute frequencies*, *relative frequencies*, and *cumulative frequencies*. Let's now examine each type.

Absolute Frequencies

Absolute frequencies are simple counts of the number of cases per category. An **absolute frequency distribution** is a table that displays the number of cases in each category of a variable. To construct an absolute frequency distribution, simply construct a table containing two columns and as many rows as there are categories in the variable you want to display. In each row of the left column, enter the value for each category. In each

Table 3.1 Partial Raw Data for 50 Cases in a Hypothetical Evaluation in a Residential Treatment Center

CASE ID NUMBER	GENDER	ETHNICITY	AGE	TREATMENT GROUP	NUMBER OF SERIOUS BEHAVIORAL INCIDENTS
1	male	Caucasian	7	new	0
2	female	Caucasian	12	new	0
3	male	Hispanic	9	new	1
4	male	African American	8	new	8
5	female	African American	10	new	1
6	female	Hispanic	9	new	2
7	female	Caucasian	10	new	0
8	female	African American	14	new	21
9	female	Hispanic	9	new	0
10	female	Other	13	new	3
11	female	Caucasian	15	new	0
12	female	African American	12	new	3
13	female	Hispanic	9	new	19
14	male	African American	11	new	2
15	female	Caucasian	8	new	22
16	male	Caucasian	13	new	20
17	female	African American	11	new	0
18	male	Hispanic	12	new	11
19	female	Caucasian	13	new	1
20	male	Caucasian	10	new	1
21	female	Caucasian	10	new	2
22	male	African American	10	new	2
23	female	Caucasian	11	new	18
24	male	African American	15	new	7
25	female	Hispanic	9	new	6
26	female	African American	10	routine	3
27	male	African American	8	routine	3
28	female	Hispanic	11	routine	4
29	male	Caucasian	12	routine	5
30	female	Caucasian	7	routine	6
31	male	Hispanic	13	routine	6
32	male	Caucasian	11	routine	4
33	male	African American	9	routine	5

Table 3.1   *Continued*

CASE ID NUMBER	GENDER	ETHNICITY	AGE	TREATMENT GROUP	NUMBER OF SERIOUS BEHAVIORAL INCIDENTS
34	male	Hispanic	9	routine	5
35	male	Other	11	routine	3
36	male	Caucasian	11	routine	6
37	male	African American	10	routine	8
38	male	Hispanic	14	routine	5
39	female	Caucasian	10	routine	5
40	male	Hispanic	13	routine	7
41	male	Caucasian	10	routine	3
42	female	African American	11	routine	4
43	male	Hispanic	12	routine	5
44	female	Caucasian	13	routine	5
45	male	Caucasian	10	routine	6
46	female	Caucasian	10	routine	5
47	male	African American	14	routine	7
48	female	Caucasian	11	routine	5
49	male	African American	13	routine	6
50	female	Hispanic	9	routine	4

row of the right column, enter the number of cases for that category. Table 3.2 displays how this is done for the variable *ethnicity* for the raw data in Table 3.1. Notice how much easier it is to see how many cases are in each category of the nominal level variable *ethnicity* than it was by examining the raw data in the 50 rows of the ethnicity column in Table 3.2.

When we construct frequency distributions for variables at the ordinal, interval, or ratio level of measurement, we arrange the rows for the quantitative values of the variable (in the left column) in ascending order. That is, we start with the smallest value in the top row, the next smallest value in the second row, and so on, with the largest value in the bottom row. To illustrate this process, let's examine an absolute frequency distribution for the ratio-level variable *number of serious behavioral incidents*, again using the raw data from Table 3.1. In Table 3.3 we can see that the frequency distribution

table makes it much easier to see how many cases had each value than it was by examining

Table 3.2   Absolute Frequency Distribution for the Variable *Ethnicity*

ETHNICITY	FREQUENCY (f)*
1 Caucasian	20
2 African American	15
3 Hispanic	13
4 Other	2
Total (N)**	50

* The symbol *f* often appears in frequency distributions as a shorthand way to represent the word *frequency*.

** The symbol *N* often appears in frequency distributions as a shorthand way to represent the total number of cases.

Table 3.3   Absolute Frequency Distribution for the Variable *Number of Serious Behavioral Incidents*

NUMBER OF SERIOUS BEHAVIORAL INCIDENTS	FREQUENCY (*f*)
0	6
1	4
2	4
3	6
4	4
5	9
6	6
7	3
8	2
11	1
18	1
19	1
20	1
21	1
22	1
Total (*N*)	50

the raw data in the 50 rows of the ethnicity column in Table 3.1. We also can see how much easier it is to get a sense of how many youths had how many serious behavioral incidents than it was by reading the relevant part of the earlier narrative paragraph:

> Six youths had no serious behavioral incidents, four had 1 serious behavioral incident, another four had 2 serious behavioral incidents, six had 3 serious behavioral incidents, four had 4 serious behavioral incidents, nine had 5 serious behavioral incidents, six had 6 serious behavioral incidents, three had 7 serious behavioral incidents, two had 8 serious behavioral incidents, one had 11 serious behavioral incidents, one had 18 serious behavioral incidents, one had 19 serious behavioral incidents, one had 20 serious behavioral incidents, one had 21 serious behavioral incidents, and one had 22 serious behavioral incidents.

Relative Frequencies

In addition to displaying absolute frequencies, most frequency distributions will also display relative frequencies. **Relative frequencies** are the proportions or percentages of cases per category. To calculate the proportion of cases for a category of a variable, we simply divide the number of cases in that category by the total number of cases that have provided data for that variable. For example, suppose our sample contains 100 cases with ordinal data on socioeconomic status (SES), using the categories low, middle, and high. If 55 of our cases are low SES, then by dividing 55 by 100 we get a proportion of 0.55 cases with low SES. If 43 of our cases are middle SES, then by dividing 43 by 100 we get a proportion of 0.43 cases with middle SES. Likewise, the remaining two cases would become a proportion of 0.02 with high SES. To convert these proportions to percentages, we simply multiply each by 100. Thus, 0.55 becomes 55%, 0.43 becomes 43%, and 0.02 becomes 2%. These proportions and percentages would comprise our *relative frequencies*.

Of course, if you are using computer software to develop a frequency distribution, you won't have to perform the above calculations manually. But it helps to know them so you'll better understand the various types of frequencies you'll generate in your own reports or encounter in other reports.

Frequency distributions that display relative frequencies are constructed in the same way as absolute frequency distributions, but additionally show the proportions or percentages of cases per category alongside the absolute frequencies, as illustrated in Table 3.4 for the variable *ethnicity* and in Table 3.5 for the variable *number of serious behavioral incidents* (again using the raw data from Table 3.1). In those tables, each absolute frequency is divided by 50 (the total number of cases) to get its proportion, and each proportion is then multiplied by 100 to get each percentage.

Cumulative Frequencies

In addition to displaying absolute and relative frequencies, frequency distributions can display how the absolute and relative frequencies of cases per category add up as we go from one category to the next. The sums of absolute or relative frequencies are called *cumulative frequencies*. Tables displaying cumulative frequencies are constructed in the same

Table 3.4 Frequency Distribution with Absolute and Relative Frequencies for the Variable *Ethnicity*

ETHNICITY	FREQUENCY (*f*)	PROPORTION	PERCENT (%)
1 Caucasian	20	0.4000	40.0
2 African American	15	0.3000	30.0
3 Hispanic	13	0.2600	26.0
4 Other	2	0.0400	4.0
Total (*N*)	50	1.000	100

Table 3.5 Frequency Distribution with Absolute and Relative Frequencies for the Variable *Number of Serious Behavioral Incidents*

NUMBER OF SERIOUS BEHAVIORAL INCIDENTS	FREQUENCY (*f*)	PROPORTION	PERCENT (%)
0	6	0.1200	12.0
1	4	0.0800	8.0
2	4	0.0800	8.0
3	6	0.1200	12.0
4	4	0.0800	8.0
5	9	0.1800	18.0
6	6	0.1200	12.0
7	3	0.0600	6.0
8	2	0.0400	4.0
11	1	0.0200	2.0
18	1	0.0200	2.0
19	1	0.0200	2.0
20	1	0.0200	2.0
21	1	0.0200	2.0
22	1	0.0200	2.0
Total (*N*)	50	1.000	100

fashion as other frequency distributions and typically show each absolute and relative frequency alongside and to the left of each cumulative frequency. Thus, the most comprehensive frequency distribution will be one showing absolute frequencies, relative frequencies, and cumulative frequencies, as displayed in Table 3.6 for the variable *number of serious behavioral incidents* (again using the raw data from Table 3.1).

Grouped Frequency Distributions

Some variables have so many categories that interpreting their frequency distributions can become

Table 3.6   Frequency Distribution Displaying Cumulative Frequencies for the Variable *Number of Serious Behavioral Incidents*

NUMBER OF SERIOUS BEHAVIORAL INCIDENTS	FREQUENCY (*f*)	CUMULATIVE FREQUENCY (*Cf*)	PROPORTION	PERCENT (%)	CUMULATIVE PERCENT (%)
0	6	6	0.1200	12.0	12.0
1	4	10	0.0800	8.0	20.0
2	4	14	0.0800	8.0	28.0
3	6	20	0.1200	12.0	40.0
4	4	24	0.0800	8.0	48.0
5	9	33	0.1800	18.0	66.0
6	6	39	0.1200	12.0	78.0
7	3	42	0.0600	6.0	84.0
8	2	44	0.0400	4.0	88.0
11	1	45	0.0200	2.0	90.0
18	1	46	0.0200	2.0	92.0
19	1	47	0.0200	2.0	94.0
20	1	48	0.0200	2.0	96.0
21	1	49	0.0200	2.0	98.0
22	1	50	0.0200	2.0	100.0
Total (*N*)	50		1.000	100	

cumbersome. To illustrate this point, compare the frequency distributions displayed for the variables *ethnicity* and *number of serious behavioral incidents*. Consider, for example, how easy it is to comprehend the full picture in the absolute frequency distribution displayed in Table 3.2 for the variable *ethnicity*, which has a small number of categories (rows). Contrast that with the larger number of categories (rows) in the tables for the variable *serious behavioral incidents*.

To simplify a frequency distribution for a variable that contains a large number of categories, it is often helpful to create a **grouped frequency distribution,** which involves combining some or all of the categories into a smaller number of meaningful groupings. Notice, for example, how Table 3.7, which displays a grouped frequency distribution of the data in Table 3.6, is easier on the eyes than Table 3.6.

How to combine categories in creating a grouped frequency distribution is an important decision. The best way to combine categories will vary, depending on the meaning and practical implications of a particular variable and the way the data are distributed for that variable. Sometimes it makes sense to create groupings that have fairly even numbers of cases per grouping. This is particularly appropriate when—before grouping—there is a fairly even distribution of cases across the original list of categories.

At other times groupings with uneven numbers of cases make more sense. How you conceptualize your study and how the prior literature has dealt with the variable in question can guide your decision as to how best to combine categories. For example, suppose you are assessing an outreach intervention aimed at motivating attendance at a 12-session outpatient treatment program for substance abuse. Suppose that the literature indicates that attending some sessions is better than none, but that clients who miss even just one session are much less likely to benefit from the treatment than those who attend all 12 sessions. Regardless of the numbers of cases per category, therefore, you may want to create three categories in your grouped frequency distribution for the variable *number of*

Table 3.7   Grouped Frequency Distribution for the Variable *Number of Serious Behavioral Incidents*

NUMBER OF SERIOUS BEHAVIORAL INCIDENTS	FREQUENCY (*f*)	CUMULATIVE FREQUENCY (*Cf*)	PROPORTION	PERCENT (%)	CUMULATIVE PERCENT (%)
0	6	6	0.1200	12.0	12.0
1–2	8	14	0.1600	16.0	28.0
3–4	10	24	0.2000	20.0	48.0
5–6	15	39	0.3000	30.0	78.0
7–11	6	45	0.1200	12.0	90.0
18–22	5	50	0.1000	10.0	100.0
Total (*N*)	50		1.000	100	

sessions attended: (1) zero sessions; (2) 1 to 11 sessions; and (3) 12 sessions.

Returning to our residential treatment center evaluation, notice that 6 of the 50 cases in Table 3.6 had zero serious behavioral incidents. Would it make sense to group them with the 4 cases that had one incident? That might be reasonable, since the other categories in our grouped frequency distribution in Table 3.7 combine values. Upon further reflection, however, you might decide to keep the zero incidents category ungrouped, since it represents the best outcome possible and since 6 cases is not an inconsequential number, comprising 12% of the total sample of 50 cases.

Looking at Table 3.6, notice that 5 cases (near the bottom of the table) had 18 or more serious incidents and that the closest three categories above them (7, 8, and 11 incidents) had a total of 6 cases. Would it make sense to lump them all together into a *seven or more* category containing 11 (22%) of the cases? That might be easy on the eyes, but there is a big difference conceptually and in terms of program implications between 7 serious behavioral incidents and 18 or more incidents. After considering such conceptual and practice-related implications, you might decide instead to combine categories as done in Table 3.7. I am not suggesting that grouping as the only "correct" way to collapse Table 3.6. It makes sense to me, but reasonable people may devise other ways to combine the categories. The important thing is that you understand how to create and interpret tables like this and that you create your groupings according to what provides the most accurate and meaningful portrayal of your data, rather than just do it in a knee-jerk fashion.

MISLEADING PERCENTAGES

Percentages can be misleading when they are based on a relatively small number of cases. So far, we have been examining percentages based on 50 cases. But what if we were comparing a larger and a smaller residential treatment program? Suppose 10% of the youths in both programs had 18 or more serious behavioral incidents, and each program implemented a different intervention aimed at reducing such incidents. Let's further suppose that one program is a national chain of residential facilities with 1000 residents, and the other is one small facility with 20 residents.

Let's say that the large program implements Intervention A, and the number of youths with 18 or more serious behavioral incidents falls from 100 out of 1000 (10%) to 50 (5%). Not bad! Let's also say that the small program implements Intervention B, and the number of youths with 18 or more serious behavioral incidents falls from 2 out of 20 (10%) to 1 (5%).

Both interventions were followed by a 50% decrease in dropout rates (from 10% to 5%). But would you be equally impressed by each decrease? Conceivably both interventions are equally effective. But it's a lot harder to get a decrease from 100 to 50 than from 2 to 1. It would be misleading, therefore, to say that both interventions appear to be equally effective even though they had the same percentage decreases.

Here's another example. Suppose the large national chain of residential facilities employed 100 therapists, but only one of them was African American. Suppose, responding to pressure from the board, its chief administrator recruited one more African American therapist and then boasted that he doubled the percentage of African American practitioners. You would not be impressed, knowing that doubling a percentage (from 1% to 2%) based on such a small number can be misleading. Let's hope that the board members would not be impressed either, especially if the proportion of African American youths in treatment were a lot larger than 2%!

So, be cautious when you are reporting or reading about percentages based on a small number of cases. With that caveat in mind, let's move on to Chapter 4, which discusses other ways to simplify the presentation of a large mass of data: using graphs or charts.

Main Points

• Frequency distributions transform a mass of unmanageable details of data into manageable summaries.

• A frequency is a statistical term pertaining to a count of how many cases there are in a particular category of a particular variable.

• A frequency distribution is a list of the frequencies for each category of a variable.

• Frequencies can be displayed in three ways: as absolute frequencies, relative frequencies, and cumulative frequencies.

• Absolute frequencies are simple counts of the number of cases per category.

• An absolute frequency distribution is a table that only displays the number of cases in each category of a variable.

• In addition to displaying absolute frequencies, most frequency distributions will also display relative frequencies.

• Relative frequencies are the proportions or percentages of cases per category. To calculate the proportion of cases for a category of a variable, we simply divide the number of cases in that category by the total number of cases that have provided data for that variable.

• In addition to displaying absolute and relative frequencies, frequency distributions can display how the absolute and relative frequencies of cases per category add up as we go from one category to the next. The sums of absolute or relative frequencies are called *cumulative frequencies*.

• To simplify a frequency distribution for a variable that contains a large number of categories, it is often helpful to create a grouped frequency distribution, which involves combining some or all of the categories into a smaller number of meaningful groupings.

• Percentages can be misleading when they are based on a relatively small number of cases.

Review Questions and Exercises

1. You administer a substance abuse program for youths. You and your staff are concerned about difficulties in engaging and retaining referred youths in your 12-session treatment program. You conduct an evaluation to assess factors that might explain differences in treatment engagement and retention. Table 3.8 provides a raw data file for three variables and 30 of the youths in your study. You are encouraged to use SPSS or other statistical software for this exercise if you have access to it. Otherwise, you can complete this exercise manually. If you use SPSS, you are encouraged to read the following sections in Appendix G: "Using SPSS to Create Frequency Distributions (Chapter 3)," and "Using SPSS to Create Grouped Frequency Distributions (Chapter 3)."

a. Create and interpret a frequency distribution for the variable *main substance abused*. Include absolute and relative frequencies in it.

b. Create and interpret a frequency distribution for the variable *age*. Include absolute, relative, and cumulative frequencies in it.

c. Create and interpret a frequency distribution for the variable *number of treatment sessions attended*. Include absolute, relative, and cumulative frequencies in it.

d. Based on the frequencies you observe in c, above, create and interpret a grouped frequency distribution for the variable *number of treatment sessions attended*.

Table 3.8

CASE NUMBER	MAIN SUBSTANCE ABUSED	AGE	NUMBER OF TREATMENT SESSIONS ATTENDED
1	Alcohol	16	10
2	Marijuana	14	12
3	Cocaine	15	3
4	Heroin	17	0
5	Other	12	4
6	Alcohol	15	9
7	Marijuana	13	11
8	Cocaine	14	5
9	Heroin	16	1
10	Alcohol	15	8
11	Marijuana	14	10
12	Alcohol	17	8
13	Marijuana	12	9
14	Alcohol	13	8
15	Alcohol	14	7
16	Cocaine	15	6
17	Heroin	16	2
18	Marijuana	14	9
19	Other	15	5
20	Heroin	16	4
21	Marijuana	13	8
22	Alcohol	17	7
23	Marijuana	14	8
24	Cocaine	15	6
25	Marijuana	12	10
26	Cocaine	16	5
27	Cocaine	17	5
28	Marijuana	14	8
29	Alcohol	15	7
30	Marijuana	14	9

2. Suppose in the following year the number of youths attending all 12 sessions of the treatment program discussed in Exercise 1 doubles from 1 (out of 30) to 2 (out of 30). Suppose your colleague wants to interpret that increase in percentage terms, and thus be able to claim a 100% increase in the number of youths completing the entire regimen: from 3.3% to 6.6%. Would you advise your colleague to make that claim? Why or why not?

InfoTrac Exercises

1. Examine and interpret one of the frequency distributions in the following article:

Johnson, H., & Pottie Bunge, V. (2001). Prevalence and consequences of spousal assault in Canada. *Canadian Journal of Criminology, 43*(1), 27.

2. Briefly interpret at least one finding of interest to you in the grouped frequency distribution in Table 1 of the following article:

Ray, D. C., Armstrong, S. A., Warren, E. S., & Balkin, R. S. (2005). Play therapy practices among elementary school counselors. *Professional School Counseling, 8*(4), 390–395.

3. Re-examine the following article (first mentioned in the InfoTrac exercises in Chapter 1):

Walsh, J., Green, R., Matthews, J., & Bonucelli-Puerto, B. (2005). Social workers' views of the etiology of mental disorders: Results of a national study. *Social Work, 50*(1), 43–52.

Briefly discuss something you find interesting and relevant to evidence-based practice in Table 1 of the article.

Graphs and Charts

INTRODUCTION

You've probably heard the expression: "A picture is worth a thousand words." People who have to read the statistical findings of program evaluation reports might say, "A picture is worth a thousand numbers." Busy administrators, clinicians, legislators or funding sources, for example, may prefer graphical representations of your findings that enable them to get a sense of the overall picture more quickly and simply than examining the numerical details in tables. Readers who are not astute with research and statistics, or perhaps have an aversion to them, might be especially appreciative of graphical presentations. Likewise, they might get turned off if such pictorial presentations are missing, forcing them to rely solely on tables with lots of numbers.

Graphical depictions of findings typically provide less detail than tables. But unless your audience consists primarily of folks who are comfortable with research and statistics, you should provide graphs or charts that will enable you to communicate more effectively with them. The graphs and charts can be supplied in addition to the tables, and for some audiences it might be wise to put all of the detailed tables in appendices, keeping the graphs and charts in the main body of the report while referring readers to the particular appendixes where they can find the more detailed table associated with each graph or chart.

Graphs and charts come in a variety of formats. Which format is best to use will depend on the purpose of the graph or chart. For example, a graph or chart showing trends over time might require a different format from one comparing proportions or averages among groups at the same point in time.

Some of the most commonly used formats in evidence-based practice and evaluation are bar graphs, pie charts, histograms, and frequency polygons. We'll examine each of these and a few others shortly. First, let's examine the general structural basis for constructing or understanding most graphs. As displayed in Figure 4.1, most graphs begin with a vertical line that goes upward and a horizontal line that begins at the bottom of the vertical line and extends to the right. The point from which the two lines begin is called the **point of origin**. The horizontal line, called the *x*-**axis** or **abscissa**, typically displays the values of a variable. The vertical line, called the *y*-**axis** or **ordinate**, often

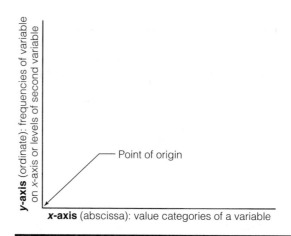

Figure 4.1   General Structure for Commonly Used Graphs

displays the number (frequency) or percentage of cases for each value of that variable. The *y*-axis might also display different levels of a second variable, thus showing whether changing levels of categories of the *x*-axis variable move in a consistent fashion with changing levels of the *y*-axis variable. Don't worry if this sounds a bit complicated now; it will become much clearer as we illustrate some commonly used types of graphs. We'll begin with bar graphs.

BAR GRAPHS

Bar graphs depict frequency distributions, using vertical bars to show the number or percentage of cases for each category of a nominal-level variable. For every category along the *x*-axis there is a bar of equal width. The bars are evenly spaced along the *x*-axis, and none of the bars touch. The more cases in a particular category, the taller the bar for that category. By looking at the number along the *y*-axis that—like the numbers on a ruler—corresponds to the top of each bar, we can see the number and/or percentage of cases for each category. Figure 4.2 displays a bar graph for the distribution of ethnicity for the 50 cases in the hypothetical evaluation in a residential treatment center that we discussed in Chapter 3. You may recall that the raw data for that evaluation were displayed in Table 3.1, and the various frequency distributions displayed and discussed in Chapter 3 were based on those raw data.

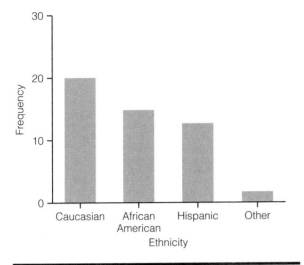

Figure 4.2 Bar Graph of Ethnicity Distribution

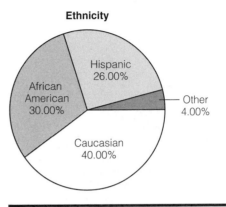

Figure 4.3 Pie Chart of Percentage Distribution for Ethnicity

The bar graph in Figure 4.2 corresponds to the frequency distribution displayed in Table 3.2 of the previous chapter (Table 3.2, Absolute Frequency Distribution for the Variable *Ethnicity*). The section of Appendix G headed "Using SPSS to Create Graphs (Chapter 4)" shows how to use SPSS to create a bar graph like the one in Figure 4.2. It also conveys how to create the other types of graphs to be discussed next in this chapter.

PIE CHARTS

Pie charts portray frequency distribution data in terms of percentages represented by slices of a pie or sections of a circle. The bigger the slice of pie, the higher the percentage of cases in the particular category of the variable being portrayed. Pie charts work best when the number of categories being portrayed is not extensive. With a large number of categories representing tiny percentages of cases, there would be so many tiny slices that readers might need a magnifying glass to see them and to decipher their corresponding percentages. Figure 4.3 displays a pie chart for the percentage distribution of ethnicity for the 50 cases in our hypothetical evaluation. These percentages correspond to the data in both our bar graph in Figure 4.2 and our frequency distribution in Table 3.1.

HISTOGRAMS

When our data are at a metric level of measurement—that is, they are at the ordinal, interval, or ratio level—they can be displayed with a **histogram**. Histograms look like bar graphs with bars that touch each other, and they can be interpreted like bar graphs. In case you are wondering, the reason that histogram bars touch each other is that—unlike bar graphs of nominal variables—they represent quantitative increments moving from one bar to the next.

When histograms represent interval- or ratio-level variables that have had their values collapsed into grouped categories of unequal ranges, the width of the bars may be equal or unequal. When they are unequal, the different widths correspond proportionately to the differences in the range of values for each grouped category. For example, a grouped age category with a 10-year range—say, from age 1 to 10—might be represented by a bar twice as wide as the next bar if that next bar represents a 5-year age range, say from 11 to 15.

Most histograms (including all done with SPSS), however, have bars of equal width, as do all bar graphs. To keep things simple, we'll just look at one with equal bar widths, as displayed in Figure 4.4. The bars in that histogram represent our grouped data on the variable *number of serious behavioral incidents* in our hypothetical evaluation, which were displayed in the grouped frequency distribution in

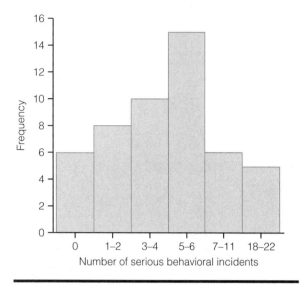

Figure 4.4 Histogram: Number of Serious Behavioral Incidents

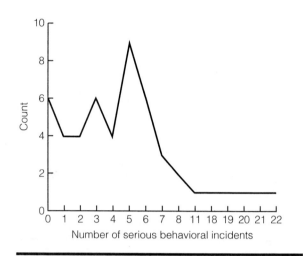

Figure 4.5 Frequency Polygon for Number of Serious Behavioral Incidents

Table 3.7. Going from left to right, the first bar represents the six cases with no incidents. The second bar represents the eight cases with 1–2 incidents. The third bar represents the ten cases with 3–4 incidents. The fourth, and tallest, bar represents the 15 cases with 5–6 incidents, and so on.

FREQUENCY POLYGONS

A graph that uses single points instead of bars to convey the *y*-axis amount for each value along the *x*-axis is called a **frequency polygon** or **line graph**. Straight lines connect adjacent points, forming a shape that depicts the frequency distribution for the *x*-axis variable. Although frequency polygons typically involve interval- or ratio-level data, they can be constructed with ordinal data if those data represent grouped values of interval- or ratio-level variables. When using grouped values along the *x*-axis, the dots in the polygon are placed above the midpoints of the grouped values. Figure 4.5 displays a frequency polygon using the ungrouped, ratio-level data on *number of serious behavioral incidents* from Table 3.3.

Notice how the shape of the frequency polygon shows, in pictorial fashion, that the values for number of cases with various numbers of serious behavioral incidents in our sample tended to vary quite a bit, with some values near 20 being quite a distance away from much smaller values and with many

more cases at some of the smaller values than at the much larger values. This variance, or dispersion, in the distribution is a very important concept. We considered it in Chapter 1, when we examined how extreme cases can distort the meaning of the arithmetic average. We'll delve into this concept in more depth in the next chapter.

LINE GRAPHS SHOWING TRENDS OVER TIME

If you compare the histogram in Figure 4.4 to the frequency polygon in Figure 4.5, you can probably see why some people prefer histograms to line graphs for illuminating the way a variable is distributed at one point in time. Frequency polygons, or line graphs, can be more difficult to grasp when used this way. But line graphs can be much clearer when our purpose is to show trends over time. Consider the line graph in Figure 4.6, for example, which is identical in shape to the one in Figure 4.5, but which represents the overall number of serious behavioral incidents in a hypothetical residential treatment center over time.

With this graph, the categories on the *y*-axis represent the number of serious behavioral incidents (for the facility as a whole) instead of the number of cases, and the categories on the *x*-axis are weeks (instead of number of serious behavioral incidents). Notice the precipitous drop in the number of incidents immediately after week 6. Notice also that the number remained low throughout the remaining weeks. What happened around week 6 or 7 that might have caused this change? Was some new policy or some new treatment introduced at the facility? If so, this graph clearly suggests that this change may have led to reduced numbers of serious

behavioral incidents. While we might not know the reason for the drop, Figure 4.6 illustrates the utility of using line graphs to display trends over time.

Even if we didn't know the reason for the drop just by looking at the graph, it would spur us to investigate further to try to find the reason. For example, we might suspect that it was a new intervention that got implemented across the facility around week 6 or 7. We might therefore conduct a study in a similar residential treatment center that had not yet implemented this new intervention. We might assess the number of serious behavioral incidents in the center for each of six weeks prior to implementing the new intervention and each of six weeks after implementing it. Suppose our results were graphed as in Figure 4.7. That line graph clearly would support our hypothesis that the new intervention is effective in reducing the number of serious behavioral incidents. Moreover, combined with the line graph results in Figure 4.6, it would offer some degree of replication and consequently strengthen the logic of that inference. (To learn more about the logic used in interpreting Figures 4.6 and 4.7, you can read about time-series designs and single-case evaluation designs in texts such as Rubin and Babbie (2005) and Bloom, Fischer, and Orme (2003).

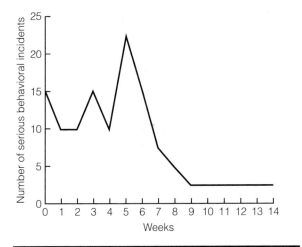

Figure 4.6 Line Graph for Number of Serious Behavioral Incidents Over Time

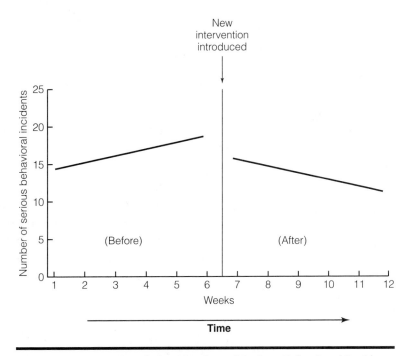

Figure 4.7 Line Graph for Number of Serious Behavioral Incidents Over Time Before and After a New Intervention is Introduced

MISLEADING GRAPHICS

Graphs can be constructed in misleading ways. Sometimes this is done mistakenly but not unethically. At other times less ethical folks might intentionally seek to distort things for propagandistic purposes. A common way this is done is by changing the spacing between categories on the vertical or horizontal axis so as to convey a more dramatic pattern or perhaps a less dramatic pattern— depending on whether a more dramatic pattern or less dramatic pattern fits the distorted impression a propagandist wants to convey.

For example, suppose some folks with a vested interest in the intervention being evaluated in Figure 4.7 want to make the after-treatment improvement during weeks 7 through 12 look even more impressive than appears in Figure 4.7. They could spread out the distance between intervals on the vertical axis, and squeeze the weeks on the horizontal axis more closely together. Thus, their graph of the same data would look like the one in Figure 4.8.

Conversely, a trend can be made to look less dramatic by squeezing the intervals on the vertical axis closer together while spreading out the intervals on the horizontal axis. Suppose an ethically challenged program administrator is worried about how his board might react upon seeing the declining trend in the agency's caseload over the past 12 months. Suppose the trend looks like the one in Figure 4.9 (A). He could attempt to mislead the board by squeezing the vertical intervals closer together and spreading out the horizontal ones, as in the graph in Figure 4.9 (B), thus making the declining caseload trend look flatter and thus less critical.

As noted at the outset of this book, people can lie with statistics. Distorting graphs is just one way they can do this. Some folks mislead unintentionally, while others might do so intentionally. If you are ethical, you'll never do so intentionally. By understanding the material in this chapter (and in the rest of this text), your chances of misleading unintentionally will be diminished. To further reduce your chances of misleading or being misled with graphics, you should ask yourself regarding every graph you construct or read whether the kinds of distortions illustrated in Figures 4.8 and 4.9 have been avoided. Obtaining the reactions of colleagues or statistical consultants can help, too.

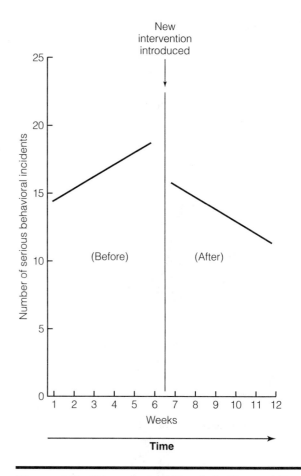

Figure 4.8   Distortion of Graph in Figure 4.7 to Make After-Treatment Improvement Trend Look More Dramatic

Main Points

• Graphs and charts come in a variety of formats. Which format is best to use will depend on the purpose of the graph or chart. For example, a graph or chart showing trends over time might require a different format than one comparing proportions or averages among groups at the same point in time.

• Most graphs begin with a vertical line that extends upward and a horizontal line that begins at the bottom of the vertical line and extends to the right. The point at which the two lines begin is called the point of origin. The horizontal line, called the x-axis or abscissa, typically displays the values of a variable. The vertical line, called the

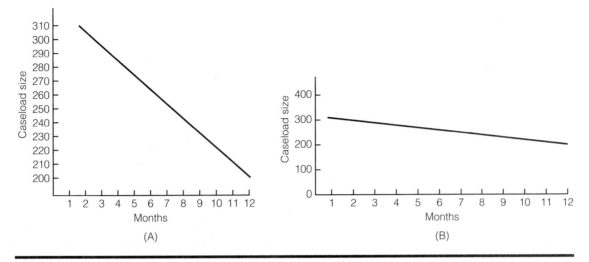

Figure 4.9   Two Graphs Displaying a Declining Trend in a Fictional Agency Caseload

y-axis or ordinate, often displays the number (frequency) or percentage of cases for each value of that variable.

• Bar graphs depict frequency distributions, using bars to show the number or percentage of cases for each category of a nominal-level variable.

• Pie charts portray frequency distribution data in terms of percentages represented by slices of a pie or sections of a circle. The bigger the slice of pie, the higher the percentage of cases in the particular category of the variable being portrayed.

• Histograms can be used to depict frequencies with ordinal-, interval-, or ratio-level variables. They look like bar graphs with bars that touch each other, and they can be interpreted like bar graphs.

• A graph that uses single points instead of bars to convey the *y*-axis amount for each value along the *x*-axis is called a frequency polygon or line graph.

• Line graphs can be difficult to read when portraying frequencies for a variable at one point in time, but can be much clearer when showing trends over time.

• Graphs can be constructed in misleading ways, such as by changing the spacing between categories on the vertical or horizontal axis so as to convey a more dramatic pattern or perhaps a less dramatic pattern.

Review Questions and Exercises

1. For this question, refer to the raw data file in Review Question 1 in Chapter 3, regarding a substance abuse program for youths and factors that might explain differences in treatment engagement and retention. (You are encouraged to use SPSS or other statistical software for this exercise if you have access to it.)

a. For the variable *main substance abused*, create and interpret a bar graph and a pie graph.

b. For the variable *age*, create and interpret a histogram and a frequency polygon.

c. For the variable *number of treatment sessions attended*, create and interpret a histogram based on combined value categories (such as the ones you may have used in your grouped frequency distribution in your answer to Exercise 1(c) in Chapter 3.

2. A new family preservation project was funded for 12 months in a statewide child welfare agency. To retain funding after the twelve months expire, it must demonstrate that it has dramatically reversed the worsening trend of an increasing number of out-of-home placements of abused children over the 12 months before the project was implemented. The number of out-of-home placements for each 12-month time period are shown in Figure 4.10 (the arrow signifies the start of the project).

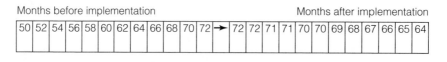

Months before implementation   Months after implementation

| 50 | 52 | 54 | 56 | 58 | 60 | 62 | 64 | 66 | 68 | 70 | 72 | → | 72 | 72 | 71 | 71 | 70 | 70 | 69 | 68 | 67 | 66 | 65 | 64 |

Figure 4.10

a. Create a line graph displaying the trends over time in out-of-home placements before and after the project was implemented.

b. Suppose an unethical administrator wanted to create a different line graph displaying the trends over time in out-of-home placements before and after the project was implemented, but in a distorted and misleading manner that would make the trend reversal in out-of-home placements look more dramatic. Create such a graph using the same data but changing the spacing on the vertical and horizontal axes. Explain why it is misleading.

InfoTrac Exercises

1. Read the following article and write down one or more of its tips for presenting charts or graphs that you think is important.

Presentation graphics should help audiences get the picture. (1987). *PC Week, 4*(49), 56.

2. Re-examine the following article and briefly summarize your interpretation of its bar graph in Figure 1.

Walsh, J., Green, R., Matthews, J., & Bonucelli-Puerto, B. (2005). Social workers' views of the etiology of mental disorders: Results of a national study. *Social Work, 50*(1), 43–52.

Measures of Central Tendency

INTRODUCTION

The frequency distributions and graphs discussed in Chapters 3 and 4 are not the only ways to transform your data into manageable summaries and convey an overall picture of your findings. When your data are at the ordinal, interval, or ratio level of measurement, you can summarize them with descriptive statistics called **measures of central tendency,** which include the *mean, median,* and *mode.* These descriptive statistics can summarize ordinal-, interval-, or ratio-level data more succinctly than can frequency distributions and graphs.

Each of these statistics provides one number that attempts to give readers a sense of the "average" or "typical" value in a distribution. Before examining each of these statistics, let's clarify what is meant—and *not* meant—by the term *average.* When the term *average* is used in reference to a group of people, it is often thought to mean *typical.* Thus, if we are describing the participants in a high school dropout prevention program, we might say that the "typical" participant is on average 16 years old and from a family earning on average less than $20,000 per year. In the previous sentence the terms *average* and *typical* are used interchangeably in a loose fashion. Although the arithmetic average of the ages of participants might be 16, most participants might not be 16 years old. Maybe 40% of them are 16, and maybe a total of 60% are at younger or older ages.

The difference between *average* and *typical* is more evident if we are describing the caseload of a family service agency that offers services to children, parents, and the elderly. It would be problematic to say that the "typical" client in such an agency has the average age of 40, even if that number is the arithmetic average age of all the agency's clients. The descriptive statistics that will be discussed in this chapter and the next, examined together, will help indicate just how typical (or perhaps *atypical*) an arithmetic average really is. That is, they will not only refer to an average, but will also show the degree to which the values in a distribution of a variable tend to be close to or not so close to that average value. When most of the values are close to the arithmetic average, then it may be reasonable to think of that average as *typical.* But the arithmetic average may not represent the *typical* case when it is merely the middle value between many values that are far above it and far below it.

In this chapter we'll look at the utility of the three different measures of central tendency, how to calculate them, and how to interpret them and not be misled by them. We'll begin with the most commonly cited measure of central tendency: *the mean.* Then we'll examine *the median.* Both of these measures are based on the notion of locating the value that best represents the *center* of a distribution of scores (thus the term *central tendency*). After we examine and compare the mean and median, we'll turn to the mode, which is less likely to be at the center of a distribution than the mean or median.

THE MEAN

In Chapter 1 we examined the arithmetic **mean** in connection with tax savings, as an illustration of how an understanding of statistics can protect you from being misled. We noted that to calculate the mean, we sum all of the values for a variable and divide that sum by the number of values being summed. The formula for calculating the mean can be found in the box labeled "Formula for Calculating the Mean."

Because calculating the mean involves adding and dividing, it is not appropriate to find a mean for nominal-level variables such as gender or ethnicity. Imagine, for example, how silly it would be to think of adding up male and female—or African American, Hispanic and so on! If we calculate a mean using the code numbers we assign to nominal variables, the average may make no sense. For example, if we have three clients of different ethnicities and we add up code 1 for Caucasian, code 2 for African American, and code 3 for Hispanic, the sum would be 6. Dividing that by 3 (there are 3 cases) would give us a mean of 2. Would that tell us that our average or typical client was African American (code 2)? Of course not.

The mean makes the most sense when it is calculated with variables that convey quantities, such as ordinal-, interval- or ratio-level variables. With variables at the ratio level of measurement, for example, if an experimental group's mean is double a routine treatment group's mean, then the experimental group has on average exactly twice as much of the quantity being measured as does the routine treatment group. Thus, if an experimental group's

---

Formula for Calculating the Mean

The formula for calculating the mean value of a variable in a sample uses the following symbols:

$\bar{X}$ = The sample mean*

Σ = The sum of all of the items to the right of the symbol Σ (which is the upper-case Greek letter *sigma*)

X_s = All the values for the variable being summed

N = The total number of values being summed (usually the total number of cases in the data file)

Using the above symbols, the formula for calculating the mean is

$$\bar{X} = \frac{\Sigma X_s}{N}$$

---

*Note: The line is placed above the X in the symbol $\bar{X}$ to signify that we are computing a mean of a sample, not a population. The symbol is read or spoken as *X-bar*. When calculating the mean of a population, the Greek letter mu (μ) is used instead of *X-bar*.

---

mean number of treatment sessions attended is 10, and the routine treatment group's is 5, we know that on average the experimental group participants attended twice as many sessions as did the control group participants who were receiving the routine treatment.

How might knowing the mean of a particular variable be useful to evidence-based practitioners? Here's an example. Suppose your first professional job is in an inpatient substance abuse treatment facility for adolescents. The program also offers weekly support group meetings for the parents of the youths in treatment. Before graduating, you learned of a new, evidence-based approach to facilitating parent support groups, and you want to try it out. To be effective, however, the new approach requires that parents attend the entire package of 12 weekly support group meetings.

You discuss your idea with your supervisor, and she informs you of a problem with your plan. The mean number of support group sessions currently attended by parents in its existing parent support groups is 2. You ask why and learn that there are many reasons—most having nothing to do with satisfaction with the service. For example, many of the parents live too far away, have transportation problems, need childcare, are substance abusers

themselves and thus not motivated or functioning adequately to attend even one session, and so on. Knowing that the mean of 2 sessions attended is so far away from the required number of 12 sessions, you would realize that before implementing the new support group approach you'd better try to come up with some ways to make it easier for the parents to attend all 12 sessions and to motivate them to do so.

Here's an administration and planning example—one that involves some real means that I recently encountered while writing a research proposal in Texas. Suppose you are seeking government funding for a small pilot project that would deliver an after-care social service intervention to prevent crimes committed by people recently released from state prisons in Texas. Suppose your small program would cost $100,000 and would intervene with 100 released prisoners. Your mean program cost per prisoner therefore would be $100,000 divided by 100, or $1,000.

If you inquired with the Texas Department of Criminal Justice (TDCJ, 2003), you would learn that the mean length of incarceration for released prisoners who become re-incarcerated in state prisons is 4.74 years, or 1731.29 days (as of this writing). You would also learn that the mean cost of re-incarceration is $44.01 per day. That comes to $76,194 over 4.74 years. (You'd get this by multiplying $44.01 times 1731.29 days.) Thus, if your $100,000 program prevented just 2 re-incarcerations per year, you would save the state $52,398 per year in re-incarceration costs alone (because 2 times $76,194 = $152,398, which is $52,398 more than your program cost), not to mention the other fiscal and emotional costs to victims and society caused by crime. Thus, knowing the mean costs and the mean length of incarceration—and thus being able to cite them in your proposal—would probably strengthen your chances of convincing a government agency to invest in your program.

When our quantitative data are at the ordinal level, however, interpreting the mean can be trickier. Suppose we ask clients to rate their satisfaction with services on a 6-point scale, with scores of 1 for very dissatisfied, 2 for moderately dissatisfied, 3 for slightly dissatisfied, 4 for slightly satisfied, 5 for moderately satisfied, and 6 for very satisfied. If our experimental group's mean is 4 and our routine treatment group's mean is 2, it would be inappropriate to conclude that our experimental group participants on average are twice as satisfied as are our routine treatment group participants.

Nevertheless, means are frequently reported with some ordinal-level variables, such as grade point average (GPA). It is useful to know that one applicant's GPA is 4.0 and another's is 2.0, even though that does not mean that the 4.0 applicant performed twice as well in school or learned twice as much as the 2.0 applicant. For example, the 2.0 applicant may have averaged 75% on his exams, while the 4.0 applicant may have averaged 95% on her exams. Ninety-five percent is not double the 75% performance, but when we assign ordinal codes to grades, with a 4 for an A and a 2 for a C, the higher average exam score gets converted to an ordinal value that is double the ordinal value for the lower average exam score. Thus, while we frequently encounter means for ordinal data, and can find some practical value in some of them, we should be careful in how we interpret them.

Before we move on to the next measure of central tendency, the median, let's calculate two means in the data set for our hypothetical evaluation in a residential treatment center. We'll calculate the mean number of serious behavioral incidents for our two treatment groups. To do so, we need to refer to the data file for that evaluation displayed in Table 3.1 on page 26. As indicated in Table 3.1, one treatment group received the new treatment, and the other received the routine treatment. From Table 3.1 we can list the number of serious behavioral incidents for the 25 cases in each group, as displayed in Table 5.1.

Table 5.1 Calculating the Mean Number of Serious Behavioral Incidents in Each of Two Treatment Groups

GROUP 1: NEW TREATMENT	GROUP 2: ROUTINE TREATMENT
0	3
0	3
1	4
8	5
1	6
2	6
0	4
21	5
0	5
3	3
0	6
3	8
19	5
2	5
22	7
20	3
0	4
11	5
1	5
1	6
2	5
2	7
18	5
7	6
6	4
Total 150	125
Mean 150/25 = 6.0	125/25 = 5.0

By summing each column and then dividing by the number of values (or cases) in each column, we find that the new treatment group's mean number of serious behavioral incidents is 6, compared to 5 for the routine treatment group. If you have access to statistical software, such as SPSS, MicroCase or Excel, you can use that software to calculate these means. If you have access to SPSS, you may want to examine the section in Appendix G headed "Using SPSS to Calculate Measures of Central Tendency (Chapter 5)."

Because serious behavioral incidents are undesirable, and the treatment being evaluated is trying to reduce them, the new treatment group's higher mean of 6 is worse than the routine group's lower mean of 5. Thus, our first inclination might be to conclude that routine treatment is more effective in preventing serious behavioral incidents than is the new treatment because the "average" case in that group did worse than the "average" case in the routine group. But as we will soon see when we examine some additional measures, we should not rush to judgment on this issue based solely on the mean. The median, for example, can give us a different sense of the central tendency of the distribution of a set of values.

THE MEDIAN

The **median** is the *middle* value in a ranked distribution of values. Because it involves only the rank order of values, it can be used with ordinal data without the problems associated with calculating the mean for ordinal data. Since the *median* represents the "middle" value, we can calculate it by seeing which value has an equal number of cases above it and below it.

Although you can use statistical software to calculate the median, let's look back at Table 5.1 to see how it's done. If we look at the 25 values in the Routine Treatment column, we can count eight values below 5 and eight values above 5. (There are nine cases with the value 5.) Therefore, 5 is the *median* for that group. It's important to keep in mind that we are not just looking at the thirteenth case in the unranked data list, which also would be a 5 for the routine treatment group. When we calculate the median we are asking, "If we arranged the numbers in rank order from lowest to highest, which number would be located in the middle?" To picture this better, let's arrange the 25 cases for the routine treatment group in rank order from lowest to highest, as shown in Figure 5.1.

Notice how there are eight numbers to the left of the median (5) and eight numbers to the right of it. Notice also that the same value gets repeated in the list if more than one case has that value. Thus, since nine cases had 5 serious behavioral incidents, 5 gets listed nine times.

When calculating the median for the new treatment group, we find ten values below 2, four 2's, and 11 values above 2. Therefore, the median for the new treatment group is 2. To picture this better, let's arrange the 25 cases for the new treatment group in rank order from lowest to highest, as shown in Figure 5.2.

Although there is one more case above 2 than below it, 2 comes closer than any other value to being the middle value and is therefore the median. (When there are unequal numbers on either side of the median, the median is sometimes calculated with decimal points, as discussed in the box titled "Calculating the Median.")

```
3  3  3  3   4  4  4  4 | 5  5  5  5  5  5  5  5  5 | 6  6  6  6  6   7  7   8
    ←——— Eight cases ———           Median            ——— Eight cases ———→
```

Figure 5.1

```
0  0  0  0  0  0  1  1  1  1 | 2  2  2  2 | 3  3  6  7  8  11  18  19  20  21  22
    ←——— Ten cases ———             Median         ——— Eleven cases ———→
```

Figure 5.2

THE INFLUENCE OF EXTREME VALUES

Notice that the median for the routine treatment group, which is 5, is the same as that group's mean, which (as we calculated above) is also 5. If we eyeball our rank-ordered list, we can see that deeming the mean of 5 to be the "typical" value is not terribly unreasonable or misleading. That's because the other values for the routine treatment group are clustered close to it.

The same cannot be said about the new treatment group, however. Looking at our rank-ordered list for that group, we see that 16 of the 25 cases fall between 0 and 3 and therefore are closer to the median of 2 than to the mean of 6. That's because 5 of the values in the list (18, 19, 20, 21, and 22) are extremely high in comparison to the other values. The statistical term for very extreme values in a distribution is *outliers*. The **outliers** inflate the sum that gets divided by the number of cases to calculate the mean. However, when calculating the median, it doesn't matter how extreme those outliers are; all that matters is that there are equal numbers of cases above and below the median, no matter how far above or below they may be.

Just as we discussed in Chapter 1 with regard to tax savings, and as we illustrated again above, sometimes outliers can make the mean misleading. Here's another example:

........the (mean) average person in Redmond, Washington, has a net worth in excess of a million dollars. If you were to visit Redmond, however, you would not find that the "average" resident lives up to your idea of a millionaire. The very high mean reflects the influence of one extreme case among Redmond's 40,000 residents—Bill Gates of Microsoft, who has a net worth (at the time this is being written) of tens of billions of dollars. Clearly, the median wealth would give you a more accurate picture of the residents of Redmond as a whole.

(Rubin & Babbie, 2005, p. 560)

Consequently, it's important not just to rely solely on the mean when presenting, interpreting, or reading about our own or someone else's data. By also taking into account the frequency distribution and the median, we can get a better sense of the meaning of the data and whether the mean really depicts the "typical" value. For example, if we see a big difference between the mean and the median, then we know that some extreme values are affecting the mean.

But even if the mean and the median are exactly the same, they may not represent the typical case. Suppose, for example, the new treatment being evaluated in our hypothetical illustration completely resolves behavioral problems for youths who have experienced only one trauma, but makes the problem twice as bad for youths who have had multiple traumas. Suppose half of the youths have experienced one trauma, and half had multiple traumas. Let's say that before treatment each half had the same mean and median of 5 behavioral incidents and that after treatment half the clients had 0 incidents and the other half had 10 incidents. Both the mean and the median after treatment for the entire group would be 5, and each would be misleading, since half of the group had the value 0 and half had the value 10. Thus, in addition to the mean and median, additional statistics help us avoid unintentionally misleading others or being misled ourselves. We'll examine some additional helpful statistics in the remaining sections of this chapter and in the next chapter. But before moving on, you may want to examine the box titled "Calculating the Median." You won't need to calculate the median if you have access to statistical software, but examining this information might be useful anyway since, for some data sets, calculating the median can be more complicated than it is with our hypothetical data set.

THE MODE

The **mode** is that value which appears *most frequently* in a distribution of values for a particular variable. Looking above at our two lists of 25 values for serious behavioral incidents for the New Treatment group and the Routine Treatment group, we can see that 0 appears most frequently for the former group and that 5 appears most frequently for the latter. Thus, 0 is the mode for the new treatment group, and 5 is the mode for the routine treatment group. Consequently, the mode (0) for the new treatment group is lower than the median (2) and much lower than the mean (6), whereas the

Calculating the Median

It is relatively easy to calculate the median when examining a small list of cases where exactly half of the values exceed a particular value in the list and half are less than that value. But often that is not the case. For example, sometimes we have an even number of cases, with no middle value, such as the following:

1   2   3   4   6   7   8   9

Notice that there are four values below 6, but also four values above 4. If we were to draw a line separating this list into the four lowest values and the four highest values, we'd draw that line halfway between the 4 and the 6. Thus, our median would be 5.

Let's modify the above list slightly now, as follows:

1   2   3   4   5   6   7   8

Now notice that if we were to draw a line separating the list into the four lowest values and the four highest values, we'd draw that line halfway between the 4 and the 5. That would make our median 4.5. Thus, the median is not always a whole number or one that actually appears in our data set.

In most large data sets the median involves decimal points. For the eight values immediately above, it is easy to see how we arrived at the 4.5 figure, since there was one 4 and one 5 and halfway between them is 4.5. But in many data sets there are unequal numbers of middle values, making the calculation of the median more complicated. Consider the following list of ten values, for example:

2   3   4   4   5   5   5   6   6   8

Notice that there are six values above 4 and four values below 5. If we called the median 4.5, we'd be overlooking the fact that there are more values above 4 than there are below 5. To adjust for that imbalance, we'd count the number of cases with the middle two values (that is, the number of cases with either a 4 or a 5). There are five such cases, and three of them have the value 5. In decimal terms, three out of five (i.e., three-fifths) is 0.6. Thus, to convey the fact that there are more fives than fours in the middle two value categories, the correct value of the median would be 4.6, *not* 4.5.

A complex mathematical formula exists for calculating the median with large data sets where the calculations are more complicated than above. But it's hard to imagine anyone these days calculating the median manually with large data sets instead of using computer software. What you have read in this box should enable you to understand the meaning of the median and the general idea underlying its calculation with small or large data sets. But if you wish to examine the more complex mathematical formula for calculating the median with large data sets, you can find it in statistics texts that put more emphasis on mathematical formulae, such as Gravetter and Wallnau (2000).

---

mode (5) for the routine treatment group is exactly the same as its mean and median. Knowing this gives us a better basis for deciding what to make of the mean and the median when thinking about what's "typical" in a distribution.

Because the mode is based only on the number of cases that have each value in a distribution, and not on the rank order of any value or the quantitative amount of that value, the mode can be used to portray nominal data as well as metric data. Thus, if we re-examine Table 3.2 in Chapter 3, we see that the modal category for ethnicity in our hypothetical evaluation is Caucasian, since that value category has more cases in it than any other category of ethnicity.

Some distributions have more than one mode. Consider the hypothetical example in which half of the cases in a group had 0 incidents, and the other half had 10 incidents. The two modes in that distribution would be 0 and 10, because each of those values were tied for having the greatest number of cases in the distribution. When there are two modes in a distribution, we call it a **bimodal distribution**.

Modes can also be reported for grouped frequency distributions. For example, if we re-examine Table 3.7 in Chapter 3, we can see that the grouped category of 5-6 for number of serious behavioral incidents had more cases than any other grouping. The mode, or modal category, for that distribution then is 5–6. Or we could call the mode 5.5, which is the midpoint of the interval from 5 to 6.

The mode, by itself, is not considered to be as useful as the mean and median in portraying the central tendency (average) of the data or the "typical" case. However, as we've seen above, it has some value, especially when considered along with the mean and median.

SELECTING A MEASURE OF CENTRAL TENDENCY

Each of the three measures of central tendency helps summarize our data and gives us a sense of the average or most frequent values for a variable. With nominal data, of course—data that lack quantitative meaning—the only measure applicable is the mode. With ordinal data, we can use all three measures, but we need to be careful using the mean because ordinal numbers don't reflect exact quantities (as discussed above). With interval or ratio data, we can use any of the three measures, and it's usually best to use all three. The mean has the advantage of taking the actual amount of all values into account when depicting the central tendency, but has the disadvantage of being influenced by outliers (assuming there are some outliers). The median has the advantage of being immune to outliers, but its disadvantage is that the presence of outliers in a distribution may be relevant and important to know about.

When a distribution contains outliers, another option is to use something called the ***trimmed mean***, which involves calculating the mean after trimming off outliers at both the high and low ends of the distribution when those outliers comprise a very small percentage of the distribution (usually 5% or less). That is, you would not include the outliers in your calculation. However, the trimmed mean, like the median, may be omitting relevant information to the extent that the outliers are important to know about.

One way to compare the meaning of the three measures of central tendency, as well as to illustrate their advantages and disadvantages, is to imagine a seesaw with the different values arrayed across it. The mean of all the values will be the balance point under the seesaw where neither side teeters higher or lower than the other side. Thus, with the *mean*, that balance point is the *central tendency*. The *median*, however, disregards the balance point and instead indicates the *central tendency* as that value that has as many values above it as below it. The *mode*, in contrast, might be anywhere on the seesaw—wherever the most common value is located—regardless of centrality or balance.

This visual comparison is illustrated in Figure 5.3, using our 25 values for the number of serious behavioral incidents in the new treatment group in our hypothetical evaluation. In examining Figure 5.3, assume that all the values are blocks of the same weight. Each block represents one case in the data file. The blocks representing the cases with the more extreme values are located at the more extreme ends of the seesaw. The more cases there are with a particular value, the more blocks are piled up at that point on the seesaw.

Since every measure of central tendency has advantages and disadvantages, it's best to report and pay heed to all of them. Whether they all have similar values or are very different gives us a partial sense of whether cases are clustering fairly close to some "average" or "typical" value and whether there may be extreme outliers above or below that value. To improve our sense of how cases are clustering near the average or scattering away from it, we need to consider another set of statistics along with measures of central tendency. Those statistics are called measures of dispersion. We'll examine them next, in Chapter 6.

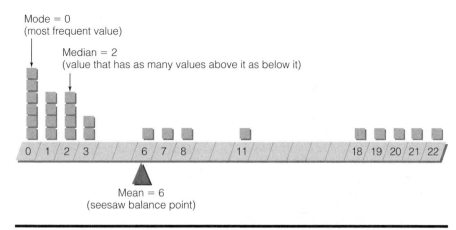

Figure 5.3   Visualizing a Seesaw to Compare the Three Measures of Central Tendency

Main Points

• Measures of central tendency can summarize data more succinctly than frequency distributions and graphs, but are best presented *in addition to*—not instead of—those displays.

• To calculate the mean, we sum all of the values for a variable and divide that sum by the number of values being summed.

• Because the mean involves adding and dividing, it does not apply to nominal-level variables.

• While we frequently encounter means for ordinal data, and can find some practical value in them, we should be careful in how we interpret them.

• The median is the *middle* value in a ranked distribution of values. Because it involves only the rank order of values, it can be used with ordinal data without the problems associated with calculating the mean for ordinal data. Since the *median* represents the "middle" value, we can calculate it by seeing which value has an equal number of cases above it and below it.

• The statistical term for very extreme values in a distribution is *outliers*. Outliers can inflate the sum that gets divided by the number of cases to calculate the mean, but outliers do not affect the median.

• The mean has the advantage of taking the actual amount of all values into account when depicting the central tendency, but has the disadvantage of being influenced by outliers. The median has the advantage of being immune to outliers, but its disadvantage is that the presence of extreme values in a distribution may be relevant and important to know about.

• You should not just rely solely on the mean when presenting or interpreting data. You should also consider the frequency distribution and the median to get a better sense of the meaning of the data.

• The mode is that value which appears most frequently in a distribution of values for a particular variable.

• Because the mode is based only on the number of cases that have each value in a distribution, and not on the rank order of any value or the quantitative amount of that value, the mode can be used to portray nominal data as well as metric data.

• Some distributions have more than one mode. When there are two modes in a distribution, we call it a bimodal distribution.

• The trimmed mean involves calculating the mean after trimming off outliers at both the high and low ends of the distribution when those outliers comprise a very small percentage of the distribution (usually 5% or less). However, the trimmed mean, like the median, may be omitting relevant information to the extent that the outliers are important to know about.

• Since every measure of central tendency has advantages and disadvantages, it's best to report and pay heed to all of them.

Review Questions and Exercises

1. Below are two rows of data on number of treatment sessions attended. The first row is for a treatment program using highly trained and experienced treatment staff. The second row corresponds to a program that lacks the funds to employ highly trained and experienced treatment staff, and therefore relies primarily on inexperienced staff with less training. Both programs are located near the US-Mexico border. Program 1 is in California, and Program 2 is in Texas. Almost all of the clients in both programs are Mexican American. Most of the clients in Program 1 were born in California. Most of the clients in Program 2 are recent immigrants whose main language is Spanish. Although the Program 1 staff have more training and experience, none of them are Mexican American, and despite their superior training and experience, they have *not* been trained to become culturally competent. Although the Program 2 staff have less training and experience, half of them *are* Mexican American, and half of them *are* culturally competent.

NUMBER OF TREATMENT SESSIONS ATTENDED BY 12 CLIENTS IN EACH OF TWO PROGRAMS:

Program 1: 3 4 4 5 6 6 6 6 7 8 8 9

Program 2: 0 0 0 1 1 2 8 9 9 10 10 10

a. Calculate each group's mean, median, and mode(s).

b. Discuss the advantages and disadvantages of each statistic in portraying the central tendency of each group's data.

c. Discuss why it helps to look at the frequency distributions for both groups in addition to the central tendency statistics in describing differences between the two groups.

d. If we assume that it takes 10 sessions to fully complete the treatment in each program, and in light of your answers to questions a through c above, which of the two programs do you think had the preferable attendance data? Why?

2. The community development agency you work for is lobbying the city council to finance construction of low-income housing in your community. The council is skeptical about the need for low-income housing in your community, based mainly on a census statistic showing that the mean income in your community is a bit higher than what you define as "low income." Based on what you've read in this chapter, what would you tell the city council about relying exclusively on the mean in its deliberations?

InfoTrac Exercise

1. Examine the article below and summarize what it says about the important uses of the mode and the median, the strengths and weaknesses of the mean, and the influence of extreme scores.

McHugh, M. L. (2003). Descriptive statistics, part II: Most commonly used descriptive statistics. (Scientific Inquiry). *Journal for Specialists in Pediatric Nursing,* 8(3), 111–116.

Measures of Dispersion

INTRODUCTION

Chapter 5 illustrated the meaning and utility of measures of central tendency while at the same time indicating that the values in a distribution may be located close to a measure of central tendency or far away from it. Consequently, we need additional measures, called **measures of dispersion,** which tell us how much **variability** exists in the distribution for a particular variable. The terms *variability* and *dispersion* both refer to the amount of **variation** that exists among the values in a distribution. That is, these measures assess how closely the values in a distribution are clustered together or how far they are scattered apart.

A clinical outcome study might find that out of a group of clients who receive the particular treatment being evaluated, the same proportions do better and worse after treatment and to roughly the same degree. When the scores of those who improve are averaged with the scores of those who do worse, the mean is near zero, indicating no change from pretest to posttest. Of course, concluding that such a treatment has no effect would be erroneous. It apparently has beneficial effects on some clients and harmful effects on others. It's important to know this, rather than being misled by relying solely on one statistic. Getting a more accurate view of the situation will keep us from dismissing a treatment that might be helping some clients and will spur us to learn more—through subsequent studies or analyses—about the kinds of clients who benefit from the treatment and the kinds who do not.

The importance of measuring dispersion was evident when we examined the mean and median number of serious behavioral incidents in each of the two groups in our hypothetical evaluation. Figure 6.1 shows the raw data on number of serious behavioral incidents again, this time listed horizontally and in order from low to high to get a better sense of the difference in dispersion between the two groups.

Recall that the mean for Group 1 is 6, and the mean for Group 2 is 5. That doesn't seem like much of a difference. But just by eyeballing the above two rows of data below you can see a big difference in the *variability,* or *dispersion,* between the two rows. For example, the Group 1 values range from 0 to 22, whereas the Group 2 values range from just 3 to 8. Six of the 25 cases in Group 1 had no serious incidents whatsoever, whereas the best outcome in Group 2 was 3 incidents. Five of the 25 cases in Group 1 had 18 or more incidents, whereas the worst outcome for Group 2 was only 8 incidents.

Why is this information important? Perhaps the small difference in means favoring the routine treatment group is misleading. Seeing the variation in the data raises the possibility that perhaps the new treatment is very effective with some traumatized youths and harmful for others. Perhaps it is more effective than routine treatment for one subgroup and less effective for the other. We would not be aware of this possibility if we restricted our information to the small difference in means between the two groups and the fact that it favors Group 2.

Now that we see the importance of measuring dispersion, let's examine the four most commonly used measures of dispersion: the range, the interquartile range, the variance, and the standard deviation.

THE RANGE

The range is the simplest measure of dispersion. It is the total number of possible values between the minimum and maximum values in a distribution. For example, suppose you fainted once in your first statistics class session this semester and the student sitting beside you fainted twice. None of the other students fainted. The range for your class would be 3. In other words, there are three possible numbers in a distribution where the lowest value is 0 and the highest is 2. Said another way, the range equals 1 plus the difference between the lowest and highest

---

Number of Serious Behavioral Incidents in Group 1 (New Treatment):
0 0 0 0 0 0 1 1 1 1 2 2 2 2 3 3 6 7 8 11 18 19 20 21 22
Number of Serious Behavioral Incidents in Group 2 (Routine Treatment):
3 3 3 3 4 4 4 4 5 5 5 5 5 5 5 5 5 6 6 6 6 6 7 7 8

Figure 6.1

values. Two minus 0 is 1. Add 1 to that and you get 3—the range. We can summarize this statement with a simple formula:

Range = Highest Value − Lowest Value + 1

Let's apply the above formula to the two lists of serious behavioral incidents for Group 1 and Group 2 in our hypothetical evaluation. The values for Group 1 *ranged* from 0 to 22. Thus, the range was 22 − 0 + 1 = 23. The values for Group 2 *ranged* from 3 to 8. Thus, the range for Group 2 was 8 − 3 + 1 = 6.

Not everyone uses the above formula. Some, for example, just subtract the lowest from the highest value without adding 1. Some might just say that the data *ranged* from 0 to 22 or from 3 to 8. It doesn't much matter which approach is used to convey the range; they all tell us what we need to know about it.

Knowing the range helps us understand the nature and meaning of our data. But the range can be misleading if it has been inflated by one or more very aberrant outliers. For example, suppose Group 2 above had only one 0 and one 22, with the remaining values ranging between 5 and 7. The range would still be 23, even though the range for all but two of the 25 cases would be only 3 (from 5 to 7). In that case, the range of 23 would be an exaggeration of the actual degree of variability in the data. In light of the range's vulnerability to outliers, and its lack of information regarding the amount of variability existing among the values between the minimum and maximum value, it is the weakest of the four most commonly used measures of dispersion. Let's turn now to another type of range that is less vulnerable to outliers.

THE INTERQUARTILE RANGE

The **interquartile range** is the range for the middle 50 percent of values in a rank-ordered distribution. We can think of this concept in terms of percentiles.

A **percentile** is a value that incorporates a certain percentage of rank-ordered values in a distribution. For example, the 25th percentile would be that value below which the lowest 25% of the values fall. In turn, the 75th percentile would be that value below which the lowest 75% of the values fall. Therefore, the interquartile range, which is the middle 50% of values, would fall between the 25th and 75th percentiles.

Here's a simple example. Suppose 25% of the clients in your agency have attended 5 or fewer treatment sessions, 25% attended 6 to 7 sessions, 25% attended 8 to 9 sessions, and 25% attended more than 9 sessions. The 25th percentile would be 5, because one-fourth of the values are at or below it, and three-fourths fall above it. The 75th percentile would be 9, because three-fourths of the values fall at or below it, and one-fourth fall above it. Therefore, the interquartile range, or middle 50% of the values, would be from 5 to 9. We could also call it an interquartile range of 4, since subtracting 5 from 9 is 4. Some might call it 5, because there are 5 possible whole number values between 5 and 9 when we include the 5 and the 9. Just saying that the middle 50% of the cases ranged from 5 to 9, however, is the simplest and most useful way to convey this measure of dispersion.

With real data, however, the interquartile range may be more difficult to calculate than in the simple example above. For example, let's re-examine the list of the number of serious behavioral incidents for Group 2 in our hypothetical evaluation, as shown in Figure 6.2.

Notice that four of the 25 values, or 16% of them, are at 3. If we include the four 4's, we would be including 8 out of the 25 values, or 32%. Consequently, deciding where to draw the line marking off the lowest 25% of the values is not so simple. Likewise, only 3 of the 25 values—12% of them—exceed 6, but 22 of the 25 values—88% of them—are at 6 or below. So it's not so clear what to call the 75th percentile, either.

If you enter the above 25 values into SPSS and ask it to calculate the interquartile range, the

Number of Serious Behavioral Incidents in Group 2:
3 3 3 3 4 4 4 5 5 5 5 5 5 5 5 6 6 6 6 6 7 7 8

Figure 6.2

answer you'll get is 4 to 6. That's the best estimate of the interquartile range, based on a complicated formula. With a much larger data set than 25 cases, it's usually possible to estimate the interquartile range just by scanning the cumulative frequency distribution and finding those values that come closest to the 25th and 75th percentiles. For example, the cumulative percent column in the frequency distribution of the number of serious behavioral incidents for *all 50* cases in our hypothetical evaluation, as was displayed in Table 3.6 in Chapter 3, shows that 28% of the cases are at 2 and below, and 78% are at 6 and below. Because only 66% are at 5 and below, we would choose 2 to 6 as the best estimate of our interquartile range when the data for Group 1 and Group 2 are combined.

Of what practical use is knowing the interquartile range? Consider the above example. The range for our 50 cases is 23, or zero to 22. Knowing that the interquartile range is 2 to 6 spurs us to wonder about the distribution of the highest 25% of cases (between 7 and 22), since half the cases are between 2 and 6 and one-fourth of them are less than 2. It also lets us know that the large majority (75%) of the cases have a value of 6 or less, despite the fact that the high end of the range is 22.

What if you were administering a large program for battered women and only knew that the age range of your clients' children was the same as our range above—zero to 22? (We'll round off the age of recently born infants to zero.) Knowing that the interquartile range was 4 to 6 would be of great value in thinking about the need for services for young children who may have witnessed domestic violence as well as the extent of need for childcare services for the women who seek shelter.

By the way, SPSS will tell us that the best estimate of the interquartile range for the wildly dispersed numbers of serious behavior incidents for Group 1 is 0.5 to 9.5. We'll re-examine that issue shortly when we put all the measures together at the end of this chapter. Before moving on to the next section of this chapter, which discusses the variance, you may want to examine the box titled "The Boxplot," which illustrates and discusses a graph that is sometimes used in research and evaluation reports to provide a pictorial representation of the median, interquartile range, and range in the distribution of a variable.

THE VARIANCE

As we've seen, a drawback of the range and interquartile range is that they do not take all of a variable's values into account when depicting the dispersion of those values. Consequently, those two measures don't give us a sense of how much on average the values are dispersed from each other. The next two measures of dispersion that we'll examine do take all of the values into account, and thus have great value. One is called the *variance.* The other is called the *standard deviation,* and it is the one you'll see the most when you read research or evaluation reports. But because it is calculated as the square root of the variance, let's examine the variance first.

To calculate the variance of a variable in a sample, we first subtract each value in the distribution of values for that variable from that distribution's mean. Then we square each of the differences we get from those subtractions. Next, we add up all the squared differences and then divide that sum (called the *sum of squares*) by the total number of values minus 1. *Thus, the* **variance** *is the average of the squared deviations from the mean.* (The reason for the "minus 1" in this formula has to do with estimating the population variance from the variance in a sample. If our data involve an entire population—or if our intent is just to describe the sample, and not to estimate the population variance—we would just divide by the total number of values. You can consult more advanced statistical texts if you want to learn more about this topic.)

If the above steps sound complicated, relax—the computer will do the calculations for you. (See the section of Appendix G headed "Using SPSS to Calculate Measures of Dispersion (Chapter 6).") But just for the fun of it and to see how easy it is (and, of course, to help you better grasp the meaning of the variance), let's illustrate the calculations using our hypothetical data on the number of serious behavioral incidents for the 25 cases in Group 2. The first column in Table 6.1 displays each of the 25 values. The second column displays the mean of 5 for the distribution of the 25 values. The third column displays the difference we obtain by subtracting the mean (in column 2) from each value (in column 1). That column is headed *Deviation,* because the differences represent *deviations* from the mean. The fourth column displays the squares of each deviation. At the bottom of that column we see the sum

The Boxplot

The **boxplot** is a graph that provides a pictorial representation of the median, interquartile range, and range in the distribution of a variable. It can also display outliers. Figure 6.3 shows boxplot diagrams for the number of serious behavioral incidents for Group 1 and Group 2 in our hypothetical evaluation. The boxplot on the left is for Group 1 (New Treatment). The thick line within the box shows that its median falls at 2. The boxplot on the right is for Group 2 (Routine Treatment). The thick line within that box shows that its median falls at 5. The top and bottom lines of the boxes depict the interquartile range. The vertical lines extending above and below each box depict the range. The horizontal lines that intersect the top and bottom of the vertical lines indicate the maximum (at the top) and minimum (at the bottom) values. However, because Group 1 has some outliers, the horizontal line at its top stops short of the outlier values, and those values are depicted with circles above it. (Some computer software programs will indicate outliers with other sorts of symbols, such as asterisks.)

Notice how the juxtaposition of the two boxplots lets us quickly compare the two distributions. It provides a picture of the lower median, greater dispersion, and outliers in Group 1, and the very small degree of disper-

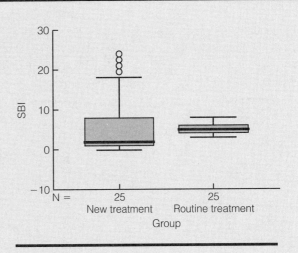

Figure 6.3

sion around the higher median in Group 2. Thus, the practical value of boxplots is like the practical value of the interquartile range. The boxplot, however, not only gives you a picture of the same information, it enables you also to visualize at a glance the median and outliers.

(You can use SPSS to create boxplots for any interval or ratio level variables. To see how to do so, study the section of Appendix H headed "Using SPSS to Create Graphs (Chapter 4)." Follow the steps described in that appendix, but click on BOXPLOT instead of BAR.)

of squares. Then we see the variance obtained when we divide that sum by $N - 1$ (N is the symbol for the total number of values in the distribution). The formula for calculating the variance is displayed in the box titled "Formula for Calculating the Variance and the Standard Deviation."

THE STANDARD DEVIATION

Because the variance is based on *squared* deviations from the mean, its square root will tell us how far the scores in a distribution are deviating from the mean, on average. This "unsquaring" step converts the variance to a more useful statistic called the **standard deviation**. In fact, the standard deviation is used more than any other measure of dispersion. In subsequent chapters, you'll see why. Right now, however, you're probably skeptical of its utility for you, especially if you don't expect to do research in your career. So let's see if your skepticism changes after we do some fairly simple calculations.

First, let's see what the standard deviation is for the data displayed in Table 6.1. Using a computer

Table 6.1   Calculating the Variance (Using the Number of Serious Behavioral Incidents for the 25 cases in Group 2)

COLUMN 1 VALUE		COLUMN 2 SUBTRACT THE MEAN		COLUMN 3 DEVIATION	COLUMN 4 SQUARED DEVIATION
3	−	5	=	−2	4
3	−	5	=	−2	4
3	−	5	=	−2	4
3	−	5	=	−2	4
4	−	5	=	−1	1
4	−	5	=	−1	1
4	−	5	=	−1	1
4	−	5	=	−1	1
5	−	5	=	0	0
5	−	5	=	0	0
5	−	5	=	0	0
5	−	5	=	0	0
5	−	5	=	0	0
5	−	5	=	0	0
5	−	5	=	0	0
5	−	5	=	0	0
5	−	5	=	0	0
6	−	5	=	1	1
6	−	5	=	1	1
6	−	5	=	1	1
6	−	5	=	1	1
6	−	5	=	1	1
7	−	5	=	2	4
7	−	5	=	2	4
8	−	5	=	3	9
				Sum of Squares =	42
				Variance =	42/24 = 1.75

or calculator, we can find in an instant that the square root of 1.75 (the variance that we calculated in that table) is 1.32. Thus, 1.32 is the standard deviation for the number of serious behavioral incidents in Group 2 (the routine treatment group). Recall that the mean for that group is 5.0. Consequently, we know that the youths in Group 2 are deviating on average 1.32 from a mean of 5 incidents.

Table 6.2 Calculating the Standard Deviation (Using the Number of Serious Behavioral Incidents for the 25 Cases in Group 1)

COLUMN 1 VALUE		COLUMN 2 SUBTRACT THE MEAN		COLUMN 3 DEVIATION	COLUMN 4 SQUARED DEVIATION
0	−	6	=	−6	36
0	−	6	=	−6	36
0	−	6	=	−6	36
0	−	6	=	−6	36
0	−	6	=	−6	36
0	−	6	=	−6	36
1	−	6	=	−5	25
1	−	6	=	−5	25
1	−	6	=	−5	25
1	−	6	=	−5	25
2	−	6	=	−4	16
2	−	6	=	−4	16
2	−	6	=	−4	16
2	−	6	=	−4	16
3	−	6	=	−3	9
3	−	6	=	−3	9
6	−	6	=	0	0
7	−	6	=	1	1
8	−	6	=	2	4
11	−	6	=	5	25
18	−	6	=	12	144
19	−	6	=	13	169
20	−	6	=	14	196
21	−	6	=	15	225
22	−	6	=	16	256

Sum of Squares = 1418

Variance = 1418/24 = 59.08

Standard Deviation = Square root of 59.08 = 7.69

The value of this information should become clearer after we calculate the standard deviation for the same variable in Group 1 (the new treatment group). To find the standard deviation we simply go through the same steps as in Table 6.1 but use the values for Group1 as well as its mean of 6. Because there are extreme scores in Group 1, squaring the deviations takes a bit more effort. If you'd like to see the arithmetic steps, you can examine Table 6.2, which shows that the standard deviation for Group 1 is 7.69. (The standard deviation formula, which simply is the square root of the variance, is presented in the box titled "Formula for Calculating the Variance and the Standard Deviation.")

Wow! The standard deviation of 7.69 for Group 1 is greater than that group's mean of 6! Knowing the means and standard deviations of each group immediately tells us that whereas the cases in Group 2 cluster pretty close to its mean of 5, the cases in Group 1 on average fall pretty far from its mean of 6. Therefore, perhaps we shouldn't put much stock in the difference between the two means. Rather than presume that Group 2's lower mean signifies a more effective treatment approach, we might wonder what on earth is explaining the extensive dispersion in outcome among the recipients of the new treatment (in Group 1).

Perhaps you are thinking, "Hey, I knew that just by eyeballing the raw data when we aligned the two groups into two rows of 25 cases each in rank order with one row atop the other." But what if there were many more cases—perhaps 100 or more—in each group? Eyeballing wouldn't work so well. Moreover, the standard deviation has additional valuable uses, as we will see in the next chapter and in some later chapters as well.

PUTTING IT ALL TOGETHER

Before we move to the next chapter, let's see how well all of the measures of central tendency and dispersion—taken as a whole—have depicted the nature of the distributions of the number of serious behavioral incidents in our two hypothetical treatment groups. Table 6.3 lists the measures for each group. (We'll omit the variance, since its square root, the standard deviation, conveys the same point in a more easily interpretable way.) Even if there were hundreds of cases (instead of only 25) in

Table 6.3   The Mean, Median, Mode, Range, Interquartile Range, and Standard Deviation by Treatment Group

	GROUP 1: NEW TREATMENT	GROUP 2: ROUTINE TREATMENT
Mean	6	5
Median	2	5
Mode	0	5
Range	23	6
Interquartile Range	0.5 to 9.5	4 to 6
Standard Deviation	7.69	1.32

Group 1, by noticing the differences among that group's mean, median, and mode and then observing its three measures of dispersion, you could tell that although its mean is worse than the mean for Group 2, many of its cases are not near that mean. Many are below it, and some are very far above it. In contrast, the data for Group 2 would tell you that most of its cases are clustering very close to its mean.

Knowing all this, which treatment do you think was more effective in preventing serious behavioral incidents? When I present these data to my students and then ask them the same question, a debate usually follows. Some say that the routine treatment (Group 2) was more effective because it had the lower mean and more consistent results from client to client. Others counter that the new treatment was more effective because 24% (6 of 25) had no incidents whatsoever, its median of 2 was lower than the median of 5 for Group 2, and the only reason its mean was higher is because it was influenced by several extreme outliers. The other side then counters that we can't ignore those outliers. The 5 outliers comprised 20% of the 25 cases. Perhaps the Group 1 treatment has harmful effects for some clients. Eventually, the two sides in this debate reach an impasse and look to me for the answer. You may be wondering the same thing. Actually, both arguments are reasonable. The remaining chapters of this book, however, will cover additional statistical procedures that are needed to

Formula for Calculating the Variance and the Standard Deviation

Recall from Chapter 5 the following symbols:

$\bar{X}$ = The sample mean

Σ = The sum of all of the items to the right of the symbol Σ (which is the upper-case Greek letter *sigma*)

X_s = All the values for the variable being summed

N = The total number of values being summed (usually the total number of cases in the data file)

Using the above symbols, the formula for calculating the variance is

$$\text{Variance} = \frac{\Sigma(X_s - \bar{X})^2}{N - 1}$$

The symbol for variance is s^2. Therefore, the above formula for the variance is usually expressed as follows:

$$s^2 = \frac{\Sigma(X_s - \bar{X})^2}{N - 1}$$

The numerator in the above formula represents the sum of squares, which is the sum of each score's squared deviation from the mean. First the mean is subtracted from the score, and then the difference is squared. After we square the difference for each score, those squared differences are added up to give us the sum of squares in the numerator. Then we divide that sum by the denominator (which is the total number of values minus 1).

The symbol s^2 is useful because the symbol s is used to represent the standard deviation. Because the standard deviation is simply the square root of the variance, the formula for calculating the standard deviation is simply the square root of the formula for calculating the variance, as follows:

$$\text{Standard Deviation} = \sqrt{\frac{\Sigma(X_s - \bar{X})^2}{N - 1}}$$

Using the symbol s to represent standard deviation, the above formula is usually expressed as follows:

$$s = \sqrt{\frac{\Sigma(X_s - \bar{X})^2}{N - 1}}$$

resolve this impasse and to determine whether it is reasonable to infer that either of the two hypothetical treatments is more effective in light of the data on these 50 hypothetical cases.

Main Points

• Measures of dispersion tell us how much variability exists in the distribution for a particular variable.

• The terms *variability* and *dispersion* both assess the extent to which the values in a distribution are clustered near each other or are scattered far from each other.

• The range is the total number of possible values between the minimum and maximum values in a distribution.

• The interquartile range is the range for the middle 50% of values in a rank-ordered distribution. We can think of this concept in terms of percentiles. A percentile is a value that incorporates a certain percentage of rank-ordered values in a distribution.

• The boxplot is a graph that provides a pictorial representation of the median, interquartile range, and range in the distribution of a variable. It can also display outliers.

• The variance is the average of the squared deviations from the mean.

• To calculate the variance, we first subtract each value in a distribution from that distribution's mean. Then we square each of the differences we get from those subtractions. Next, we add up all the squared differences and then divide that sum (called the sum of squares) by the total number of values minus one.

• Because the variance is based on *squared* deviations from the mean, its square root will tell us how far the scores in a distribution are deviating from the mean on average. This "unsquaring" step converts the variance to a more useful statistic called the standard deviation. The standard deviation is used more than any other measure of dispersion.

Review Questions and Exercises

1. Figure 6.4 displays the same data on number of treatment sessions attended that were presented in Review Question 1 in Chapter 5. The first row is for a treatment program using highly trained and experienced treatment staff. The second row is for a program that lacks the funds to employ highly trained and experienced treatment staff and therefore relies primarily on inexperienced staff with less training. Both programs are located near the US-Mexico border. Program 1 is in California, and Program 2 is in Texas. Almost all of the clients in both programs are Mexican American. Most of the clients in Program 1 were born in California. Most of the clients in Program 2 are recent immigrants whose main language is Spanish. Although the Program 1 staff have more training and experience, none of them are Mexican American, and despite their superior training and experience, they have not been trained to become culturally competent. Although the Program 2 staff have less training and experience, half of them are Mexican American, and half of them are culturally competent.

Program 1: 3 4 4 5 6 6 6 6 7 8   8   9

Program 2: 0 0 0 1 1 2 8 9 9 10 10 10

Figure 6.4

a. Calculate each group's range, interquartile range, variance, and standard deviation.

b. Which group had more dispersion? In light of the above description of the two programs, what do you think might explain the difference in dispersion?

2. Calculate the range, interquartile range, variance, and standard deviation for the following values regarding how many times a group of 12 adolescents had used drugs or alcohol in the past month:

0 0 1 2 2 3 5 5 6 7 8 9

InfoTrac Exercises

1. Examine Tables 1 through 4 in the article listed below. Based on the means and standard deviations displayed in those tables, list at least four variables in which the values are clustering on average very near the mean and at least four variables in which many values are scattered relatively far away from the mean.

Slonim-Nevo, V. (2001). The effect of HIV/AIDS prevention intervention for Israeli adolescents in residential centers: Results at 12-month follow-up. *Social Work Research, 25*(2), 71.

2. Examine Table 1 in the article listed below. Briefly interpret the implications of the size of the standard deviations relative to the size of the means for most of the variables reported in that table.

Edmond, T., Rubin, A., & Wambach, K. G. (1999). The effectiveness of EMDR (eye movement desensitization and reprocessing) with adult female survivors of childhood sexual abuse. *Social Work Research, 23*(2), 103.

3. Interpret the boxplot in Figure 5 in the article below:

McHugh, M. L. (2003). Descriptive statistics, part II: Most commonly used descriptive statistics. *Journal for Specialists in Pediatric Nursing, 8*(3), 111–116.

Normal Distributions

INTRODUCTION

As you can tell from the discussion so far, the values for a variable can be distributed in different ways. Sometimes they cluster close to the mean, and sometimes they don't. They may even be scattered far away from the mean. Sometimes there are extreme outliers above the mean, and sometimes the outliers are below the mean. Sometimes extreme outliers are on both sides of the mean.

Sometimes the mean and the median are close together or even identical; sometimes they are quite different. Sometimes the mode is near them, and sometimes it is not. Some distributions have a great deal of dispersion (with a high variance and standard deviation), and some have much less dispersion (with a low variance and standard deviation).

In this chapter we will examine how to use frequency polygons to convey pictures of different shapes of distributions of interval- and ratio-level variables. We'll also examine the distinguishing attributes of and labels given to the different shapes. We'll see how knowing the shape of a distribution gives a more complete understanding of that distribution and enhances our interpretation of its central tendency and dispersion.

Let's begin by examining the concepts of normal and skewed distributions. An understanding of these distributions will help us comprehend the basis for the inferential statistics that we'll take up in subsequent chapters. We'll look at skewed distributions first, before we take up the more comprehensive topic of normal distributions.

SKEWED DISTRIBUTIONS

A **skewed distribution** is one in which many more values fall on one side of the mean than on the other

side of the mean. This imbalance creates a difference between the mean and the median. You may recall from the earlier discussions of our hypothetical evaluation in a residential treatment center that this was the case with the distribution of serious behavioral incidents for the 25 cases that had received the new treatment. Although the mean for this group is 6, we can see in Figure 7.1 that 16 of its 25 values are below 6, and only 8 values are above 6.

When there are a lot more values below the mean because the mean is being inflated by some extremely high values above the mean, we have a **positively skewed distribution.** Figure 7.2 (A) illustrates a positively skewed distribution. Notice how most of the x-axis values in the distribution are on the low end, to the left, and how a smaller number of extreme values are on the high end, to the right, pulling the mean to the right of the median. The part of the distribution curve containing the smaller number of extreme values is commonly called the **tail.** In a positively skewed distribution, the tail is on the right, at the higher end of x-axis values (and lower level of vertical y-axis values).

In a **negatively skewed distribution,** more values are above the mean, but the mean is lowered by some extremely low values below it. Figure 7.2 (B) illustrates a negatively skewed distribution. Notice how most of the x-axis values in the distribution are on the high end, to the right, and how the smaller number of extremely low values on the low end are pulling the mean to the left of the median. Thus, in a negatively skewed distribution, the tail is on the left, at the lower end of x-axis values.

NORMAL DISTRIBUTIONS

Unlike skewed distributions, which are *asymmetrical,* **normal distributions** are **symmetrical.** That is,

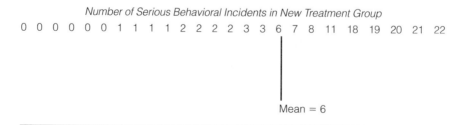

Number of Serious Behavioral Incidents in New Treatment Group

0 0 0 0 0 0 1 1 1 1 2 2 2 2 3 3 6 7 8 11 18 19 20 21 22

Mean = 6

Figure 7.1

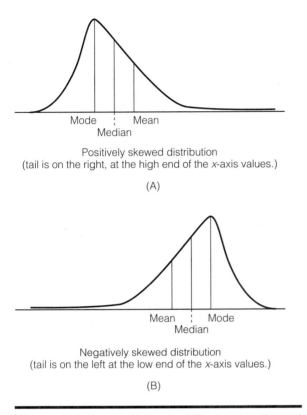

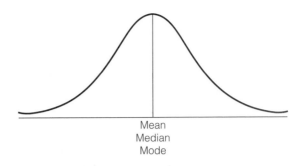

Mode ⋮ Mean
Median
Positively skewed distribution
(tail is on the right, at the high end of the x-axis values.)

(A)

Mean ⋮ Mode
Median
Negatively skewed distribution
(tail is on the left at the low end of the x-axis values.)

(B)

Figure 7.2 Examples of a Positively Skewed Distribution and a Negatively Skewed Distribution

Mean
Median
Mode

Figure 7.3 The Normal Distribution (Also Known as the Bell-Shaped Curve, the Bell Curve, or the Normal Curve)

the right and left halves of the curve are mirror images of each other. Consequently, the mean, median, and mode in a normal distribution are identical and are located at its center, as illustrated in Figure 7.3. Suppose you cut out the distribution in Figure 7.3 and then folded it on the centerline depicting the mean, median, and mode. Suppose you next held up the folded curve to the light. You would see only one line, because the right and left halves of the curve would completely overlap each other.

You can also see in Figure 7.3 that the normal distribution is curved in the shape of a bell. Thus, it is often referred to as a **bell-shaped curve** or more simply as a **bell curve.** It is also often called the **normal curve.**

Mathematicians have determined that the symmetry of the normal curve enables us to ascertain what proportion of the cases in a normal distribution fall any specified number of standard deviations above or below the mean. Let's suppose we

have a data set for a variable whose values are distributed according to the normal curve. In other words, the frequency polygon for that variable would look like the normal distribution depicted in Figure 7.3. Right off the bat, we would know that the area under the curve represents 100 percent of all the cases—or values—for that variable in our data set and that half of the cases would fall to the left of the center line (the mean, median, and mode), and half would fall to the right of it. To see how the standard deviation comes into play, let's examine Figure 7.4. As we do, we will keep things simple by referring to the centerline as the mean, although we know that it also represents the median and the mode.

As illustrated in Figure 7.4, the x-axis of any normal curve consists of six standard deviation intervals. To the left of the mean are three standard deviation intervals representing x-axis values that are less than the mean. To the right of the mean are three standard deviation intervals representing x-axis values that are greater than the mean.

The two standard deviation intervals closest to the mean, and dissected by it where the curve is the highest on the y-axis, have a greater proportion of cases than those intervals further away from the mean. One of those two closest intervals falls to the right of the mean; the other falls to the left. Each contains approximately 34% (0.3413) of the cases. In other words, approximately 34% of the cases in any normal distribution fall between the mean and the value at one standard deviation greater than the mean, and approximately 34% of the cases fall between the mean and the value at one standard deviation less than the mean. Thus, approximately 68%

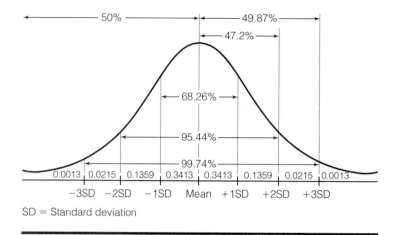

Figure 7.4 Standard Deviation Proportions of the Normal Curve

(0.6826) of all the cases in any normal distribution fall between the x-axis values that are one standard deviation less than the mean and one standard deviation greater than the mean.

Let's put this in more practical terms that may be easier to fathom. Figure 7.5 reproduces Figure 7.4 for a normal distribution with a mean of 10 and a standard deviation of 2. Let's assume that this distribution depicts something positive, such as how many tokens youths received for positive behaviors. With a mean of 10 and a standard deviation of 2, Figure 7.5 shows that approximately 68% of the youths in our study received between 8 and 12 tokens. With a mean of 10 and a standard deviation of 2, 8 would be one standard deviation below the mean ($10 - 2 = 8$), and 12 would be one standard deviation above the mean ($10 + 2 = 12$).

As Figures 7.4 and 7.5 further show, 13.59% of the cases in any normal distribution fall between the x-axis values at one and two standard deviations greater than the mean, and another 13.59% of the cases fall between the x-axis values at one and two standard deviations less than the mean. Thus, Figure 7.5 shows that with a mean of 10 and a standard deviation of 2, 13.59% of the youths would have received between 6 and 8 tokens, and another 13.59% would have received between 12 and 14 tokens.

Combining the above intervals, we could add the two intervals that each contain 13.59% of the cases to the two intervals that together contain 68.26%

of the cases. Two times 13.59% is 27.18%. Adding that to the 68.26% tells us that 95.44% of the youths would have received between 6 and 14 tokens (between two standard deviations below the mean and two standard deviations above the mean).

Likewise, we could split that 95.44 into two halves on both sides of the mean. There would be 47.72% in each half. That would tell us that 47.72% of the cases fall between the mean and two standard deviations above the mean, and 47.72% of the cases fall between the mean and two standard deviations below the mean. Thus, a value that is two standard deviations above the mean is at the 97.72 percentile. How do we know that? Because the 50% of the cases below the mean plus the 47.72% of the cases that fall between the mean and two standard deviations above the mean add up to 97.72%.

Figure 7.5 shows that with a normal distribution having a mean of 10 tokens and a standard deviation of 2, we can know that 97.72% of the youths would have received 14 tokens or less and that only 2.28% of them would have received more than 14 tokens. Using the same calculations on the left side of the mean, we can know that only 2.28% of the youths would have received 6 tokens or less.

Figures 7.4 and 7.5 also show that 99.74% (or almost all) of the cases in any normal distribution fall between the x-axis values that are three standard deviations above and below the mean. We

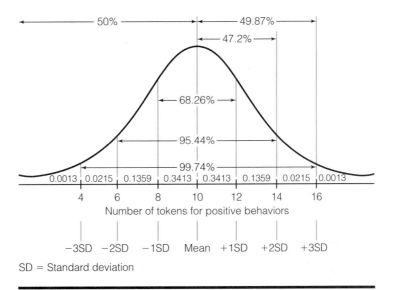

Figure 7.5 Standard Deviation Proportions of the Normal Curve for a Normal Distribution of Tokens for Positive Behaviors with a Mean of 10 and a Standard Deviation of 2

could perform the same calculations as above to see what the corresponding values would be. For example, Figure 7.5 shows that with a mean of 10 and a standard deviation of 2, almost all of the cases would fall between the values 4 and 16.

Perhaps you are dubious as to whether any of this has much practical value to a non-statistician. If so, consider the following. Suppose you are reading or conducting an evaluation comparing two interventions. Let's assume that the results of the evaluation approximate a normal curve and that the aim of each intervention is to increase a desirable behavior.

Let's further assume that Intervention A has a mean of 12 and a standard deviation of 2, and that Intervention B has a mean of 10 and the same standard deviation of 2. Thus, the mean (12) for Intervention A would be one standard deviation better (higher) than the mean (10) for Intervention B. Just knowing that information alone would enable us to determine that the mean for the cases receiving Intervention A was better than 84.13% (50% plus 34.13%) of the outcomes for the cases receiving Intervention B. Pretty impressive! Likewise, if the mean for Intervention A was 14, then it would be two standard deviations better than the mean (10) for Intervention B, indicating that the mean for the cases receiving Intervention A was better than

97.72% (50% plus 47.72%) of the outcomes for the cases receiving Intervention B. Even more impressive!

KURTOSIS

Before leaving this chapter's discussion of normal distributions, we should consider the term **kurtosis.** Don't worry; we won't digress weirdly into a discussion of foot abnormalities involving curved toes! The term *kurtosis* refers to the fact that while all normal curves are symmetrical, some are more peaked or flatter than others. The degree to which a normal curve is peaked or flat depends on the size of its standard deviation relative to the size of its mean and its range.

Figure 7.6 illustrates three normal curves with different degrees of kurtosis. They all have the same mean, but the flattest curve (a) has the most dispersion, and thus a greater standard deviation, than the other two curves. The tallest curve (c) has the least dispersion, and thus the smallest standard deviation. Its values cluster closer to the mean than do the values in the other two curves. Curve b is in the middle in terms of dispersion. Its shape more closely resembles a bell than the other two curves.

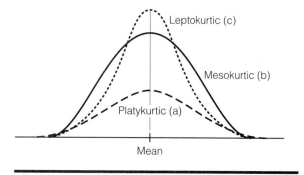

Figure 7.6   Three Normal Curves with the Same Mean but Different Degrees of Kurtosis

A normal curve that is very close to being bell-shaped (like curve b) will have a kurtosis near zero. Curves that are more peaked will have a positive kurtosis and thus less dispersion while curves that are flatter will have a negative kurtosis and thus more dispersion.

You may encounter the term *kurtosis* when you use computer programs, such as SPSS, to calculate various descriptive statistics. You may also encounter it as a factor influencing your choice of an appropriate inferential statistic. (We'll discuss inferential statistics in Part 3 of this book.) SPSS (as well as other statistical software) can tell you the degree of kurtosis in the distribution of your data for a particular variable based on a complex statistical formula. Kurtosis statistics that exceed +1.0 signify tall, narrow, peaked curves with scores clustering closer to the mean. These curves are called **leptokurtic.** Kurtosis statistics less than –1.0 signify flatter curves with scores scattered farther from the mean, and are called **platykurtic.** Kurtosis statistics near zero signify curves that are approximately bell-shaped, which are called **mesokurtic.** The section of Appendix G headed "Using SPSS to Calculate Measures of Kurtosis and Skewness (Chapter 7)" provides more detail about the implications of these statistics and using SPSS to calculate them.

SOME CLARIFICATION

Many students get a bit overwhelmed with the various types of curves and proportions that this chapter has discussed. So before moving on to the next chapter, let's engage in a bit of review that might clarify things.

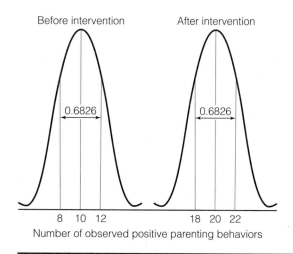

Number of observed positive parenting behaviors

Figure 7.7   Two Normal Curves with Different Means (10 and 20) but Equal Standard Deviations (2)

To begin, let's clarify the difference between the number representing the standard deviation, and the number representing its proportion under the normal curve. Figure 7.7 displays two normal curves that have different means but equal standard deviations. Let's suppose that the normal curve on the left represents the distribution of the frequency of positive parenting behaviors observed *before* clients participated in a parenting skills intervention, and the curve on the right represents the frequency of positive parenting behaviors observed *after* the clients participated in a parenting skills intervention. Before intervention, their mean is 10 and their standard deviation is 2. After intervention, their mean jumps to 20, though their standard deviation is still 2.

Because the distributions are both normal and have the same standard deviation of 2, 68.26% (2 X 0.3413) of the parents in both distributions scored between 2 points less than the mean and 2 points above it. (Thus, if there were 100 parents in our evaluation, 68 of them would have scored between 2 points less than the mean and 2 points above it.) Although both curves have the same standard deviations and the same proportions, the actual numbers of positive behaviors on the x-axis are different. On the left, for example, 8 positive behaviors is one standard deviation less than the mean of 10, and 12 positive behaviors is one standard deviation more than the mean of 10. On the right, 18 positive behaviors is one standard deviation less than the mean of 20, and 22 positive behaviors is one standard deviation more than the mean of 20. On the left, 68.26% of parents scored between 8 and 12. On the right, 68.26% of parents scored between 18 and 22. In other words, the proportions on the x-axis in both distributions are the same, as are the standard deviations, but the actual numbers of observed positive behaviors in each curve are different.

One more thing is worth mentioning about the two curves in Figure 7.7. They both have the same degree of kurtosis because they have the same range and standard deviation. Let's now examine Figure 7.8 to see what the two curves would look like if they had different degrees of kurtosis.

In Figure 7.8, the curve on the left is the same as in Figure 7.7. However, the curve on the right is flatter (more platykurtic), with a higher standard deviation indicating more dispersion around the mean of 20. Because the standard deviation on the right is 4, 68.26% of the parents scored between 16 and 24. Notice that the proportion scoring between one standard deviation above and below the mean after intervention is the same as in Figure 7.7, but the actual number of positive behaviors on the x-axis falling at those proportions of the normal curve has changed from 18 and 22 to 16 and 24. That's because the standard deviation increased from 2 to 4.

BIMODAL DISTRIBUTIONS

With the hope that you have a good grasp of the features of normal curves, let's look at one more type of curve that is *not* normal before moving on. Earlier in this chapter normal curves were contrasted with skewed curves. We saw that normal curves are *symmetrical*, while skewed curves are *asymmetrical*. Not all symmetrical curves are normal, however. That is, symmetry is necessary for a curve to be normal, but it is not sufficient.

Examine Figure 7.9, for example. It is symmetrical because the mean and median are the same. But it is not normal because it has modes that are not the same as the mean and median. Because it has two modes, it is called a **bimodal distribution.** If we suppose that the bimodal curve in Figure 7.9 represents the distribution of scores after the parenting skills intervention, with the before-intervention scores distributed as in Figures 7.7 and 7.8, how would you interpret the practical implications of the bimodal curve in Figure 7.9? I'm with you if your answer is that it appears that half of the parents seem to have possibly benefited from the intervention, and half appear perhaps not to have benefited.

I've thrown a lot of curves at you in this chapter. I hope you see their utility in evidence-based practice. I also hope you are comfortable with the concepts discussed in this chapter, because understanding them will help you grasp the concepts to be discussed in the remaining chapters of this book.

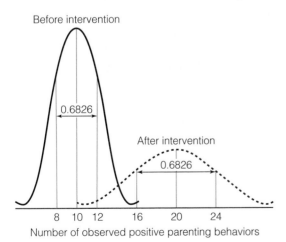

Figure 7.8 Two Normal Curves with Different Means (10 and 20) and Different Standard Deviations (2 and 4)

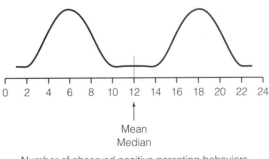
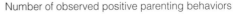
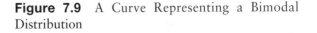

Figure 7.9 A Curve Representing a Bimodal Distribution

Main Points

• A skewed distribution is one in which many more values fall on one side of the mean than on the other side of the mean.

• A positively skewed distribution has more values below the mean than above it, and a negatively skewed distribution has more values above the mean than below it.

• Unlike skewed distributions, which are asymmetrical, normal distributions are symmetrical. That is, the right and left halves of the curve are mirror images of each other. Consequently, the mean, median and mode in a normal distribution are identical and are located at its center.

• A normal distribution is curved in the shape of a bell. Thus, it is often referred to as a bell-shaped curve or more simply as a bell curve. It is also often called the normal curve.

• In a normal distribution, 68.26% of the cases fall between the x-axis values that are one standard deviation less than the mean and one standard deviation greater than the mean, with 34.13% on each side of the mean.

• In a normal distribution, 95.44% of the cases fall between two standard deviations less than the mean and two standard deviations greater than the mean, with 47.72% on each side of the mean.

• The term *kurtosis* refers to the fact that while all normal curves are symmetrical, some are more peaked or flatter than others. The degree to which a normal curve is peaked or flat depends on the size of its standard deviation relative to the size of its mean and its range.

• A normal curve that is very close to being bell-shaped will have a kurtosis near zero. Curves that are more peaked will have a positive kurtosis and thus less dispersion. Curves that are flatter will have a negative kurtosis and thus more dispersion.

• Kurtosis statistics that exceed +1.0 signify tall, narrow, peaked curves with scores clustering closer to the mean. These curves are called *leptokurtic*.

• Kurtosis statistics less than –1.0 signify flatter curves with scores scattered farther from the mean, and are called *platykurtic*.

• Kurtosis statistics near zero signify curves that are approximately bell-shaped and are called *mesokurtic*.

• Bimodal distributions have two modes, and thus their curves have two peaks (or humps). Therefore, even if their curves are symmetrical, they are not normal, because their modes are not the same as their mean and median.

Review Questions and Exercises

1. Figure 7.10 shows three lists of distributions of values.

a. Which list reflects a positively skewed distribution?

b. Which list reflects a negatively skewed distribution?

c. Which list reflects a more normal distribution?

d. In which list will the mean be:
   d1. To the left of the median?
   d2. To the right of the median?
   d3. The same as the median and the mode?

2. In a normal distribution with a mean of 30 and a standard deviation of 3:

a. What proportion of the area under the normal curve falls between 0 and 33?

Distribution A:

1 2 2 3 3 3 4 4 4 4 5 5 5 5 5 5 6 6 6 6 6 7 7 7 7 8 8 8 9 9 10

Distribution B:

3 3 3 3 3 3 3 3 3 4 4 4 4 4 4 5 5 5 5 5 6 6 6 7 7 8 12 14 18 19 20

Distribution C:

1 2 3 4 5 10 14 18 20 25 30 35 45 45 48 48 48 50 50 50 50

Figure 7.10

b. What proportion of the area under the normal curve falls between 27 and 33?

c. What proportion of the area under the normal curve falls between 24 and 36?

d. What proportion of the area under the normal curve falls between 21 and 39?

3. An evaluation is conducted on the effectiveness of three different interventions for students with high absentee rates. The dependent variable is number of unexcused absences over a two-year period. There is a normal distribution of results for that variable for each intervention. For Intervention A, the mean is 12 and the standard deviation is 2. For Intervention B, the mean is 12 and the standard deviation is 4. For Intervention C, the mean is 16 and the standard deviation is 1.

a. Which intervention's distribution has the least kurtosis?

b. Which intervention's distribution has the most kurtosis?

c. Which intervention's distribution is the most peaked?

d. Which intervention's distribution is the flattest?

e. Which curve comes closest to being normal (bell-shaped)?

InfoTrac Exercise

1. Examine the article below and briefly summarize what you learn in it about skewness and kurtosis.

McHugh, M. L. (2003). Descriptive statistics, part II: Most commonly used descriptive statistics. *Journal for Specialists in Pediatric Nursing, 8*(3), 111–116.

CHAPTER **8**

z-Scores, Percentiles, and Effect Size

INTRODUCTION

In Chapter 7 we saw that when a variable's values in a data set are distributed normally, we can depict any value in terms of where it falls within the standard deviation intervals above or below the variable's mean. In the illustration involving how many tokens youths received for positive behaviors, for example, we saw that if the mean number of tokens is 10 and the standard deviation is 2, and Joe has 12 tokens, then Joe's value is one standard deviation greater than the mean. A statistic that is used to represent how many standard deviation intervals a value falls above or below the mean is called the **z-score**. (*z*-scores are also referred to as *standard scores*.) Joe's *z*-score, for example, would be 1.0, a *positive* *z*-score because it is *above* the mean. Likewise, if Joe has 8 tokens, then his *z*-score value is –1.0, a *negative* *z*-score (one standard deviation *below* the mean).

As illustrated in Figure 8.1, we can see that with a positive *z*-score of 1.0, Joe would be at the point on the *x*-axis of the normal curve that is higher than 0.8413 (84.13 %) of the cases. How do we know that? By adding the 0.3413 proportion between the mean and one standard deviation above it to the 0.50 below the mean. Likewise, if Joe had a negative *z*-score of –1.0, we can easily figure out that 0.8413 (84.13%) of the cases had more tokens than

Joe. To get that result, we simply change directions and add the 0.3413 proportion between the mean and one standard deviation unit below the mean to the 0.50 above the mean.

Using the same logic, we could determine that if Joe had a positive *z*-score of 1.0, there would be 0.1587 (15.87%) of the cases with more tokens than Joe. We would know that simply by subtracting 0.8413 from 1.0 (or 84.13% from 100%). Likewise, if Joe had a negative *z*-score of –1.0, we would know that 0.1587 (15.87%) of the cases had fewer tokens than he had.

CALCULATING *z*-SCORES

What if Joe had 9 tokens? That would be one-half of a standard deviation below the mean because the standard deviation is 2, and Joe was half that distance below the mean of 10. Thus, Joe's *z*-score would be –0.50. Likewise, if Joe had 11 tokens, his *z*-score would be +0.50 (or one-half of a standard deviation *above* the mean).

The simple formula for converting a raw value into a *z*-score is as follows:

$$z\text{-Score} = \frac{\text{Raw Value} - \text{Mean}}{\text{Standard Deviation}}$$

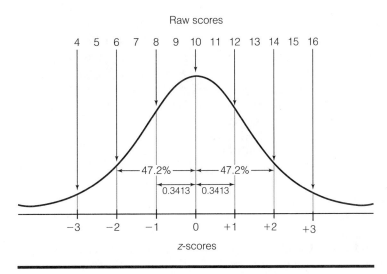

Figure 8.1 Location of Some *z*-scores on the Normal Curve with a Raw Score Mean of 10 and a Standard Deviation of 2

Thus, if Sam has 13 tokens, with a mean of 10 and a standard deviation of 2, Sam's z-score would be as follows:

$$\text{Sam's } z\text{-score} = \frac{13 - 10}{2} = \frac{3}{2} = 1.5$$

Likewise, if Ben has 7 tokens, with a mean of 10 and a standard deviation of 2, Ben's z-score would be as follows:

$$\text{Ben's } z\text{-score} = \frac{7 - 10}{2} = \frac{-3}{2} = -1.5$$

Figure 8.1 depicts the relationship of the above raw scores to their z-scores, the relation of z-scores to their standard deviation units, and the location of z-scores on the normal curve. The section of Appendix G headed "Using SPSS to Calculate z-Scores (Chapter 8)" shows how to use SPSS to (guess what?) calculate z-scores.

PRACTICAL USES OF z-SCORES

One of the neat things about z-scores is that they can enable us to compare scores on different kinds of measures of the same variable. Suppose, for example, that you work in a child and family agency and are forming a play therapy group for children who have been traumatized. Many children served by your agency might benefit from the group, and you don't have room for all of them. You want to make sure that those children with the most severe posttraumatic stress symptoms are invited to participate in the group. So you examine their case files to find the scores they received on a standardized scale measuring posttraumatic stress symptoms. You find, however, that some children were measured with one standardized scale (we'll call it Scale A) and some were measured with another (Scale B).

The two scales are different in the number of items and the number of response categories. Scale A has 20 items, each asking about the frequency of a different symptom, and each followed by three response categories: often, sometimes, and rarely. The scores on each item range from 1 to 3, so across the 20 items the total scale score can range from 20

to 60. Scale B has 100 items. Each item asks about the presence or absence of a different symptom, with response categories limited to yes or no. "Yes" is scored as 1, and "No" is scored as 0. Thus, Scale B's total scores can range from 0 to 100.

How do you decide whether a child with a raw score of 35 on Scale A has more or less severe trauma symptoms than a child with a raw score of 50 on Scale B? Because the two measurement approaches are so different, you wouldn't want to conclude that the Scale B score depicted worse symptoms than the Scale A score just because 50 is greater than 35. Your dilemma would be resolved, however, if you knew the means and standard deviations of the two scales derived from studies of them with large samples of children. (Such data are called *norms* and are known for some prominent clinical measurement scales.)

Suppose you learned that the mean and standard deviations for the two scales were 25 and 5 for Scale A and 40 and 10 for Scale B. From that information you could derive the z-scores for the two children. A raw score of 35 on Scale A would be 2 standard deviations (2 times the standard deviation of 5) above the Scale A mean of 25. As shown in Figure 7.4, that z-score would be higher than 97.2% of Scale A scores in the normative data. A raw score of 50 on Scale B would be one standard deviation (10) above the Scale B mean of 40. As shown in Figure 7.4, that z-score would be higher than 84.13% of Scale B scores in the normative data. Assuming that higher scores on each scale signified worse trauma symptoms, you would know that although both children have worse trauma symptoms than most other children, the child with a raw score of 35 on Scale A is experiencing more posttraumatic stress than the child with the (higher) raw score of 50 on Scale B.

USING A z-SCORE TABLE

So far we've been examining z-scores (such as 1 and 2) that make it fairly simple to ascertain corresponding proportions of the normal curve just by looking at Figure 8.1 or Figure 7.4. However, real studies tend to produce z-scores that involve fractions or decimals that cannot be converted to normal curve proportions just by looking at figures like these. For example, suppose our z-score was 0.74

or 1.65. Figure 8.1 or Figure 7.4 won't show you normal curve proportions for those z-scores.

Fortunately, we can look up any z-score in a table to find the proportion of the area under the normal curve between the mean and the z-score. Suppose our z-score was 1.65, for example. That z-score would depict a value that is 1.65 standard deviations above the mean. Using Table 8.1, we'd start with the left-hand column, headed z, and find the row for 1.6. That row would cover all the proportions above the mean for z-scores between 1.60 and 1.69. Next, we'd locate the column for the second decimal point of the z-score (0.05). The intersection between the 1.6 row and the 0.05 column would show us that for a z-score of 1.65, 45.05% of the normal curve falls between the mean and the value that is 1.65 standard deviations above the mean. Adding the 50% of the normal curve area on the other side (below) the mean, we would know that a value that is 1.65 standard deviations above the mean exceeds 95.05% (50% + 45.05%) of the cases in the distribution. Rounding off the 95.05% to 95%, we could say that a z-score of 1.65 is at the 95th percentile, since the definition of the term *percentile* is the percentage of the normal distribution exceeded by a particular value.

Suppose our z-score was negative, at −1.65. Using the same row and column, we would know that it was at the 5th percentile. Thus, it would exceed only 5% of the cases in the distribution. We would know that because the area between the mean and 1.65 standard deviations below it is 0.4505. By adding the 45% (after rounding off 0.4505) below the mean to the 50% above it, we get 95% of the cases with higher values.

SOME PRACTICE EXAMPLES

To practice using Table 8.1, you can look up the percentile for a z-score of 0.74. I suggest you do that now, and jot down your answer before reading any further. Okay, assuming you have done so, let's see if you followed the right steps and found the correct answer.

You should have started with the row headed 0.7 in the left-hand column. Next, you should have found the intersection of that row with the column headed 0.04. There you should have found the number 27.04. That would tell you that 27.04% of

the normal curve falls between the mean and the value that is 0.74 standard deviations above the mean. Adding the 50% of the normal curve area on the other side (below) the mean, we would know that a value that is 0.74 standard deviations above the mean exceeds 77.04% (50% + 27.04%) of the cases in the distribution. Rounding off the 77.04% to 77%, we could say that a z-score of 0.74 is at the 77th percentile.

Perhaps one more example will help. This time, instead of telling you the z-score, I'll just tell you the mean, the value, and the standard deviation. Suppose we had a normal distribution with a mean of 50 and a standard deviation of 10. Suppose Jane's score was 56. What would her z-score and percentile be? Again, you may want to jot down your answer before reading any further.

Here are the steps we would take to find the answers. First, we would plug the above numbers into the z-score formula and thus subtract 50 from 56 and then divide by 10 (the standard deviation). That would give us a z-score of 0.60. Next we would look up 0.60 in Table 8.1. There we would begin with the row in the left-hand column labeled 0.6 and then move over to the column headed 0.00 (because our second decimal point is a zero). At that intersection we would find the number 22.57. That would tell us that that 22.57% of the normal curve falls between the mean (50) and the value that is 0.60 standard deviations above the mean (56). Adding the 50% of the normal curve area on the other side (below) the mean, we would know that a value that is 0.60 standard deviations above the mean exceeds 72.57% (50% + 22.57%) of the cases in the distribution. Rounding off 72.57% to 73%, we could say that a z-score of 0.60 is close to the 73rd percentile.

POSITIVE AND NEGATIVE z-SCORE PERCENTILES

So far, we have been practicing with positive z-scores; that is, z-scores for values that are *greater* than the mean. Let's now practice with a z-score for a value that is *less than* the mean.

Suppose in the example immediately above that Jane's score was 44 instead of 56, and that the mean (50) and standard deviation (10) were the same as above. To calculate the z-score, we would subtract

TABLE 8.1   Percent of Area under Normal Curve between the Mean and the z-Score

Z	0.00	0.01	0.02	0.03	0.04	0.05	0.06	0.07	0.08	0.09
0.0	00.00	00.40	00.80	01.20	01.60	01.99	02.39	02.79	03.19	03.59
0.1	03.98	04.38	04.78	05.17	05.57	05.96	06.36	06.75	07.14	07.53
0.2	07.93	08.32	08.71	09.10	09.48	09.87	10.26	10.64	11.03	11.41
0.3	11.79	12.17	12.55	12.93	13.31	13.68	14.06	14.43	14.80	15.17
0.4	15.54	15.91	16.28	16.64	17.00	17.36	17.72	18.08	18.44	18.79
0.5	19.15	19.50	19.85	20.19	20.54	20.88	21.23	21.57	21.90	22.24
0.6	22.57	22.91	23.24	23.57	23.89	24.22	24.54	24.86	25.17	25.49
0.7	25.80	26.11	26.42	26.73	27.04	27.34	27.64	27.94	28.23	28.52
0.8	28.81	29.10	29.39	29.67	29.95	30.23	30.51	30.78	31.06	31.33
0.9	31.59	31.86	32.12	32.38	32.64	32.90	33.15	33.40	33.65	33.89
1.0	34.13	34.38	34.61	34.85	35.08	35.31	35.54	35.77	35.99	36.21
1.1	36.43	36.65	36.86	37.08	37.29	37.49	37.70	37.90	38.10	38.30
1.2	38.49	38.69	38.88	39.07	39.25	39.44	39.62	39.80	39.97	40.15
1.3	40.32	40.49	40.66	40.82	40.99	41.15	41.31	41.47	41.62	41.77
1.4	41.92	42.07	42.22	42.36	42.51	42.65	42.79	42.92	43.06	43.19
1.5	43.32	43.45	43.57	43.70	43.83	43.94	44.06	44.18	44.29	44.41
1.6	44.52	44.63	44.74	44.84	44.95	45.05	45.15	45.25	45.35	45.45
1.7	45.54	45.64	45.73	45.82	45.91	45.99	46.08	46.16	46.25	46.33
1.8	46.41	46.49	46.56	46.64	46.71	46.78	46.86	46.93	46.99	47.06
1.9	47.13	47.19	47.26	47.32	47.38	47.44	47.50	47.56	47.61	47.67
2.0	47.72	47.78	47.83	47.88	47.93	47.98	48.03	48.08	48.12	48.17
2.1	48.21	48.26	48.30	48.34	48.38	48.42	48.46	48.50	48.54	48.57
2.2	48.61	48.64	48.68	48.71	48.75	48.78	48.81	48.84	48.87	48.90
2.3	48.93	48.96	48.98	49.01	49.04	49.06	49.09	49.11	49.13	49.16
2.4	49.18	49.20	49.22	49.25	49.27	49.29	49.31	49.32	49.34	49.36
2.5	49.38	49.40	49.41	49.43	49.45	49.46	49.48	49.49	49.51	49.52
2.6	49.53	49.55	49.56	49.57	49.59	49.60	49.61	49.62	49.63	49.64
2.7	49.65	49.66	49.67	49.68	49.69	49.70	49.71	49.72	49.73	49.74
2.8	49.74	49.75	49.76	49.77	49.77	49.78	49.79	49.79	49.80	49.81
2.9	49.81	49.82	49.82	49.83	49.84	49.84	49.85	49.85	49.86	49.86
3.0	49.87									
⋮	⋮									
4.0	49.997									

Originally from *Tables for Statisticians and Biometricians*, K. Pearson (ed.). Used by permission of The Biometrika Trustees. Present layout from El Lundquist, A First course in Statistics, used by permission from Houghton Mifflin Co.

the mean of 50 from Jane's score of 44 and then divide by 10. Since 44 is less than 50, subtracting 50 from 44 yields a negative number, −6. Dividing −6 by 10 gives us a *negative z*-score of −0.60. Using Table 8.1, and following the same steps as we did for a positive *z*-score of +0.60, we would again find that 22.57% of the normal curve falls between the mean and the value that is 0.60 standard deviations away from the mean.

However, this time—since our negative *z*-score of 0.60 standard deviations is *below* the mean, rather than above it—we cannot add the 50% of the normal curve below the mean to the 22.57%. Instead, we would *subtract* the 22.57% from the 50%. That would tell us that Jane's score exceeded 27.43% of the cases in the distribution. In other words, approximately 27% of the cases in the distribution would be to the left of the position of Jane's score on the *x*-axis. Thus, Jane's score would be approximately at the 27th percentile, as illustrated in Figure 8.2.

To summarize, to find the percentile for a *positive z*-score, we *add* the 50% of the normal curve below the mean to the percent of the normal curve between the mean and the *z*-score. To find the percentile for a *negative z*-score, we subtract the percent of the normal curve between the mean and the *z*-score from the 50% of the normal curve below the mean.

SOME NEGATIVE *z*-SCORES CAN BE POSITIVE!

A negative *z*-score can be desirable if the variable in question represents some behavior or score that is undesirable. For instance, the variable *serious behavioral incidents* that we've been discussing in the hypothetical residential treatment center evaluation is something that an intervention would attempt to prevent or reduce. There are countless other possible examples of undesirable things that we might attempt to prevent or reduce, such as abusive behaviors, school absenteeism or tardiness, scale scores indicating higher degrees of depression or stress, and so on.

When we intervene to prevent or reduce any of these undesirables, we would like the mean score for clients receiving our intervention to be lower than the mean score for clients not receiving our intervention. Thus, if the mean number of serious behavioral incidents for all the clients in our residential treatment center is 10, with a standard deviation of 2, and we test out a new intervention with Mary, we would want Mary's number of incidents to be well below 10. Suppose Mary had only 4 incidents after the new intervention was introduced. Her *z*-score would be: |4 − 10|/2 = −3.0. Table 8.1 tells us that the distance between the mean and a value that is 3.0 standard deviations

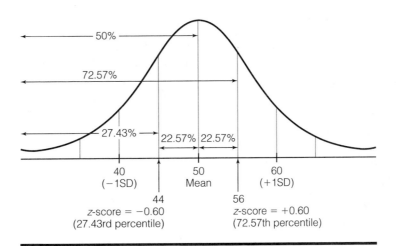

Figure 8.2 Normal Curve Depiction of Positive and Negative *z*-Score Percentiles for a Mean of 50, a Standard Deviation of 10, and Values of 44 and 56

away from the mean covers 49.87% of the normal curve. Since Mary's z-score is negative, we could subtract 49.87% from 50% and get 0.13% (which is much less than 1% because it represents the proportion 0.0013). Thus, we could say that Mary's z-score is below the 1st percentile.

However, because we *want* Mary's z-score to be low, we could say that she is doing *better* than 99% of the cases. We could then reverse our wording and say that Mary is at the 99th percentile in terms of *not* getting into trouble with serious behavioral incidents.

If all of this seems a bit confusing, just remember that positive z-scores are not always desirable and that negative z-scores are not always undesirable. It all depends on whether the variable in question represents something desirable that we'd like to be high or something undesirable that we'd like to be low. This should become clearer as we turn now to another practical use of z-scores: the *effect size* statistic.

EFFECT SIZE

In addition to their utility in converting the scores of individuals into percentiles, z-scores can be used to compare the means of two groups in terms of how many standard deviations one group's mean is above or below another group's mean. This comes in handy when we are evaluating the effectiveness of an intervention, program, or policy.

For example, suppose a new treatment is being compared to a routine treatment in reducing serious behavioral incidents (as in the residential treatment center evaluation we've been referring to throughout this text). Suppose the mean for the new treatment is 6 incidents, and the mean for the routine treatment is 8 incidents. Suppose further that the standard deviation for both treatments is 2. Subtracting the new treatment mean of 6 from the routine treatment mean of 8, we get a difference of 2 incidents between the two means. That difference of 2 is the same value as our standard deviation. Thus, the new treatment mean of 6 is one standard deviation better than the routine treatment mean of 8. (This is a situation in which a negative z-score is desirable, because the variable in question—number of serious behavioral incidents—refers to undesirable behaviors.)

Depicting the difference in means between two groups in standard deviation units is the same as converting that difference to a z-score. Thus, when we say that the mean for the new treatment is one standard deviation better than the mean for the routine treatment, we are saying that the z-score for the difference between the means is 1. Because one standard deviation better than the mean is at the 84.13 percentile (as discussed earlier in this chapter), we can say that the mean score for the new treatment is better than 84.13% of the scores for the routine treatment.

When we use z-score calculations to compare the difference between two means in standard deviation units, we call the z-score statistic the **effect size.** We call it that because it compares the effect one variable (such as type of intervention) has on another variable (such as treatment outcome).

You are most likely to encounter the term *effect size* when you read reports of experimental or quasi-experimental evaluations of the effectiveness of interventions in which group means are compared. The effect size (ES) formula is simply a z-score formula, except that instead of comparing one case's score to the group mean in the numerator, it compares two group means in the numerator. The formula is as follows (ES stands for *effect size*):

$$ES = \frac{|(\text{Experimental Group Mean}) - (\text{Control Group Mean})|}{\text{Control Group Standard Deviation}}$$

Thus, if an experimental group had a mean number of serious behavioral incidents of 5, and the control group's mean and standard deviation were 6 and 2, respectively, then the effect size would be as follows:

$$ES = \frac{|5 - 6|}{2} = \frac{|-1|}{2} = |0.5|$$

You're probably wondering, "What's with all the vertical lines in the above formula and calculations?" Good question. When calculations appear between those vertical lines, the lines signify that we are dealing only with absolute values, ignoring plus or minus signs. It's important to keep that in mind when interpreting the ES statistic because a higher experimental group mean signifies a desirable treatment outcome only when the dependent variable is a desirable thing that we are trying to increase. When the dependent variable is something undesirable that we want to decrease, then a higher experimental group mean would signify an undesirable treatment outcome and perhaps a harmful treatment.

Notice in the above ES calculation that the dependent variable, number of serious behavioral incidents, refers to negative behaviors that are undesirable. Thus, if we neglected the vertical lines in the formula, our ES would be −0.5 instead of +0.5. On the other hand, if the means were reversed, with the experimental group having the 6 and the control group having the 5, we'd get a positive ES (+0.5) if we neglected the vertical lines in the formula when the intervention's effects were negative (i.e., undesirable).

After we calculate the absolute value ES, as above, we insert a plus or minus sign according to whether the difference between the group means represents a desirable or undesirable effect. If the dependent variable is a desirable thing that the intervention seeks to increase, then a positive difference in the formula's numerator signifies a positive effect. We would therefore report the ES as positive (i.e., ES = +0.50). If the dependent variable is an undesirable thing that the intervention seeks to decrease, then a positive difference in the formula's numerator signifies a negative effect. We would therefore insert a minus sign and report the ES as negative (i.e., ES = −0.50).

Thus, the ES tells us how many control group standard deviation intervals the experimental group's mean falls above or below the control group's mean. Thus, we would interpret an ES of +0.5 by observing that the experimental group's mean was one-half of a standard deviation better than the control group's mean. Assuming that the control group's values are distributed normally, we can examine Table 8.1 to see what proportion of the control group's values are better or worse than the experimental group's mean. There we can see that with an ES of 0.500 (which is the same as a z-score of 0.500) the experimental group's mean exceeds 69.15% of the control group's values, because 19.15% of the area under the normal curve falls between the control group's mean and the experimental group's mean. Thus, the 50th percentile in the experimental group is better than the 69th

percentile of the control group. Still using Table 8.1, we can also see that if an ES were to equal +2.00, then the experimental group mean would be better than 97.72% of the control group values.

The same effect size formula can be used to compare two different intervention groups, instead of comparing one intervention group to a control group. For example, if an evaluation compared Intervention A to Intervention B, the means of those two groups would go in the numerator, and the overall standard deviation for the cases in both groups combined would go in the denominator.

Practical Use of Effect Size Statistics

Effect size statistics can be very useful to practitioners by enabling them to compare the effects of different interventions across studies using different types of outcome measures. Suppose one study in a residential treatment center finds that Intervention A reduces serious behavioral incidents from a control group mean of 6 to an experimental group mean of 5, with a standard deviation of 1. The ES therefore would be 5 minus 6 divided by 1, or 1.0. Thus, the experimental group's mean is better than 84% of the control group values.

Suppose another study in a similar residential treatment center finds that Intervention B improves scores on a conduct disorder scale by 5 points, but with a standard deviation of 10. The ES therefore would be 5 divided by 10, or 0.5. Thus, the experimental group's mean is better than 69% of the control group values (as found in Table 8.1). Although the two studies used completely different measures of behavior problems, and although the raw score difference between the experimental group and control group for Intervention B is 5 times that of Intervention A, we can conclude that because Intervention A had the stronger effect size, it therefore had stronger treatment effects than Intervention B.

So far I have been careful to use the terms "stronger" and "strongest" when comparing the effect sizes of different studies rather than the terms "better" or "best." That's because not all dependent variables in outcome evaluations are of equal value. Suppose a third study finds an ES of 2.0 in connection to Intervention C's effectiveness in increasing the amount of time the youths spend praying each night before going to bed. Unless we assume that praying has a strong beneficial impact on behavior, we might not deem that "stronger" ES as "better" or more valuable than the "weaker" ES of 1.0 for Intervention A, since the latter measured actual behavioral incidents.

Before concluding this chapter, let's consider one more example to further illustrate the utility of effect size statistics to practitioners. Suppose an evaluation finds that Intervention A reduces the number of times youths are re-arrested for substance abuse from a mean of 2 to a mean of 1. Suppose a different evaluation finds that after receiving Intervention B a similar sample of youths self-report different attitudes about substance abuse. Before treatment, their mean score on a self-report scale was 50. After treatment the mean score increased to 60, indicating a desired change in which the youths now express more criticism of substance abuse.

It would make no sense to say that Intervention B is more effective because its 10-point differential far exceeds Intervention A's 1 point differential. That would make no sense because we would be comparing apples and oranges. We would have no basis for determining how many points of improvement on one measure are equivalent to how many points of improvement on the other. If the self-report scale scores have a possible range from 0 to 100, then a 10-point improvement on that scale might be less meaningful than a 1-point improvement in re-arrests. By the same token, we would have no basis for knowing how much improvement in terms of re-arrests was equivalent to how much improvement in terms of self-report scores.

The solution to this dilemma would be to convert each outcome into a *z*-score. Doing this would require that we assume that the outcome data in both evaluations have a normal distribution. This is an important assumption, and we should not make it without checking the shape of the two distributions. Let's assume that the two distributions *are* normally distributed, and that the standard deviation in the evaluation of Intervention A is 0.50, while the standard deviation in the evaluation of Intervention B is 10. Converting the 1-point differential in the evaluation of Intervention A to an effect size, we would divide the 1-point difference by 0.50 (its standard deviation) and get an effect size of 2. Converting the 10-point differential in the evaluation of Intervention B to an effect size, we

would divide the 10 by its standard deviation of 10 and get a *z*-score of 1.

Now we can compare the relative effectiveness of the two interventions even though they were evaluated with different measures. Intervention A resulted in a mean improvement of 2 standard deviation units, while Intervention B resulted in a mean improvement of 1 standard deviation unit. Thus, Intervention A had a greater impact on its dependent variable even though its (non-standardized) difference (1) was less than the (non-standardized) difference (10) for Intervention B.

Referring to Figure 8.1, we could also say that the mean for the youths receiving Intervention A is better than 97.2% of the values for its control group, whereas the mean for the youths receiving Intervention B is better than 84.13% of the values for its control group. Although the raw score mean difference for Intervention B is 10 times that of Intervention A, the standardized effect size statistics tell us that Intervention A is more effective.

But what if Intervention B had the stronger effect size? Would that automatically mean it is "better" than Intervention A? Not necessarily. As I mentioned above, not all dependent variables in outcome evaluations have the same value. Practitioners might be skeptical about the meaningfulness of what youths *say* in a self-report scale. They might put more stock in what the youths actually *do*. Thus, those practitioners might deem re-arrest rates as a more valid and more clinically meaningful indicator of the effectiveness and value of an intervention than self-report scores. We'll return to the issue of making judgments about the comparative value of different kinds of outcome variables in Chapter 16, when we discuss the substantive, or clinical, significance of varying effect sizes.

Main Points

• A *z*-score (or standard score) shows how many standard deviation intervals a value falls above or below the mean.

• *z*-scores enable us to compare outcomes of evaluations that use very different outcome measures.

• We can look up any *z*-score in a table to find the proportion of the area under the normal curve between the mean and the *z*-score.

- A percentile is the percentage of the normal distribution exceeded by a particular value.

- To find the percentile for a *positive z*-score, we *add* the 50% of the normal curve below the mean to the percent of the normal curve between the mean and the *z*-score. To find the percentile for a *negative z*-score, we subtract the percent of the normal curve between the mean and the *z*-score from the 50% of the normal curve below the mean.

- Positive *z*-scores are not always desirable, and negative *z*-scores are not always undesirable. It depends on whether the variable in question represents something desirable that we'd like to be high or something undesirable that we'd like to be low.

- When we use *z*-score calculations to compare the difference between two means in standard deviation units, we call the *z*-score statistic the *effect size*.

- The effect size (ES) formula is simply a *z*-score formula, except that instead of comparing one case's score to the group mean in the numerator, it compares two group means in the numerator.

- The *ES* tells us how many control group standard deviation intervals the experimental group's mean falls above or below the control group's mean.

- After we calculate the absolute value *ES* we insert a plus or minus sign according to whether the difference between the group means represents a desirable or undesirable effect.

- Effect size statistics can be very useful to practitioners by enabling them to compare the effects of different interventions across studies using different types of outcome measures.

- Not all dependent variables in outcome evaluations are of equal value; therefore, when we are comparing the effect sizes of different studies "stronger" does not necessarily mean "better" or "best."

Review Questions and Exercises

1. Based on the normal curve in Figure 8.3, which has a mean of 12 and a standard deviation of 3, what are the *z*-scores and percentiles for the following outcomes?

a. 15 positive behaviors

b. 18 positive behaviors

c. 21 positive behaviors

d. 9 positive behaviors

e. 6 positive behaviors

f. 3 positive behaviors

g. 12 positive behaviors

2. Suppose a valid scale exists to measure risk of child abuse in a family. Lower scores indicate less risk of abuse and are therefore more desirable than higher scores. Suppose the mean and standard deviation of the scale for all families receiving child welfare interventions are 50 and 6, respectively. Atop the next page is a list of families receiving child welfare interventions and their scores on the scale. For each family, calculate its *z*-score and percentile (using Table 8.1). Then identify which families are most and least in need of further intervention.

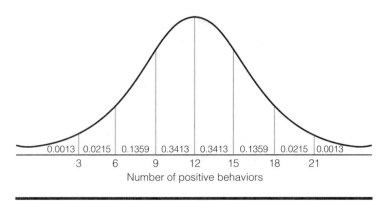

Figure 8.3

NAME	SCORE	z-SCORE	PERCENTILE
Adams	52		
Doe	40		
Jones	57		
Smith	61		
Woods	37		

3. Nursing home A evaluated the effectiveness of staff retreats in improving the job satisfaction of its patient care staff. It found that after the retreat the mean score improved from 30 to 60 on a self-report scale of job satisfaction. The standard deviation was 10. Nursing home B evaluated the effectiveness of a new in-service training course for its patient care staff. The dependent variable was the number of reported incidents of patient abuse by each staff member. The experimental group's mean was 0.34 after receiving the training. The control group's mean was 1, and its standard deviation was 0.33.

a. Calculate the effect size for each nursing home's evaluation results.

b. Using Table 8.1, interpret the two effect sizes in terms of percentiles, and explain the practical meaning of the two percentiles.

c. Which evaluation had the stronger effect size?

d. All things considered, including your judgment of the comparative value of the two dependent variables, which intervention would you choose to implement if you were a nursing home administrator? Why?

e. Compare your answer to d, above, with the answers of your classmates. If your answers differ, engage in a dialogue about each other's reasoning.

InfoTrac Exercises

1. Briefly describe at least one way in which the following articles illustrate the practical use of effect size statistics:

Robinson, D. H., Fouladi, R. T., Williams, N. J., & Bera, S. J. (2002). Some effects of including effect size and "what if" information. *The Journal of Experimental Education, 70*(4), 365–382.

Kowatch, R. A., Suppes, T., Carmody, T. J., Bucci, J. P., Hume, J. H., Kromelis, M., Emslie, G. J., Weinberg, W. A., & Rush, A. J. (2000). Effect size of lithium, divalproex sodium, and carbamazepine in children and adolescents with bipolar disorder. *Journal of the American Academy of Child and Adolescent Psychiatry, 39*(6), 713.

2. Briefly describe how the following article used percentiles in its data analysis, and explain how that illustrates the utility of using percentiles.

Meilman, P. W., Presley, C. A., & Cashin, J. R. (1997). Average weekly alcohol consumption: Drinking percentiles for American college students. *Journal of American College Health, 45*(5), 201.

Inferential Statistics

In the previous six chapters (in Part 2) we focused on various descriptive statistics whose purpose is limited to organizing, summarizing, and displaying the data collected in a particular study. But what if we have a broader purpose? What if we want to use the data collected in our study not just to describe our sample, but also to make inferences about a larger population? For the latter purpose we'll need **inferential statistics,** which will be the focus of the remaining ten chapters of this book.

Probability and Sampling Distributions

INTRODUCTION

The purpose of using inferential statistics is to see if we can generalize our findings beyond our particular study or sample. To illustrate the difference between descriptive and inferential statistics, suppose you are administering a substance abuse treatment program for women. One of your practitioners tells you that based on her clinical experience she believes that a large proportion of your program's clients have been sexually abused in the past and that she therefore thinks your treatment program ought to incorporate some new interventions focusing on that problem. In response, you conduct an anonymous survey of all of your program's clients. You find that 50% of them report having been victims of sexual abuse. This finding spurs you to convene a committee assigned to find ways to improve your agency's responsiveness to that problem in its treatment approach. You don't really need to know about the population of female substance abuse clients in other programs nationally or internationally to recognize that because 50% of *your* program's clients need a new intervention approach, then such an approach is worth pursuing in *your* agency. The *descriptive* statistics dealing with the frequency of that problem among *your* program's clients are sufficient since you are not generalizing beyond your program.

Suppose, however, you attend a conference where you happen to informally discuss your findings with some colleagues who administer similar programs in other cities. Should they infer, based solely on your findings, that approximately 50% of their clients have been victims of sexual abuse and therefore need some new intervention approach, too? Leaping to that conclusion would be unwarranted without first determining the likelihood that your findings can be generalized to the broader population of women in treatment for substance abuse. Assessing that likelihood requires the use of inferential statistics.

Likewise, suppose a year later you tell the same colleagues that you evaluated the effectiveness of the new intervention approach you adopted and found that the clients who received it had a lower relapse rate than those who did not receive it. You might report the difference using the effect size statistic, as discussed in Chapter 8. Again, your colleagues should not infer that the treatment will be associated with the same relapse rate in their agencies.

There are many reasons why your results may not generalize to the population. Most of the reasons have to do with potential sampling error. For example, maybe your clients are older (or younger) on average than the population as a whole. Maybe they have better social support systems and fewer psychiatric symptoms. Maybe they are more (or less) likely to be minorities or in poverty. Maybe the clients who received the new treatment approach were more motivated to change than the ones who did not receive it.

The foregoing reasons all have to do with methodological issues. You don't need inferential statistics to spot methodological flaws, such as sampling bias or experimental design biases, to be wary about generalization. (Appendix A reviews methodological issues like these.) But there is another problem affecting our ability to generalize that can occur even in the best designs, and for that problem you *do* need inferential statistics. That problem has to do with **chance**. The term *chance*, in this context, refers to sampling error. But it is not sampling error based on bias; rather, it is based on *random* error.

CHANCE (SAMPLING ERROR)

To comprehend the concept of chance, or sampling error, you should understand what the terms *population* and *sample* mean. A **population** is the entire universe of cases to which you seek to generalize. It may be all men and/or women in treatment for substance abuse, all registered voters, all nursing home residents, all statistics textbooks, all mental health clinics, and so on. If you are only interested in the caseload of one agency, and have no wish to know about or generalize to others, then that one agency's caseload can be the population for your study's limited purpose. If, however, you study some agency caseloads with the intent to generalize to all agencies, then all caseloads in the universe of all agencies as a whole will be your population.

In reality, the concept of a *population* is somewhat theoretical. That's because it is ever changing. The population of registered voters tomorrow will be different from today due to deaths and new registrations. Likewise, the population of any country changes from minute to minute, as people die, are born, emigrate, immigrate, and so on.

A **sample** is that part of the population from which you have data. It might be a small part of the population or a large part. If we seek to generalize from our sample data to the population, our sample should be representative of the population. That is, the sample should have the same distribution of characteristics as the population from which it was drawn. Thus, if we seek to generalize to all people in treatment for substance abuse, our sample should match the population of people in treatment for substance abuse in terms of the distribution of background attributes such as gender, age, ethnicity, type of substance abused, motivational level, socioeconomic status, and so on. The best way to maximize the likelihood of getting a representative sample is to use **probability sampling,** which involves using **random sampling** procedures that avoid sampling bias. (See Appendix A for a review of research methods and concepts like these.)

But while random sampling prevents sampling bias, it does not prevent random sampling error. Imagine, for example, trying to predict the outcome of a presidential election in the United States by randomly selecting only two voters in an election eve poll. Assuming that voters will be choosing between only two nominated candidates, the chances of the two respondents saying they'll vote for the same candidate are fairly high. (We'll see shortly that the two voters are just as likely to support the same candidate as they are to support different candidates.) Thus, the poll is apt to predict that one candidate will get 100% of the votes. If so, despite the random sampling, the poll would most likely have a great deal of **sampling error,** since most presidential elections in the United States are close to a 50/50 split.

Sometimes, however, one candidate gets closer to 60% of the vote. Let's suppose that will be the case in the election we are discussing. With a random sample of two voters, the only possible results of the poll are that both respondents will say they are voting for the same candidate (thus leading to a prediction that one candidate will get 100% of the votes) or that the respondents will say they are voting for different candidates (thus leading to a prediction that each candidate will get 50% of the votes). Thus, the prediction is certain to be off by either 40% or 10% in an election where one candidate gets 60% of the votes and the other gets 40%.

Likewise, if the poll randomly selected three voters, the only possible outcomes of the poll would be all three voters (100%) supporting the same candidate, or two of the three (67%) supporting one candidate and one of the three (33%) supporting the other. Since we cannot slice people in half and then poll each half (especially if we don't want to alienate them and discourage their participation in future polls), there would be no way with three voters to get 50% (1.5 voters) of the poll respondents supporting one candidate and 50% supporting the other. Thus, if the results of the election were close to 50/50, our poll results would be off by either about 50% or 17% despite random sampling.

Highly regarded scientific presidential election polls using random sampling typically poll about 1000 or more people and tend to be fairly accurate in their election eve predictions. But even they are usually off by a tiny percentage (perhaps 1 to 3% or so). In other words, while random sampling avoids bias in sample selection, it does not ensure the avoidance of some degree of random sampling error.

The same concept applies to research and evaluation in evidence-based practice. For example, suppose we survey three clients in an agency providing services to children, teens, adults, and the elderly. Even if we select our sample of three randomly, the chances are slim that its mean age will exactly match the mean age of the entire agency caseload. Also slim are the chances that the three clients sampled will mirror the overall caseload distribution of ethnicity, service needs, and so on. For reasons to be examined later, the larger our random sample, the lower the amount of sampling error to be expected. But, as with election eve polls with very large samples, there is always some chance of sampling error no matter how large our sample is. That's where inferential statistics come into play. Inferential statistics tell us about the influence of sampling error on our findings and on our ability to generalize those findings beyond our sample.

PROBABILITY

In order to understand how inferential statistics inform us about the influence of sampling error, we must first become comfortable with some basic concepts underlying the calculation of **probability.** *The* probability of a particular outcome occurring is equal to the number of ways that particular outcome can occur divided by the total number of all possible outcomes. For example, if we flip a coin, there are two possible outcomes: heads or tails. There is only one way a coin can come up heads, so the probability that the coin will come up heads is one divided by two, or 0.50 (one over two). The same goes for tails. Probability can be depicted in terms of proportions—such as 0.50, 0.33, and so on—or in terms of percentages, such as 50%, 33%, and so on.

Let's assume that we flip a coin to determine whether a client gets assigned to Treatment A or Treatment B. If the coin comes up heads, then the client is assigned to Treatment A. Tails means assignment to Treatment B. Thus, the probability of being assigned to Treatment A is 0.50 (1/2), or 50%, and the probability of being assigned to Treatment B is also 0.50 (1/2), or 50%.

Suppose our agency serves 100 clients, and only one of our clients is a Native American. If we were to randomly select one client for a case study, then the probability of selecting a Native American client would be 1 out of 100 (1/100), or 0.01 (1%). If two of our clients are Native Americans, then the probability of selecting a Native American client would be 2 out of 100 (2/100), or 0.02 (2%).

There is another way to calculate probability that is consistent with the statement above that the probability of a particular outcome occurring is equal to the number of ways that particular outcome can occur divided by the total number of all possible outcomes. The other way comes into play when we want to know the probability that two particular outcomes will occur. That probability is determined by multiplying one outcome's probability by the other outcome's probability.

For example, suppose we were to select two clients for case study out of our agency's caseload of 100 clients. Also suppose that 2 out of the 100 clients are Native American. The probability of a Native American client being selected first would be 2 out of 100 (2/100), or 0.02 (2%). That would leave 99 clients not selected, one of whom would be Native American. The probability of selecting that Native American next, therefore, would be 1/99, or 0.0101. Thus, the probability of selecting not just one of them, but both of them, would be $0.02 \times 0.0101 = 0.000202$ (or $2/100 \times 1/99 = 2/9900 = 1/4950$).

In the above example, the selections of each Native American client were not independent events. That is, the selection of one influenced the probability of selecting the other. To illustrate how this multiplication rule works with independent events, let's switch from a study in which we are randomly selecting clients from our caseload of 100 clients to a study in which we will conduct a clinical experiment requiring that we randomly assign half of the clients in a substance abuse treatment program to Intervention A and the other half to Intervention B. We'll use a coin toss to randomly assign each client. If the client's toss comes up heads, we'll assign the client to Intervention A. If tails, they get Intervention B.

Suppose the first two clients that we assign, whose names are Dan and Tom, are both very highly motivated to change. The probability that *either* one gets assigned to Intervention A is 0.5 (or 1/2), since the probability of heads or tails is 50/50. But the probability that *both* get assigned to Intervention A is $0.5 \times 0.5 = 0.25$ (or 1/4). Below are all the possible outcomes for assigning Dan and Tom, and each has the same probability of occurring.

Outcome 1: Dan and Tom both get heads, and both are assigned to Intervention A.

Outcome 2: Dan and Tom both get tails, and both are assigned to Intervention B.

Outcome 3: Dan gets heads and Intervention A; Tom gets tails and Intervention B.

Outcome 4: Dan gets tails and Intervention B; Tom gets heads and Intervention A.

Notice that Dan and Tom both are assigned to Intervention A in one of the four (0.25) possible outcomes—the same as multiplying their individual probabilities of 0.5 by each other. Also notice that in half of the four possible outcomes of random assignment both of our very highly motivated clients are assigned to the same group (i.e., either Intervention A or B) and that in half of them they are assigned to different groups.

The purpose of random assignment in a clinical outcome evaluation comparing the effectiveness of two alternative treatments is to maximize the probability that the two groups will be equivalent in terms of client characteristics before treatment (as discussed in Appendix A). Thus, if our most highly motivated clients all are assigned to the same treatment condition, we have a big problem.

But sometimes flukes occur in random assignment that result in important differences in the before-treatment characteristics of treatment groups. Sometimes, for example, more clients who are so highly motivated to change that they would have done so without treatment are assigned to one group than to the other. Above, we saw that the probability that two such highly motivated clients (Dan and Tom) would both get assigned to Intervention A via a coin toss is 0.25, and the probability that they would both get assigned to Intervention B is 0.25. Thus, the probability of *either* outcome occurring is 2 out of 4 possibilities, or 0.50. (We also can get this result by adding the two individual probabilities.) But suppose the first eight clients being assigned to either Intervention A or B are all highly motivated like Dan and Tom. What is the probability that all eight of these clients would get heads and thus be assigned to Intervention A? To find out, we multiply each of the eight individual probabilities (1/2 or 0.5) of getting heads by each other, as follows:

$$1/2 \times 1/2 \times 1/2 \times 1/2 \times 1/2 \times 1/2 \\ \times 1/2 \times 1/2 = 1/256$$

or

$$0.5 \times 0.5 \times 0.5 \times 0.5 \times 0.5 \times 0.5 \times 0.5 \times 0.5 \\ = 0.004$$

Thus, the probability that all eight would be assigned to Intervention A is less than 1/2 of 1%. The probability that all 8 would get tails and be assigned to Intervention B is the same. Therefore, the probability of either outcome occurring—that is, all eight clients being assigned to the same group—would be $0.004 + 0.004 = 0.008$. That total is still less than 1% (0.008 is less than 0.01).

This example illustrates that as our sample size increases, the probability of flukes in random selection or random assignment decreases. Another way to illustrate the same point is to suppose that we have a caseload of ten clients, half (five) of whom are male and half (five) of whom are female. If we select a random sample of those clients, the more clients we select, the better our chances are of approximating the proportion of males and females in our population of ten. For example, if we select one client, we have no chance of getting a 50% split between males and females. If we select two clients,

we have a 0.22 chance of getting two men and a 0.22 chance of getting two women. (We get 0.22 by multiplying $5/10 \times 4/9 = 20/90 = 2/9 = 0.22$. We don't just multiply 1/2 times 1/2 because once we've selected one client, there will be nine clients left, four of whom will be of the same gender as the first client selected.) We will therefore have a 0.44 chance of getting either outcome and thus having only one gender in our sample. But as we select more clients, the probability decreases that they all will be of the same gender and thus increases that they will be more representative of the distribution of males and females in our population.

Another way to think about this is as follows. Suppose the first two clients we select are both male. Remaining unselected are three males and five females. Thus, the next client we select has a five out of eight probability of being a female and a lower (three out of eight) probability of being a male. Suppose of the first five clients we select, four are male and one is female. That leaves five of the ten clients unselected, four of whom will be female and only one of whom will be male. Thus, the probability that the next client will be female is 4/5 (0.8), while the probability that the next client will be male is only 1/5 (0.2). With each client selected, therefore, the probability that the next client selected will have the same attribute (regardless of whether the attribute in question pertains to gender or some other variable) decreases. Likewise, the probability increases that we will select someone with an attribute not previously selected.

Using the same principles of probability, suppose we find a big difference between Intervention A and Intervention B in substance abuse relapse rates, with all eight of the clients receiving Intervention B relapsing and none of the eight clients receiving Intervention A relapsing. Inferential statistics will tell us the probability that we could have obtained that difference just through a fluke in the random assignment of cases who were or were not going to relapse regardless of which intervention they received.

Likewise, if we randomly select a sample of cases from our agency caseload, inferential statistics will tell us the probability that our population has the same proportions or mean as our sample, within various margins of sampling error. Thus, inferential statistics can be used to assess two kinds of probabilities: (1) the probability that differences between groups can be attributed to sampling error (chance); and (2) the probability that attributes of a sample are accurate estimates of population attributes within certain margins of sampling error. With either purpose, as our sample size increases, the probability of sampling error decreases, and the probability that our sample statistics accurately reflect the population's statistics increases. With either purpose, the concepts we discussed in Chapter 7 and 8 regarding normal curves are key. Therefore, before we examine further each of the purposes of inferential statistics, let's examine the role of the normal curve in inferential statistics.

THEORETICAL SAMPLING DISTRIBUTIONS

When we select a sample for the purpose of generalizing to a population, we use our sample statistics as estimates of the population's statistics. For example, if we find that the mean family size (number of people residing in the household) among our sample of ten clients is 5.5, then we would estimate that the mean for our entire agency caseload is about 5.5. In statistical terminology, the term **parameter** is used instead of *statistic* when referring to a summary statistic for an entire population. The term *statistic* is reserved for summarizing a sample. Thus, we call our sample mean of 5.5 a *statistic* and our population mean of 5.5 a *parameter*. Although you might be tempted to dismiss this distinction in terminology as rather tedious semantics, it's important that you know it so things will seem less complicated when you read reports using these terms.

Probability theory enables us to estimate a population parameter based on statistics from a sample by using the features of the normal curve in something called a *theoretical sampling distribution*. A **theoretical sampling distribution** is a normal distribution (depicted in a normal curve) of all possible sample statistics produced by an infinite number of randomly drawn samples from a population. The theoretical sampling distribution shows the proportion of times each sample statistic would be found merely due to chance. In other words, it identifies the probability of obtaining a particular outcome in a sample merely as a result of chance.

To see how this works, suppose we have a small agency caseload of ten clients, and each client has a different number of persons residing in his or her household, ranging from 1 to 10. Thus one client lives alone, another lives with one other person, another has a family size of three, and so forth up to the client with a family size of ten. Figure 9.1 depicts this population of ten clients.

If we add all the family sizes in Figure 9.1, we'll get a total of 55. Dividing that by the total number of cases in our small agency population, we get a mean household size of 5.5. Thus, our population parameter for mean household size is 5.5. Now, suppose we randomly selected a sample of only one client from our population of ten. Whichever client gets selected will be our estimate of the parameter. If Client 1 is selected, we'd estimate that the population mean is 1 (because Client 1 lives alone). If Client 10 gets selected, we'd estimate it to be 10 (because that client lives with nine other people).

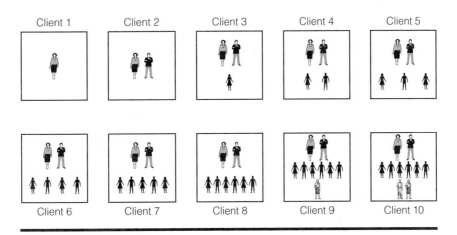

Figure 9.1   A Population of ten Clients with ten Different Household Sizes

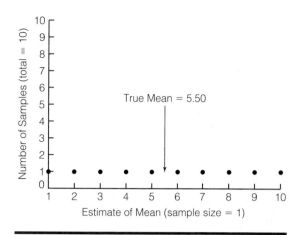

Figure 9.2   Theoretical Sampling Distribution of Samples of one

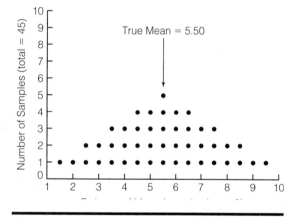

Figure 9.3   Theoretical Sampling Distribution of Samples of two

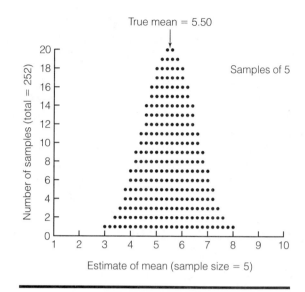

Figure 9.4   Theoretical Sampling Distribution of Samples of five

Figure 9.2 displays a graph of the ten possible estimates we'd get. The distribution of dots is called the theoretical sampling distribution. We can see at a glance that with a sample size of only one client, many of our possible samples would miss the true population mean of 5.5 by a lot.

Figure 9.3 shows what our theoretical sampling distribution would look like if we took samples of two clients each. Notice how the increase in sample size has reduced sampling error by producing more samples that are closer to the true mean than in Figure 9.2. Instead of only 10 possible samples, we now have 45. And five of those samples now hit the true mean of 5.5 exactly. Those five samples would be the following pairs of clients: Client 1 and Client 10;

Client 2 and Client 9, Client 3 and Client 8; Client 4 and Client 7; and Client 5 and Client 6. (For each of the foregoing five pairs, the household numbers add up to 11. Dividing that sum by 2 gives us 5.5.) Eight other samples are at mean household sizes of either five or six—only 0.5 away from the true population mean.

Notice also how the overall distribution begins to resemble a normal curve, in which the closer we get to the true population mean, the more possible sample means there are. With each incremental increase in sample size, the closer the sample means cluster near the true population mean. This is further illustrated in Figure 9.4, based on taking samples of 5 each.

The idea underlying the progressive decrease in sampling error illustrated in Figures 9.2 through 9.4 is called the **central limit theorem.** According to this theorem, as the size of the sample increases, the theoretical sampling distribution based on that sample size will become increasingly normal in shape, and its mean will become increasingly closer to the population mean.

But as discussed earlier in this chapter, even large samples will usually have some degree of sampling error. Most election eve polls, for example, will be off by a percent or two in predicting the distribution of votes in the population of actual votes cast. In the same vein, recall from Chapters 7 and 8 that approximately 68% of the values in a normal curve

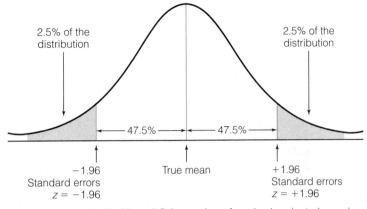

2.5% of the distribution

2.5% of the distribution

47.5% 47.5%

−1.96
Standard errors
$z = -1.96$

True mean

+1.96
Standard errors
$z = +1.96$

Sample means obtained in an infinite number of randomly selected samples

Figure 9.5 Illustration of a Theoretical Sampling Distribution with Percentages of the Distribution Beyond and Between 1.96 Standard Errors Above and Below the Mean

fall between one standard deviation below the mean and one standard deviation above it. Therefore, the remaining 32% of the values in a normal curve are at least one standard deviation away from the mean. Thus, regardless of sample size, there is approximately a 32% probability of obtaining a sample mean that is at least one standard deviation away from the true population mean.

In fact, if you re-examine Table 8.1 (page 76), you'll see that 19.15% of the values in a normal curve fall between the mean and a z-score of 0.50. Thus, 19.15% of the values fall between the mean and one-half (0.50) standard deviation above the mean, and another 19.15% of the values fall between the mean and one-half standard deviation below the mean. Adding the two percentages together, we see that only 38.30% of the values in a normal curve are as close as 0.5 standard deviations above or below the mean. Subtracting 38.30% from 100%, we find that 61.70% of the values in a normal curve are at least 0.5 standard deviations away from the mean. In other words, in any theoretical sampling distribution the majority of possible outcomes will have some sampling error.

Said another way, anytime we take a sample of a population, no matter how rigorously scientific our sampling techniques might be, we are likely to have some degree of inaccuracy in our estimate of the population parameter. Theoretical sampling distributions, which have the properties of normal curves, enable us to estimate our likely degree of

sampling error. As displayed in Figure 9.5, when dealing with an interval- or ratio-level variable, the y-axis in a theoretical sampling distribution represents the proportion of random selections that would obtain each x-axis mean if we were to select an infinite number of samples of a particular sample size. Also as displayed in Figure 9.5, the mean of the various sample means arrayed across the x-axis would be the true population mean.

The Standard Error

The standard deviation of the theoretical sampling distribution is called the **standard error of the mean.** It is called that because it represents the *sampling error* involved in estimating the true population mean based on an infinite number of random selections of sample means. The standard error of the mean is usually referred to more simply as the *standard error*. As we've seen, the larger the sample size, the lower the standard deviation of the theoretical sampling distribution (and thus the lower the standard error).

In order to factor in the influence of sample size, the *standard error* equals the standard deviation of the sample divided by the square root of the sample size. (The mathematical derivation of this formula goes beyond the scope of this book.) We cannot know the standard deviation of a population based on the data from a sample, so we just use our sample standard deviation as an estimate of the population standard deviation when calculating the standard error. Thus, if our sample size is 100, its square root is 10. If our sample standard deviation is 10, then the standard error would be 10/10 = 1. If our sample size is 400, then its square root would be 20. With our sample standard deviation remaining at 10, our standard error would be 10/20 = 0.5. Thus, since the standard error is the standard deviation of our theoretical sampling distribution, by increasing our sample size we reduce the dispersion in our theoretical sampling distribution (as indicated by the smaller standard deviation).

You may wonder why we don't just use the standard deviation of the sample to estimate the standard deviation of the population instead of dividing it by something. After all, you might reason, didn't we use the sample mean as the estimated mean of the theoretical sampling distribution? Without getting into the complexities of the math, the answer has to do with the difference in the number of values in a sample and the number of values in a theoretical sampling distribution. More values in a distribution means that the sample size of that distribution is larger. As illustrated earlier, the larger the sample size, the less dispersion there is around the mean. That is, the closer the distribution of values will cluster near the mean. The lower the dispersion, the lower the standard deviation.

Because the x-axis values of the theoretical sampling distribution have been derived from a theoretically *infinite* number of randomly drawn samples from a population, its *infinite* sample size dwarfs the size of any sample that was used to estimate the theoretical sampling distribution. Thus, the dispersion (as depicted by its standard error) of the theoretical sampling distribution is going to be much less than the sample dispersion (as depicted by its standard deviation). How much less dispersion will be in the theoretical sampling distribution will depend on the size of the sample being used to estimate the standard error. If you re-examine Figures 9.2, 9.3, and 9.4, you'll see how the sample means cluster closer and closer to the mean of the sampling distribution with each incremental increase in sample size.

Confidence Intervals for Estimating Population Parameters

Calculating the standard error of a sampling distribution enables us to estimate with a certain degree

of confidence how close the true population mean is likely to be to our sample mean. For example, suppose we conduct a needs assessment survey of a random sample of 400 people living in a community containing a high proportion of recent immigrants and having a high poverty rate. Let's further suppose we are conducting the survey in order to get data that can be used in a proposal for funding a new service, and that we need to show that there is a lot of economic deprivation in the area to justify the need for funding. One indicator of that need would be the population's mean income. If the mean income of our survey sample was $15,000, and our standard deviation was $4000, we could divide the $4000 by 20 (which is the square root of our sample size of 400) to get the standard deviation of our theoretical sampling distribution (the standard error of the mean). Dividing $4000 by 20 would give us $200.

Since $200 is the standard deviation of our theoretical sampling distribution, approximately 95% of that distribution would fall between a mean of $14,600 and $15,400. Why? Because $14,600 is two standard deviations (2 × $200) below the mean of $15,000, and $15,400 is two standard deviations above $15,000.

But let's not deal in approximations; let's get precise. To find the means that would border exactly 95% of the theoretical sampling distribution, we would have to use z scores of plus or minus 1.96 instead of plus or minus 2.0 (as discussed in Chapter 8). Multiplying $200 by 1.96, we would get $392. Subtracting and adding that figure to $15,000 would tell us that 95% of the theoretical sampling distribution falls between $14,608 and $15,392. We would therefore be 95% confident that the true mean income of the town was somewhere between $14,608 and $15,392. That interval, between $14,608 and $15,392, would be termed our 95% **confidence interval.** The 95%, which is an estimate of the probability that the true population mean lies somewhere within our confidence interval, is called our **confidence level.** Thus, we would have a *confidence level* of 95% that the population mean falls within the *confidence interval* of $14,608 and $15,392.

What if we wanted to have less than a 0.05 probability of being wrong about our confidence interval? What if we wanted to lower that probability to 1%? Then we would need to construct a 99% confidence interval. Using Table 8.1 (page 76), we

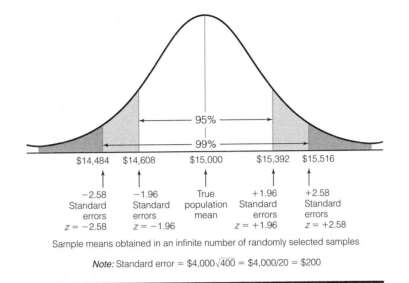

95%

99%

| $\$14,484$ | $\$14,608$ | $\$15,000$ | $\$15,392$ | $\$15,516$ |

-2.58 Standard errors $z = -2.58$ -1.96 Standard errors $z = -1.96$ True population mean $+1.96$ Standard errors $z = +1.96$ $+2.58$ Standard errors $z = +2.58$

Sample means obtained in an infinite number of randomly selected samples

Note: Standard error $= \$4,000\sqrt{400} = \$4,000/20 = \$200$

Figure 9.6 Illustration of a Theoretical Sampling Distribution with 0.95 and 0.99 Confidence Interval Estimates for a Sample Size of 400 with a Mean of $15,000 and a Standard Deviation of $4,000

would find that 99% of the theoretical sampling distribution would fall between plus or minus 2.58 standard deviations away from the mean. Multiplying 2.58 times our standard error of the mean (standard deviation of our theoretical sampling distribution) of $200 gives us $516. Subtracting and adding $516 to $15,000 gives us a 99% confidence interval of $14,484 and $15,516. Thus, when we reported our findings as part of our proposal for funding, in addition to saying that the mean income in our survey was $15,000, we could assert that we have only a 1% probability of being wrong in estimating that the population's mean income is somewhere between $14,484 and $15,516. (See Figure 9.6.)

Estimating Confidence Intervals Involving Proportions

So far we have been examining estimates of standard errors and confidence intervals with variables at the interval or ratio level of measurement. We can do the same with nominal-level variables, but instead of dealing with means and standard deviations, we must deal with proportions. This is what is done in election polls that predict what proportions of the vote two candidates will get within a certain margin of error. On the eve of the 2004 presidential election in the United States, for example,

various presidential polls predicted a dead heat between candidates Bush and Kerry—with each getting 50% of the popular vote cast between those two candidates—but with a 3% margin of error. With that margin of error, therefore, they were saying that they are confident that of all the votes cast for those two candidates, either candidate will get between 47% and 53% of the vote. (After the actual election votes were tallied, we learned that the actual results were well within the pollsters' confidence intervals, with Bush receiving 51.5% of the votes cast between those two candidates and Kerry getting 48.5%.)

How confident were the pollsters making their prediction? It depends on whether they used a 95% or a 99% confidence interval. If their confidence interval was between plus and minus 1.96 standard errors of the proportions they found in their poll, then they were 95% confident. That's because 95% of the normal curve (the theoretical sampling distribution) falls between plus and minus 1.96 standard deviations (standard errors). If their confidence interval was between plus and minus 2.58 standard errors of the proportions they found in their poll, then they were 99% confident. That's because 99% of the normal curve (the theoretical sampling distribution) falls between plus and minus 2.58 standard deviations (standard errors).

How do they calculate the standard error, not having interval or ratio data with which means and standard deviations can be calculated? They use a different formula. That formula is as follows:

$$s = \sqrt{\frac{P \times (1 - P)}{N}}$$

where s = standard error (an estimate of the standard deviation of the theoretical sampling distribution of proportions)

P = sample proportion

N = sample size

Here's how the formula works in an election poll that predicts a dead heat in which each of two candidates gets 0.50 of the votes. The 0.50 would be the P in the above formula. Multiplying 0.50 times $(1 - 0.50)$ gives us 0.25. The 0.25 would therefore be the numerator under the square root sign. The denominator will depend on the sample size. Let's suppose it is 1000. The fraction under the square root sign thus becomes 0.25/1000, or 0.00025. The square root of that number is 0.0158. Thus, the standard error (s) is 1.58%. Because the 95% confidence interval is between plus and minus 1.96 standard errors, we multiply 0.0158 by 1.96. This gives us 0.031. Rounding off, that is 3%. Thus, the 95% confidence interval is between 3% below the 0.50 sample proportion (47%) and 3% above it (53%). From this we now can tell that the 2004 pollsters were 95% confident of their prediction, since their stated margin of error was plus or minus 3%.

Now let's see how this works in an administrative practice illustration. Suppose you survey a random sample of 100 community residents to assess whether they would support or oppose establishing a substance abuse treatment facility in their community. Suppose 50% say they'll support it, and 50% say they'll oppose it. Plugging those numbers into the above formula, we get

$$s = \sqrt{\frac{0.5 \times (1 - 0.5)}{100}} = \sqrt{\frac{0.25}{100}} = \sqrt{0.0025} = 0.05$$

Thus, our standard error is 0.05. Multiplying 0.05 by 1.96, we get 0.098. We'll round that off to 0.10, or 10%. Therefore, our 95% confidence interval tells us that we can be 95% confident that the true

population proportion of residents supporting or opposing the facility is between 40% (1.96 standard errors below the sample proportion) and 60% (1.96 standard errors above the sample proportion).

Figure 9.7 illustrates what theoretical sampling distributions involving proportions look like. They look just like the distributions involving means. The only difference is that each x-axis value is a proportion from a sample rather than a mean from a sample. Although the data in each sample are nominal, a mean can be calculated from the various proportions across the many samples. Each sample's proportion is plotted in the distribution. After many sample proportions are plotted, the distribution takes on the shape and properties of a normal curve, with the same standard deviation proportions as in the normal curves examined earlier regarding interval- or ratio-level variables. And with each increase in sample size, the normal curve becomes more peaked, with the sample proportions clustering closer and closer to the mean proportion.

Practical Use

Of what practical use would this information be? Suppose the administrator in your agency is eager to establish the substance abuse facility, and is convinced that the community will support it overwhelmingly. In fact, she insists that less than a few percent of community residents will oppose the facility.

You tell her that your survey indicates otherwise, noting that 50% of the residents you sampled said they'd oppose the facility. She responds by arguing that your 50% figure is just based on one sample; perhaps it is a fluke. Perhaps another survey would be closer to her belief.

Your 95% confidence interval will enable you to tell her that not only do 50% of your respondents oppose the facility, but that there is less than a 2.5% probability that fewer than 40% of the residents will oppose it. (That's because the 5% outside the confidence interval is split with 2.5% on one end of the x-axis and 2.5% at the other end.) In fact, with a 99% confidence interval, you could tell her that there is less than a 1% chance that fewer than 37% of the residents will oppose the facility. (You would know that because 99% of the theoretical sampling distribution falls between 2.58 standard errors above and below the sample

Small sample size (N = 25) with 50% sample proportion

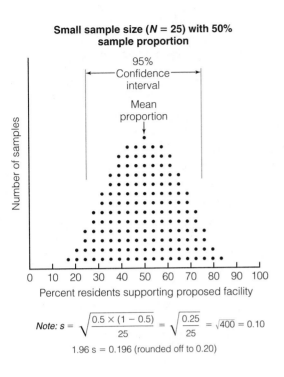

$$\textit{Note: } s = \sqrt{\frac{0.5 \times (1 - 0.5)}{25}} = \sqrt{\frac{0.25}{25}} = \sqrt{400} = 0.10$$

1.96 s = 0.196 (rounded off to 0.20)

Larger sample size (N = 100) with 50% sample proportion

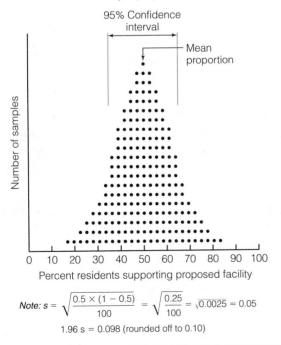

$$\textit{Note: } s = \sqrt{\frac{0.5 \times (1 - 0.5)}{100}} = \sqrt{\frac{0.25}{100}} = \sqrt{0.0025} = 0.05$$

1.96 s = 0.098 (rounded off to 0.10)

Figure 9.7 Theoretical Sampling Distributions of Proportions

proportion, and 2.58 times 0.05 equals 0.13. Subtracting 13% from the sample proportion of 50% gives you a minimum of 37% of residents in opposition.)

This is important information. You wouldn't want to waste time and other resources trying to establish a facility in a location where community opposition is going to block your efforts. Moreover, being able to anticipate such opposition will enable you to formulate a strategy to try to reduce it before implementing your program, rather than attempting to implement it first and then having to shut down in the face of community wrath.

With this statistical information, therefore, you could try to persuade your administrator to either find a more receptive site for your program or delay implementing it until you garner more community support for it. But would she be persuaded? Perhaps she sneers at statistics as "damn lies." Perhaps she is someone who doesn't like facts to get in the way of her beliefs. If so, no matter how reasonable your argument, she may have to learn the hard way that she is wrong. It wouldn't be the first time an executive didn't want facts to get in the way of his or her beliefs! But if your administrator learned and remembers the concepts you are reading right now, she'll probably be persuaded. More importantly, someday you may be in her position, and what you are learning right now will come in handy. (You therefore may want to keep this book for future reference!)

Main Points

• Whereas descriptive statistics organize, summarize, and display data collected in a particular study, inferential statistics are used to make inferences about a larger population.

• The term *chance* refers to sampling errors that inevitably occur in random sampling.

• A population is the entire universe of cases to which you seek to generalize, whereas a sample is that part of the population from which you have data.

• The probability of a particular outcome occurring is equal to the number of ways that particular outcome can occur divided by the total number of all possible outcomes.

• The probability that two particular outcomes will occur is determined by multiplying one outcome's probability by the other outcome's probability.

• As sample size increases, the probability of flukes in random selection or random assignment decreases.

• Inferential statistics can be used to assess two kinds of probabilities: (1) the probability that differences between groups can be attributed to sampling error (chance); and (2) the probability that attributes of a sample are accurate estimates of population attributes within certain margins of sampling error.

• When we select a sample for the purpose of generalizing to a population, we use our sample statistics as estimates of the population's statistics.

• The term *parameter* is used instead of *statistic* when referring to a summary statistic for an entire population.

• A theoretical sampling distribution is a normal distribution (depicted in a normal curve) of all possible sample statistics produced by an infinite number of randomly drawn samples from a population. The theoretical sampling distribution shows the proportion of times each sample statistic would be found merely due to chance.

• According to the central limit theorem, as the size of the sample increases, the theoretical sampling distribution based on that sample size will become increasingly normal in shape, and its mean will become increasingly closer to the population mean.

• Theoretical sampling distributions, which have the properties of normal curves, enable us to estimate our likely degree of sampling error.

• The standard deviation of the theoretical sampling distribution is called the *standard error of the mean*, or more simply, the *standard error*. The larger the sample size, the lower the standard deviation of the theoretical sampling distribution (and thus the lower the standard error).

• In order to factor in the influence of sample size, the standard error equals the standard deviation of the sample divided by the square root of the sample size.

• Calculating the standard error of a sampling distribution enables us to estimate with a certain degree of confidence how close the true population mean is likely to be to our sample mean.

• Confidence intervals are the areas of the theoretical sampling distribution that fall between a specified number of standard errors above and below the mean.

• A confidence level is the degree of probability that the true population mean will be within a particular confidence interval.

• The standard error for confidence intervals for nominal data involving proportions is calculated by multiplying the sample proportion by 1 minus that proportion, next dividing by the sample size, and then taking the square root.

Review Questions and Exercises

1. You conduct a client satisfaction survey with a descriptive purpose. A random sample of 100 clients (out of your agency's caseload of 2000 clients) participates in the survey. The overall mean satisfaction score is 6.8, with a standard deviation of 1.0. (On a scale from 1 to 10, a score of 7 depicts a moderate degree of satisfaction.) Your administrator concludes that this shows that the typical client in your agency's client population is moderately satisfied.

a. Why is his inference incorrect?

b. What would you tell him to explain the difference between descriptive and inferential statistics?

c. What other statistics would you say he needs to consider before making any inference?

2. Calculate 95% and 99% confidence intervals for the data in question 1 above. (Remember to calculate the standard error of the mean by dividing the standard deviation by the square root of the sample size.) How would you explain your confidence interval results to your administrator?

3. Suppose your survey was repeated with a sample size of 400 clients, and the same mean and standard deviation were found. Would that change your conclusions? How and why?

4. A faith-based program is introduced in prisons across your state to prevent re-arrests of released prisoners. In a random sample of 210 released prisoners who participated in the program, 30% of them are re-arrested within three years.

a. Calculate and interpret a 95% and a 99% confidence interval for the sample proportion of 0.30.

b. Suppose the statewide proportion of all released prisoners (not just those who participated in the faith-based program) who are re-arrested within three years is 0.35. Suppose that the administrator of the faith-based program concludes that since only 0.30 of the sample of faith-based program participants were re-arrested within three years, that proves that the faith-based program reduces re-arrests from 35% to 30%. Would you agree? Explain why or why not.

InfoTrac Exercises

1. Read the article below and then explain one of the following:

a. Why you would switch doors as a contestant on "Let's Make a Deal."

b. The conditions under which you would or would not buy a lottery ticket.

c. Something in the article that enhanced your understanding of the concept of *probability*.

Murphy, P., & Doherty, P. What are the odds? (2002). *The Magazine of Fantasy and Science Fiction, 102*(5), 128–136.

2. After reading the two articles below, discuss whether the concept of probability should influence our thinking about the debate between those believing in creationism and those believing in evolution or the debate between those who believe the world is the result of a grand design versus those who believe it is the result of chance.

Devlin, K. (2000). Snake eyes in the Garden of Eden. *The Sciences, 40*(4), 14.

Kaplan, M. A. (2000). Probability, design, and the limits of explanation. *World and I, 15*(7), 16.

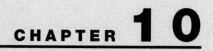
Hypothesis Testing and Statistical Significance

INTRODUCTION

In Chapter 9 we saw how theoretical sampling distributions can be used to calculate the probability that a population parameter falls within a certain distance from sample statistic. That is, by calculating a confidence interval, we can calculate the probability that a population mean (for interval or ratio measures) or a population proportion (for nominal measures) is between plus or minus a certain number of standard errors (standard deviations of the theoretical sampling distribution) away from our sample statistic. In this chapter we'll see how theoretical sampling distributions can be used in the same way to test hypotheses.

Testing hypotheses means making decisions about whether or not to attribute to sampling error a relationship between variables that we observe in a sample. When the probability that sampling error accounts for the relationship observed in a sample is very low, that relationship (or finding) is said to be *statistically significant.* Two rival hypotheses come into play here. One is our *research hypothesis.* The other is called the *null hypothesis.*

As discussed in Appendix A, a **research hypothesis** is a tentative and testable prediction about how changes in one (independent) variable are proposed to cause or explain changes in another (dependent) variable. For example, we might predict that one type of intervention will prevent more students from dropping out of school than will another type of intervention. In such a hypothesis, a nominal variable (type of intervention) would be our independent variable and another nominal variable (whether a student drops out) would be our dependent variable. Another hypothesis might predict a relationship between ordinal-, interval-, or ratio-level independent *and* dependent variables. For example, we might predict that the more often high school students use drugs or alcohol, the more often they'll be absent from school.

The **null hypothesis,** in contrast, supposes that there really is *no* relationship between our hypothesized variables in the population. Even if there is some relationship between the variables in our sample, the null hypothesis postulates that our findings can be attributed to sampling error and that the relationship does not really exist in the population or in a theoretical sense. Thus, if we evaluate our dropout prevention intervention and find that a sample of students who receive it have a somewhat lower dropout rate than a sample of students who do not receive it, the null hypothesis would attribute our difference in dropout rates to sampling error.

Testing for **statistical significance** means assessing the probability that the null hypothesis is true. When that probability is low enough to reject the null hypothesis as a plausible explanation for the relationship observed in a sample, we call that relationship **statistically significant.** We'll return to the role of the null hypothesis soon. First we'll examine the role that theoretical sampling distributions play in testing for statistical significance.

THEORETICAL SAMPLING DISTRIBUTIONS IN HYPOTHESIS TESTING

In testing whether a finding is statistically significant, the theoretical sampling distribution represents the distribution of the null hypothesis. That is, the theoretical sampling distribution is based on the premise that no relationship exists between the variables in our research hypothesis. Thus, it shows the likelihood of getting a particular finding—such as a difference in dropout rates between a treatment group and a control group—just due to sampling error. If the relationship observed in our sample data falls in that area of the theoretical sampling distribution that comprises a tiny percentage of the normal curve—usually about two or more standard errors away from the mean—then there is a low probability that our results are attributable to sampling error. When that happens, we can call the relationship *statistically significant* and reject the null hypothesis.

When we are comparing outcomes between two treatment groups (or between a treatment group and a control group), the theoretical sampling distribution in hypothesis testing is based on the assumption that there is no difference in outcome between two theoretical populations: the population represented by the sample in one treatment group and the population represented by the sample in the other treatment group. Said another way, if recipients of Treatment A and Treatment B are two treatment groups, then the theoretical sampling distribution is based on the assumption that there is no difference in outcome between two theoretical populations: the population

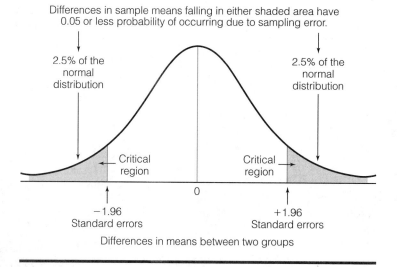

Figure 10.1 Theoretical Sampling Distribution of Differences in Means Between Two Groups

of recipients of Treatment A and the population of recipients of Treatment B.

To illustrate the use of theoretical sampling distributions in statistical significance testing, let's return to our fictional evaluation in a residential treatment center, in which we are assessing whether a new treatment is more effective than routine treatment in reducing the number of serious behavioral incidents. Recall from Chapter 4 that the *sample* mean for the new treatment group was 6, and the *sample* mean for the routine treatment group was 5. Therefore, if we were using a theoretical sampling distribution to construct a confidence interval to estimate the mean number of serious behavioral incidents for the population of new treatment recipients, the mean of the theoretical sampling distribution would be 6.

However, if we want to test the hypothesis that the *population* of new treatment group recipients will have fewer serious behavioral incidents than the *population* of routine treatment group recipients, then the mean of the theoretical sampling distribution would be 0, even though the difference in our *sample* was not 0. (With the two means being 6 and 5, the sample difference was 1.) That's because the theoretical sampling distribution assumes no difference in outcome between two theoretical *populations*. In other words, it assumes that sampling error explains any between-group difference in our

sample data, and therefore the true difference in the *population* is zero.

As displayed in Figure 10.1, we can examine the theoretical sampling distribution to see what degree of difference falls 1.96 or more standard errors away from the null hypothesis mean of 0 (no difference). Since 95% of the values in a theoretical sampling distribution fall between plus or minus 1.96 standard errors from the mean (as discussed in Chapter 9), we know that only 5% of the values fall outside that interval. Thus, in Figure 10.1 we can infer that differences in outcome between the new treatment group and routine treatment group that are at least 1.96 standard deviations away from the mean of no difference would be found in no more than 5% of an infinite number of random samples. In other words, we can infer that the probability of differences that large being due to sampling error is 0.05 or less.

The area of the theoretical sampling distribution where our sample statistic needs to fall in order to be deemed statistically significant (that is, too unlikely to be attributable to sampling error) is called the **critical region.** The cutoff point that separates the critical region probability from the rest of the area of the theoretical sampling distribution is called the **level of significance.** Sometimes it is called the **rejection level** or the **alpha level.** All of these terms mean the same thing. They refer to the probability—

which we select in advance—that we are willing to risk of being wrong in rejecting the null hypothesis. Usually that probability is set at 0.05 (for reasons we'll examine later in this chapter). When it is, then 0.05 can be called the *level of significance,* the *rejection level,* or the *alpha level.* Whichever term is used, it means that the critical region is that area of the theoretical sampling distribution containing values with no more than a 0.05 probability of being caused by sampling error.

To simplify things, suppose the sample size in our evaluation is ridiculously small, consisting of only four boys. Suppose we flip coins to assign two of the boys to one treatment group and two to the other treatment group. After treatment, one of the two boys who got randomly assigned to the new treatment group had 0 incidents. The other boy had 2. Thus, their mean is 1. Of the two boys assigned to the routine treatment group, one had 7 incidents and the other had 9. Thus, their mean is 8.

Although the difference in means (1 versus 8) for our two groups is large, it very easily could be due to chance. Even if there is no difference in the effectiveness of the two treatments, the probability that two of the boys with a small number of incidents will just happen by chance to get heads on a coin toss and therefore be assigned to the same group is a lot higher than 0.05. (In Chapter 9, we saw that the probability of getting two heads in a row is 0.25, and the probability of getting two tails in a row is also 0.25. Therefore, the probability that the first two boys will both get *either* two heads or two tails is $0.25 + 0.25 = 0.50$.)

In contrast, assume we got the same difference in means between 20 boys in one group and 20 in the other. The probability of that difference happening by chance would be a lot lower due to the much larger sample. How much lower would depend on the standard error, which is influenced by sample size (calculated using the standard deviation of our sample, as discussed in Chapter 9). Let's assume that the standard error is 3. Because the difference between 1 and 8 is 7, the mean of the 20 boys in the new treatment group (1) would be more than two standard errors ($2 \times 3 = 6$) better than the mean for the routine treatment group (8). Therefore, the probability of that difference occurring by chance would be less than 0.05. In other words, the probability that the null hypothesis is true would be less than 0.05. With a probability that

low, most researchers would reject the null hypothesis and therefore deem the difference to be *statistically significant.* Let's now examine further the use of the null hypothesis.

THE NULL HYPOTHESIS

So far we have been discussing chance, or sampling error, as a rival explanation to our research hypothesis for sample data that appear to support our research hypothesis. But if you've studied research methods or read Appendix A of this text (which reviews major research methods concepts), you may recall that various possible research design flaws serve as additional rival explanations.

Suppose a relatively unknown therapist (let's call him Joe) develops a new intervention that he hopes will make him rich and famous in addition to gratifying his altruistic need to help people. Not well versed in research methods and eager to obtain findings that will support his hypothesis, Joe uses the following method to evaluate whether his intervention is effective in helping clients improve their social functioning: he provides it only to those clients who need it the most (based on his clinical judgment). For his other clients, he provides whatever approach he routinely provided before developing his new intervention. Joe compares the effectiveness of the two approaches by giving each client—upon termination of treatment—his own subjective rating on a scale from 1 to 10 of how much improvement he "thinks" they made. The higher the rating, the more Joe thinks the client improved. He gives a mean rating of 9 to clients who received his intervention and a mean rating of 2 to those who received the routine intervention. Let's assume that Joe's results have less than a 1% probability of being explained by sampling error. Therefore, Joe rejects the null hypothesis and thus deems his results statistically significant.

In light of the very low probability that the null hypothesis is true, we can agree with Joe in ruling out the plausibility of sampling error as the explanation for the huge difference in ratings between his two treatment groups. But does that make his research hypothesis—that his new intervention is effective in helping clients improve their social functioning—the only plausible explanation for the huge difference? Of course not! Glaring research design flaws—such as measurement bias, therapist bias, and selectivity bias—remain as very plausible alternative explanations. (Biases like those are discussed in Appendix A.) In fact, if we bias a research design as much as Joe did, it's pretty easy to get findings that will not be due to sampling error. That is, there is nothing at all chancy about his findings since he (perhaps unintentionally) stacked the deck so egregiously that his "significant" findings were a foregone conclusion.

Therefore, when we get findings that warrant rejecting the null hypothesis, we should remember that while those findings may be consistent with our research hypothesis, and while they let us rule out sampling error as their explanation, they do not mean that we can overlook design issues as alternative explanations for our findings. Having a statistical term called the *null hypothesis* serves to remind us of that caution. It also reminds us that the theoretical sampling distribution is not the distribution of our research hypothesis, but instead is the distribution of the null hypothesis—the distribution of results that can be obtained by chance if our research hypothesis is *not* true.

Can We Confirm the Null Hypothesis?

Failing to reject the null hypothesis is not the same as confirming it. Suppose we find a 0.25 probability that sampling error explains the sample data supporting our hypothesis. Assuming that we use a lower cutoff point for refuting sampling error, such as 0.05 or 0.10, we would not rule out sampling error as a plausible explanation for our results and would therefore *not* reject the null hypothesis. But that would *not* mean that we *confirmed* the null hypothesis. The probability of the null hypothesis being true is still low at only 0.25. Although that probability is too high to reject the plausibility that the null hypothesis might be true, it is a far cry from proving it to be true.

For example, suppose you and I are about to go on a five-mile afternoon walk on a nippy autumn day to raise money for a charity. As we are about to leave, we hear the weather report, which forecasts a 30% chance of rain during the afternoon. Upon hearing this you go get your umbrella. I then chide you for being too cautious, arguing that with only a 0.30 probability of rain we can safely assume that it won't rain. Thus, my prediction is for no rain. There is only a 30% probability that my

prediction is wrong. Nevertheless, you decide to play it safe and take your umbrella. With a bit of autumn chill in the air, it's not the kind of day for getting drenched! But even though it is less likely to rain than to not rain, in taking your umbrella you are not implying that my prediction is wrong. You just don't want to take the risk that I'm wrong. Refusing to reject the null hypothesis works the same way. If we refuse to reject it when it has only a 0.30 (or perhaps a 0.15 or 0.20) probability of being wrong, we are not accepting it as true. We just are unwilling to take even that much risk in rejecting it mistakenly.

To be on the safe side, researchers and evaluators typically are willing to reject the null hypothesis only when the probability that the results are due to sampling error is extremely small—usually 0.05 or less (though sometimes 0.10 or less). You probably would not bother schlepping your umbrella with a rain probability that low. But having a higher probability of 0.15 or 0.20 that our results are due to sampling error is a far cry from *proving* sampling error as the explanation for our results.

But what if the aim of our research really is to support, rather than reject, the null hypothesis? That is, what if we are seeking to *disconfirm* a hypothesis that was supported in one or more previous studies? Suppose, for example, that Joe submits an article reporting his evaluation of his intervention to a journal that assigns it to editorial reviewers who are not well versed in research methods and that it consequently gets published. Suppose we read the published article and are appalled by its methodology and the fact that it got published. Suppose we decide to do a better evaluation, with the intent of refuting not the null hypothesis, but Joe's findings. That is, we would seek to show that his intervention is *not* more effective than existing alternative interventions.

Now, if we want to show that Joe's intervention is actually worse than alternative interventions, we would seek to reject the null hypothesis of no difference—but in the opposite direction from Joe's hypothesis. But if, instead of predicting that Joe's intervention is worse, we are simply predicting that it is no better than the alternative intervention, then we are predicting no difference. Thus, we are seeking to support, rather than reject, the null hypothesis.

What can we do statistically to support our prediction—that is, to support the null hypothesis?

We could examine whether Joe's intervention has a significantly better outcome than the alternative intervention. If it does, then our hypothesis of no difference is dead in the water. What if there is no difference whatsoever between the two outcomes? That also would provide evidence supporting our notion that Joe's intervention is no better.

But what if Joe's intervention has better results but with approximately a 0.15 or 0.20 probability of being due to sampling error? With that high a probability that Joe's intervention's better outcome is due to sampling error, we have not proven that Joe's intervention is no better than alternative interventions. We have only shown that the probability that the difference in outcomes can be explained by sampling error is too high for the difference in outcomes to be deemed statistically significant.

The bottom line is that when we are seeking to support the null hypothesis, we can't really come up with probabilities that we are wrong in supporting it, in the same way that we can come up with probabilities that we are wrong in rejecting it. The best we can do is to come up with results that show virtually no relationship whatsoever—for example, showing that the mean outcomes for two treatment groups in our sample are identical or nearly so. To the extent that our findings show no relationship, those findings support (but do not confirm) the null hypothesis. To the extent that our findings have a low probability of being due to chance, but not as low as 0.05 (or whatever alternative significance level we choose), those findings may raise some doubt about the relationship we are seeking to disconfirm, but they do not confirm the null hypothesis.

In many studies, it is a mistake to view the null hypothesis as the opposite of the research hypothesis. When Joe hypothesizes that his intervention is more effective than routine treatment, the opposite hypothesis is that routine treatment is more effective than Joe's intervention. The null hypothesis, in contrast, predicts no difference between the two.

The only time when the null hypothesis is the opposite of the research hypothesis is when the research hypothesis predicts some form of relationship between two variables, but does not predict the direction of that relationship. Suppose, for example, that Joe developed two types of interventions and was equally enthralled with each. Suppose he compared the two interventions in an evaluation without predicting which one would be more

effective. Let's just say he wanted to test the hypothesis that type of treatment is related to improvement in social functioning. Because he would not be predicting *which* type is more effective—just that a relationship exists—he would be postulating a **nondirectional hypothesis.** Since Joe is only predicting that *some* relationship exists, without predicting which categories of the independent variable will have higher or lower values on the dependent variable, the opposite of his hypothesis would be the null hypothesis that *no* relationship exists.

ONE-TAILED AND TWO-TAILED TESTS OF STATISTICAL SIGNIFICANCE

As illustrated in Figure 10.1, if our critical region combines the areas of the theoretical sampling distribution that are at least 1.96 standard deviations above or below the mean, we account for 5% (0.05) of the possible random assignment outcomes that occur just due to sampling error. In so doing, we'd be combining *two tails* of the distribution: the *tail* with the 2.5% of the area that lies farthest above the mean and the *tail* with the 2.5% of the area that lies farthest below the mean.

Suppose we are testing a nondirectional hypothesis, in which we have predicted a relationship between type of treatment and our dependent (outcome) variable without specifying which type will be more or less effective. In that case, we'd use a **two-tailed test of significance** because a sufficient difference between means that favors *either* Treatment A or Treatment B would support our hypothesis. In order to have no more than a 0.05 (5%) probability that the difference between means was due to sampling error, then to *reject the null hypothesis* we'd need to find a difference between means that is *either* 1.96 standard errors above the mean or 1.96 standard errors below the mean. (Thus, we would need a 2-score of at least 1.96.) This is illustrated in Figure 10.2.

Suppose we have postulated a **directional hypothesis,** one in which we predict which categories of the independent variable will have higher or lower values on the dependent variable. For example, we might predict that Treatment A will be more effective than Treatment B. In that case, we could use a **one-tailed test of significance** because a sufficient difference between means that favors

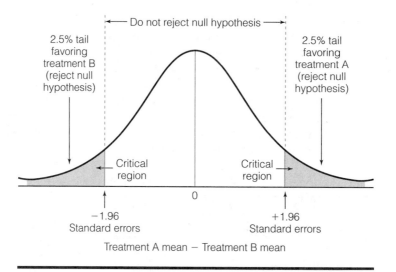

Figure 10.2   Illustration of a Two-Tailed Test of Significance with a 0.05 Probability of Incorrectly Rejecting the Null Hypothesis

only Treatment A would support our hypothesis. With a one-tailed test, we place the entire critical region at the predicted end of the theoretical sampling distribution. There would be no critical region at the other end. In order to have no more than a 0.05 (5%) probability in a one-tailed test that the difference between means favoring Treatment A was due to sampling error, then to *reject the null hypothesis* we'd need to find a difference between means in the critical region *above* the mean that comprises 5% of the theoretical sampling distribution. As explained in Chapter 8, a *z*-score of 1.65 is at the 95th percentile of the normal curve. (That is, 50% of the values in the curve are less than the mean, and 45% are between the mean and the value that is 1.65 standard deviations above the mean.) Thus, in a one-tailed test, to reach the point above the mean that comprises 5% of the area of the theoretical sampling distribution, the amount of difference in means favoring Treatment A mean would have to be 1.65 standard errors above the null hypothesis mean of no difference.

As illustrated in Figure 10.3, a one-tailed test of significance does not require as great a margin of difference between the two means to warrant rejecting the null hypothesis. However, that margin must be in the predicted direction; that is, in the predicted *tail*. If it is in the opposite tail—the one *not*

included in our directional prediction—then we cannot reject the null hypothesis. Why not? Because we would then be taking a 10% risk that our results were really due to sampling error since we would have rejected the null hypothesis had our results been in *either* 0.05 tail (above as well as below the mean).

Many studies will use a two-tailed test of significance even with a *directional* hypothesis. That's because sometimes our findings are in the opposite direction from the one we predicted, and we want to be able reject the null hypothesis if that happens to be the case. For example, suppose our directional hypothesis predicts that Treatment A will be more effective than Treatment B, but our results show the opposite: that Treatment B is much more effective than Treatment A. If Treatment B really is much more effective, then we would be doing a disservice to future clients (and practitioners) not to say so. Consequently, we would choose to use a two-tailed test of significance so that if the opposite of what we predict is the case, we can still rule out sampling error as the explanation. But we must decide how many tails we'll use *before* we test for significance. If we were willing to reject the null hypothesis with a one-tailed test, but then switch to a two-tailed test only *after* we see that our results are the opposite of what we predicted, then we are

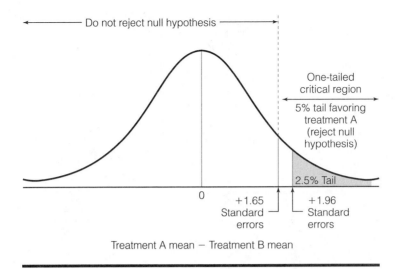

Figure 10.3 Illustration of a One-Tailed Test of Significance with a 0.05 Probability of Incorrectly Rejecting the Null Hypothesis

really doubling the probability that the results can be attributed to sampling error. The only appropriate way we could use both tails, each of which comprise 0.05 of the theoretical sampling distribution, would be to specify *in advance* that we will use a two-tailed test and reject the null hypothesis if it has no more than a 0.10 probability of being true (0.05 at both tails).

In previous chapters we saw that the normal curve is flatter with small sample sizes and more peaked with large sample sizes. In other words, there is greater dispersion—and thus a greater standard error—in the theoretical sampling distributions for findings based on smaller samples. Hence, the smaller the sample, the more extreme the difference between the means needs to be in order to fall in either tail of the theoretical sampling distribution, as illustrated in Figure 10.4. The top distribution in part A of Figure 10.4 is more peaked than the one below it (in part B) because it is based on a study with a larger sample size. A difference of plus or minus 3 mean raw score increments reaches the two-tailed critical regions in the top distribution, but a plus 3 difference falls short of even the one-tailed critical region in the bottom distribution. A difference of plus 4 is needed in the bottom distribution to reach the one-tailed critical region. But even that

difference falls short of the two-tailed critical region in the bottom distribution.

With some very small samples, the between-group differences need to be so extreme that we may not be able to reject the null hypothesis even when our results are reflecting a very effective intervention. Consequently, if our sample size is small, we might choose to use a one-tailed test of significance even though we'd prefer to use a two-tailed test. By using a one-tailed test, we sacrifice the option of being able to reject the null hypothesis with results that are in the opposite of the predicted direction, but we increase our chances of being able to reject the null hypothesis with results that are in the predicted direction since the between-group difference won't need to be as extreme.

If we use a one-tailed test but then get results that are in the opposite tail, we *cannot* call the results statistically significant. For example, in Figure 10.4(B) no difference in the negative direction—no matter how extreme—reaches the critical region. That's because with a one-tailed test, the side that is not predicted has *no* critical region. Thus, we *cannot* reject the null hypothesis. But we *can* inform our readers of what we found. We *can* tell them the probability that the results are due to sampling error. Although we must tell them that this probability does not meet our criterion for rejecting the

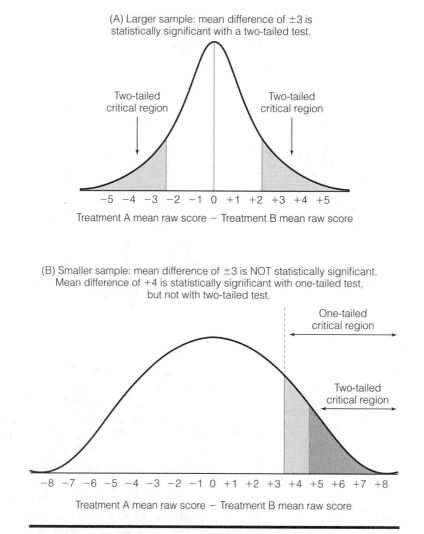

(A) Larger sample: mean difference of ±3 is statistically significant with a two-tailed test.

Two-tailed critical region

Two-tailed critical region

−5 −4 −3 −2 −1 0 +1 +2 +3 +4 +5

Treatment A mean raw score − Treatment B mean raw score

(B) Smaller sample: mean difference of ±3 is NOT statistically significant. Mean difference of +4 is statistically significant with one-tailed test, but not with two-tailed test.

One-tailed critical region

Two-tailed critical region

−8 −7 −6 −5 −4 −3 −2 −1 0 +1 +2 +3 +4 +5 +6 +7 +8

Treatment A mean raw score − Treatment B mean raw score

Figure 10.4 Illustration of Varying Extents of Difference Between Means Needed to Be Statistically Significant Depending on Sample Size and One- Versus Two-Tailed Tests

null hypothesis, we can point out that neither does it confirm the null hypothesis. Thus, even when our results are not statistically significant, if they *suggest the possibility* that the intervention that we thought would be effective is really less effective than alternative approaches—or perhaps is even harmful—then practitioners should be alerted to that possibility. We can inform them of the probability that our results were due to sampling error even when that probability exceeds 0.05 or 0.10, and then based on

that information they can make their own decisions about using or not using the intervention we've tested. Perhaps some readers will decide, based on our results, to test the intervention with a larger sample and with a two-tailed hypothesis.

The box titled "Illustrations of One- and Two-Tailed Tests with Directional and Non-directional Hypotheses" displays some additional examples that you might find helpful in understanding one- and two-tailed tests and determining when to use them.

Illustrations of One- and Two-Tailed Tests with Directional and Non-directional Hypotheses

Hypothesis and Rationale	Critical Region(s) of Theoretical Sampling Distribution

Hypothesis:

The more foster care changes children have, the more behavioral problems they will have.

Rationale for one-tailed test:

The hypothesis is directional, predicting a positive relationship.

One-tailed test with critical region for a positive relationship:

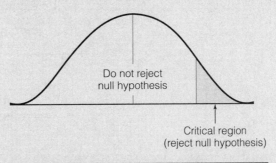

Figure 10.5

Hypothesis:

The more contact they have with a positive adult role model, the fewer behavioral problems abused children will have.

Rationale for one-tailed test:

The hypothesis is directional, predicting a negative relationship.

One-tailed test with critical region for a negative relationship:

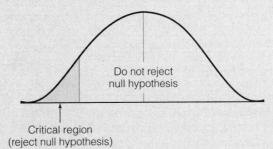

Figure 10.6

Hypothesis:

There is a difference in effectiveness between faith-based social services and secular social services.

Rationale for two-tailed test:

The hypothesis is non-directional; it does not predict which service will be more effective.

Two-tailed test with two critical regions for a non-directional hypothesis:

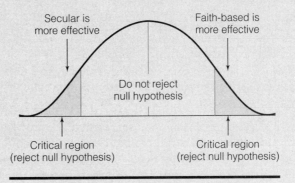

Figure 10.7

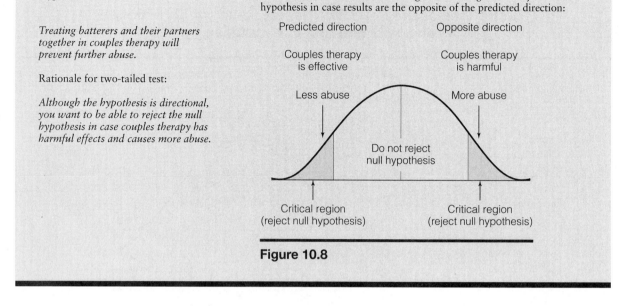

Hypothesis:

Treating batterers and their partners together in couples therapy will prevent further abuse.

Rationale for two-tailed test:

Although the hypothesis is directional, you want to be able to reject the null hypothesis in case couples therapy has harmful effects and causes more abuse.

Two-tailed test with two critical regions for being able to reject the null hypothesis in case results are the opposite of the predicted direction:

Predicted direction — Opposite direction

Couples therapy is effective — Couples therapy is harmful

Less abuse — More abuse

Do not reject null hypothesis

Critical region (reject null hypothesis) — Critical region (reject null hypothesis)

Figure 10.8

Main Points

• Testing hypotheses means making decisions about whether or not to attribute to sampling error a relationship between variables that we observe in a sample.

• The null hypothesis supposes that there really is *no* relationship between our hypothesized variables in the population. Even if there is some relationship between the variables in our sample, the null hypothesis postulates that our findings can be attributed to sampling error and that the relationship does not really exist in the population or in a theoretical sense.

• Testing for statistical significance means assessing the probability that the null hypothesis is true. When that probability is low enough to reject the null hypothesis as a plausible explanation for the relationship observed in a sample, we call that relationship *statistically significant.*

• The theoretical sampling distribution represents the distribution of the null hypothesis. It is based on the premise that no relationship exists between the variables in a research hypothesis. Thus, it shows the likelihood of getting a particular finding just due to sampling error.

• The area of the theoretical sampling distribution where our sample statistic needs to fall in order to be deemed statistically significant (that is, too unlikely to be attributable to sampling error) is called the *critical region.*

• The cutoff point that separates the critical region probability from the rest of the area of the theoretical sampling distribution is called the *level of significance*. Sometimes it is called the *rejection level* or the *alpha level*. All of these terms mean the same thing. They refer to the probability—which we select in advance—that we are willing to risk being wrong in rejecting the null hypothesis.

• Usually level of significance is set at 0.05, meaning that the critical region is that area of the theoretical sampling distribution that contains values that have no more than a 0.05 probability of occurring due to sampling error.

• When we get findings that warrant rejecting the null hypothesis, we should remember that while those findings may be consistent with our research hypothesis, and while they let us rule out sampling error as their explanation, they do not mean that we can overlook design issues as alternative explanations for our findings.

• Failing to reject the null hypothesis is not the same as confirming it.

• When seeking to support the null hypothesis, we can't really come up with probabilities that we are wrong in supporting it in the same way that we can come up with probabilities that we are wrong in rejecting it. The best we can do is to come up with results that show virtually no relationship whatsoever. To the extent that our findings show no relationship, those findings support (but do not confirm) the null hypothesis. To the extent that our findings have a low probability of being due to chance but are not in the critical region, those findings may raise some doubt about the relationship we are seeking to disconfirm, but they do not confirm the null hypothesis.

• When testing a nondirectional hypothesis, we use a two-tailed test of significance.

• A two-tailed test of significance splits the critical region at both ends of the theoretical sampling distribution.

• When testing a directional hypothesis, one in which we predict which categories of the independent variable will have higher or lower values on the dependent variable, we could use a one-tailed test of significance.

• With a one-tailed test, we place the entire critical region at the predicted end of the theoretical sampling distribution. There will be no critical region at the other end.

• Many studies will use a two-tailed test of significance even with a directional hypothesis because sometimes findings are in the opposite direction from the one predicted, and we want to be able reject the null hypothesis if that happens to be the case.

• With some very small samples the between-group differences need to be so extreme that we may not be able to reject the null hypothesis even when our results reflect a very effective intervention. Consequently, we might choose to use a one-tailed test of significance even though we'd prefer to use a two-tailed test. By using a one-tailed test, we sacrifice the option of being able to reject the null hypothesis with results that are in the opposite of the predicted direction, but we increase our chances of being able to reject the null hypothesis with results that are in the predicted direction since the between-group difference won't need to be as extreme.

Review Questions and Exercises

1. Suppose you test the hypothesis that Intervention A is more effective in preventing high school dropout than Intervention B.

a. How would you word the null hypothesis?

b. What would be the mean of the theoretical sampling distribution?

c. If you were able to obtain only a very small sample, would you use a one-tailed or two-tailed test of significance? Why?

d. If you were able to obtain a large sample, would you use a one-tailed or two-tailed test of significance? Why?

2. Suppose you administer a public child welfare agency that investigates reports of child abuse and neglect, recommends whether to place abused or neglected children into foster care, and provides services to abusive or neglectful parents whose children have not been placed into foster care. The aim of the latter services is to prevent further abuse or neglect. Suppose most units in your agency provide routine child welfare services to families in which the priority of protecting the child takes precedence over preserving the family when there is doubt about whether foster care placement is warranted. However, suppose a demonstration project is being carried out in one small family preservation unit that is providing more intensive services to families in an effort to preserve families and to avoid placing children in foster care when in doubt.

Suppose the small family preservation unit evaluates its effectiveness in an experiment with a small sample size of 20 families. Ten of the families get randomly assigned to the family preservation approach, and ten get assigned to the routine approach. The dependent variable is whether or not the child gets placed in foster care. Some practitioners in other units are critical of that dependent variable, arguing that it doesn't take into account the possibility that some children who are not placed in foster care perhaps should have been, due to ongoing abuse or neglect in their family of origin. Thus, those critics are concerned that in attempting to avoid out-of-home placement as the chief priority, the family preservation approach risks harmful effects for some children.

a. Would you recommend using a one-tailed or a two-tailed test of significance? Why?

b. Suppose the results of the above evaluation show a difference favoring the family preservation approach, but the probability that the difference is due to chance is slightly higher than the significance level. How would you recommend interpreting those results? What implications would they have for practice or further research?

c. Suppose upon seeing the above results some critics of the family preservation approach argue that the results prove that the family preservation approach is no more effective than the routine approach. Would you agree with them? Why or why not?

d. Suppose the above evaluation used a one-tailed test with a 0.05 significance level for a second dependent variable: whether or not there is further abuse or neglect. Suppose that its results are in the opposite of the predicted direction, showing a difference favoring the routine approach that falls within the 0.05 tail at the other end of the theoretical sampling distribution. Upon seeing those results, some critics of the family preservation approach argue that the results prove that the routine approach is more effective than the family preservation approach. Would you agree with them? Why or why not? What implications for practice or future research should be drawn from this finding?

3. Suppose a very biased research design gets findings that are statistically significant. Would rejecting the null hypothesis imply that the research hypothesis is the most plausible explanation for the findings? Explain.

InfoTrac Exercises

1. In explaining hypothesis testing and inferential statistics, the article below states that "the inferential statistic should equal zero." In light of what you read in Chapter 10 of this text, do you agree? Why or why not?

Martelli, J. T. (1997). Using statistics in HRD. *Training & Development, 51*(2), 62–63.

2. Read the following article and briefly summarize its main point.

Coolican, H. (2002). Of cricket, screws and the null hypothesis. *Psychology Review, 9*(2), 17–22.

Type I and Type II Errors and Significance Levels

INTRODUCTION

In Chapter 10 we saw that the main purpose of significance testing is to assess the probability that rejecting the null hypothesis would be an error. For example, with a significance level of 0.05, there is a 0.05 probability that the null hypothesis is true. Because that probability is so low, we reject the null hypothesis when our findings fall within the critical region. But in rejecting the null hypothesis, we are risking a 0.05 probability of being wrong. Maybe the null hypothesis really is true. After all, statistical flukes can happen just due to sampling error.

For example, suppose I claim to be a mind reader. To prove it, I ask you to pull a card out of a deck of cards and look at it without showing it to me. Let's say you pull the queen of hearts. I then correctly guess you pulled the queen of hearts. Because there are 52 cards in the deck, the probability of a correct guess is 1/52, or less than 0.02. Would the fact that 0.02 is such a low probability (and less than the typical significance level of 0.05) convince you that I am a mind reader? Probably not. Instead, you'd suspect two rival explanations. One would be that it's just some magic trick I've learned involving deception. (Maybe there's a mirror behind you. Or maybe it's a trick deck containing 52 queens of hearts.) That rival explanation is like suspecting that a research study's impressive findings might be due to bias in the research design.

Another rival explanation for my correct guess is that it was just dumb luck. Recognizing that flukes can happen, you'd probably challenge me to repeat my impressive feat. So you pull another card. This time it's the ace of spades, and I guess it's the four of clubs. "Oops! I just wasn't concentrating enough. Let's try again," I plead. We do, and I'm wrong again a bunch of times in a row. Now you'd be convinced that my first correct guess was just dumb luck. Accepting that rival explanation is the same as recognizing that even when a research study obtains statistically significant findings, there is a chance—albeit a small one—that the findings might be due to sampling error. In research terminology, we call that type of error a *Type 1 error*—a type of error that we risk whenever we reject the null hypothesis. But when we do *not* reject the null hypothesis we risk making another type of error, called a *Type II error*. This chapter is about both types of errors and their useful implications for evidence-based practice and evaluation.

TYPE I ERRORS

We risk making a Type I error every time we have statistically significant results and therefore reject the null hypothesis. A **Type I error** occurs whenever we reject a true null hypothesis. In other words, if our hypothesized relationship does not really exist in a general or theoretical sense, and only appears in our sample data due to sampling error, then the null hypothesis is true. If that is the case, yet a sampling fluke produces a statistically significant result that leads us to reject the null hypothesis, then we are committing a Type I error.

If we reject the null hypothesis because it has only a 0.05 probability of being true, then there is a 0.05 probability that we erroneously have rejected a true null hypothesis. If we reject the null hypothesis because it has only a 0.01 probability of being true, then there is a 0.01 probability that we erroneously have rejected a true null hypothesis. There will always be some chance, no matter how small, that our results are due to sampling error. Although the null hypothesis may be implausible, it is never impossible.

For example, suppose we are evaluating the effectiveness of a new intervention for court-referred teens who have been arrested for driving under the influence of alcohol. Suppose we have a sample of 10 teens, five of whom never drank and drove before, who are truly remorseful and so highly motivated to change that even without any intervention they'll never drink and drive again. Suppose the other five are repeat offenders, not at all motivated to change, and certain to get arrested again in the future for the same crime no matter what intervention they receive.

Suppose we flip a coin for each teen. Heads, they receive our new intervention; tails, they receive routine services. The chance that the five first-time, remorseful offenders will all get heads, while the others all get tails, is slim (less than 0.05), but not impossible. If that happens, our results would be statistically significant and lead us to reject the null hypothesis since none of the teens receiving our intervention would get re-arrested for drinking and driving, while all the others eventually would get re-arrested (assuming our study lasted long enough). This illustrates how we can find a statistically significant relationship in our data just due to sampling error. If we opt for a 0.05 significance level in our evaluation, we therefore are taking a 0.05 risk of a Type I error. In taking a 0.05 risk, we can expect to make a Type I error five times for every 100 hypotheses we test.

TYPE II ERRORS

The only times that we avoid risking a Type I error are when we refuse to reject the null hypothesis. We refuse to do so when the probability is too high (such as greater than 0.05) that the relationship between our variables can be attributed to sampling error. In other words, we refuse to reject the null hypothesis when our results are not statistically significant. However, whenever we opt *not* to reject the null hypothesis, we inescapably risk making a Type II error. A **Type II error** occurs when we fail to reject a *false* null hypothesis. Table 11.1 illustrates the impossibility of avoiding one risk or the other when statistically testing hypotheses.

We are most susceptible to committing Type II errors when our sample is small. We saw in Figure 10.4 in Chapter 10, for example, that with smaller sample sizes we need more extreme differences between means to reach the critical region. As explained in Chapter 10, findings that do not permit rejecting the null hypothesis do not confirm the null hypothesis. If there is a 0.20 probability that our results are due to sampling error, and we therefore fail to reject the null hypothesis, the probability is still only 0.20 that sampling error explains our results. Thus, whenever we opt *not*

to rule out sampling error—that is, whenever we opt *not* to reject the null hypothesis—we risk the possibility that we have opted not to reject a false null hypothesis, which means we risk committing a Type II error.

Calculating the probability of a Type II error is much more complicated than calculating the probability of a Type I error. As implied above, we calculate the probability of a Type I error by seeing where our results fall in the theoretical sampling distribution of the null hypothesis. To calculate the probability of a Type II error, instead of just examining the theoretical sampling distribution of the null hypothesis, we would also have to create another theoretical sampling distribution based on the assumption that our research hypothesis is true and that the null hypothesis is false. The mean of the theoretical sampling distribution of our research hypothesis would depend on a prediction we make about how strongly our hypothesized variables really are related in the population. Then we would examine the overlap between the two hypothetical distributions in order to find the proportion of the predicted sampling distribution that falls short of the significant tail of the null hypothesis sampling distribution.

For example, in our evaluation of a new intervention to prevent re-arrests for drinking and driving, suppose we predict that it will cut the re-arrest rate in half. Let's say that we know that the statewide re-arrest rate for drinking and driving is 30%, and we predict that recipients of our intervention will have a 15% re-arrest rate (versus 30% for our control group). The mean of the theoretical sampling distribution of the null hypothesis would be no difference in the re-arrest percentage for our experimental and control group. The mean of the theoretical sampling distribution of our research hypothesis would be a difference of 15% (30% minus 15% = 15%).

As mentioned above, calculating the probability of a Type II error in our evaluation is complicated. We would need computer software like SPSS to do it. By examining Figure 11.1, however, you can conceptualize in pictorial terms the difference between calculating the probability of Type I and Type II errors and of the fact that the Type II error probability is not merely one minus the Type I error probability.

Table 11.1 Type of Error Risked When We Reject or Fail to Reject the Null Hypothesis

| TYPE OF ERROR | DECISION ABOUT NULL HYPOTHESIS | |
	REJECT	DO NOT REJECT
Type I	Risked	Not Risked
Type II	Not Risked	Risked

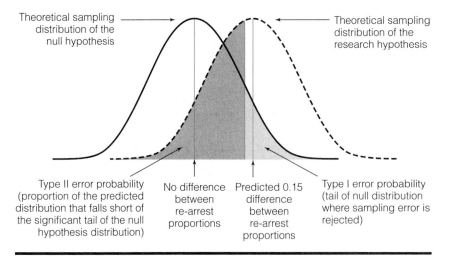

Figure 11.1   Illustration of the Difference Between Calculating the Probability of Type I and Type II Errors

WHICH TYPE OF ERROR IS MORE SERIOUS?

Historically, social scientists have tended to be very concerned about Type I errors and to virtually ignore the risk of committing Type II errors. This probably can be attributed to their wish to avoid appearing biased in favor of supporting their research hypotheses. They protect their public image of scientific caution and objectivity by refraining from inferring support for their hypotheses unless there is only a tiny probability that their results can be attributed to sampling error.

But much social scientific research does not evaluate the effectiveness of interventions that aim to alleviate human suffering and to promote social justice. Committing a Type II error may not seem too tragic in a study testing a hypothesis connected to the conditions that enhance learning among laboratory rats or in a study testing a hypothesis about social conformity among fraternity and sorority members. But committing such an error could be tragic if we incorrectly deem ineffective an intervention that really is effective in substantially reducing recidivism among perpetrators of various forms of abuse or domestic violence. The latter error would be particularly tragic if the tested intervention really is more effective than any existing alternative interventions.

In evaluation research, the reason for testing the effectiveness of an intervention, a program, or a policy is often connected to dissatisfaction with the effectiveness of alternative approaches. Sometimes the alternatives have been previously tested and found to be wanting. Sometimes we just don't know what, if anything, is effective with a particular target problem or target population. Under those conditions, committing a Type II error about an intervention that truly is effective could mean that practitioners won't use that intervention with people who would be helped by it. That would be a serious error—perhaps even a tragic one. The risk of committing Type II errors, therefore, should be taken very seriously when evidence-based practitioners evaluate services or policies.

But acknowledging the seriousness of Type II errors does not necessarily mean that they are *more* serious than Type I errors. Which error is deemed more serious will vary from study to study, depending on the value judgments we make about various considerations. Suppose we are evaluating the effectiveness of a policy involving the early release and community aftercare of incarcerated sex offenders. If we make a Type I error and deem the policy effective in preventing recidivism when it really is not effective, the harm that could result from implementing the ineffective policy would probably outweigh the harm of being wrong if we deemed the policy ineffective when it really was effective. We wouldn't want to release these offenders early if they are going to commit more sex offenses!

Likewise, suppose we commit a Type I error in deeming effective an intervention to reduce trauma symptoms that is actually ineffective. Suppose further that the particular intervention in question is one that has a big risk of unwanted side effects. Perhaps some clients' trauma symptoms worsen as they mentally "relive" the trauma as part of the intervention. If the intervention that we are evaluating has a substantial risk of harming some clients— or of just causing them some temporary yet severe emotional distress—then we might want to take very little risk indeed of incorrectly recommending an ineffective intervention. In such contexts we might deem a Type I error to be more serious than a Type II error.

On the other hand, suppose we are evaluating an intervention or policy that has no apparent risk of harmful side effects. Maybe we want to see if child welfare practitioners with social work degrees are more effective in preventing child abuse than child welfare practitioners with degrees in other areas. Suppose the true abuse rate for the population of clients is 20% less for those served by social workers than for those served by other practitioners, but our study fails to reject the null hypothesis (perhaps due to a small sample size). In that case, we might deem committing a Type II error as more serious than committing a Type I error. I do not wish to imply that a Type I error would be trivial in that instance. It is never a trivial matter when we (unintentionally) mislead the field into thinking that something will help people when it really won't. My point is simply that even when Type I errors are serious, some circumstances may lead us to judge Type II errors as equally serious or perhaps more serious. To reiterate, which error is deemed more serious will vary from study to study, depending on the value judgments we make about considerations like those above.

SELECTING A SIGNIFICANCE LEVEL

How we judge the relative seriousness of Type I errors and Type II errors will influence the degree of risk we are willing to take of committing either error. As noted earlier, the degree of risk we take of committing a Type I error is the probability we are willing to risk of being wrong in rejecting the null hypothesis. Also, as noted above, that probability is determined by where we draw the cutoff point along the x-axis of the theoretical sampling distribution to place the critical region that separates results that we deem statistically significant and thus not attributable to sampling error from results that have too high a probability of being due to sampling error to be considered statistically significant.

In the following chapters of this text we will examine alternative tests of statistical significance. We will also examine the criteria for choosing the appropriate test. Although the alternative tests will differ in various ways, they all have the same function: to calculate the probability that a study's findings are attributable to sampling error. That probability is called a *p*-value.

It is important not to equate *p*-values with significance levels. *P*-values can range from 0.0 to 1.0 and are calculated from our data, not selected by us. Our level of significance, on the other hand, is what we say it is before we calculate our *p*-value. If our *p*-value turns out to be equal to or less than our level of significance, that means it is falling in the critical region of the theoretical sampling distribution. That in turn means that our finding is statistically significant and we can reject the null hypothesis because our *p*-value indicates a sufficiently low probability that our results were produced by sampling error.

For example, if our level of significance is 0.05, and our *p*-value is 0.04, then our finding is statistically significant, and we would risk a Type I error. If our level of significance is 0.05, but our *p*-value is 0.06 or even 0.051, then we cannot call our finding statistically significant, and we would risk a Type II error.

Typically, we will use a computer software program such as SPSS to calculate our *p*-value. (The computer won't tell us our level of significance; we choose that in advance ourselves.) Our main concern when examining our computer output is to see whether the *p*-value falls within our selected critical region. The *p*-value in the computer output will typically read as $p = $ [some probability value] or $p < $ [some probability value]. For example, if our level of significance was set at 0.05, and we see $p = 0.04$, then we know we have statistical significance. We would also have statistical significance if the computer output reads $p < 0.05$ or $p = 0.01$. The symbol "$<$" means *less than*; thus, $p < 0.001$ means there is less than a 0.001 probability that our results were produced by sampling error. When the p-value is extremely low, the output will typically use the "less than" symbol instead of the exact probability. Likewise, if we see $p = 0.000$, it means that the p-value is less than 0.001 and the computer is just letting us know this instead of giving us the exact minuscule probability. But knowing that p is less than our level of significance is enough to deem our findings statistically significant.

But now that we are familiar with these terms and symbols, let's return to the question of where to set our level of significance. As noted earlier, many social scientists automatically set it at 0.05 just to conform to tradition, perhaps not even considering any alternative. Also as noted earlier, in some research studies with small sample sizes, setting the level of significance at a higher probability, such as 0.10, might be warranted. You might even see some rare studies with very large samples that set the level of significance much lower, say at 0.01.

If we are more worried about a Type I error than a Type II error, we might opt for a lower significance level. If we are more worried about a Type II error, we might choose a higher significance level. The lower our significance level, the less we risk a Type I error. We know that by definition, as discussed earlier. The higher our significance level, the more we risk a Type I error, but the less we risk a Type II error. Why the lower risk of a Type II error with a higher level of significance? Because the larger our critical region, the lower the proportion of the theoretical sampling distribution of the research hypothesis that falls short of the critical region of the theoretical sampling distribution of the null hypothesis. To clarify this, I suggest reexamining Figure 11.1. As you do that, imagine enlarging the critical region of the null hypothesis distribution by moving the cutoff point for that region to the left. Notice that as that cutoff moves left, the greater the proportion of the distribution on the right (the theoretical sampling distribution of the research hypothesis) falls to the right of that cutoff point and thus within the critical region.

THE INFLUENCE OF SAMPLE SIZE

Increasing our sample size is another way to reduce the probability of committing a Type II error. Figure 10.4 in Chapter 10, for example, showed that

the smaller our sample size, the more extreme the difference between group means needs to be in order to fall in the critical region. That's because larger samples have less sampling error than smaller samples. Therefore, as sample size increases, the standard deviation of the theoretical sampling distribution decreases. As that happens, the critical region moves closer toward the no-difference mean of the theoretical sampling distribution. Thus, the smaller the between-groups difference in means needs to be in order to reach the critical region, the greater the probability that a true population difference between the two group means will fall within the critical region. By definition, then, an increase in that probability decreases the probability of a Type II error because it will lower the probability of incorrectly rejecting a false null hypothesis.

Perhaps the simplest way to illustrate the influence of sample size on statistical significance testing is with dichotomous independent and dependent variables (i.e., variables that have only two categories). Let's suppose we are evaluating an intervention designed to prevent school dropout. The first three tables in Table 11.2 illustrate what would happen to our p-value with a 20% difference in dropout rates at three different sample sizes. The bottom two tables in Table 11.2 illustrate what would happen to our p-value with a 4% difference in dropout rates at two different sample sizes. As in most research reports, the symbol N in Table 11.2 refers to sample size.

In the first three tables our experimental group has a 40% dropout rate, and our control group has a 60% dropout rate. Thus, our experimental group's dropout rate is 20% better than our control group's rate. Those results would not be significant at the 0.05 level with 10 students per group. But with 50 students per group that same difference in rates would be significant at the 0.05 level, and with 100 students per group it would be significant at the 0.01 level.

In the last two tables in Table 11.2 our experimental group has a 48% dropout rate, and our control group has a 52% dropout rate. Thus, our experimental group's dropout rate is only 4% better than our control group's rate. Those results would not be significant at the 0.05 level with 50 students per group. But with 5000 students per group that same tiny difference in rates would be significant at the 0.001 level. Thus, a 4% difference with $N = 10,000$

Table 11.2 Illustration of the Influence of Sample Size on the Statistical Significance of Differences in Dropout Rates

RESULT A: $N = 20$; $p > 0.05$; 20% DIFFERENCE IN RATES

OUTCOME	EXPERIMENTAL GROUP		CONTROL GROUP	
Dropout	4	(40%)	6	(60%)
Graduate	6	(60%)	4	(40%)
Total	10	(100%)	10	(100%)

RESULT B: $N = 100$; $p < 0.05$; 20% DIFFERENCE IN RATES

OUTCOME	EXPERIMENTAL GROUP		CONTROL GROUP	
Dropout	20	(40%)	30	(40%)
Graduate	30	(60%)	20	(60%)
Total	50	(100%)	50	(100%)

RESULT C: $N = 200$; $p < 0.01$; 20% DIFFERENCE IN RATES

OUTCOME	EXPERIMENTAL GROUP		CONTROL GROUP	
Dropout	40	(40%)	60	(40%)
Graduate	60	(60%)	40	(60%)
Total	100	(100%)	100	(100%)

RESULT D: $N = 100$; $p > 0.05$; 4% DIFFERENCE IN RATES

OUTCOME	EXPERIMENTAL GROUP		CONTROL GROUP	
Dropout	24	(48%)	26	(52%)
Graduate	26	(52%)	24	(48%)
Total	50	(100%)	50	(100%)

RESULT E: $N = 10{,}000$; $p < 0.001$; 4% DIFFERENCE IN RATES

OUTCOME	EXPERIMENTAL GROUP		CONTROL GROUP	
Dropout	2400	(48%)	2600	(52%)
Graduate	2600	(52%)	2400	(48%)
Total	5000	(100%)	5000	(100%)

has a lower probability of being due to sampling error than a much larger (20%) difference with $N = 200$.

If it is feasible to increase the size of our sample, then that is a better way to reduce the probability of a Type II error than by increasing our significance level. As we'll see in Chapter 16, a sufficiently large sample can enable us to have a 0.05 or lower probability of both a Type I error and a Type II error. With smaller samples, however, setting our Type I error probability (our level of significance) at 0.05 might require having a Type II error probability many times larger. When feasibility constraints force us to have only a small sample, then we may want to increase our level of significance. And if our results are in the direction we predicted, but fall a bit short of the critical region, then we need to give ample consideration to the possibility of a Type II error and its potential seriousness.

Because it is possible to get statistical significance with very weak relationships when our sample size is very large, some statistics texts advise readers not to use huge samples. Their concern is that readers will be misled into thinking that a statistically significant difference is an important difference regardless of the magnitude of the difference. Said another way, they are concerned that readers will ignore the magnitude of the difference and only be concerned about its statistical significance. Moreover, readers might misconstrue a lower p-value as signifying a stronger or more important relationship. In the Table 11.2 illustration, for example, their concern is that readers would mistakenly think that the difference in p-values makes the 4% difference in Result E more impressive or more meaningful than the 20% difference in Result C. Why would that be a mistake? Because the p-value only refers to the probability that sampling error explains the difference in rates. It does *not* represent the magnitude or practical importance of the difference.

Which of the following would you prefer in your practice? Being 99% confident that you were making a 20% difference in dropout rates? Or being 99.9% confident that you were making only a 4% difference in dropout rates? We will return to this issue in Part 4 of this text, which deals with assessing the strength and importance of relationships. As we leave this chapter, you may be wondering how to find the p-values for Table 11.2. The next four chapters will show how to calculate *p*-values, as we examine the calculation and meaning of some commonly used tests of statistical significance.

Main Points

• A Type I error occurs whenever we reject a true null hypothesis.

• The probability of committing a Type I error is the *p*-value.

• There will always be some chance, no matter how small, that our results are due to sampling error. Although the null hypothesis may be implausible, it is never impossible.

• The only times that we avoid risking a Type I error are when we refuse to reject the null hypothesis. We refuse to do so when the probability is too high (such as greater than 0.05) that the relationship between our variables can be attributed to sampling error. In other words, we refuse to reject the null hypothesis when our results are not statistically significant.

• Whenever we opt *not* to reject the null hypothesis, we inescapably risk making a Type II error.

• A Type II error occurs when we fail to reject a *false* null hypothesis.

• We are most susceptible to committing Type II errors when our sample is small.

• The probability of a Type II error can be visualized by juxtaposing a theoretical sampling distribution of the null hypothesis alongside a theoretical sampling distribution based on the assumption that our research hypothesis is true and that the null hypothesis is false. The Type II error probability is the proportion of the predicted sampling distribution that falls short of the significant tail of the null hypothesis sampling distribution.

• Although social scientists historically have tended to be much more concerned about committing Type I errors than Type II errors, in evaluation research sometimes Type II errors can be at least as serious as Type I errors.

• If we are more worried about a Type I error than a Type II error, we might opt for a lower significance level. If we are more worried about a Type II error, we might choose a higher significance level.

• The probability that a study's findings are attributable to sampling error is called a *p*-value.

• Increasing the significance level (and thus expanding the critical region) and increasing sample size are two ways to reduce the probability of committing a Type II error.

• A lower *p*-value does not necessarily signify a stronger or more important relationship; with large samples weaker relationships can become statistically significant because sampling error diminishes as sample size increases.

Review Questions and Exercises

1. Returning to a review question in Chapter 10, suppose you administer a public child welfare agency that investigates reports of child abuse and neglect, recommends whether to place abused or neglected children out of their home and into foster care, and provides services to abusive or neglectful parents whose children have not been placed into foster care. The aim of the latter services is to prevent further abuse or neglect. Suppose most units in your agency provide routine child welfare services to families in which the priority of protecting the child takes precedence over preserving the family when there is doubt about whether foster care placement is warranted. However, suppose a demonstration project is being carried out in one small family preservation unit that is providing more intensive services to families in an effort to preserve families and to avoid placing children in foster care when in doubt.

Suppose the small family preservation unit evaluates its effectiveness in an experiment with a small sample size of 20 families. Ten of the families get randomly assigned to the family preservation approach, and ten get assigned to the routine approach. The dependent variable is whether or not the child gets placed in foster care. Some practitioners in other units are critical of that dependent variable, arguing that it doesn't take into account the possibility that some children not placed in foster care perhaps should be due to ongoing abuse or neglect in their family of origin. Thus, those critics are concerned that in attempting to avoid out-of-home placement as the chief priority, the family preservation approach risks harmful effects for some children.

a. Which type of error—Type I or Type II—would you deem more serious in the above evaluation? Why?

b. What level of significance would you recommend to your staff conducting the above evaluation? Why?

c. What would be the mean of the theoretical sampling distribution of the null hypothesis in the above evaluation?

2. Suppose the above evaluation was conducted on a national basis with a much larger sample of 10,000 families.

a. What level of significance would you recommend? Why?

b. Suppose the evaluation finds that 48% of the families receiving the family preservation approach had a child placed in foster care, as compared to 52% of the families receiving routine services. In light of the extremely low p-value for that difference ($p < 0.001$), family preservation approach advocates conclude that the family preservation approach is tremendously more effective than the routine services approach. Would you agree with them? Why or why not?

3. Explain why increasing the critical region of the theoretical sampling distribution increases the risk of a Type I error and decreases the risk of a Type II error.

InfoTrac Exercises

1. Read the article below particularly in respect to selecting a significance level and the issues of Type I and Type II errors. Do you agree with how the authors dealt with these issues in their data analysis and interpretations? Briefly state why or why not.

Sharma, S. B., Elkins, D., van Sickle, A., & Roberts, C. S. (1995). Effect of predischarge interventions on aftercare attendance: Process and outcome. *Health and Social Work, 20*(1), 15–20.

2. In the article below, do you agree with the authors' decision to use a 0.10 significance level? Briefly state your reason.

Roberts, C. S., Piper, L., Denny, J., & Cuddeback, G. (1997). A support group intervention to facilitate young adults' adjustment to cancer. *Health and Social Work, 22*(2), 133–138.

The *t*-Test

INTRODUCTION

In this chapter we'll begin examining specific tests of statistical significance, all of which share the aim of calculating the probability that our results are due to sampling error. As noted in Chapter 11, that probability is signified by the *p*-value. With each significance test, then, our main concern is to see whether the calculated *p*-value is lower than our significance level. If it is, we can reject the null hypothesis. Which significance test to use depends on a variety of considerations about the purpose of our research and the nature of our variables and our data, as displayed in the chart inside the front and back covers of this book. In this chapter, we will focus on one popular test of significance, the *t*-Test.

THE *t*-TEST

The *t*-Test can be used with an interval- or ratio-level dependent variable and a dichotomous nominal independent variable that has only two categories. The most common use of the *t*-Test in evaluating programs and practice is to compare the mean outcome scores of groups assigned to two different treatment conditions (such as an experimental group versus a control group or a new treatment versus a routine treatment). It does this by using the concepts discussed in Chapters 9 and 10 regarding the standard error of the theoretical sampling distribution.

In Chapter 9, we saw that the standard error estimates the standard deviation of the population by dividing the standard deviation of the sample by the square root of the sample size. In Chapter 10 we saw that when we are testing a hypothesis about whether one group's mean differs from another group's mean, the theoretical sampling distribution is based on the null hypothesis assumption that there is no difference between the two means in two theoretical populations: the population represented by the sample in one group and the population represented by the sample in the other group. Therefore, the values along the *x*-axis of the theoretical sampling distribution are differences between the means.

Because the theoretical sampling distribution of the null hypothesis assumes no difference between the group means in the population, the mean of that distribution is 0. In other words, it assumes that sampling error explains any between-group difference in our *sample* data, and therefore the true difference in the *population* is 0.

For example, I have been involved in various studies evaluating whether a controversial psychotherapy for trauma victims, called eye movement desensitization and reprocessing (EMDR), is really as effective as many think it is. In one study my co-investigators and I found almost no difference in mean scores on a scale measuring behavioral problems between a group of children who received EMDR and a control group who received routine treatment only. In another study we found a statistically significant difference ($p < 0.05$) in mean scores on a scale measuring trauma symptoms between a group of sexually abused girls who received EMDR and their control group counterparts.

Figure 12.1 illustrates how a theoretical sampling distribution is used when testing the statistical significance of the difference between two group means in those two evaluations. The *x*-axis values represent the experimental group's mean score minus the control group's mean score. The 0 in the middle of the *x*-axis represents the null hypothesis notion that there is no difference between the two means in the population of those who do and do not receive EMDR treatment. In Study A, the difference in our sample was very small and not near the critical region, and thus was not statistically significant. In Study B, the difference in our sample was large enough to reach the critical region, and thus was statistically significant. In other words, with Study B's results reaching the 0.05 critical region, the difference was of a magnitude that occurs less than 5 times out of 100 just due to sampling error. Consequently, we rejected the null hypothesis.

The *t*-Test applies a complex formula to ascertain whether the difference between two means is statistically significant. Although you won't have to use that formula when relying on statistical software to calculate *t*-Tests, you should know that the *t*-Test formula involves calculating a *t*-score by dividing the difference between two means by the standard error of the difference between means in the theoretical sampling distribution. If you'd like to see the formula represented in terms of its mathematical symbols (or if your instructor requires you to learn that formula), you can examine the box "*t*-Test Formula: Summary Version."

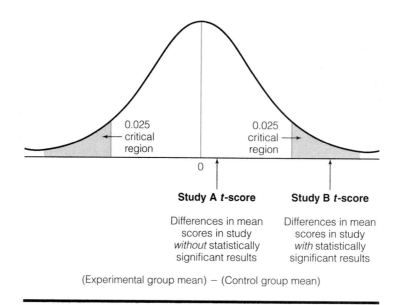

Figure 12.1 Theoretical Sampling Distribution of Differences in Mean Scores Between Two Groups

We will soon examine several different kinds of *t*-Tests. Each is based on a normal distribution of differences between means, called the *t* distribution. There are a variety of *t* distributions. Each *t* distribution is normally shaped with a mean of 0. (That's because each *t* distribution represents a theoretical distribution of the null hypothesis of no difference between means in the population.)

The *t* distributions will vary depending on the size of our sample and its standard deviation. The smaller the sample and the greater its standard deviation, the greater the estimate of the standard error in the theoretical sampling distribution will be. Consequently, the smaller our sample and the greater its standard deviation, the flatter and more spread out the *t* distribution will be. Since *t*-scores are calculated by dividing the difference between means by the standard error of the difference between means, larger differences between means will be required for statistical significance with theoretical sampling distributions that are flatter and more spread out. Conversely, smaller differences between means can be statistically significant for *t* distributions with lower standard errors of the difference between means.

You may be wondering why we need *t* distributions, recalling our use of *z*-scores in discussing the-

oretical sampling distributions in previous chapters. The prime reason is that *t* distributions provide better estimates of population means and standard errors when our sample sizes are very small or badly skewed. Unlike *z*- scores, the number of standard errors needed to reach the critical region in *t* distributions will vary depending on sample size. You may recall from Chapter 8 that if our significance level with a two-tailed test is 0.05, we need a *z*-score of 1.96 standard errors to reach the critical region that comprises 5% (0.05) of the area under the normal curve. Unless our sample size is very large, we would need a higher *t*-score than 1.96 to reach the critical region.

As our sample size increases, the closer the needed *t*-score gets to 1.96. With larger sample sizes, the needed *t*-score becomes 1.96, the same as the needed *z*-score. This is illustrated in Table 12.1, which shows what *t*-scores are needed with different sample sizes to reach different significance levels with one- and two-tailed tests. When you examine Table 12.1 you will notice that there is no column for sample size. In its place is a column labeled *df*. What the heck is that?! The symbol *df* stands for a statistical term called ***degrees of freedom.***

The term **degrees of freedom** refers to how many values are *free to vary* in a set of values if we

---

t-Test Formula: Summary Version

In the formula below, the *t*-score is a ratio that is calculated by dividing the difference between two means by the standard error of the difference between means in the theoretical sampling distribution.

$$t = \frac{\bar{x}_1 - \bar{x}_2}{s_{\bar{x}_1 - \bar{x}_2}}$$

where

$\bar{x}_1$ is the mean of the first sample
$\bar{x}_2$ is the mean of the second sample
$s_{\bar{x}_1 - \bar{x}_2}$ is the estimate of the standard error of the difference between means

---

know the summary statistic and the number of values in the set. That is, how many values would we need to know in order to deduce the remaining values? Here's a simple example. Suppose we know that the mean of a set of three values is 2. How many values would we need to know in order to deduce the remaining values? The answer is two. How do we know that?

In order to get a mean of 2 the three values would have to add up to 6. If we know only one of the three values, we are unable to deduce the missing values. Suppose we know that one of the three values is 2. To get to 6, the other two values might also be 2. Or they may be a 1 and a 3. They might also be a zero and a 4. Since knowing only one of the values won't let us determine the remaining values, we have more than one degree of freedom.

But if we know two of the values, we can deduce the missing value. For example, suppose we know that two values are 1 and 3, which add up to 4. Since we know that we need the sum of the three values to be 6 in order to have a mean of 2, we can deduce that the missing value is a 2. Likewise, if we know that two of the three values are 1 and 2, then we can deduce that the value of 3 is needed to achieve a sum of 6 and thus a mean of 2. Thus, we have two degrees of freedom, because two of the numbers are free to vary before the third one becomes predetermined.

When dealing with means, the degrees of freedom (*df*) will be one less than the sample size. Since sample size is signified by the letter *N*, *df* will equal *N* – 1. In other words, if we know the mean and the sample size, we can always deduce what remaining value is needed to get that mean if we know all but one of the values. Thus, the values are *free to vary* in *N* – 1 ways, but once we know those *N* – 1 values, there are no more *degrees of freedom*; the remaining value becomes predetermined.

I'll bet you are muttering to yourself right now something like the following: "Gee whiz (we'll keep it clean!), wasn't all this rigmarole confusing enough? Why not just use sample size (*N*) instead of all this mumbo jumbo about freaking *df*'s?" If you really want to know why we use degrees of freedom, you can examine a text on advanced statistical theory. For now, however, it is sufficient to know that when examining Table 12.1, *df* refers to the size of the sample.

When we are using a *t*-Test to compare the means of two groups, the *df* value will be the sum of each group's *df*. Thus, if we have a total overall sample size of 50, with 25 cases in each group, each group's *df* will be 24, and the overall *df* for the *t*-Test will be 48. Another way to think of this is by subtracting two from the overall sample size of the two groups combined (which is the same as subtracting 1 from each group's sample size and then adding the two individual group *df*'s).

The term *degrees of freedom*, or its symbol *df*, will reappear later in this text. It will also appear in your results when using statistical software like SPSS. Don't let it throw you. You don't need to

Table 12.1 Critical Values of *t*

df	LEVEL OF SIGNIFICANCE FOR A ONE-TAILED TEST					
	0.10	0.05	0.025	0.01	0.005	0.0005
	LEVEL OF SIGNIFICANCE FOR A TWO-TAILED TEST					
	0.20	0.10	0.05	0.02	0.01	0.001
1	3.078	6.314	31.821	31.821	63.657	636.619
2	1.886	2.920	4.303	6.965	9.925	31.598
3	1.638	2.353	3.182	4.541	5.841	12.941
4	1.533	2.132	2.776	3.747	4.604	8.610
5	1.476	2.015	2.571	3.365	4.032	6.859
6	1.440	1.943	2.447	3.143	3.707	5.959
7	1.415	1.895	2.365	2.998	3.499	5.405
8	1.397	1.860	2.306	2.896	3.355	5.041
9	1.383	1.833	2.262	2.821	3.250	4.781
10	1.372	1.812	2.228	2.764	3.169	4.587
11	1.363	1.796	2.201	2.718	3.106	4.437
12	1.356	1.782	2.179	2.681	3.055	4.318
13	1.350	1.771	2.160	2.650	3.012	4.221
14	1.345	1.761	2.145	2.624	2.977	4.140
15	1.341	1.753	2.131	2.602	2.947	4.073
16	1.337	1.746	2.120	2.583	2.921	4.015
17	1.333	1.740	2.110	2.567	2.898	3.965
18	1.330	1.734	2.101	2.552	2.878	3.922
19	1.328	1.729	2.093	2.539	2.861	3.883
20	1.325	1.725	2.086	2.528	2.845	3.850
21	1.323	1.721	2.080	2.518	2.831	3.819
22	1.321	1.717	2.074	2.508	2.819	3.792
23	1.319	1.714	2.069	2.500	2.807	3.767
24	1.318	1.711	2.064	2.492	2.797	3.745
25	1.316	1.708	2.060	2.485	2.787	3.725
26	1.315	1.706	2.056	2.479	2.779	3.707
27	1.314	1.703	2.052	2.473	2.771	3.690
28	1.313	1.701	2.048	2.467	2.763	3.674
29	1.311	1.699	2.045	2.462	2.756	3.659
30	1.310	1.697	2.042	2.457	2.750	3.646
40	1.303	1.684	2.021	2.423	2.704	3.551
60	1.296	1.671	2.000	2.390	2.660	3.460
120	1.289	1.658	1.980	2.358	2.617	3.373

Source: From Table III of R. A. Fisher and F. Yates, *Statistical Tables for Biological, Agricultural, and Medical Research,* published by Longman Group, Ltd., London (previously published by Oliver and Boyd, Ltd., Edinburgh) and by permission of the authors and publishers.

comprehend advanced statistical theory about it in order to utilize and interpret tests of statistical significance.

Calculating the *t*-Score

Different formulas for calculating the *t*-score are used, depending on whether we are comparing means from two independent groups, examining changes within a group, comparing the means of matched groups, or comparing a sample statistic to a population statistic. When I was a student, in the olden days before computers, we had to learn to use each formula to hand calculate *t*-scores and then look up those values in tables like Table 12.1 to see if they reached the critical region (usually a *p*-value of 0.05 or less). Today, statistical software programs like SPSS will calculate the *t*-score for you and will give you its *p*-value. If the *p*-value is at or below the significance level that you had already selected in advance, you know the difference between group means is statistically significant, and you reject the null hypothesis (thus risking a Type I error). If the *p*-value is above the significance level that you had already selected in advance, you know the difference between group means is *not* statistically significant, and you do *not* reject the null hypothesis (thus risking a Type II error).

Although you no longer need to know the different formulas for calculating the various *t*-scores, you should know that each of them finds a *t*-score by dividing the difference between two means by the standard error of the difference between means in the theoretical sampling distribution. You should also remember that with each formula the chances of attaining a *t*-score that is statistically significant will be better the greater the difference is between means. Those chances will be worse the smaller the sample and the greater its standard deviation. You can see this in the box titled "*t*-Test Formula for Groups with Equal Variances," which displays one of the more commonly used formulas. It is a more detailed extension of the summary *t*-Test formula presented in the earlier box in this chapter. If that formula seems too complex, remember that you just need to know how to command your statistical software program to do the calculations for you. For example, a section of Appendix G shows how easy using such software can be. That

section is headed: "Using SPSS to Calculate *t*-Tests (Chapter 12)."

The Independent-Samples *t*-Test

The **independent-samples *t*-Test** is used when we want to compare the means of two independent groups. The term *independent* in this context means that the two groups to be compared are not connected or related to each other. A common way to achieve independent groups is to use random numbers or a coin toss to randomly assign cases to one group or the other. Thus, if we randomly assign a pool of cases to either Treatment A or Treatment B, or if we randomly assign them to either an experimental group or a control group, we will have independent groups. (We'll discuss examples of groups that are not independent when we examine the paired-samples *t*-Test.)

Let's suppose we have used SPSS to conduct an independent-samples *t*-Test to compare the mean number of serious behavioral incidents (SBI) of Group 1 and Group 2 in our hypothetical evaluation in a residential treatment center. You may recall that Group 1 received the new treatment, and Group 2 received the routine treatment. You may recall that the mean number of serious behavioral incidents was 6.0 for Group 1 and 5.0 for Group 2. The *t*-Test will tell us if we can refute chance (sampling error) as the explanation for that difference in means. The results of our *t*-Test using SPSS are displayed in Table 12.2.

The first table in Table 12.2 (at the top) shows the number of cases (N), the mean, the standard deviation, and the standard error of the mean for each group. Thus, we see that each group contains 25 cases, the means are 6.0 and 5.0, and the standard deviation (and consequently the standard error, as well) is much higher for the new treatment group than for the routine treatment group.

The next table displays Levene's Test for Equality of Variances, which shows whether there is a significant difference in the variances of the two groups. Different *t*-Test formulas are used depending on whether the variances of the two groups are significantly different. If the *p*-value is greater than 0.05, then the formula that assumes equal variances is used. If the *p*-value is less than 0.05, then the formula that does *not* assume equal variances is used. You don't have to worry about those formulas; you

t-Test Formula for Groups with Equal Variances

In a previous box a summary version of the *t*–Test formula was stated as follows:

$$t = \frac{\overline{x}_1 - \overline{x}_2}{s_{\overline{x}_1 - \overline{x}_2}}$$

where

$\overline{x}_1$ is the mean of the first sample
$\overline{x}_2$ is the mean of the second sample
$s_{\overline{x}_1 - \overline{x}_2}$ is the estimate of the standard error of the difference between means

Below the formula is elaborated so that you can see the calculations for the denominator:

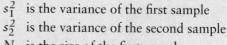

which is the estimate of the standard error of the difference between means in the theoretical sampling distribution.

$$t = \frac{\overline{x}_1 - \overline{x}_2}{\sqrt{\left(\dfrac{N_1 s_1^2 + N_2 s_2^2}{N_1 + N_2 - 2}\right)\left(\dfrac{N_1 + N_2}{N_1 N_2}\right)}}$$

where

s_1^2 is the variance of the first sample
s_2^2 is the variance of the second sample
N_1 is the size of the first sample
N_2 is the size of the second sample

---

just have to know which row to use in the next table—the row for *Equal variances assumed* or the row for *Equal variances not assumed*. (You also don't have to worry about the meaning of *F* in the table, but we will be discussing it in the next chapter when we examine analysis of variance.) Notice in our Levene's Test results that the *p*-value is 0.000—much less than 0.05. This should not surprise us if we remember from earlier chapters how much more dispersion there is among the 25 values in Group 1 as compared to the relatively little dispersion there is among the 25 values in Group 2. That huge difference in dispersion (or variance) is reflected in the huge difference between the standard deviations of Group 1 and Group 2.

Having determined that equal variances cannot be assumed, we are now ready to examine the third table in Table 12.2. Since equal variances cannot be assumed, the relevant row for us in that table is the second one, headed *Equal variances not assumed*. There we see a relatively small *t*-score of less than 1.0 (0.641 to be exact). The next column displays

our degrees of freedom. Since there are 50 cases in our sample, with 25 in each of the two groups, there would be 48 degrees of freedom if we were assuming equal variances. However, when we cannot assume equal variances, a different approach is used to calculate degrees of freedom, but you do not have to deal with that. The important thing is to examine the next column, which displays the *p*-value, which is our main interest. The column heading for the *p*-values indicates that it refers to a two-tailed test of significance. (If you are using a one-tailed test, you can look up the *t*-score in Table 12.1 to see if it is significant.) Seeing that our *p*-value is 0.527, which is much higher than 0.05 (or even 0.10 had we chosen that significance level), we know that the difference between the two group means is *not* statistically significant. Therefore we cannot reject the null hypothesis, and we choose to risk a Type 2 error. In fact, with a *p*-value greater than 0.50, we know that there is better than a 50/50 probability that our results can be attributed to sampling error.

Table 12.2 Results of Independent-Samples *t*-Test Using SPSS to Analyze Data for Hypothetical Evaluation of Practice Effectiveness in a Residential Treatment Center

GROUP STATISTICS				
GROUP	*N*	MEAN	STANDARD DEVIATION	STD. ERROR MEAN
SBI New Treatment	25	6.00	7.69	1.54
Routine Treatment	25	5.00	1.32	0.26

INDEPENDENT SAMPLES TEST		
	LEVENE'S TEST FOR EQUALITY OF VARIANCES	
	F	SIGNIFICANCE
SBI Equal variances assumed	36.09	0.000
Equal variances not assumed		

INDEPENDENT SAMPLES TEST				
	t-TEST FOR EQUALITY OF MEANS			
	t	*df*	SIGNIFICANCE (2-TAILED)	MEAN DIFFERENCE
SBI Equal variances assumed	0.641	48	0.525	1.00
Equal variances not assumed	0.641	25.42	0.527	1.00

Our results do *not* mean that anytime we get a difference between two means like the one we got (i.e., 6 versus 5) that difference will *not* be statistically significant. A difference like that very easily could be significant if our sample size were much larger or if Group 1's standard deviation were much smaller. Remember, the *t*-Test formula is based on dividing the difference between the means by the standard error of the difference between means, which in turn depends on the sample sizes and the standard deviations of the two groups. If the standard error using the *t*-Test formula were only 0.4, for example, then a difference of 1 between two means, divided by that standard error, would yield a *t*-score of 2.5. Looking that value up in Table 12.1, we see that it would be significant at the 0.05 level in a two-tailed *t*-Test even if we had a *df* of only 6.

We could also get a significant *p*-value if our data were unchanged but based on a sample size of 500, with 250 cases per group. To illustrate this, you can download our data set based on $N = 500$ from the Wadsworth website <http://humanservices .wadsworth.com /rubin_statistics> and then run a *t*-Test, following the steps in the section of Appendix G headed: "Using SPSS to Calculate *t*-Tests (Chapter 12)." That data set was created by copying the data set of 50 cases and then pasting the set of 50 nine times to add 450 cases to the original set of 50 cases. Thus, the data set of 500 cases has the exact same attributes as the data set of 50 cases, except it is for a hypothetical sample 10 times as large.

With the much larger sample size, the standard error decreases so much, and the degrees of freedom increase so much, that the *p*-value becomes 0.04, which is significant at the 0.05 level. This further illustrates the influence of sample size on statistical significance.

The Paired-Samples *t*-Test

The **paired-samples *t*-test** is used when the two groups of values that we want to compare are connected or related to each other in some way. Perhaps pairs of individuals are matched because they are similar to each other on certain variables and then split into two comparable groups that receive different interventions. Pairs of siblings, for example, might be split into two groups that receive different forms of intervention. Or maybe we want to compare the mean score of a group of husbands on some attitude scale to the mean score of a group of their wives.

The most common use of the paired-samples *t*-test, however, is when we are assessing changes that take place between two points in time within one group. For example, maybe we want to see if attitudes about the causes of poverty change among students in a class on poverty between the first and last day of class. Or perhaps we want to assess whether one group of clients improve on some measure of well-being from a pretest (administered before an intervention begins) to a posttest (administered after an intervention is completed).

Let's suppose that in our hypothetical evaluation in a residential treatment center that, in addition to comparing the effectiveness of the new and routine intervention, we want to assess whether the youths improve on a measure of trauma symptoms between their admission to the residential treatment center and their graduation from it. We'll assume that the measure is a 15-item self-report scale that the youths complete by indicating how often they experience or do certain undesirable things resulting from the trauma they suffered before admission to the center. These things might include nightmares, angry outbursts, sadness, bad thoughts, flashbacks, fear, withdrawal, and so on. Since the items on our hypothetical scale all refer to undesirable things, lower scores on the scale will be more desirable.

The hypothetical scores on that scale appear in our data set with the SPSS variable acronyms *presum* and *postsum*. The *presum* variable is the pretest scale score, which is the sum of the scores assigned to the response to each item. For example, youths who answer "occasionally" to each item might get a score of 3 on each item and thus a total scale score of 45 on the 15 items. Youths who answer "rarely" to each item might get a score of 2 on each item and thus a total scale score of 30 on the 15 items. The *postsum* variable is scored the same way, and is the posttest scale score. Thus, if the youths' trauma symptoms improve between admission to the center and graduation from it, their posttest scores should be lower than their pretest scores.

Following the steps for conducting a paired-samples *t*-Test delineated in Appendix G, in the section headed "Using SPSS to Calculate *t*-Tests (Chapter 12)," would produce the results displayed in Table 12.3. The top table in Table 12.3 shows the mean, the number of cases (N), the standard deviation, and the standard error of the mean for the pretest and the posttest. Although the N of 50 is listed twice, this does not mean that there are 100 youths split into two groups of 50 each. Since this is a pretest and a posttest using the same sample of 50 youths for each, the N of 50 in each row refers to the same 50 youths. Since each youth has two scores on the scale—a pretest score and a posttest score—there is a total N of 100 scores from a total of 50 youths. The table also shows a sharp decrease in mean scores, from 44.68 at pretest to 19.42 at posttest. Since lower scale scores are more desirable, this decrease reflects a big improvement in self-reported trauma symptoms from admission to graduation.

But is the improvement statistically significant? That is, what is the probability that it can be attributed to sampling error? The bottom table in Table 12.3 shows that the improvement of 25.26 points in the mean score on the scale is indeed statistically significant, with less than a 0.001 ($p < 0.001$) probability of being attributable to sampling error. Therefore we would reject the null hypothesis, since our risk of a Type 1 error is extremely small—less than one chance in a thousand.

But while the results in Table 12.3 allow us to reject *sampling error* as a plausible explanation for

Table 12.3 Results of Paired-Samples *t*-Test Using SPSS to Analyze Pretest to Posttest Change in Trauma Symptom Scale Scores in Hypothetical Evaluation in a Residential Treatment Center

PAIRED SAMPLES STATISTICS				
	MEAN	N	STANDARD DEVIATION	STANDARD ERROR MEAN
Pretest Score	44.68	50	8.17	1.16
Posttest Score	19.42	50	5.33	0.75

PAIRED SAMPLES TEST						
	PAIRED DIFFERENCES					
	MEAN	STANDARD DEVIATION	STANDARD ERROR MEAN	*t*	*df*	SIGNIFICANCE (2-TAILED)
Pair 1	25.26	11.36	1.61	15.718	49	0.000

the huge improvement in trauma symptom scale scores, they do *not* imply that the improvement necessarily can be attributed to the therapeutic effects of the residential treatment center. Remember, tests of statistical significance pertain only to ruling out sampling error; they do *not* rule out alternative explanations such as history, maturation, measurement bias, and so on. Maybe the improvement in the scores has more to do with the passage of time. Perhaps the trauma symptoms dissipate on their own over time as the trauma recedes further and further into the past. Or maybe at posttest the youths were more inclined than at pretest to want to please the center's staff and therefore understate the degree to which they continued to experience trauma symptoms. When conducting paired-samples *t*-Tests of change over time within one group, we need to be careful not to become so enamored with impressive statistical results that we forget about methodological limitations and alternative explanations other than sampling error.

The One-Sample *t*-Test

The **one-sample *t*-Test** is used when we want to compare a sample statistic to a population statistic. (As noted earlier, the term for a population statistic is *parameter*.) In order to use a one-sample *t*-Test, we first have to know the population parameter. For example, perhaps we know from reading a report of the findings of a national survey of residential treatment centers that the mean age of the national population of youths residing in the centers is 11.0 years old. Suppose we want to see if the sample of 50 youths in our hypothetical evaluation is atypical in regard to age. Perhaps they are younger or older than the national mean. If we have other population parameters regarding gender, ethnicity, diagnosis, and so on, we could also compare our sample statistics to those parameters in an overall examination of whether our sample is representative of the population.

Let's limit our first illustration of the one-sample *t*-Test to a comparison of mean age. We can use SPSS to conduct our one-sample *t*-Test by following the referent steps in the section of Appendix G headed "Using SPSS to Calculate *t*-Tests (Chapter 12)." SPSS will calculate the mean age of our sample and assess whether it is significantly different from the population's mean age of 11. Following those steps with our hypothetical data set, we would get the results that appear in the top two tables in Table 12.4.

Table 12.4 Results of Two One-Sample *t*-Tests Using SPSS to Compare Sample Mean Age and Sample Mean SBI to Population Mean Age and Population Mean SBI for Hypothetical Evaluation in a Residential Treatment Center

AGE			
ONE-SAMPLE STATISTICS			
	N	MEAN	STANDARD DEVIATION	STANDARD ERROR MEAN
AGE	50	10.84	1.98	0.28

ONE-SAMPLE TEST					
TEST VALUE = 11					
					95% CONFIDENCE INTERVAL OF THE DIFFERENCE
	t	*df*	SIGNIFICANCE (2-TAILED)	MEAN DIFFERENCE	LOWER	UPPER
AGE	−0.570	49	0.571	−0.16	−0.7236	0.4036

SRI			
ONE-SAMPLE STATISTICS			
	N	MEAN	STANDARD DEVIATION	STANDARD ERROR MEAN
SBI	50	5.50	5.48	0.77

ONE-SAMPLE TEST					
TEST VALUE = 6					
					95% CONFIDENCE INTERVAL OF THE DIFFERENCE
	t	*df*	SIGNIFICANCE (2-TAILED)	MEAN DIFFERENCE	LOWER	UPPER
SBI	−0.645	49	0.522	−0.50	−2.06	1.06

In the top table, we see that the mean age for our sample of 50 youths in the site of our evaluation is 10.84. We also see the standard deviation (1-98) regarding the ages of our 50 youths. The next table shows the *t*-score and its probability when we compare our sample data on age to the test value of 11. With a *p*-value of 0.571, we know that our sample is not significantly different in age from the population, since 0.571 is far above any significance level that we might choose (such as

0.05, 0.10, or even 0.20). Although the table shows that our sample mean is 0.16 less than the population parameter, we cannot rule out sampling error as the explanation for that difference. The two columns on the far right of the second table tell us that we can be 95% confident that the mean age of the population of youths in our center is between 0.72 less than and 0.40 more than the population parameter.

If we have results like this when we compare all the background attributes of our sample to their corresponding population parameters, we would have evidence supporting the notion that our sample does not appear to be atypical. Instead, it would appear to be representative of the population, at least in regard to the background variables in our data. But we have to exercise caution in the way we interpret this evidence. Remember, the lack of statistical significance does not confirm the null hypothesis—it merely means we cannot reject it. Perhaps we are making a Type II error. That is, perhaps there really is a difference between our sample and the population despite the fact that our p-value fell short of our critical region. If our significance level is 0.05 and our p-value is 0.06, then we have results that are not statistically significant despite the fact that there is only a 0.06 probability that the difference between our sample mean and the population parameter is a function of sampling error.

Thus, if we want to interpret our findings as evidence that our sample is representative of the population, it is important that the t-Test not only produce a t-score whose p-value is above our significance level, but also that the mean differences be negligible in magnitude. Just saying that the differences between our sample and the population are not statistically significant does not necessarily mean that they are trivial or don't exist. Some authors of research articles (and of some statistics texts!) make the mistake of arguing that a sample is representative on a particular variable just because a one-sample t-Test did not produce a statistically significant t-score. When I read research articles that make that claim without indicating the magnitude of the mean differences, I can't help but wonder whether the mistake is one of misunderstanding or of biased (and therefore unethical!) reporting.

One-sample t-Tests can be used not only when we hope to find that our sample is representative of a population, but also when we hope to find some difference between our sample and the population. Suppose in our hypothetical evaluation, for example, we want to see if the treatment approaches used in our residential treatment center—as a whole—produce better results than the national average in regard to serious behavioral incidents. In other words, with this aim we would not be concerned with comparing the two treatment groups of 25 youths apiece in our center to each other, but rather with whether our center as a whole does significantly better than the national mean. Let's suppose that from a national survey we know that the population parameter for the particular time period of concern is 6.0 serious behavioral incidents (SBI).

Using SPSS to conduct a one-sample t-Test, we would get the results displayed in the bottom two tables of Table 12.4. There we see that the 0.50 difference between the mean of 5.5 for the 50 youths in our sample and the 6.0 population parameter is not statistically significant, with a t-score of only -0.645 and a p-value of 0.522, again way above any reasonable significance level. The fact that our t-score is preceded by a minus sign only means that our sample mean is less than the population parameter. The minus sign is desirable, since we want our sample mean to be lower because SBIs are undesirable. Because our p-value is above any reasonable significance level that we may have chosen, we cannot reject the null hypothesis. Therefore we cannot rule out sampling error as the explanation for why the evaluated center's mean was lower than the population parameter.

A COMMON MISTAKE

So far we have examined comparisons of only two means. But many evaluations of practice or programs assess whether two groups differ in terms of improvement over time. Doing such assessments usually involves four means: two pretest means and two posttest means. The t-Test procedure cannot handle more than two means.

You may wonder why we can't just rely on the independent-samples t-Test and compare the posttest means of the groups without complicating things with the pretest mean. The answer is that there may be important differences in pretest scores between the groups we are comparing. If Group A and Group B have the same mean posttest scores regarding trauma symptoms, but if the mean pretest score was worse for Group A than Group B, then Group A made more *improvement* than Group B.

Conversely, if Group A has a better posttest score than Group B, but its pretest score was also better, then it may not have improved more than Group B. Suppose, for example, that Group A improved from a mean of 40 to a mean of 30, while Group B improved from 45 to 35. (Remember, lower scores are more desirable on our hypothetical measure of trauma symptoms.) Each group then would have had the same ten-point increment in improvement, and therefore it would be misleading to interpret the five-point difference at posttest as an indicator of better outcome for Group A.

Consequently, to assess the probability that sampling error might explain why one group changed more than another, we have to use one of two procedures: (1) Create a new dependent variable composed of the difference between each participant's pair of pretest and posttest scores; or (2) Conduct a multivariate analysis called *analysis of covariance (ANCOVA)*.

We'll examine the latter option in the next chapter. Before we examine the first option, let's consider a mistake novice researchers make all too often when they don't use either of the foregoing two procedures. That mistake involves conducting separate paired-sample *t*-Tests for the groups being compared. If one group has a significant *t*-score, and the other does not, some researchers misinterpret this as meaning that there is a significant difference between the groups—as if they had conducted an independent-samples *t*-Test. Why is that a mistake? Recall that the paired-sample *t*-Test calculates the probability that sampling error might explain the change from a pretest mean to a posttest mean *in one group only*. If one group has a significant change in a paired-sample *t*-Test, and another group does not in its (separate) paired-sample *t*-Test, that does not mean that there is a significant difference *between* the groups. Here's a simplified illustration of why this is so.

Let's suppose there are 5 clients who receive Treatment A and 5 who receive Treatment B, and

that they have the following pairs of pretest and posttest scores on our trauma symptoms scale (with lower scores indicating fewer symptoms):

TREATMENT A

CLIENT	PRETEST SCORE MEAN = 38 ST. DEV. = 1.58 STD. ERROR = 0.71	POSTTEST SCORE MEAN = 36
Al	40	40
Bill	39	38
Carl	38	36
Donna	37	34
Eve	36	32

TREATMENT B

CLIENT	PRETEST SCORE MEAN = 38 ST. DEV. = 1.58 STD. ERROR = 0.71	POSTTEST SCORE MEAN = 37
Gina	40	41
Hal	39	39
Jill	38	37
Lois	37	35
Mark	36	33

Notice that the mean pretest score for both groups is 38, with a standard deviation of 1.58. Dividing the standard deviation by the square root of the sample size ($N = 5$), the standard error for the pretest in both groups is 0.71. Keeping the math simple, we'll say that to reach the critical region in a paired-sample *t*-Test, each group would need a posttest mean more than two standard errors below its pretest mean. Thus, their posttest mean would have to be $38 - (2 \times 0.71)$, or $38 - 1.42 = 36.58$. Notice that the posttest mean (36) for Treatment A barely makes it into that critical region, while the posttest mean (37) for Treatment B barely falls short of it.

The fact that Treatment A's results were significant and Treatment B's were not does not mean that Treatment A's degree of change (which was significant when compared to itself at pretest) was significantly different from Treatment B's degree of change. To illustrate this, below is a list of the five pretest to posttest change scores for each case in each group (subtracting the posttest score from the pretest score for each case):

CHANGE SCORES:

Treatment A:	0	1	2	3	4
Treatment B:	−1	0	1	2	3

Notice that four of the five cases in each group have the change scores of 0, 1, 2, and 3. The only difference is that one case in Treatment A is a 4 whereas one case in Treatment B is a –1. The mean change score for Treatment A is 2, and the mean change score for Treatment B is 1—a difference in mean change scores of 1. Analyzing these change scores with an independent-samples *t*-Test yields a *t*-score of 1.0, with 8 degrees of freedom, which falls well short of the critical value of *t* needed for statistical significance (as shown in Table 12.1). Consequently, the probability that the difference in change scores is due to sampling error (chance) is too high to reject the null hypothesis. In other words, the fact that Treatment A's mean posttest score was significantly lower than its mean pretest score—and Treatment B's was not—does not imply that we can rule out the plausibility of sampling error as an explanation of the small difference in the degree of change *between* the two groups.

INDEPENDENT-SAMPLES *t*-TEST WITH CHANGE SCORES

Instead of erroneously conducting two paired-samples *t*-Tests, we could conduct an independent-samples *t*-Test with change scores. We would do this following the same steps discussed in the earlier section on the independent-samples *t*-Test, with only one difference. Instead of using the raw posttest data entered in our data file for our dependent variable, we would first have to create a new

dependent variable in which the posttest score for each case is subtracted from the pretest score of the same case. Alternatively, the pretest score might be subtracted from the posttest score. Which to subtract from which would depend on whether we desire an increase or a decrease in scores. For example, if higher scores mean worse trauma symptoms, we'd want a decrease, and therefore we'd subtract the posttest scores from the pretest scores. Conversely, if higher scores mean better social functioning, we'd subtract the pretest scores from the posttest scores.

Instead of manually subtracting scores, you can use statistical software to do all the subtractions and create a new, change score, dependent variable. How to do so using SPSS is shown in a section of Appendix G. That section is headed: "Using the COMPUTE Procedure in SPSS to Create Change Scores (Chapter 12)." (It follows the section headed "Using SPSS to Calculate *t*-Tests (Chapter 12)." Once the change score is computed, we simply use that new variable as our dependent variable in our independent-samples *t*-Test. Table 12.5 displays the SPSS results when we do this for the 50 cases in our hypothetical evaluation.

The first table in Table 12.5 (at the top) shows the number of cases (*N*), the mean change score, the standard deviation, and the standard error of the mean change score for each group. We see that the groups have similar degrees of variance and that the new treatment group's change score of 29.96 is higher than the routine treatment group's mean change score of 20.56. Thus, the new treatment group showed greater mean improvement than the routine treatment group.

The next table displays Levene's Test for Equality of Variance. It shows that there is not a significant difference in the variances of the two groups. Having determined that equal variances can be assumed, we can examine the first row in the third table. There we see a *t* score of 3.186. We also see that with 48 degrees of freedom the *p*-value for that *t*-score is 0.003. Since the *p*-value is below 0.05 (or even 0.01 had we chosen a more stringent significance level), the difference between the two group mean change scores is statistically significant. Therefore we can reject the null hypothesis and take a tiny 0.003 risk of a Type 1 error in refuting sampling error as the explanation for the difference in means.

Table 12.5 Results of Independent-Samples *t*-Test Using SPSS to Analyze Change Score Data for Hypothetical Evaluation of Practice Effectiveness in a Residential Treatment Center

GROUP STATISTICS					
GROUP		N	MEAN	STANDARD DEVIATION	STD. ERROR MEAN
CHANGE	New Treatment	25	29.96	10.94	2.19
	Routine Treatment	25	20.56	9.90	1.98

INDEPENDENT SAMPLES TEST			
		LEVENE'S TEST FOR EQUALITY OF VARIANCES	
		F	SIGNIFICANCE
CHANGE	Equal variances assumed	0.149	0.701
	Equal variances not assumed		

INDEPENDENT SAMPLES TEST				
		t-TEST FOR EQUALITY OF MEANS		
		t	*df*	SIGNIFICANCE (2-TAILED)	MEAN DIFFERENCE
CHANGE	Equal variances assumed	3.186	48	0.003	9.4
	Equal variances not assumed	3.186	47.52	0.003	9.4

Main Points

• The *t*-Test can be used with an interval- or ratio-level dependent variable and a dichotomous nominal independent variable.

• To find out whether the difference between two means is statistically significant, the *t*-Test calculates a *t*-score by dividing the difference between two means by the standard error of the difference between means in the theoretical sampling distribution.

• There are a variety of *t* distributions. Each *t* distribution is normally shaped with a mean of 0. (That's because each *t* distribution represents a theoretical distribution of the null hypothesis of no difference between means in the population.)

• The *t* distributions will vary depending on the size of our sample and its standard deviation. The smaller the sample and the greater its standard deviation, the larger the difference between the means needs to be for statistical significance. Conversely, smaller differences between means can be statistically significant with *t* distributions with lower standard errors of the difference between means.

• *t* distributions provide better estimates of population means and standard errors than do *z*-scores when our sample sizes are very small or badly skewed. Unlike *z*-scores, the number of standard errors needed to reach the critical region in *t* distributions will vary depending on sample size.

• The term *degrees of freedom* refers to how many values are *free to vary* in a set of values if we know the summary statistic and the number of values in the set. That is, how many values would we need to know in order to deduce the remaining values?

• When dealing with means, the degrees of freedom (*df*) will be one less than the sample size. When using a *t*-Test to compare the means of two groups, the *df* value will be the sum of each group's *df*. Thus, if we have a total overall sample size of 50, with 25 cases in each group, each group's *df* will be 24, and the overall *df* for the *t*-Test will be 48.

• The independent-samples *t*-Test is used when we want to compare the means of two independent groups.

• The paired-samples *t*-Test is used when the two groups of values that we want to compare are connected or related to each other in some way. The most common use of the paired-samples *t*-Test is when we are assessing changes that take place between two points in time within one group.

• The one-sample *t*-Test is used when we want to compare a sample statistic to a population parameter.

• A common mistake is to think that if one group has a significant change in a paired-sample *t*-Test, and another group does not in its (separate) paired-sample *t*-Test, that signifies a significant difference *between* the groups. It does *not*.

• To assess the probability that sampling error might explain why one group changed more than another, we can create a new dependent variable comprised of the difference between each participant's pair of pretest and posttest scores and then compare the mean change scores using an independent-samples *t*-Test.

Review Questions and Exercises

1. Which type of *t*-Test should be used for each of the following scenarios?

a. Spouse abusers participate in group therapy. A pilot study assesses the potential effectiveness of the therapy by comparing the abusers' pretest and posttest scores on a scale measuring anger management.

b. Spouse abusers are assigned randomly to one of two treatment groups. Those assigned to Group A participate in group therapy with other abusers, and their partners do not participate. Those assigned to Group B participate in group therapy with other abusers and with their partners. The dependent variable is the number of future incidents of abuse reported by each partner.

c. Substance-abusing immigrant teens and their parents complete a scale measuring their degree of acculturation. The purpose of the study is to test the hypothesis that substance-abusing immigrant teens are more acculturated than their parents.

d. The mean age of the parents in the above study is 38. A national survey found that the mean age of the population of parents of immigrant teens is 42. The researchers want to see if the above difference in mean age is statistically significant.

e. A treatment program for teens arrested for the first time for substance abuse finds that three years after treatment, the mean number of re-arrests is 0.2. Statewide data show that among the state population of teens arrested for substance abuse the mean number of re-arrests three years after the first arrest is twice 0.2, at 0.4. The researchers want to see if the mean for the treated teens is significantly lower than the statewide mean.

2. An independent *t*-Test with a 0.05 significance level is conducted to see whether 100 children in treatment after being abused score significantly higher on a newly developed scale measuring trauma symptoms than 100 children not in treatment and never abused. The purpose of the study is to assess the validity of the scale. The means of the two groups are in the predicted direction, at 20 and 17. In conducting an independent samples *t*-Test on the data, however, the researchers first see that there is a significant difference in the variances of the two groups. After that, they see the results for their *t*-Test on the equality of means, which appear in the box below. Which row should they use to decide whether the difference in means is statistically significant? Should they reject the null hypothesis? Why or why not? What type of error would they be risking? Explain.

t-TEST FOR EQUALITY OF MEANS

	t	SIGNIFICANCE (2-TAILED)
Equal variances assumed	2.2	0.04
Equal variances not assumed	1.9	0.07

3. Suppose the study in question 2, above, were done with a much smaller sample, but obtained the same means. Do you think the data in the above box would therefore be different? If you think they would be different, describe whether the numbers in each column would be increased or decreased, and explain why. If you think they would not be different, explain why not.

4. Cosmo Kramer conducts a study to see if his yoga sessions are effective in reducing stress among the participants. He administers a stress scale at pretest and posttest to an experimental group and a control group and then conducts a paired-samples *t*-Test for each group. For the experimental group (i.e., the session participants), the results are statistically significant, with a lower (better) mean stress score at posttest. For the control group, however, the lower mean at posttest is not statistically significant. Because his experimental group made significant change, and his control group's mean improvement did not reach the critical region, Cosmo concludes that his sessions were effective in lowering participants' stress levels. Do you agree with Cosmo's conclusion? Why or why not?

InfoTrac Exercise

1. Briefly identify the reasons why, in the article below, the paired-samples *t*-Test was used in Table 1 and the independent-samples *t*-Test was used in Table 2.

Vinson, T. S., & Neimeyer, G. J. (2003). The relationship between racial identity development and multicultural counseling competency: A second look. *Journal of Multicultural Counseling and Development, 31*(4), 262–277.

Analysis of Variance

INTRODUCTION

In Chapter 12 we saw that *t*-Tests can compare only two means at a time. Many evaluations, however, involve comparisons of means among three or more groups. Doing so requires using a procedure called **analysis of variance,** or **ANOVA.**

Whereas a *t*-Test produces a *t*-score that reflects the difference in two means in relation to the standard error of the difference, *ANOVA* produces an analogous statistic called the *F-ratio.* The **F-ratio** reflects the variation among the means of several groups in relation to the variation within the groups. The numerator in the *F*-ratio is called the *between-groups mean square,* which refers to the variation *between* the means of each group divided by the *between-groups* degrees of freedom. The degrees of freedom for the numerator is simply the number of groups minus one. The denominator in the *F*-ratio is called the *within-groups mean square,* which refers to the variation in the dependent variable among the individual cases *within* each group divided by the within-groups degrees of freedom. The within-groups degrees of freedom is the sum of the degrees of freedom for each of the groups. The total degrees of freedom is one less than the total number of cases in the entire sample across all of the groups.

Like the *t*-score, the *F*-ratio is compared to a table showing what *F*-ratios are needed to reach the critical region for various degrees of freedom. But unlike ancient times when I was a student, you don't need a table; your statistical software program (like SPSS) will calculate the *F*-ratio for you and will give you its *p*-value.

An Illustration of ANOVA

So far this discussion of ANOVA probably seems pretty abstract, so let's apply it to our hypothetical evaluation in a residential treatment center. Recall from Chapter 12 that our *t*-Tests involving serious behavioral incidents in our hypothetical evaluation failed to produce statistically significant differences in outcome between our new treatment group and our routine treatment group. But before we even began any inferential analyses, our descriptive statistics—such as the standard deviation—indicated a rather large amount of dispersion in the number of serious behavioral incidents in our sample. Since our independent-samples *t*-Test results did not support the hypothesis that the independent variable *treatment group* explains the variation in the dependent variable *number of serious behavioral incidents,* we might therefore look for alternative explanations of the large amount of variance in that variable.

Let's suppose we have a hunch that the variation might be related to which of three cottages the youths are bunked in. We'll call them Cottage A, Cottage B, and Cottage C. If we calculate the mean number of serious behavioral incidents in each cottage, we'll find that the means are 3.3 for Cottage A, 2.8 for Cottage B and 10.8 for Cottage C. Wow; what on earth is going on in Cottage C? Is its higher mean merely a function of sampling error?

With more than two cottages, we cannot use the *t*-Test to compare their means. Remember, the *t*-Test can be used only when comparing the means of two groups and cannot be used to compare more than two means. To compare the three means, we'll need to conduct an ANOVA. The ANOVA we'll conduct is called a **one-way analysis of variance.** To conduct the ANOVA, we will follow the steps delineated in Appendix G under the heading, "Using SPSS to Conduct a One-Way ANOVA (Chapter 13)."

The results of our one-way ANOVA are displayed in Table 13.1. We see that our *F*-ratio is

Table 13.1 ANOVA Results Comparing Mean Differences in SBIs among Three Cottages

	SUM OF SQUARES	*df*	MEAN SQUARE	*F*	SIGNIFICANCE
Between groups	650.912	2	325.456	18.618	0.000
Within groups	821.588	47	17.481		
Total	1472.500	49			

18.618 and that its p-value is less than 0.001. We also see the various statistics used to calculate the F-ratio, but our prime interest involves whether the p-value reaches our critical region. Assuming that our significance level is 0.05, the F-ratio certainly does reach our critical region, since less than 0.001 is far less than 0.05. Thus, our results would be statistically significant even if we had chosen a more stringent significance level such as 0.01 or even 0.001. Therefore, we can reject the null hypothesis that sampling error explains the differences among the three cottages' mean number of serious behavioral incidents.

Post Hoc Tests

So far, our ANOVA results tell us only that there is a statistically significant difference *somewhere* among the multiple groups being compared. They do not tell us which particular comparisons of group means are statistically significant. Is the difference between Cottage C's mean and Cottage A's mean statistically significant? How about comparing Cottage C with Cottage B, or Cottage A with Cottage B? To find out which particular comparisons of group means are statistically significant, we would conduct a **post hoc test.** There are various types of post hoc tests, all of which can tell us which pair or pairs of group means differ significantly from each other. The post hoc tests should be employed only when the F-ratio is significant for the overall data across the multiple groups.

You might be wondering why we can't conduct a t-Test separately for each paired comparison. The reason is that doing so would inflate our probability of a Type I error. Let's assume our significance level is 0.05. The likelihood of getting significant results due to chance (sampling error), then, is 5 out of 100, or 1 out of 20. That means if we conduct a very large number of statistical significance tests, we would get 5 significant results due to chance for every 100 tests we conducted.

Suppose I gave you the same odds on guessing a number between 1 and 20 that I've written down. If you guess the correct number, you win a prize. What if I wrote down another number between 1 and 20 on a separate piece of paper and said you can win the prize if you guess either number correctly? Suppose I offered you the option of guessing just one of the numbers or of taking a guess at the second number, too. You can try to guess just one of the numbers or try to guess the second if you are wrong on your first guess.

Knowing that you had nothing to lose by taking two chances to win the prize instead of just one, you'd try to guess the second number if you were wrong on the first guess. You'd do so because you'd know intuitively—without doing any math—that your odds of ultimately lucking out with a correct guess increase the more numbers you get to guess. (Of course, this assumes you'd want to win the prize. If the prize were an audiotape of this book to entertain you and your passengers during long automobile trips, you might opt to take no guesses!)

The same logic would apply if we were to conduct a t-Test separately for each of the multiple paired comparisons. With two significance tests the probability of getting one p-value of 0.05 or less is actually greater than 0.05. And that probability keeps increasing the more significance tests we conduct. For example, the probability of *not* making a Type 1 error in one significance test at the 0.05 significance level is $1 - 0.05 = 0.95$. The probability of that happening twice with two separate significance tests is $0.95 \times 0.95 = 0.903$. Thus, with two separate tests at the 0.05 level, our real probability of a Type I error would be $1 - 0.903 = 0.097$. With three separate tests it would be $1 - 0.858 = 0.142$. With four separate tests it would be 0.185, and with five tests it would be 0.23.

Post hoc tests involve statistical procedures that enable us to make multiple comparisons without inflating the probability of finding a statistically significant relationship that is really due to chance and thus without inflating the probability of a Type I error. If you conduct your post hoc multiple comparisons by using SPSS, you can click on the POST HOC button to be given several post hoc test options to choose from, such as the Bonferroni procedure, the Scheffe method, the Tukey procedure, and others. Which one to use depends on various considerations that go beyond the scope of this text, but the results are likely to be similar whichever one you use.

Table 13.2 is a simplified version of an SPSS output displaying the results for our hypothetical multiple comparisons of the three cottages, using the Bonferroni procedure. This procedure guards

Table 13.2   Results of Post Hoc Test Using the Bonferroni Procedure

(I) COTTAGE	(J) COTTAGE	MEAN DIFFERENCE (I-J)	STANDARD ERROR	SIGNIFICANCE	95% CONFIDENCE INTERVAL	
					LOWER BOUND	UPPER BOUND
A	B	0.53	1.43	1.0	−3.03	4.09
A	C	−7.46*	1.46	0.000	−11.07	−3.84
B	C	−7.99*	1.46	0.000	−11.60	−4.37

*The mean difference is significant at the 0.05 level.

against inflating the risk of a Type I error by multiplying the p-value for each comparison by the total number of comparisons being made. In Table 13.2 we see the mean differences for each of the three possible pairings of Cottages A, B, and C. The differences that are statistically significant at the 0.05 level have an asterisk beside them. The column headed *Significance* displays the p-value for each comparison multiplied by the total number of comparisons. We can see that two of the three paired comparisons are statistically significant. Cottage A and Cottage B each have significantly lower mean SBI's than Cottage C, whose mean is much higher than either Cottage A or B. We can also see that the negligible difference between Cottage A and Cottage B is not statistically significant.

ANALYSIS OF COVARIANCE (ANCOVA)

In Chapter 12 we discussed what to do when we want to compare two groups in terms of their mean improvement over time. We examined the option of conducting an independent-samples t-Test using change scores, and mentioned that a second option is to conduct an **analysis of covariance**, or **ANCOVA**. The ANCOVA procedure can examine whether there are significant differences among groups on posttest scores when the effects of the pretest scores are controlled. It accomplishes this by running the ANOVA procedure just as before, but with the additional step of entering the pretest score variable as a control variable called a **covariate**. Let's examine the logic of this procedure with a simple table involving the comparison of two treatment

groups' posttest scores using pretest scores as a covariate. Let's suppose we have the following results:

	TREATMENT GROUP A			TREATMENT GROUP B		
YOUTH	PRETEST SCORE	POSTTEST SCORE	YOUTH	PRETEST SCORE	POSTTEST SCORE	
A1	10	5	B1	10	5	
A2	10	5	B2	10	5	
A3	10	5	B3	30	25	
A4	30	25	B4	30	25	
Mean	15	10		20	15	

Notice that Group A has a lower posttest mean than Group B, but that difference is explained by the fact that Group A's youths also had lower pretest scores. Notice also that regardless of which group a youth is in, the youths with pretest scores of 10 had posttest scores of 5, and youths with pretest scores of 30 had posttest scores of 25. Thus, the *Group* variable doesn't explain the differences in posttest scores. What really explains the differences is the *covariate*: pretest score.

Had we done only an independent-samples t-test analysis without the covariate, we would know only whether the difference in posttest scores is statistically significant. If it is significant, we might erroneously infer that Group A's treatment was more effective than Group B's. But by controlling for the pretest score covariate in ANCOVA, we learn that there was *not* a significant difference between the two groups in *improvement* from pretest to posttest

Table 13.3 Results of SPSS ANCOVA Comparing Posttest Scores by Group, Controlling for Pretest Scores

DESCRIPTIVE STATISTICS

DEPENDENT VARIABLE: POSTSUM

GROUP	MEAN	STANDARD DEVIATION	N
New treatment	15.200	3.391	25
Routine treatment	23.640	3.067	25
Total	19.420	5.33	50

TESTS OF BETWEEN-SUBJECTS EFFECTS

DEPENDENT VARIABLE: POSTSUM

SOURCE	TYPE III SUM OF SQUARES	df	MEAN SQUARE	F	SIG.
Corrected Model	1053.818	2	526.909	73.190	0.000
Intercept	1369.367	1	1369.367	190.211	0.000
PRESUM	163.398	1	163.398	22.697	0.000
GROUP	842.681	1	842.681	117.052	0.000
Error	338.362	47	7.199		
Total	20249.000	50			
Corrected Total	1392.180	49			

and that the posttest difference is explained by pretest differences between the two groups.

With the foregoing logic in mind, let's now conduct an ANCOVA on the 50 cases in our hypothetical evaluation, comparing the amount of change from pretest to posttest on our trauma symptoms scale. The posttest score on our measure of trauma symptoms is our dependent variable, pretest score is the covariate, and treatment group is our independent variable. Thus, we will be assessing whether there was a significant difference in improvement in trauma symptoms between the groups receiving the new treatment versus the routine treatment. A section in Appendix G headed "Using SPSS to Conduct an ANCOVA (Chapter 13)" provides the steps for conducting our analysis with SPSS.

The SPSS results of the ANCOVA are displayed in Table 13.3. The table at the top displays the mean posttest scores of our two treatment groups, along with their standard deviations. We see that on a *descriptive* basis, at least, the new treatment group had a better (lower) mean trauma symptoms posttest score than did the routine treatment group. But those descriptive statistics on posttest means do *not* tell us two things: (1) whether there was a difference in *change* from pretest to posttest; and (2) whether that difference in change was statistically significant.

To answer the latter two questions, we need to examine the *inferential* results of our ANCOVA, which are displayed in the second table. Our main concern in the data displayed in that table is whether our independent variable, GROUP, has a statistically significant relationship with our dependent variable, POSTSUM (our SPSS acronym for posttest score). By examining the intersection of the row headed GROUP (under the Source column) and the column headed Sig. (for significance), we find that the p-value is less than 0.001 for the difference in mean posttest score between groups when the pretest score covariate is controlled.

The low p-value for the PRESUM row simply means that pretest scores also had a significant relationship with posttest scores. But the ANCOVA controls for that relationship, and our significant p-value for our independent variable (GROUP) means that even when we control for the fact that youths with lower posttest scores also had lower pretest scores, the new treatment group had a significantly lower (better) mean posttest score than did the routine treatment group. In other words, their degree of improvement was greater than that of the routine treatment group, and we can rule out sampling error as a plausible explanation for the difference.

Finally, notice that the results of this ANCOVA are consistent with the results of the independent-samples t-Test with change scores that we conducted in Chapter 12. Both procedures produced a statistically significant p-value well below our significance level.

Several things might puzzle you right now. Perhaps you are remembering that t-Tests are used when comparing the means of two groups, while ANOVA is used to compare the means of more than two groups. In the ANCOVA in Table 13.3, however, we compared the means of only two groups. While it is simpler to conduct a t-Test when comparing the means of only two groups without controlling for a covariate, you actually can use the ANOVA procedure instead. It will give you exactly the same results as the t-Test. But when we want to control for a covariate we must use ANCOVA because the t-Test procedure can't handle more than two variables.

Perhaps you are also wondering whether it is better to conduct an ANCOVA or an independent-samples t-Test on change scores. Some statisticians favor using ANCOVA, arguing that using change scores involves data that are less reliable. [That may be the reason that our p-value in the ANCOVA ($p < 0.001$) was lower than our 0.003 p-value in the independent-samples t-Test on change scores.] Others argue that the difference in reliability is negligible, and they even favor using change scores in some instances. This unresolved debate involves statistical complexities that go beyond the scope of this text. In my experience, I have always gotten essentially the same results using both procedures on the same data, as we did above. So my advice to you would be to use whichever procedure you feel more comfortable with, and if somebody criticizes your choice, you can refer them to the following statistical article on this issue: Malgady & Colon-Malgady, 1991 (for more information, turn to the References section at the end of this book).

Finally, you may be remembering that in our residential treatment center evaluation the new treatment group had a higher (worse) mean than the routine treatment group on the SBI variable. Why, then, does it have a significantly better outcome on the trauma symptoms measure? Remember, however, that our independent-samples t-test found that the difference between mean SBIs was *not* statistically significant. Also, it is possible that the youths with more SBI's were more traumatized and had more severe behavioral problems to begin with. Although they had more SBI's over the course of their residential stay, perhaps by the end of it they had made a great deal of improvement in the overall range of their symptoms. There are other possible explanations for the different results on the two outcome measures, explanations that are best assessed using multivariate ANOVA procedures like the ones we'll examine next.

But first we should note that ANCOVA itself is a multivariate procedure. That is, it simultaneously examines more than two variables. The additional variables it can examine, as noted above, are called *covariates*. So far we have illustrated only one type of covariate: pretest score. But any interval- or ratio-level variable can be controlled as a covariate in an ANCOVA, using the same logic and procedures as above. For example, if we suspect that differences in age between groups might account for their differences in mean scores, we can enter age as a covariate. In fact, several covariates can be entered in a given ANCOVA, yielding results showing whether differences in mean scores are significant when all of the covariates are controlled. Let's now turn to some other multivariate forms of ANOVA.

TWO-FACTOR ANALYSIS OF VARIANCE

The covariates in ANCOVA are extraneous variables that we seek to control. We can also conduct ANOVAs with two or more nominal *independent* variables, called *factors*. Thus, there can be a two-factor ANOVA, three-factor ANOVA, and so on, depending on how many nominal independent variables we seek to analyze simultaneously. Evaluations using ANOVA with more than two factors are rare, and since the same logic is involved with more than two factors, let's keep things simpler by focusing on the **two-factor ANOVA.**

Whereas ANCOVA includes a third variable as a metric control variable, two-factor ANOVAs include a third variable as a second nominal independent variable. Often the two factors refer to different interventions that are being evaluated in a combined fashion. For example, let's suppose that we want to evaluate the effectiveness of two interventions for hospitalized people with the dual diagnosis of schizophrenia and chemical dependency (substance abuse). The ultimate aim of our intervention is to prevent rehospitalization after discharge.

One intervention is a pre-discharge, inpatient educational program about the particularly harmful effects substance abuse has on people suffering from schizophrenia. The other intervention is a new case management approach provided after discharge. Evaluating both interventions simultaneously requires a 2-by-2 factorial design, as illustrated in Table 13.4. In that table we see four possibilities: (1) pre-discharge psychoeducational intervention + new case management approach; (2) pre-discharge psychoeducational intervention + routine case management approach; (3) routine inpatient care only + new case management approach; (4) routine inpatient care only + routine aftercare approach.

A two-way ANOVA identifies the **main effect** of each independent variable on the dependent variable as well as any **interaction effect** between the two of them on the dependent variable. The dependent variable is number of days in the community before rehospitalization. We can visualize the main effect of each independent variable in Table 13.4 by comparing the two categories of each separately. For example, we see that the overall mean for the pre-discharge psychoeducational intervention (750) is greater (better) than the overall mean (500) for routine inpatient care only. Likewise, we see that the overall mean for the new case management approach (800) is higher (better) than the overall mean for the routine case management approach (450). Thus, we also see that the main effect for the new case management approach is somewhat greater than the main effect for the pre-discharge psychoeducational intervention.

But we also see that the best (highest) mean is in the cell representing those clients who received *both* the psychoeducational intervention *and* the new case management approach. They averaged 1000 days before rehospitalization. This signifies an interaction effect, meaning that the two treatment

Table 13.4 Two-Factor ANOVA Hypothetical Results for an Evaluation of a Pre-Discharge Psychoeducational Intervention and of a New Case Management Approach, Displaying Mean Number of Days Before Rehospitalization

CASE MANAGEMENT TREATMENT CONDITION	PRE-DISCHARGE TREATMENT CONDITION		
	PSYCHOEDUCATIONAL INTERVENTION	ROUTINE CARE ONLY	OVERALL ROW MEAN
New Approach	1000	600	800
Routine Approach	500	400	450
Overall Column Mean	750	500	625

conditions interact and have a combined effect on the dependent variable. Another way to see the interaction effect is to subtract the second row mean from the first row mean in the two columns (not including the total column). When we do that, we get a remainder of 500 (1000 − 500) in one column and a remainder of 200 (600 − 400) in the other. The degree of difference in the remainders between the two columns represents the degree to which there is an interaction effect between the two treatment conditions.

Two-way ANOVA does not require that both (or either) nominal factors be treatment conditions. For example, Brannen and Rubin (1996) compared two alternative approaches to spouse abuse treatment in which the second factor was whether the perpetrator abused alcohol. They found that one type of treatment worked better when alcohol abuse was involved, but produced no difference in treatment effects when alcohol abuse was not involved. Thus, their findings showed an interaction effect, but no main effect for type of treatment.

The output of a two-factor ANOVA regarding statistical significance is similar to that of a one-way ANOVA. It will display sums of squares, degrees of freedom, mean squares, F-ratios and p-values for each factor and for interaction effects. Your primary interest will be in the p-values, to see which main or interaction effects are statistically significant.

MULTIVARIATE ANALYSIS OF VARAIANCE (MANOVA)

So far we have examined ANOVA in terms of whether one or more *independent* variables are involved. Many evaluations, however, conduct analyses of variance when more than one *dependent* variable is involved. Doing so requires conducting a **multivariate analysis of variance (MANOVA).**

For example, what if in our hypothetical evaluation of a pre-discharge psychoeducational intervention or a new case management intervention we wanted to use a scale measuring quality of life as a dependent variable in addition to days in the community. One option would be to conduct two separate ANOVAs—one using days in community as the dependent variable and one using quality of life as the dependent variable. There are two prime rea-

sons, however, why conducting a MANOVA would be more appropriate than conducting separate ANOVAs.

One reason has to do with inflating the probability of a Type I error. Recall our discussion above regarding using a post hoc comparisons procedure instead of multiple t-Tests when multiple paired comparisons are involved for three or more categories of an independent variable. The same logic applies when we test the effects of an intervention with multiple dependent variables. With separate ANOVAs for each dependent variable, the probability of getting one "significant" p-value keeps rising the more bivariate significance tests we conduct.

Many evaluations of interventions use more than one dependent variable. Many use more than two or three. That's because we often have no strong reason to suppose that there is only one way that an intervention will have valuable effects, and we want to cast a wide net so as not to miss any variables it might be affecting.

For example, suppose we are evaluating the effectiveness of a Big Brother/Big Sister program in terms of its effects on the little brother/little sister. Do we measure effects on self-esteem? How about grades in school? How about school conduct? What about mood states, like depression? How about involvement in social and recreational activities? Perhaps the program affects some youths in some of these ways and other youths in other ways. Not wanting to miss any important effects and thus erroneously deem the program ineffective, we might use a bunch of dependent variables. If we were to find statistical significance on only one of them on a series of separate bivariate significance tests, we would be incorrect in ruling out chance.

With MANOVA, however, we would be using a statistical procedure that takes our multiple dependent variables into account and gives us an overall probability for ruling out chance in light of all of them combined. (The statistical calculations involved rely on matrix algebra and go way beyond the purview of this text.) Several statistics are used to report the overall p-value regarding group differences on a calculated combined dependent variable. Of these, Wilks' Lambda is the most commonly reported. Depending on the number of categories in the independent variable and the degree of homogeneity of variance in the data, alternative statistics include Pillai's Trace, Hotelling's Trace (Hotellings T^2), and Roy's Largest Root.

The important thing to remember as a consumer of studies reporting MANOVA results is that regardless of which of these statistics is reported, the meaning is the same: the probability of making a Type 1 error in light of the combined dependent variables. If that probability is statistically significant, it permits the researcher to proceed to conduct a series of ANOVAs separately with each dependent variable to see which ones are being affected by the intervention.

So far we have been discussing the need to use MANOVA in order to avoid inflating the probability of a Type 1 error. There is, however, another reason to use MANOVA—one that is more positive. Often the dependent variables being used are correlated with one another in such a way that an intervention will not have significant effects on any one of them alone, but will have a significant effect on a linear combination of them. Separate ANOVAs in such a case will fail to produce significant results, but a MANOVA will detect such a result on a *combined* dependent variable.

Some studies report using MANCOVA instead of MANOVA. The *C* between the *MAN* and the *OVA* simply means that at least one covariate was included in the analysis, which then becomes a multivariate analysis of covariance. Like ANCOVA, MANCOVA enables researchers to see whether and how any covariates may have influenced the relationships between the independent variables and the set of dependent variables.

This chapter's sections on ANCOVA, two-factor ANOVA, and MANCOVA have introduced the concept of multivariate analysis, in which more than two variables are analyzed simultaneously. There are various other forms of multivariate analysis. We'll examine two of them in Chapter 17 when we discuss multiple correlation and multiple regression. You can find a conceptual overview of several others in Appendix D. But before we move on to those advanced topics, we need to examine some additional bivariate inferential statistics. Whereas ANOVAs and *t*-Tests are used with a nominal independent variable and an interval- or ratio-level dependent variable, the next two chapters will discuss statistics that are appropriate when our independent and dependent variables are at the same level of measurement.

Main Points

• ANOVA is a statistical significance test that we use when we want to compare the means of more than two groups. Whereas a *t*-Test produces a *t*-score that reflects the difference in two means in relation to the standard error of the difference, *ANOVA* produces an analogous statistic called the *F-ratio*.

• The *F*-ratio reflects the variation among the means of several groups in relation to the variation within the groups.

• The numerator in the *F*-ratio is called the *between-groups mean square*, which refers to the variation *between* the means of each group divided by the *between-groups* degrees of freedom. The degrees of freedom for the numerator is simply the number of groups minus one.

• The denominator in the *F*-ratio is called the *within-groups mean square*, which refers to the variation in the dependent variable among the individual cases *within* each group divided by the within-groups degrees of freedom. The within-groups degrees of freedom is the sum of the degrees of freedom for each of the groups. The total degrees of freedom is one less than the total number of cases in the entire sample across all of the groups.

• Like the *t*-score, the *F*-ratio is compared to a table showing what *F*-ratios are needed to reach the critical region for various degrees of freedom.

• ANOVA results tell us only that there is a statistically significant difference *somewhere* among the multiple groups being compared. They do not tell us which particular comparisons of group means are statistically significant. To find out which particular comparisons of group means are statistically significant, we would conduct a post hoc test.

• There are various types of post hoc tests, all of which can tell us which pair or pairs of group means differ significantly from each other.

• Post hoc tests should be employed only when the *F*-ratio is significant for the overall data across the multiple groups.

• We can't conduct a *t*-Test separately for each paired comparison because doing so would inflate our significance level.

- The ANCOVA procedure examines whether there are significant differences among groups on posttest scores when the effects of the pretest scores or other interval- or ratio-level variables are controlled. The variables controlled in ANCOVA are called *covariates*.

- ANOVAs can be conducted with two or more nominal *independent* variables called *factors*. There can be a two-factor ANOVA, three-factor ANOVA, and so on, depending on how many nominal independent variables we seek to analyze simultaneously.

- A two-way ANOVA identifies the main effect of each independent variable on the dependent variable as well as any interaction effect between the two of them on the dependent variable.

- Multivariate analyses of variance (MANOVA) should be used when more than one dependent variable is involved in an analysis of variance.

- MANOVA avoids inflating the probability of a Type 1 error that would occur with separate ANOVAs for each dependent variable. Another reason to use MANOVA is that often the dependent variables being used are correlated with one another in such a way that an intervention will not have significant effects on any one of them alone, but will have a significant effect on a linear combination of them. Separate ANOVAs in such a case will fail to produce significant results, but a MANOVA will detect such a result on a *combined* dependent variable.

Review Questions and Exercises

1. An ANOVA tests the significance of findings comparing the mean scores of three treatments aimed at increasing self-esteem scores, and gets a significant F-ratio, with $p < 0.05$. Because Treatment 1 had a mean of 70, Group 2 had a mean of 67, and Group 3 had a mean of 50, the researchers conclude that Treatment 1 is the most effective, Treatment 2 is the second most effective, and Treatment 3 is the least effective. Do you agree with their conclusion? If yes, explain why. If no, explain why and specify what you would conclude from their findings.

2. An evaluation of a new intervention to improve self-esteem finds that the experimental group's mean score increased from 60 to 70 and that the control group's mean score increased from 50 to 60. A t-Test finds a statistically significant difference between the two groups' posttest scores, but an ANCOVA fails to find a statistically significant difference between the groups. From these results, what would you infer about the effectiveness of the new intervention? Explain.

3. How would you interpret the main effects and interaction effect in the two-factor ANOVA results in the table below, assuming that any main effect or interaction effect greater than zero is statistically significant? The dependent variable is an undesirable behavior (such as number of abusive incidents). The numbers in the table represent the mean number of incidents.

4. You want to evaluate the effects of a new type of support group intervention for caregivers of disabled relatives. You have three groups. One group receives the new intervention. Another receives a routine support group intervention. A third group receives individual counseling instead. You are uncertain as to the best way to measure treatment effects, so you decide to use three measures, including separate

(Table for Exercise 3)

GENDER	TREATMENT CONDITION INTERVENTION A	INTERVENTION B	OVERALL ROW MEAN
Male	6	6	6
Female	3	1	2
Overall Column Mean	4.5	3.5	8

scales measuring depression, anxiety, and stress. What statistical procedure should you use? Explain your answer.

InfoTrac Exercises

1. Re-examine the results of multiple *t*-Tests in Tables 1 and 2 of the article below. (This article was previously mentioned in the InfoTrac exercises in Chapter 12.) In light of what you read about post hoc tests in this chapter, do you think the way the authors of the article below conducted and analyzed their various *t*-Tests was adequate? Briefly state why or why not.

Vinson, T. S., & Neimeyer, G. J. (2003). The relationship between racial identity development and multicultural counseling competency: A second look. *Journal of Multicultural Counseling and Development, 31*(4), 262–277.

2. Critically appraise the way the author of the article below conducted and interpreted the study's ANOVA. Be sure to consider the issue of post hoc tests in your appraisal.

Weinberg, N. (1995). Does apologizing help? The role of self-blame and making amends in recovery from bereavement. *Health and Social Work, 20*(4), 294–299.

Cross-Tabulation and Chi-Square

INTRODUCTION

In the last few chapters we've been dealing with dependent variables that are at the interval or ratio level of measurement. Such variables allow us to calculate means and standard deviations and use **parametric tests** of statistical significance. One assumption of parametric tests is that at least one variable in the test has an interval or ratio level of measurement. Another is that the tested parameters of those variables are distributed normally in the population. A third is that the groups being compared are independent of each other and have been randomly assigned or selected.

Sometimes parametric tests are used even when one or more of their assumptions cannot be met. The reasons for this vary. Some researchers may use them without considering their appropriateness. Others may use them for a couple of reasons even though their assumptions cannot be met. One reason may be that advanced statistics tests commonly cite instances where the violation of certain assumptions is minor. Related to that, some (not all) statisticians believe that parametric tests have more statistical power than their nonparametric counterparts. (The explanation goes beyond the scope of this introductory text.) Having more statistical power means having a lower risk of committing a Type II error, which we will address in a later chapter.

When it is inadvisable or impossible to use parametric tests of statistical significance, nonparametric tests can be used. **Nonparametric tests** do not require all of the same assumptions as parametric tests. The most common reason to use nonparametric tests is when our variables are not at the interval or ratio level of measurement. Some nonparametric tests apply only when the variables being tested are at the nominal level of measurement. Other nonparametric tests are used when dealing with ordinal levels of measurement. Still others are used when one or more variables are at the interval or ratio level of measurement, but when the variable of study cannot be assumed to be normally distributed in the population. In this chapter we'll examine the most commonly used nonparametric test, *chi-square*, and some other tests closely related to it. Appendix E will provide an overview of some less commonly used nonparametric tests.

The **chi-square test of statistical significance** assesses the probability that sampling error explains the relationships we observe between nominal-level variables displayed in cross-tabulation tables. **Cross-tabulation tables** show whether and how two or more nominal-level variables are related. They display the frequency and/or percentages of the categories of one variable cross-tabulated with the frequencies and/or percentages of another variable or variables.

TWO-BY-TWO CROSS-TABULATION TABLES

To illustrate cross-tabulation tables and the use of chi-square, let's return to our hypothetical evaluation in a residential treatment center. Suppose we use a nominal-level dependent variable when comparing the effectiveness of the new treatment with the routine treatment. Suppose that variable is whether or not the youth's behavior and school performance were sufficiently positive to earn off-campus privileges. (That variable is in our SPSS data file with the label *campus*.) Since that variable has only a yes and a no category, it is not reasonable to calculate means and standard deviations on it. Likewise, our independent variable—which treatment group the youth is in—also is nominal. Thus, if we want to display the relationship between these two variables in a table, we must use frequencies (head counts) instead of means, medians, or other parametric statistics. The cross-tabulation table in Table 14.1 illustrates how this is done, based on the results of an SPSS cross-tabulation analysis of our hypothetical evaluation data.

Our independent variable, *treatment group*, is located in the columns in Table 14.1. Our dependent variable, *whether off-campus privileges were earned*, is in the rows. The far-right column displays the total for each category of our row (dependent) variable, and the bottom row displays the total for each category of our column (independent) variable.

The boxes that contain numbers in the table are called *cells*. Within each cell are three numbers. The first, *count*, is simply the *observed* count of the raw number of cases in the referent column category that had the referent row category. Thus, the 16 in the cell that intersects *New* with *Yes* means that 16 of the 25 youths in the new treatment group earned off-campus privileges. The second number in each cell is

Table 14.1   Cross-Tabulation of Treatment Group by Whether Off-Campus Privileges Were Earned

EARNED OFF-CAMPUS PRIVILEGES?		TREATMENT GROUP		
		NEW	ROUTINE	TOTAL
Yes	Count	16	9	25
	Expected Count	12.5	12.5	
	% Within Group	64.0%	36.0%	50%
No	Count	9	16	25
	Expected Count	12.5	12.5	
	% Within Group	36.0%	64.0%	50%
Total	Count	25	25	50
	% Within Group	100%	100%	100%

the number of cases that we would have *expected* to find in that cell if there were no relationship whatsoever between the column and row variables. It comes into play when calculating the chi-square statistic, as discussed in the box titled "Formula for Calculating Chi-Square" (pp. 156–158). (The two variables in the table are related to the extent that the observed and expected counts differ.)

The third number in each cell is the percentage pertaining to dividing the observed count in each cell by the total count for that column. Thus, the 16 youths in the new treatment group who are in the *yes* row comprise 64% of the total of 25 youths in the new treatment group.

You may wonder why the percentages in this table were calculated by column and not by row. Typically, we calculate according to the categories of our independent variable. That's because we are interested in how the rate of something in one category of our independent variable compares to the rate in another category. It does not matter whether you put the categories of the independent variable in the columns or rows. What does matter is that if you put the categories of the independent variable in the columns, your percentages should be based on the column totals, and if you put the categories of the independent variable in the rows, then your percentages should be based on the row totals.

The results of our cross-tabulation analysis in Table 14.1 show that of the 25 youths who received the new treatment, 16 (64%) earned off-campus

privileges, as compared to only 9 (36%) of the 25 youths who received the routine treatment. Thus, we can see a relationship between our two variables in this table, in which recipients of the new treatment were more likely to earn off-campus privileges than recipients of the routine treatment. But what is the probability that the difference in percentages observed in our sample does not really exist in the theoretical population of youths receiving the new or the routine treatment and is merely attributable to sampling error? To answer that question, we need to calculate the chi-square statistic.

CALCULATING CHI-SQUARE

The formula for calculating chi-square is discussed in the box "Formula for Calculating Chi-Square." Statistical software like SPSS will calculate chi-square values for you and tell you whether or not they are statistically significant, so you can get by without knowing the formula for calculating chi-square. But you may want to examine the box on its calculation anyway, just to get a better grasp of its meaning. On the other hand, if you are one of many who get a bit overwhelmed by mathematical formulas and find that those formulas consequently interfere with learning the bigger picture—and if you have access to statistical software like SPSS—you may just want to rely instead on the section in

Table 14.2 SPSS Results of Cross-Tabulation Data from Table 14.1 on the Association Between Treatment Group and Whether Off-Campus Privileges Were Earned

	VALUE	df	ASYMP. SIG. (2-SIDED)	EXACT SIG. (2-SIDED)	EXACT SIG. (1-SIDED)
Pearson Chi-Square	3.920[b]	1	0.048		
Continuity Correction[a]	2.880	1	0.090		
Fisher's Exact Test				0.089	0.044
N of Valid Cases	50				

a. Computed only for 2 × 2 table.
b. 0 cells (0.0%) have expected count less than 5. The minimum expected count is 12.50.

Appendix G titled "Using SPSS to Calculate Chi-Square (Chapter 14)." (You might also want to find out whether your instructor expects you to learn the formula!)

The SPSS results of a chi-square analysis of the cross-tabulation data in Table 14.1 are displayed in Table 14.2. The most important column in that table is the one with the heading "Asymp. Sig. (2-sided)." That column displays our *p* value, which indicates the probability that our results can be attributed to sampling error. (The abbreviated term "Asymp. Sig. (2-sided)" stands for the term *asymptotic significance*, and refers to using both tails as the critical regions of a normal theoretical sampling distribution to ascertain statistical significance.) Which row to use depends on whether we can use the normal chi-square statistic, which is displayed in the row headed *Pearson Chi-Square*, or a different formula that is required when any of the expected counts in our 2-by-2 table are too low for the Pearson chi-square.

The results using alternative formulas are displayed in the other rows in Table 14.2, headed *Continuity Correction* and *Fisher's Exact Test*. You need to be aware of those alternative formulas whether you use SPSS to calculate chi-square or calculate it yourself manually. The *Continuity Correction* row refers to the **correction for continuity,** which is also called the *Yate's correction.* The correction for continuity is used whenever our cross-tabulation table has only two rows and two columns (i.e., is a 2-by-2 table) and has any expected frequencies less than 10. The correction is needed because the

regular chi-square formula produces an inflated chi-square value under those conditions. As discussed in the box titled "Formula for Calculating Chi-Square," part of the calculation of chi-square involves subtracting the expected count (also called the *expected frequency*) from the observed count (also called the *observed frequency*). The correction for continuity involves reducing the absolute difference (ignoring any minus signs) between the observed and expected counts by 0.5.

You need to know this even if you use SPSS to calculate chi-square because the SPSS output will automatically show you values for chi-square both with and without the continuity correction. You need to know which one to report. If yours is a 2-by-2 table with any expected frequencies under 10, you should use and report the result with the correction for continuity. If all the expected frequencies in your 2-by-2 table exceed 10, then you should use and report the Pearson chi-square result. In Table 14.2, we would use the Pearson chi-square result even though we had a 2-by-2 table, because our expected frequencies (in Table 14.1) all exceeded 10. But note that had we used the result with the continuity correction, our chi-square value and *p*-value would have been higher. Also note footnote a, which reminds us that the continuity correction is computed only for a 2-by-2 table.

The **Fisher's exact test** is used whenever any cells in our 2-by-2 cross-tabulation table have an expected count of less than 5. If that is the case, SPSS will alert us that our expected frequencies are too low to use the Pearson chi-square result. Footnote b in the SPSS results in Table 14.2 tells us that since we had no cells with an expected frequency less than 5, we can use the Pearson's chi-square results in the first row.

Using the Pearson's chi-square results in the first row, the most important datum in that row is the 0.048 probability displayed in the column headed "Asymp. Sig. (2-sided)." As mentioned above, that is the probability that our results can be attributed to sampling error. Assuming that we selected (in advance) a 0.05 level of significance, we would be able to reject the null hypothesis because 0.048 is less than 0.05. Table 14.2 also displays the chi-square value and the degrees of freedom. Again, how to calculate each value is explained in the box titled "Formula for Calculating Chi-Square." If you calculate them manually, you'll need to look up the chi-square value in a table—like Table 14.3—showing what chi-square values are needed to reach the critical region for various degrees of freedom and levels of significance for one- and two-tailed tests.

If we look up our chi-square value of 3.92 (from Table 14.2) in Table 14.3, we'll find that it would be significant at the 0.025 level for a one-tailed test. But the same chi-square value would have been calculated if our findings had been reversed, with the routine group having 64% earning off-campus privileges and the new treatment group having 36%. Had we selected (in advance) a one-tailed test in which we predicted that the new treatment group would have the higher percentage earning off-campus privileges, but got the reverse finding, that 3.92 chi-square value would *not* be significant, because it would pertain to the opposite tail of the theoretical sampling distribution—the one in which the routine treatment group's rate is better than the new treatment group's.

Perhaps you are wondering why there is a significant difference favoring the effectiveness of the new treatment group when looking at whether off-campus privileges were earned when there was not a significant difference favoring the new treatment group when we looked at number of serious behavioral incidents (SBI). In fact, the mean of 6 SBIs for the new treatment group was a bit higher than the mean of 5 for the routine group. Remember, however, that the median for the new treatment group was lower than the median for the routine group, and that the mean for the new treatment group was inflated by some extreme values. If you look back in Chapter 3 at the frequency distribution of SBIs

for the two groups, you'll see that the new treatment group actually had more youths than the routine group at the lowest SBI levels. Thus, it stands to reason that the new treatment group, despite not having a lower mean number of SBIs than the routine group, could have more youths exhibiting positive behaviors and earning off-campus privileges. We'll return to this issue later in this chapter, when we examine another nonparametric statistical test: the *median test*.

TABLES WITH MORE THAN TWO ROWS OR COLUMNS

Cross-tabulation tables can have more rows and columns than the one displayed in Table 14.1, which contained the minimum number of two rows and two columns. For example, if we wanted to compare the three cottages in our residential treatment center evaluation in terms of their frequencies of youths earning and not earning off-campus privileges, we would construct a cross-tabulation table like the one in Table 14.4.

Table 14.4 shows that a large majority (64.7% and 82.4%) of the youths in Cottage A and in Cottage B earned off-campus privileges, whereas none of the 16 youths in Cottage C did. Thus, we can see a relationship between our two variables in this table, in which Cottage C youths were less likely to earn off-campus privileges than residents of the other two cottages. But what is the probability that this apparent relationship is attributable to sampling error? To answer that question, we need to calculate the chi-square statistic. Using SPSS to do so, we would get a chi-square value of 24.588 and a p-value of less than 0.001 ($p < 0.001$), which would allow us to reject the null hypothesis and thus refute sampling error as a plausible explanation for the relationship displayed in Table 14.4. The box titled "Formula for Calculating Chi-Square" shows how to calculate the expected values for each cell and the chi-square statistic. Appendix G shows how to use SPSS to construct the table as well as conduct the chi-square analysis (see the section titled "Using SPSS to Calculate Chi-Square (Chapter 14)."

As noted earlier, if any of the cells in a cross-tabulation table have an expected count of less than 5, it is necessary to use the Fisher's exact test instead

Table 14.3 Critical Values of Chi-Square

	LEVEL OF SIGNIFICANCE FOR A ONE-TAILED TEST					
	0.10	0.05	0.025	0.01	0.005	0.0005
	LEVEL OF SIGNIFICANCE FOR A TWO-TAILED TEST					
df	0.20	0.10	0.05	0.02	0.01	0.001
1	1.64	2.71	3.84	5.41	6.64	10.83
2	3.22	4.60	5.99	7.82	9.21	13.82
3	4.64	6.25	7.82	9.84	11.34	16.27
4	5.99	7.78	9.49	11.67	13.28	18.46
5	7.29	9.24	11.07	13.39	15.09	20.52
6	8.56	10.64	12.59	15.03	16.81	22.46
7	9.80	12.02	14.07	16.62	18.48	24.32
8	11.03	13.36	15.51	18.17	20.09	26.12
9	12.24	14.68	16.92	19.68	21.67	27.88
10	13.44	15.99	18.31	21.16	23.21	29.59
11	14.63	17.28	19.68	22.62	24.72	31.26
12	15.81	18.55	21.03	24.05	26.22	32.91
13	16.98	19.81	22.36	25.47	27.69	34.53
14	18.15	21.06	23.68	26.87	29.14	36.12
15	19.31	22.31	25.00	28.26	30.58	37.70
16	20.46	23.54	26.30	29.63	32.00	39.29
17	21.62	24.77	27.59	31.00	33.41	40.75
18	22.76	25.99	28.87	32.35	34.80	42.31
19	23.90	27.20	30.14	33.69	36.19	43.82
20	25.04	28.41	31.41	35.02	37.57	45.32
21	26.17	29.62	32.67	36.34	38.93	46.80
22	27.30	30.81	33.92	37.66	40.29	48.27
23	28.43	32.01	35.17	38.97	41.64	49.73
24	29.55	33.20	36.42	40.27	42.98	51.18
25	30.68	34.38	37.65	41.57	44.31	52.62
26	31.80	35.56	38.88	42.86	45.64	54.05
27	32.91	36.74	40.11	44.14	46.94	55.48
28	34.03	37.92	41.34	45.42	48.28	56.89
29	35.14	39.09	42.69	46.69	49.59	58.30
30	36.25	40.26	43.77	47.96	50.89	59.70

Table 14.3 *Continued*

df	LEVEL OF SIGNIFICANCE FOR A ONE-TAILED TEST					
	0.10	0.05	0.025	0.01	0.005	0.0005
	LEVEL OF SIGNIFICANCE FOR A TWO-TAILED TEST					
	0.20	0.10	0.05	0.02	0.01	0.001
32	38.47	42.59	46.19	50.49	53.49	62.49
34	40.68	44.90	48.60	53.00	56.06	65.25
36	42.88	47.21	51.00	55.49	58.62	67.99
38	45.08	49.51	53.38	57.97	61.16	70.70
40	47.27	51.81	55.76	60.44	63.69	73.40
44	51.64	56.37	60.48	65.34	68.71	78.75
48	55.99	60.91	65.17	70.20	73.68	84.04
52	60.33	65.42	69.83	75.02	78.62	89.27
56	64.66	69.92	74.47	79.82	83.51	94.46
60	68.97	74.40	79.08	84.58	88.38	99.61

Source: From Table IV of R. A. Fisher and F. Yates, *Statistical Tables for Biological, Agricultural, and Medical Research,* published by Longman Group, Ltd., London (previously published by Oliver and Boyd, Ltd., Edinburgh) and by permission of the authors and publishers.

Table 14.4 Cross-Tabulation of Cottage by Whether Off-Campus Privileges Were Earned

EARNED OFF-CAMPUS PRIVILEGES?		COTTAGE			TOTAL
		A	B	C	
Yes	Count	11	14	0	25
	Expected Count	8.5	8.5	8.0	
	% Within Group	64.7%	82.4%	0%	50%
No	Count	6	3	16	25
	Expected Count	8.5	8.5	8.0	
	% Within Group	35.3%	17.6%	100%	50%
Total	Count	17	17	16	50
	% Within Group	100%	100%	100%	100%

of the Pearson's chi-square formula. Using that test, however, requires having a 2-by-2 table. Consequently, if any cells in a table with more than two rows or two columns have an expected count of less than 5, it will be necessary to combine categories for the variable(s) with more than two categories (i.e., more than two rows or columns) so that both variables become dichotomous and the table collapses to a 2-by-2 format. Then we can run our SPSS chi-square analysis on the two collapsed variables. If, after collapsing the variables into a 2-by-2 table we still have a cell with an expected count of less than 5, we would use the Fisher's exact test results in our SPSS output.

THE GOODNESS-OF-FIT TEST

So far we have been applying the use of chi-square to relationships between two nominal variables. Chi-square can also be used in connection to a single variable when we know in advance the expected frequencies for the categories of that nominal variable. We then test the *goodness of fit* between our observed frequencies and the frequencies that we expect in advance. A common use of the **goodness-of-fit test** is to compare proportions in a sample to proportions known to exist in the broader population.

For example, suppose in our hypothetical evaluation we know from national data that the proportion of youths residing in residential treatment centers like ours who earn off-campus privileges is 30%, and the proportion who do not is 70%. Those percentages would tell us that we could use 15 (30% of our 50 cases) as the expected frequency for the *yes* cell and 35 (70% of our 50 cases) as the expected frequency for the *no* cell. Since half of our 50 cases earned off-campus privileges, the observed frequency in both the *yes* and *no* cells would be 25. Applying the chi-square formula, we would get an absolute value of 10 after subtracting the expected from the observed counts in each of our two cells. Then we would square each 10 (making 100) and divide each square by the expected value in each cell, getting $100/15 = 6.667$, and $100/35 = 2.857$. Adding the 6.667 and 2.857 would give us the chi-square value of 9.524. Our *df* would be the number of cells minus 1: $2 - 1 = 1$. Looking those results up in Table 14.3, we would find that they are significant at the 0.01 level for a two-tailed test.

Table 14.5 SPSS Results Using Goodness-of-Fit Test to Compare Proportion Earning Off-Campus Privileges in Our Hypothetical Sample to Hypothetical Proportion in Population

EARNED OFF-CAMPUS PRIVILEGES?

	OBSERVED N	EXPECTED N	RESIDUAL
Yes	25	15	10.0
No	25	35	−10.0
Total	50		

TEST STATISTICS

	EARNED OFF-CAMPUS PRIVILEGES?
Chi-Square[a]	9.524
df	1
Asymp. Sig.	0.002

a. 0 cells (0.0%) have expected frequencies less than 5. The minimum expected cell frequency is 15.0.

Thus, we could reject the null hypothesis that the difference between our proportions and the population proportions was due to sampling error. The box titled "Using SPSS to Calculate Chi-Square" shows the steps for conducting the goodness-of-fit test. SPSS would give us the results displayed in Table 14.5, which mirror the results that we calculated by hand a few sentences ago.

THE MEDIAN TEST

The chi-square formula also can be used with another nonparametric test of statistical significance, called the *median test*. The **median test** is used when we have a nominal dichotomous independent variable (i.e., one containing only two categories, or groups) and we have a severely skewed dependent variable that is at the ordinal, interval or ratio level of measurement. Recall that this was the case in our hypothetical evaluation when we conducted a *t*-Test to see if the difference in mean SBIs between the new treatment group and the routine treatment group was statistically significant. We found that it

Formula for Calculating Chi-Square

Our first step in manually calculating chi-square is to calculate the expected frequencies in the cells of our cross-tabulation table. We do this by multiplying each cell's corresponding column total by its corresponding row total and then dividing by the total number of cases for the entire table (N). The following model shows how to do this in a 2-by-2 table, and later we'll extend this to tables with more rows or more columns.

a	b	$a + b$
c	d	$c + d$
$a + c$	$b + d$	N

The letters a, b, c, and d represent the observed values in our 2-by-2 table. The bottom row and the far right column contain the row and column totals, which are also called *marginals*. Thus, $a + c$ represents the total for the column containing a and c, and so on. The cell at the bottom right is the grand total, signified by N. It is our total sample size, and equals the total of $a + b + c + d$.

To obtain the expected frequency for the cell containing the observed a value, we multiply $a + c$ (the column total) times $a + b$ (the row total), and then divide the product by N. To obtain the expected frequency for the cell containing the observed b value, we multiply $b + d$ (the column total) times $a + b$ (the row total), and then divide the product by N. To obtain the expected frequency for the cell containing the observed c value, we multiply $a + c$ (the column total) times $c + d$ (the row total), and then divide the product by N. To obtain the expected frequency for the cell containing the observed d value, we multiply $b + d$ (the column total) times $c + d$ (the row total), and then divide the product by N. Thus, the formula for calculating each expected frequency is

(column total) $\times$ (row total)/N

For the cell containing the observed a value, for example, this formula would mean:

$(a + c) \times (a + b)/N$

Let's now apply the above formula to the data from Table 14.1 to see how SPSS came up with 12.5 as the expected frequency for each cell in that table. Remember, the letters a, b, c, and d are the *observed* values in each cell. We can see that the reason the expected frequency of 12.5 is the same for each cell is that in this simplified example, all the row and column totals have the same value (25). In most real studies the row and column totals will vary, and therefore the expected frequencies in each cell will vary, too.

Observed Frequency: $a = 16$	Observed Frequency: $b = 9$	$a + b = 25$
Expected Frequency: $25 \times 25/50 = 12.5$	Expected Frequency: $25 \times 25/50 = 12.5$	
Observed Frequency: $c = 9$	Observed Frequency: $d = 16$	$c + d = 25$
Expected Frequency: $25 \times 25/50 = 12.5$	Expected Frequency: $25 \times 25/50 = 12.5$	
$a + c = 25$	$b + d = 25$	$N = 50$

After calculating the expected frequencies for each cell, we are ready to apply the chi-square formula to the observed and expected frequencies. That formula (*without the correction for continuity*) is as follows:

$$X^2 = \sum \frac{(F_o - F_e)^2}{F}$$

In the above chi-square formula, X^2 stands for the chi-square value being calculated. The Greek letter sigma (Σ) means that we are to sum all the values that we get from the equation to its right. The observed frequencies are signified by F_o. The expected frequencies are signified by F_e. Thus, the formula means that for every cell in our table we should subtract the expected frequency from the observed frequency, square the difference, and then divide the square by the expected frequency. The sigma means that our final step is to sum the results for each cell.

Applying the chi-square formula to the observed and expected frequencies in the above table, we get the following results:

For the *a* cell:

16 − 12.5 = 3.5
3.5 squared = 12.25
12.25/12.5 = 0.98

For the *b* cell:

9 − 12.5 = −3.5
−3.5 squared = 12.25
12.25/12.5 = 0.98

For the *c* cell:

9 − 12.5 = −3.5
−3.5 squared = 12.25
12.25/12.5 = 0.98

For the *d* cell:

16 − 12.5 = 3.5
3.5 squared = 12.25
12.25/12.5 = 0.98

Summing the results for every cell, we get $X^2 = 0.98 + 0.98 + 0.98 + 0.98 = 3.92$.

So far, we have calculated our chi-square value of 3.92, but we do not yet know if that value is statistically significant. To find that out, we have to consult Table 14.3. But Table 14.3 also asks for our degrees of freedom (*df*). With chi-square, the degrees of freedom always equals the number of rows in our table minus 1 times the number of columns in our table minus 1. The rows and columns refer only to the cells containing observed and expected frequencies. They do *not* refer to the totals (marginals) row or column containing *a* + *b*, *b* + *d*, and so on. The formula for calculating degrees of freedom

is $df = (\text{rows} - 1)(\text{columns} - 1)$. Thus, the *df* for our 2-by-2 table above is $df = (2-1)(2-1) = 1$.

Now that we know our chi-square value and our *df*, we can consult Table 14.3. There we see that for 1 *df*, and the 0.05 level of significance for a two-tailed test, we need a chi-square value of at least 3.84. Since our chi-square value of 3.92 is greater than 3.84, our results are statistically significant at the 0.05 level. We can also see in Table 14.3 that our results would have been significant at the 0.025 level had we used a one-tailed test. If we refer back to the SPSS results in Table 14.2, we can see that SPSS gave us an exact *p*-value of 0.048. SPSS is capable of calculating the exact *p*-values of chi-square values, and is not limited to just seeing if a chi-square value is above or below critical values listed in a table.

Calculating Chi-Square with the Correction for Continuity

Whenever any cells in a 2-by-2 table have any expected frequencies less than 10, the above chi-square formula produces an inflated chi-square under those conditions. Had that been the case with our data, we would need to modify the chi-square formula using the correction for continuity, which involves reducing the absolute difference (ignoring any minus signs) between the observed and expected counts by 0.5. The formula is as follows:

$$X^2 = \sum \frac{(|F_o - F_e| - 0.5)^2}{F_e}$$

The two vertical lines surrounding $F_o - F_e$ in the above formula simply mean that we should ignore any minus signs and just subtract 0.5 from the absolute difference between the observed and expected counts. Applying this correction for continuity to the data in Table 14.1, we would simply subtract 0.5 from each of the (absolute) 3.5 differences in each of our four cells. Thus, instead of squaring 3.5 four times and then summing the squares, we would square 3.5 minus 0.5, or 3, each time and get four 9's instead of 12.25 each time. Each of the four 9's would be divided by the expected count of 12.5, giving us 0.72 four times instead of 0.98 four times. The four 0.72 values would add up to 2.88, which would be our chi-square value with the correction for continuity, as displayed in the second row of Table 14.2. However, since none of the expected counts in our data were less than 10, we would not use the correction for continuity results, and instead would use the Pearson chi-square results without the correction for continuity.

Calculating Chi-Square with More Rows or Columns

So far, we have been illustrating the calculation of chi-square with the simplest type of cross-tabulation table—one with only two rows and two columns. If we had more rows and/or more columns in the table, the chi-square formula would not change. The only difference would be in calculating expected frequencies for more cells. The 2-by-3 table below illustrates how the expected frequencies would be calculated, following the same rules as with a 2-by-2 table. The

numbers in the 2-by-3 table are based on the data in Table 14.4. If we plug its values into the chi-square formula, we would get a chi-square value of 24.588, as follows:

$$X^2 = \frac{(11 - 8.5)^2}{8.5} + \frac{(14 - 8.5)^2}{8.5} + \frac{(0 - 8.0)^2}{8.0}$$
$$+ \frac{(6 - 8.5)^2}{8.5} + \frac{(3 - 8.5)^2}{8.5} + \frac{(16 - 8.0)^2}{8.0}$$
$$= \frac{6.25}{8.5} + \frac{30.25}{8.5} + \frac{64}{8.0} + \frac{6.25}{8.5}$$
$$+ \frac{30.25}{8.5} + \frac{64}{8.0}$$
$$= 0.735 + 3.559 + 8 + 0.735 + 3.559 + 8$$
$$= 24.588$$

With two rows and three columns, we'd have $(2 - 1)(3 - 1) = 2$ degrees of freedom. Consulting Table 14.3, we find that with 2 *df* we would need a chi-square of 5.99 to reach the critical region. Therefore, our chi-square value of 24.588 would be statistically significant.

Observed Frequency: a = 11 Expected Frequency: 17 × 25/50 = 8.5	Observed Frequency: b = 14 Expected Frequency: 17 × 25/50 = 8.5	Observed Frequency: c = 0 Expected Frequency: 16 × 25/50 = 8.0	a + b + c = 25
Observed Frequency: d = 6 Expected Frequency: 17 × 25/50 = 8.5	Observed Frequency: e = 3 Expected Frequency: 17 × 25/50 = 8.5	Observed Frequency: f = 16 Expected Frequency: 16 × 425/60 = 8.0	d + e + f = 25
a + d = 17	b + e = 17	c + f = 16	N = 50

was not. But the *t*-Test assumes that the variable of interest is distributed normally in the population. That assumption cannot be made in light of the severe positive skew in the distribution of SBIs among the 25 youths in the new treatment group. Recall that the median for that group was lower than the other group's median, and that its mean was pulled

up by a handful of outliers. Since the median test makes no assumption of a normal distribution, and since it focuses on the median rather than the mean, perhaps it would be a more appropriate significance test when comparing the number of SBIs in our two hypothetical treatment groups. Let's see what we'd find if we used the median test instead of the *t*-Test.

To use the median test, we first calculate the median for the overall sample. In our hypothetical evaluation, the overall sample would be 50 cases (combining the 25 in each group to make the total N of 50). The overall median for our sample of 50 cases is 4.61. Next, we collapse the interval or ratio data in each group into two (dichotomous) categories: (1) the scores that fall above the median, and (2) the scores that fall below the median. Note that we now have ordinal data, because we know that one category is higher than the other. Nevertheless, we can still analyze those two categories using the chi-square formula.

Why don't we just call this procedure *chi-square with recoded variables*, then, instead of having to remember yet another statistical test label? The only good answer that I can fathom is that if we use SPSS, we don't have to do any collapsing. By just asking SPSS to conduct a median test, SPSS will do the collapsing for us. All we have to do is identify what our independent and dependent variables are. How to do so is explained in Appendix G under the heading "Using SPSS to Conduct Chi-Square (Chapter 14)."

If we use SPSS to conduct our median test, it will round off our median of 4.61 to 5.0 and then lump the cases that have the value of 5.0 for the SBI variable in with the cases that are below the median—that is, those with less than 5.0 SBIs.

Thus, with SPSS the two categories of the independent variable will be (1) above the median; and (2) equal to or below the median. That would be a problem, because in our hypothetical sample there are 9 cases with the value 5 for the SBI variable. Those 9 cases comprise 45% of our 50 cases. When the number of cases falling exactly at the median is relatively large, it is best to exclude them from the median test. (If you use SPSS you can exclude those cases by clicking on DATA in the top menu and then clicking on SELECT CASES. Then you click on the button beside "If condition is satisfied" and then click on the IF button. Next you would move the variable of concern into the black box and then click on the symbol for not equal ($\sim =$) and then enter the median value.)

Because SPSS would round off our median of 4.61 to 5 and then lump the nine cases with 5 SBIs in with the group below the median, it's better to use chi-square to conduct our median test, as discussed above, collapsing our ratio data in each group into two (dichotomous) categories: (1) the scores that fall above the 4.61 median, and (2) the scores that fall below the 4.61 median.

Table 14.6 displays the cross-tabulation results of our median test. It shows that 64% of the youths receiving the new treatment had less than the median number of SBIs, as compared to only 32% of the youths receiving the routine treatment. Thus,

Table 14.6 Median Test of Treatment Group by SBI

WHETHER THE NUMBER OF SERIOUS BEHAVIORAL INCIDENTS IS ABOVE OR BELOW THE MEDIAN OF 4.61		TREATMENT GROUP		
		NEW	ROUTINE	TOTAL
Above Median	Count	9	17	24
	Expected Count	13.0	13.0	
	% Within Group	36.0%	68.0%	48%
Below Median	Count	16	8	26
	Expected Count	12.0	12.0	
	% Within Group	64.0%	32.0%	52%
Total	Count	25	25	50
	% Within Group	100%	100%	100%

Table 14.7 SPSS Results of Median Test of Data from Table 14.6

	VALUE	df	ASYMP. SIG. (2-SIDED)	EXACT SIG. (2-SIDED)	EXACT SIG. (1-SIDED)
Pearson Chi-Square	5.128[b]	1	0.024		
Continuity Correction[a]	3.926	1	0.048		
Fisher's Exact Test				0.046	0.023
N of Valid Cases	50				

a. Computed only for a 2-by-2 table.

b. 0 cells (0.0%) have expected count less than 5. The minimum expected count is 12.00.

the percentage of youths below the median was twice as high for the new treatment group as compared to the routine group. Likewise, the percentage of youths above the median was much lower for the new treatment group than the routine group.

Plugging the figures in Table 14.6 into the chi-square formula, we would calculate chi-square as 5.128. Consulting Table 14.3, we find that with one *df* (because we have a 2-by-2 table), our chi-square value is significant at the 0.05 level. Using SPSS to conduct our chi-square test, we would learn that our exact *p*-value is 0.024, as displayed in Table 14.7. Because 0.024 is less than 0.05, we would reject the null hypothesis and rule out sampling error as a plausible explanation for the difference between the two treatment groups.

Thus, the results of our median test give us a very different result from our *t*-Test with regard to the same two variables (treatment group and number of SBIs.). Our *t*-Test found that the difference in mean SBIs between the new treatment group and the routine treatment group was not statistically significant. In contrast, our median test found that when we collapse the ratio data on SBIs into two ordinal categories, the new treatment group's outcome was significantly better than the routine treatment group's outcome. The reason we got different results is that, as noted above, the *t*-Test assumes that our SBI is distributed normally in the population. Because we had a severe positive skew in the distribution of SBIs among the 25 youths in the new treatment group, it had a significantly larger percentage of youths below the overall median (4.61) than did the routine treatment group, even though the new treatment

group's mean of 6 was a bit higher than the routine treatment group's mean of 5.

The contrast between the findings of our *t*-Test and our median test illustrates the importance of making the proper choice between parametric and nonparametric statistics. It shows that when the assumptions of parametric tests are violated—in this case, that would be the assumption of a normal distribution—a nonparametric test might be more appropriate and might yield a very different result from what a parametric test would give.

In light of the contrasting findings between our *t*-Test and our median test, let's return to the question of which treatment approach appears to be more effective in our findings. A comprehensive and balanced report might conduct both the *t*-Test and the median test and discuss why the results of the parametric and nonparametric procedures are different. It might point out that the new treatment appears to be more effective for a larger proportion of youths as reflected in the median test results, but perhaps less effective for a small group of youths who had the extremely high SBI values and who made the mean for the new treatment group somewhat larger than the mean for the routine treatment group.

It is not uncommon to obtain inconsistent findings like these when we evaluate services. That's one reason why we have a *Discussion* section in journal articles that report research results. That section allows evaluators to offer some reasonable conjectures on different ways to interpret the results, based on an understanding of research methodological issues and statistical concepts. Many discussion sections will include recommendations for replications of the reported study as a way to try to sort out which interpretation is the soundest.

Main Points

• Parametric tests of statistical significance assume that at least one variable in the test has an interval or ratio level of measurement, that the tested parameters of those variables are distributed normally in the population, and that the groups being compared are independent of each other and have been randomly assigned or selected.

• Nonparametric tests do not require all of the same assumptions as parametric tests. The most common reason to use nonparametric tests is when our variables are not at the interval or ratio level of measurement. Some parametric tests apply only when the variables being tested are at the nominal level of measurement. Other nonparametric tests are used when dealing with ordinal levels of measurement. Still others are used when one or more variables are at the interval or ratio level of measurement but when the variable of study cannot be assumed to be normally distributed in the population.

• The most commonly used nonparametric test, *chi-square*, assesses the probability that sampling error explains the relationships we observe between nominal-level variables displayed in cross-tabulation tables.

• Cross-tabulation tables show whether and how two or more nominal-level variables are related. They display the frequency and/or percentages of the categories of one variable cross-tabulated with the frequencies and/or percentages of another variable or variables.

• The correction for continuity is used whenever our cross-tabulation table has only two rows and two columns (i.e., is a 2-by-2 table) and has any expected frequencies less than 10.

• The Fisher's exact test is used whenever any cells in our 2-by-2 cross-tabulation table have an expected count of less than 5.

• The chi-square formula involves subtracting in every cell the expected frequency from the observed frequency, squaring the difference, and then dividing the square by the expected frequency. The final step is to sum the results for each cell.

• Chi-square can be used in connection with a single variable when we know in advance the expected frequencies for the categories of that nominal variable. We then test the *goodness of fit* between our observed frequencies and the frequencies that we expect in advance. A common use of the goodness-of-fit test is when we want to compare our sample proportions to proportions known to exist in the broader population.

• The chi-square formula also can be used with another nonparametric test of statistical significance, called the *median test*, which is used when we have a nominal dichotomous independent variable and a severely skewed dependent variable that is at the ordinal, interval, or ratio level of measurement.

• To use the median test, we first calculate the median for the overall sample. Next, we collapse the interval or ratio data in each group into two (dichotomous) categories: (1) the scores that fall above the median, and (2) the scores that fall below the median. Then we analyze those categories using the chi-square formula.

Review Questions and Exercises

1. In an evaluation of an outreach intervention to motivate parents of substance-abusing adolescents to participate in their child's treatment, 30 of the 50 parents who receive the intervention participate and 20 do not. Of the 50 parents who do not receive the motivational intervention, 20 participate and 30 do not. Construct a cross-tabulation table displaying the above results. Be sure to percentage the table in the appropriate manner.

2. On descriptive grounds only, does there appear to be an association between whether parents received the motivational intervention and whether they participated in their child's treatment? Explain.

3. In assessing the statistical significance of the above results, should the correction for continuity be used? Why or why not?

4. Either using SPSS and entering the data for the two variables in question 1, or using the chi-square formula manually, calculate the chi-square value for the above results.

5. How many degrees of freedom are in the above chi-square calculation?

6. What is the probability that sampling error accounts for the above results, and are those results statistically significant?

7. Suppose the above program wanted to see if its proportion of parental participation was higher than the national proportion of parental participation in comparable programs. What type of significance test, based on chi-square, should be used?

8. If the expected frequency in any cell of a cross-tabulation table is less than 5, what type of significance test, based on chi-square, should be used?

9. Suppose the evaluation of the above program assesses not just whether parents participate, but how many treatment sessions they attend. Suppose that the data on number of sessions attended are heavily skewed (i.e., not distributed normally). Suppose that in the group receiving the motivational intervention, 10 cases are below the median, 10 cases are at the median, and 30 are above the median. Suppose that in the group not receiving the motivational intervention, 30 cases are below the median, 10 cases are at the median, and 10 are above the median.

a. What significance test should be used?

b. What should be done in the analysis with the cases that are at the median?

c. Calculate and interpret the significance test, using either the appropriate manual formula or SPSS.

InfoTrac Exercise

1. Re-examine the article below (originally mentioned in the Chapter 11 InfoTrac exercises). Using the data presented in Table 1 of this article, manually calculate chi-square, determine its statistical significance, and see if you come up with the same results as the authors do. If your results are different, discuss the possible reasons with your classmates or instructor.

Sharma, S. B., Elkins, D., van Sickle, A., & Roberts, C. S. (1995). Effect of predischarge interventions on aftercare attendance: Process and outcome. *Health and Social Work, 20*(1), 15–20.

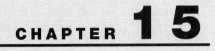
Correlation

INTRODUCTION

The term **correlation** refers to the degree to which the values of two variables vary together in a consistent fashion. With *t*-Test or ANOVA data, for example, we can say that two variables are *correlated* if the different categories of the nominal-level independent variable vary with respect to their mean value on the interval- or ratio-level dependent variable. Likewise, with chi-square data we can say that two nominal-level variables are *correlated* to the extent that the observed and expected frequencies differ in a table that cross-tabulates the two variables.

Although *correlation* is a generic term that can convey relationship strength regardless of the level of measurement of our variables, it is most commonly used when both variables in a relationship are at the ordinal, interval, or ratio level of measurement. Two ordinal-, interval-, or ratio-level variables are correlated when increases or decreases in one are accompanied by increases or decreases in the other. Thus, if adolescents who engage in greater levels of substance abuse also have higher levels of school absenteeism, while adolescents with lower levels of substance abuse also have lower levels of absenteeism, than there is a correlation between level of substance abuse and level of absenteeism. Moreover, the two variables would have a **positive correlation** because they move in the same direction. As the values of one variable increase, the values of the other tend to increase. Likewise, as the values of one decrease, the values of the other tend to decrease.

Level of substance abuse might also be correlated with the quality of the parent-child relationship. If adolescents with higher levels of substance abuse score lower on a measure of the quality of their relationship with their parents, that would be a **negative correlation,** which is also known as an *inverse correlation.* Variables are negatively (inversely) correlated if when one goes up, the other goes down. That is, they co-vary together but in opposite directions.

You can probably think of countless examples of positive and negative correlations. Some positive correlations that might quickly come to mind are height and weight, level of education and income, time spent studying and test scores, and so on. Some negative correlations that might come to mind are weight and amount of exercise, income and number of criminal arrests, and time spent smoking marijuana and test scores.

When two ordinal-, interval-, or ratio-level variables are correlated, then knowing whether one variable is high, medium, or low helps us predict whether the other variable is high, medium, or low. Thus, the two variables *co-vary* in a *predictable* fashion. For example, suppose you have a caseload of 20 adolescents. Ten have relatively high levels of substance abuse and relatively high numbers of school absences. The other 10 have relatively low levels of substance abuse and relatively low numbers of school absences. Suppose another adolescent is referred to you with a very high level of substance abuse. Based on what you know about the other 20 adolescents you would probably predict that he or she would also have a relatively high number of school absences.

Being correlated is not an all-or-nothing phenomenon. There usually are many exceptions. Although most tall people weigh more than most short people, some short people weigh more than some tall people. Some highly gifted students who study very little might score better on some exams than less gifted students who need to study more. Likewise, although most highly educated people earn more than most people with less education, some people with less education earn a lot more than some people with more education. For example, Michael Dell dropped out as an undergrad at the University of Texas to found Dell Computers and now is one of the richest people in the world. Today he probably has a higher net worth than all the faculty members at the University of Texas combined.

CORRELATION COEFFICIENTS

The fewer exceptions there are to a correlation between two variables, the stronger the correlation will be. The more exceptions, the weaker the correlation will be. The statistic that depicts the strength of a correlation between two variables that are at the ordinal, interval, or ratio level of measurement is called a **correlation coefficient.**

Correlation coefficients between variables at the ordinal, interval, or ratio level of measurement can range from -1.0 to $+1.0$. The plus or minus sign in front of the correlation coefficient indicates whether the correlation is positive or negative (inverse). Having a minus sign does not mean that the correlation is weaker than if it had a plus sign. The minus sign only means that the variables are negatively (inversely) related: As one goes up, the other goes down.

Suppose, for example, that we found a $+0.50$ correlation between level of substance abuse and number of school absences and a -0.50 correlation between level of substance abuse and quality of parent-child relationship. Both correlations would be equally strong, and the minus sign in the latter correlation means only that one variable goes down as the other goes up. The minus sign would not reduce our ability to predict one variable's value based on the other variable's value. The minus sign would only indicate the direction of the prediction (higher or lower).

Correlations of $+1.0$ and -1.0 are equally strong, and both predict perfect correlations in which there are no exceptions. A correlation of $+1.0$, for example, would mean that for every increase in one variable, there is a corresponding increase in the other variable. There would be no cases that had an increase in one without an increase in the other. Likewise, a correlation of -1.0 would mean that for every increase in one variable, there is a corresponding decrease in the other variable. There would be no cases that had an increase in one without a decrease in the other.

The weakest possible correlation is 0, which signifies no relationship whatsoever. The closer a relationship is to 0, the less we are able to predict the relative value of one variable by knowing the other. For example, knowing how many letters are in your client's first name probably is of no value to you in predicting the number of days he or she will abstain from substance abuse after completing treatment. The correlation between number of letters in first name and number of abstinence days is probably 0. In contrast, there is probably a very strong correlation between number of abstinence days and number of days employed, and if so, knowing one would help you predict the other.

The box titled "Imaginary Illustration of Strength of Correlation Coefficients" illustrates how negative correlations can be as strong as positive correlations. It also displays some correlations that are generally considered to be weak, moderate, or strong. In addition, it shows how a minus sign in front of a correlation coefficient does not necessarily signify an undesirable relationship, just as a plus sign does not necessarily signify a desirable relationship.

SCATTERPLOTS

A graphical representation of the degree of correlation between two ordinal-, interval-, or ratio-level variables is called a **scatterplot** (or **scattergram**). Scatterplots display the values of one variable (usually the independent variable) on the horizontal axis (the abscissa) and the values of the other variable on the vertical axis (the ordinate). Unlike the graphs discussed in Chapter 4, which displayed one frequency count on the vertical axis for each value on the horizontal axis, scatterplots present a dot for each case representing that case's value on two variables. Thus, if several cases with the same value on the independent variable have different values on the dependent variable, there will be multiple dots at different levels on the vertical axis above the same value on the horizontal axis. Let's examine some scatterplots so we can visualize how correlations work.

The scatterplot in Figure 15.1 depicts a perfect correlation of $+1.0$ between number of abstinence days and number of days employed for four hypothetical clients. Notice how each value on the horizontal axis has only one value on the vertical axis. Notice that every increase in abstinence days is accompanied by a twofold increase in days employed. Notice also that each client's days employed is exactly double their days abstinent. There are no exceptions. Each time abstinence days increases, days employed increases by double the increase in abstinence days. Because there are no exceptions, if we know the value of one variable, we can know the exact value of the other variable. And if we learned that a new case had 20 abstinence days, we would predict, based on the correlation observed in Figure 15.1, that the number of days worked would be 40. If that new client had a different value for days worked, then the correlation

Imaginary Illustration of Strength of Correlation Coefficients

Suppose two different intervention programs aimed at reducing substance abuse are evaluated in two different studies that use different outcome measures. Study 1—illustrated in the column on the left—assesses whether the more treatment sessions students attend, the better their scores are on a measure of knowledge about the harmful effects of substance abuse. Study 2—illustrated in the column on the right—assesses whether the more treatment sessions students attend, the lower their extent of

substance abuse. The strength of the correlations in either column is the same regardless of the plus or minus sign. However, because the outcome measure in the column on the right is an undesirable behavior (substance abuse), the positive signs indicate undesirable outcomes (i.e., more treatment sessions are accompanied by more substance abuse). In contrast, the positive signs in the left-hand column indicate desirable outcomes (i.e., more treatment sessions accompanied by improved knowledge).

Illustrative Possible Correlations Between Number of Treatment Sessions Attended and:

Scores on a Measure of Knowledge About the Harmful Effects of Substance Abuse (Study 1)	Extent of Substance Abuse (Study 2)
+1.00 (Perfect positive, desirable correlation)	+1.00 (Perfect positive, undesirable correlation)
+0.50 (Strong positive, desirable correlation)	+0.50 (Strong positive, undesirable correlation)
+0.30 (Moderate positive, desirable correlation)	+0.30 (Moderate positive, undesirable correlation)
+0.10 (Weak positive, desirable correlation)	+0.10 (Weak positive, undesirable correlation)
0.00 (No correlation)	0.00 (No correlation)
−0.10 (Weak negative, undesirable correlation)	−0.10 (Weak negative, desirable correlation)
−0.30 (Moderate negative, undesirable correlation)	−0.30 (Moderate negative, desirable correlation)
−0.50 (Strong negative, undesirable correlation)	−0.50 (Strong negative, desirable correlation)
−1.00 (Perfect negative, undesirable correlation)	−1.00 (Perfect negative, desirable correlation)

between the two variables would no longer be a perfect 1.0.

Because there are no exceptions with perfect correlations, the line drawn in the graph depicting the correlation is a straight line that includes every data point. We see this again in Figure 15.2, which depicts a perfect negative correlation of −1.0. Notice that unlike the line in Figure 15.1 which ran from lower left to upper right, depicting increasing values in both variables, the line in Figure 15.2 runs from upper left

to lower right, depicting descending values on the vertical axis as values increase on the horizontal axis. Although the line is slanted in the opposite direction from the line in Figure 15.1, it still depicts a perfect correlation in which each day of increase on the horizontal axis is accompanied by a decrease of twice as many days on the vertical axis.

In contrast to the above two scatterplots, the scatterplot in Figure 15.3 depicts a zero correlation—that is, no correlation whatsoever between number

Four hypothetical clients have the following values on each variable:

CLIENT	NO. OF ABSTINENCE DAYS	NO. OF DAYS EMPLOYED
Dick	4	8
Harry	6	12
Tom	10	20
Walt	15	30

Four hypothetical clients have the following values on each variable:

CLIENT	NO. OF ABUSE DAYS	NO. OF DAYS EMPLOYED
Dick	26	8
Harry	24	12
Tom	20	20
Walt	15	30

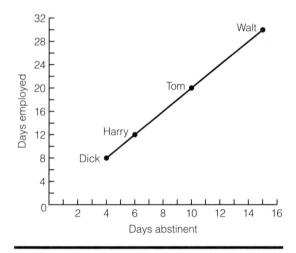

Figure 15.1   Scatterplot Depicting a Perfect +1.0 Hypothetical Correlation Between Number of Abstinence Days and Number of Days Employed for Four Hypothetical Clients

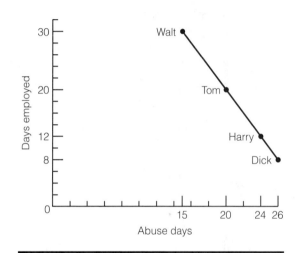

Figure 15.2   Scatterplot Depicting a Perfect –1.0 Hypothetical Correlation Between Number of Substance Abuse Days and Number of Days Employed for Four Hypothetical Clients

of treatment sessions and number of days abstinent. Notice that there are three cases for each value on the horizontal axis for the independent variable, number of treatment sessions. Notice also that each set of three cases has different values on the vertical axis, and that those three values are the same for every horizontal axis value. Thus, increases in the number of treatment sessions are not accompanied by increases or decreases in abstinence days. Therefore, the two variables do not co-vary in any way, and the correlation coefficient between them would be 0. If we obtained findings like that in a real study, it might mean that the treament sessions had no bearing on abstinence. It might also mean that the cases with the worst addictions before treatment received more treatment sessions than the cases with

less severe substance abuse problems. We cannot tell from a correlation coefficient what is or is not really causing what (an issue we'll return to later). What matters now is that you understand the concept of a zero correlation. You should also understand that real studies almost never report correlations of exactly 0. Even when there is no relationship between two variables in a population, studies will typically find some minuscule correlation between them just due to sampling error. We'll return to that issue soon, when we discuss testing the statistical significance of coerrelation coefficients.

Correlations can be strong even when the same values on the horizontal axis have multiple values on the vertical axis, as long as the sets of values move up or down together in a consistent, predictable fashion. To illustrate this point, let's take the same nine hypothetical cases depicted in Figure 15.3, except this time let's suppose that there is a fairly strong correlation between number of treatment sessions and number of days abstinent. We'll assume that each case has the same number of treatment sessions as he or she did in Figure 15.3, but this time with more days abstinent as number of treatment sesions increases. The hypothetical findings are displayed in Figure 15.4. Notice that although the vertical values vary for each horizontal value, their mean moves up as each horizontal value increases. The correlation is not perfect because knowing the value on one variable would not ensure a perfectly accurate prediction of the value on the other variable. For example, knowing that someone attended 15 treatment sessions doesn't tell us whether they had 30, 40, or 50 days abstinent. But we can predict

Nine hypothetical clients have the following values on each variable:

CLIENT	NO. OF TREATMENT SESSIONS	NO. OF ABSTINENCE DAYS
John	5	8
Mary	5	12
Peter	5	20
Sally	10	8
Paul	10	12
Alice	10	20
Don	15	8
Carol	15	12
Bob	15	20

Nine hypothetical clients have the following values on each variable:

CLIENT	NO. OF TREATMENT SESSIONS	NO. OF ABSTINENCE DAYS
John	5	10
Mary	5	20
Peter	5	30
Sally	10	20
Paul	10	30
Alice	10	40
Don	15	30
Carol	15	40
Bob	15	50

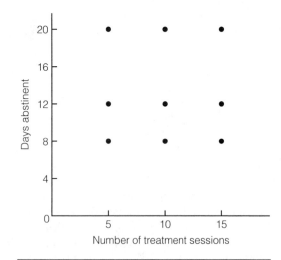

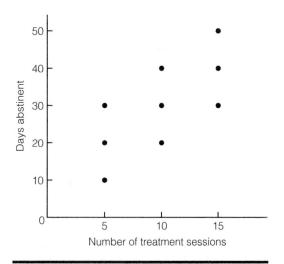

Figure 15.3 Scatterplot Depicting a Hypothetical Zero Correlation Between Number of Treatment Sessions and Number of Abstinence Days for Nine Hypothetical Clients

Figure 15.4 Scatterplot Depicting a Strong Hypothetical Correlation Between Number of Treatment Sessions and Number of Abstinence Days for Nine Hypothetical Clients

that a client attending 15 treatment sessions is likely to have more abstinence days than a client attending only 5 or 10 sessions.

CURVILINEAR CORRELATION

The scatterplots that we've examined so far all represent **linear correlations,** or **linear relationships.** They are called *linear* because the nature of the relationship, or the lack thereof, can be accurately depicted with a straight line. Sometimes, however, the direction or degree of a correlation (relationship) changes at different levels of each variable. Such relationships are portrayed by a curved line, and are therefore called **curvilinear relationships,** or **curvilinear correlations.**

Consider, for example, the relationship between duration of caregiving and degree of caregiver burden. Here we are referring to people who take care of a parent, spouse, child, partner, or other loved one who is disabled. The disability might be connected to Alzheimer's disease, severe mental illness, physical paralysis, AIDS, or some other tragic condition. The burden the caregiver experiences might be objective in terms of time and money sacrificed due to caregiving, or it might be subjective in terms of undesirable emotional effects.

If we hypothesize that caregivers experience more *objective* burden the longer they care for their loved one, then we are predicting a linear correlation. But what if we hypothesize that with Alzheimer's disease their *subjective* burden will be heaviest early and late over the course of caregiving, and lower during the middle phase. Our thinking might be that the emotional toll is greatest early when they first have to come to terms with their loved one's disability and the demands of caregiving and then again later when they anticipate the imminent loss of their loved one. During the middle phase, perhaps they have learned to accept the tragedy and become accustomed to caregiving. If our hypothesis is correct, our results would look something like the U-shaped curvilinear correlation depicted in the scatterplot displayed in Figure 15.5. Notice how the correlation is negative (inverse) in the early stage and then positive later on.

In contrast with the above hypothesis, we might predict with Alzheimer's disease that objective burden will be heaviest during the middle course of caregiving, and lower during its earliest and latest stages.

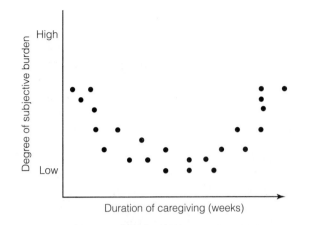

Figure 15.5 Scatterplot Depicting a Hypothetical U-Shaped Correlation Between Duration of Caregiving and Degree of Subjective Caregiver Burden

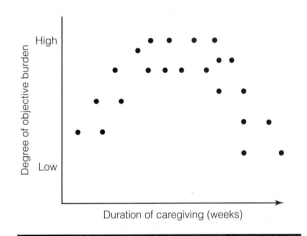

Figure 15.6 Scatterplot Depicting a Hypothetical Arch-Shaped Correlation Between Duration of Caregiving and Degree of Objective Caregiver Burden

Our thinking might be that the costs and time sacrificed in caregiving are lower when their loved one still knows who they are and is less incapacitated and later when things get so bad that nursing home care relieves the burden. The middle phase, however, might be when the demands on the caregiver are the heaviest. If our hypothesis is correct, our results would look something like the arch-shaped curvilinear correlation depicted in the scatterplot displayed in Figure 15.6. Notice how the correlation is positive in the early stage and then negative (inverse) later on.

Curvilinear correlations complicate the interpretation of correlation coefficients because the positive and negative directions can cancel each other out, resulting in an overall correlation coefficient near zero. Before we discuss the calculation of correlation coefficients, keep in mind that those calculations should be accompanied by an examination of the corresponding scatterplot. If the scatterplot depicts a curvilinear correlation, it would be inaccurate to just report the overall correlation coefficient. It might be more appropriate to calculate separate coefficients for different levels of the independent variable. Advanced statistics texts explain how to do this.

Why Would a Practitioner Want to Look at Scatterplots and Correlations?

Scatterplots and correlations can be helpful in guiding practice decisions. Suppose you are administering a program that offers supportive interventions for caregivers of family members with Alzheimer's disease. Your program has meager funding, and the number of caregivers you can serve therefore is limited. To maximize the value of your services, therefore, you want to provide assistance to caregivers experiencing the greatest degree of burden. To guide you in whom to target, you examine a report assessing the correlation between the duration of caregiving and the degree of caregiver burden.

If the report shows a strong positive correlation, you might decide to target your services to caregivers of relatives in the later stages of Alzheimer's disease. If the report shows a strong negative correlation, you might target your services to caregivers of relatives in the earlier stages. By looking at the scatterplot, you can get a quick picture of the direction and degree of the correlation. Looking at the scatterplot would also be useful if the report cites a weak or no relationship between the duration of caregiving and the degree of caregiver burden. If the scatterplot resembles the one in Figure 15.3, you can drop the duration of caregiving variable as a basis for targeting your services, because that scatterplot clearly depicts no relationship between that variable and degree of burden.

But what if the scatterplot resembles one of the curvilinear relationships displayed in Figures 15.5 and 15.6? In that case, you would recognize that the zero (or weak) correlation reported is misleading. Depending on which scatterplot the data resemble, you might end up targeting your services either to caregivers in the middle stages of caregiving or, alternatively, to those in the early and late stages.

Another possibility with a weak correlation is that outliers may be weakening the correlation. We'll return to the influence of outliers later in this chapter. For now, suffice it to say that seeing them in a scatterplot might influence you not to rely solely on the reported correlation in making practice decisions.

Here's another practice example. Suppose you are administering a nursing home that has had its funding slashed. You have no choice but to cut some programs. One possible area of cuts is in paying people to come in once a week to lead various activities for the residents. Perhaps you pay a musician to do a weekly sing-a-long on Wednesdays and a name-that-tune trivia game on Thursdays. Perhaps you pay several other people to do similar things on a weekly basis. To help guide your decision about what program(s) you might (reluctantly) cut, you look at the correlation between a measure of change in resident functioning and the number of sessions residents attend for each weekly activity. Maybe you'll see a moderate correlation for most activities and no correlation for the sing-a-long and trivia activities. You might decide to cut the musician's services. But what if you examined a scatterplot and found that those residents who've only just begun to attend the musician's activities, as well as those who have attended the most sessions, have had great improvements in functioning, while those in the middle have had little or no improvement? In that case, you might surmise that perhaps certain subgroups of residents are really being helped by those activities, and therefore you might choose not to cut them. (Perhaps they are the newer and longer-term residents who are not too impaired to benefit from the activities.)

COMPUTING THE CORRELATION COEFFICIENT

Either a parametric or a nonparametric formula is used in calculating the correlation coefficient. Nonparametric formulas apply when one or both variables are at the nominal or ordinal level of measurement or are not distributed normally within the population. A parametric formula can be used when both variables are at the interval or ratio level of measurement and are distributed normally within the population.

The most commonly used formula is a parametric one, called the **Pearson's product-moment correlation coefficient.** It is usually referred to more briefly as **Pearson's *r*** or simply as *r.* The Pearson's *r* correlation coefficient can range from the perfect correlation of −1.0 to the perfect correlation of +1.0, with zero representing no correlation, just as we've discussed above. To calculate Pearson's *r* manually, we would have to list all the pairs of values for each case in our sample and then do some extensive arithmetic calculations with them. Because the calculations are so tedious, especially with adequate sample sizes, researchers stopped doing them manually decades ago, since the advent of computer software like SPSS. Nevertheless, examining the manual formula can help you better understand the meaning of correlation coefficients. Therfore, the formula is presented and explained in the box "Formula for Calculating Pearson's *r.*" The section in Appendix G titled "Using SPSS to Calculate Correlation Coefficients and Scatterplots (Chapter 15)" shows how to use one statistical software program that will calculate Pearson's *r* for you.

The two most commonly used nonparametric formulas for calculating correlation coefficients with variables that are at the ordinal level of measurement, or with interval- or ratio-level data that are not distributed normally, are **Spearman's rho** and **Kendall's tau-*b.*** They both produce correlation coefficients ranging from −1.0 to +1.0 that have the same meaning as Pearson's *r.* Instead of using the actual variable values in their calculations, however, these two nonparametric formulas require that we first rank-order the values for each of the two variables being correlated and then plug the ranks into the formula instead of the raw values. When there are many ties in the rank ordering, Kendall's tau-*b* is the more appropriate of the two nonparametric formulas. Otherwise, Spearman's rho is commonly used. (The formula for Spearman's rho is presented in Appendix E.)

To illustrate the use and interpretation of these correlation coefficients, let's return to our hypothetical data from our hypothetical evaluation in a residential treatment center. Suppose we want to see whether the quality of the therapist-client relationship is related to the amount of change clients make from pretest to posttest on our scale measuring trauma symptoms (as discussed in Chapter 12). We'll suppose that the quality of the therapist-client relationship was measured by asking the client to rate that quality on a scale from 1 (lowest possible quality) to 10 (highest possible quality). There may be better ways to measure the quality of the therapist-client relationship, but let's keep it simple since our focus here is on statistics. The variable for the rating in our hypothetical data set has the SPSS label *qual.* (You can download the full data set by going to the Wadsworth web site at <http://humanservices.wadsworth.com/rubin_statistics>.)

Following the steps in the section of Appendix G headed "Using SPSS to Calculate Correlation Coefficients and Scatterplots (Chapter 15)," we would find that Pearson's *r* = 0.561, Spearman's rho = 0.517, and Kendall's tau-*b* = 0.399. The scatterplot depicting the relationship is displayed in Figure 15.7. Notice that despite the various exceptions, a pattern can be detected in which most of the cases with the lowest ratings of relationship quality have relatively low change scores, while most of the cases with high ratings of relationship quality have relatively high change scores. Although this relationship

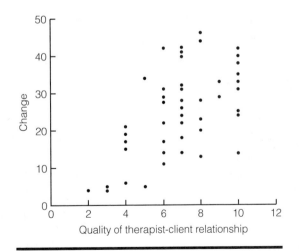

Figure 15.7   Scatterplot Depicting a Positive Correlation Between Quality of Therapist-Client Relationship and Pretest-Posttest Improvement in Trauma Symptom Scale Scores

Formula for Calculating Pearson's *r*

The following steps are necessary to calculate Pearson's *r* manually:

1. List all the pairs of values for two variables for each case in the sample.

2. Sum the values separately for each variable.

3. Square each value for each case.

4. Multiply each pair of values for each case.

5. Sum the product of the two values mutiplied in Step 4.

6. Sum the squares (from Step 3) for the first variable.

7. Sum the squares (from Step 3) for the second variable.

8. Plug the sums, squares, and products obtained in the above steps into the following formula:

$$r = \frac{N\Sigma XY - \Sigma X\Sigma Y}{\sqrt{[N\Sigma X^2 - (\Sigma X)^2][N\Sigma Y^2 - (\Sigma Y)^2]}}$$

where

ΣX is the sum of the values for the first variable (X)

ΣY is the sum of the values for the second variable (Y)

ΣXY is the sum of the products from multiplying each X value by each Y value

ΣX^2 is the sum of the squares of each X value

ΣY^2 is the sum of the squares of each Y value

To illustrate how to apply the above formula, suppose we have an N of 10 clients, with two variables. Variable X will be a score signifying the client's score on a scale measuring motivation to change. Variable Y will be the number of substance abuse treatment sessions attended. The column headed X^2 will list the square of each scale score. The column headed Y^2 will list the square of each value for number of treatment sessions attended. The column

Client	Scale Score X	Number of Treatment Sessions Attended Y	X^2	Y^2	XY
A	1	1	1	1	1
B	1	2	1	4	2
C	2	4	4	16	8
D	2	5	4	25	10
E	3	5	9	25	15
F	3	8	9	64	24
G	4	12	16	144	48
H	4	10	16	100	40
I	5	10	25	100	50
J	5	11	25	121	55
SUMS	$\Sigma X = 30$	$\Sigma Y = 68$	$\Sigma X^2 = 110$	$\Sigma Y^2 = 600$	$\Sigma XY = 243$

headed XY will list the products from multiplying each X value by each Y value.

Plugging the above sums for our N of 10 into the formula for r, we get the following:

$$r = \frac{(10)(243) - (30)(68)}{\sqrt{[(10)(110) - (30)^2][(10)(600) - (68)^2]}}$$

$$= \frac{2430 - 2040}{\sqrt{[1100 - 900][6000 - 4624]}}$$

$$= \frac{390}{\sqrt{[200][1376]}}$$

$$= \frac{390}{\sqrt{275,200}}$$

$$= \frac{390}{524.6} = 0.743$$

Thus, there is a strong correlation ($r = 0.743$) between the variables of motivation to change (reflected in the scale score) and number of treatment sessions attended. Clients who are more motivated to change tend to attend more treatment sessions.

is far from a perfect 1.0 correlation, it is nevertheless visually clear in the scatterplot.

Notice also in the scatterplot that there are many cases with tie ratings of relationship quality. For example, the nine dots above the 10 rating mean that nine cases gave the highest possible rating (10) of relationship quality. Many ties can also be seen for the ratings between 6 and 8. Considering the number of ties, and the fact that rating relationship quality on a 10-point scale is at the ordinal level of measurement, the more appropriate of the three correlation coefficients would be Kendall's tau-b.

To further illustrate the use and interpretation of correlation coefficients, let's now suppose we want to see whether the amount of change in trauma symptoms is related to the number of therapy sessions that the client's therapist had to cancel. This time we'd predict a negative (inverse) correlation, supposing that the more therapy sessions that get cancelled, the less effective the therapy is likely to be. The variable for the number of therapy sesssions cancelled in our hypothetical data set has the label *cancel*.

Following the steps in the section of Appendix G headed "Using SPSS to Calculate Correlation Coefficients and Scatterplots (Chapter 15)," we would find that Pearson's $r = -0.550$, Spearman's rho $= -0.538$, and Kendall's tau-$b = -0.416$. As discussed above, the minus sign in front of these correlations doesn't pertain to their strength or

weakness; it only signifies that the relationship is negative (inverse), as we predicted.

The scatterplot depicting the negative (inverse) relationship is displayed in Figure 15.8. Notice that despite the various exceptions, a pattern can be detected visually in which most of the cases with the fewest cancellations have relatively high change scores, while most of the cases with the greatest number of cancellations have relatively low change

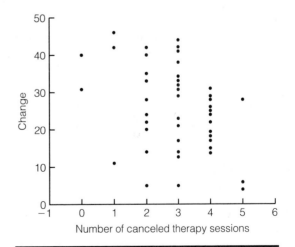

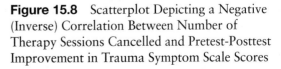

Figure 15.8 Scatterplot Depicting a Negative (Inverse) Correlation Between Number of Therapy Sessions Cancelled and Pretest-Posttest Improvement in Trauma Symptom Scale Scores

scores. Because number of cancellations is at the ratio level of measurement, and since the scatterplot provides no clear basis for not assuming a normal distribution in the population, it would be appropriate to use the parametric correlation coefficient, Pearson's *r*.

CORRELATION COEFFICIENTS FOR NOMINAL DATA

Additional nonparametric correlation coefficients can be calculated when one or more variables in a hypothesized relationship is at the nominal level of measurement. Which one to use depends on whether both variables are nominal, or just one is, and the number of categories in each nominal variable. For example, when comparing the means of two or more categories of a nominal variable (such as which treatment group a participant is in), we can use the *eta* statistic. *Eta* is interpreted like the above correlation coefficients, and can range from a zero correlation to a perfect correlation of 1.0. The main difference (in addition to its formula) is that because one variable in *eta* is nominal, negative (inverse) correlations are not applicable since only the other variable can be high or low. Thus, *eta* only contains positive values.

The manual calculation formula for *eta* goes beyond the scope of this text, but you can compute it easily with a statistical software program like SPSS, as explained in Appendix G. All you have to do is click on ANALYZE in the top menu, then on COMPARE MEANS, then on MEANS, and then, after clicking on the variables involved, click on OPTIONS. The options dialog box will allow you to check a box beside ANOVA TABLE AND ETA which, after you click CONTINUE and then OK, will give you an ANOVA analysis along with the *eta* statistic. (You can do this even if your significance test is a *t*-Test with a nominal independent variable that is dichotomous. That is because ANOVA is identical to the *t*-Test with dichotomous independent variables. Thus, eta has the same meaning regardless of whether you use a *t*-Test or ANOVA for significance testing.)

When both variables are nominal, two commonly used measures of correlation are the **phi coefficient (Φ)** and **Cramer's V.** *Phi* is used when both nominal variables have only two categories (i.e., they are each dichotomous), and thus form a

2-by-2 table. To illustrate the use of *phi*, let's reconsider the hypothesis we examined in Chapter 14, in connection with chi-square, in which we compared the effectiveness of the new treatment with the routine treatment in terms of whether or not the youth's behavior and school performance were sufficiently positive to earn off-campus privileges.

Suppose both groups had exactly the same percentage of youths who earned off-campus privileges. Then knowing whether a particular youth was in one group or the other would not improve our ability to predict whether he or she earned off-campus privileges. Consequently, the correlation coefficient would be 0.

On the other hand, if all of the cases in the new treatment group earned off-campus privileges and none of the cases in the routine group did so, then knowing which group a case was in would enable us to predict with 100% accuracy whether that case earned off-campus privileges. Consequently, the correlation coefficient would be 1.0, a perfect relationship.

Table 15.1 illustrates the above two correlations. The 2-by-2 table at the top shows a zero correlation, because each group has the same percentages in each category of the dependent variable. In the

Table 15.1 Illustrations of a Zero Correlation and a Perfect Correlation Between Two Dichotomous Nominal Variables

EXAMPLE OF A ZERO CORRELATION

OFF-CAMPUS PRIVILEGES EARNED?	NEW TREATMENT GROUP %	ROUTINE TREATMENT GROUP %
Yes	70	70
No	30	30

EXAMPLE OF A PERFECT CORRELATION

OFF-CAMPUS PRIVILEGES EARNED?	NEW TREATMENT GROUP %	ROUTINE TREATMENT GROUP %
Yes	100	0
No	0	100

Table 15.2 Illustration of a Moderate Correlation Between Two Dichotomous Nominal Variables

OFF-CAMPUS PRIVILEGES EARNED?	NEW TREATMENT GROUP	ROUTINE TREATMENT GROUP
Yes	16	9
	64.0%	36.0%
No	9	16
	36.0%	64.0%

second 2-by-2 table, the correlation coefficient is 1.0 because all of the cases in the new treatment group earned off-campus privileges, whereas none of the cases in the routine treatment group did. Thus, knowing which group a youth was in would be all the information we needed to predict with perfect accuracy whether or not the youth earned off-campus privileges.

So far we have contrasted a perfect correlation with a zero correlation. But what about something in between—for example, results similar to those we obtained regarding the above two variables in Table 14.1, as displayed again above in Table 15.2. To determine the correlation for the data displayed in that table (as well any 2-by-2 table, including those in Table 15.2), we can calculate the phi coefficient (Φ). The phi coefficient is used to assess the strength of relationships that are assessed in chi-square tests of statistical significance involving 2-by-2 tables. Its formula is as follows:

$$\Phi = \sqrt{\frac{X^2}{N}} \quad \begin{array}{l} X^2 = \text{The calculated chi-square value} \\ N = \text{Total number of cases} \end{array}$$

In Chapter 14 we saw that the chi-square value for the data in Table 15.1 is 3.92. Plugging that value along with our N of 50 into the above formula, we get the following results:

$$\Phi = \sqrt{\frac{3.92}{50}}$$
$$= \sqrt{0.0784}$$
$$= 0.280$$

Although the formula for manually calculating the phi coefficient is relatively simple, an even easier way to calculate it is simply to ask for it when you use a statistical software program to calculate chi-square, as discussed in Appendix G. Using SPSS, for example, all that is required is to check the box beside PHI AND CRAMER'S V when you request the chi-square statistic. The prompt includes Cramer's V along with phi because Cramer's V is the correlation coefficient to use when at least one of the two nominal variables you are examining has more than two categories. Phi can be used only with a 2-by-2 table. When there are more than two rows or two columns, then Cramer's V is used. The manual formula for Cramer's V is very similar to the phi formula. The only difference is that in the denominator N is multiplied by the number of rows or columns minus one, whichever is smaller, as follows:

$$V = \sqrt{\frac{X^2}{N(k-1)}} \quad \begin{array}{l} V = \text{Cramer's } V \\ N = \text{Total number of cases} \\ k = \text{number of rows or columns, whichever is smaller} \end{array}$$

Suppose we obtained a chi-square value of 10.0 in a 3-by-3 table with a total number of 100 cases. Plugging those numbers into the above formula, we would get the following somewhat weak correlation:

$$V = \sqrt{\frac{10.0}{100(3-1)}}$$
$$= \sqrt{\frac{10.0}{200}}$$
$$= \sqrt{0.05}$$
$$= 0.224$$

Notice that in the above example the number of rows (3) and columns (3) are identical. When that happens, the k in the formula will be either the number of rows or columns, since they are the same. Of course, you need not worry about the formula if you simply check the box beside PHI AND CRAMER'S V when you request the chi-square statistic in SPSS.

TESTING THE STATISTICAL SIGNIFICANCE OF CORRELATION COEFFICIENTS

Examining the strength of relationships involving at least one nominal-level variable typically comes after we have assessed the statistical significance of that relationship, such as by using chi-square, the t-Test, or ANOVA. But when both variables in a relationship are at the ordinal, interval or ratio level of measurement, we have to calculate the correlation coefficient first and then conduct a significance test to assess the probability that the correlation can be attributed to sampling error.

It is necessary to test the significance of correlation coefficients because, as I noted earlier, even when there is no relationship between two variables in a population, studies will typically find some minuscule correlation between them due to sampling error. Likewise, studies with very small samples might find strong correlations due to sampling error. For example, suppose we ask four clients to rate our services as excellent, good, fair, or poor. Two clients, named Dan and Jan, rate our services as poor. The other two, named Thelma and Louise, rate our services as excellent. We would therefore find a perfect +1.0 correlation between number of letters in the client's first name and rating of service quality, but we would strongly suspect that the correlation was just a fluke that would disappear with a larger sample size.

Testing the statistical significance of correlation coefficients involves the same logic as testing the statistical significance of differences between group means or proportions. For example, whereas the null hypothesis in the latter tests states that there is no real difference between groups in the population and that any observed difference in our sample is due to sampling error, the null hypothesis with correlation coefficients states that there is no real correlation in the population (i.e., $r = 0.00$) and that any observed correlation in our sample is due to sampling error. Just as in other tests of significance, sampling error when testing the statistical significance of correlation coefficients involves the use of theoretical sampling distributions with an assumed mean correlation of 0. Thus, with small sample sizes, the sampling distribution is relatively flat and with more dispersion, requiring a relatively large observed correlation coefficient (i.e., further from 0) to reach the critical region (i.e., to be statistically significant).

With large sample sizes, the sampling distribution has less dispersion, and therefore smaller observed correlation coefficients (i.e., closer to 0) can reach the critical region and thus be statistically significant.

Different formulas are used to test the significance of Pearson's r, Spearman's rho, Kendall's tau-b, or lesser-used nonparametric alternatives. It is no longer necessary to use these formulas, however, for two reasons. First and foremost, statistical software programs like SPSS will calculate whether our correlation coefficients are statistically significant at the same time that they calculate the coefficients. Second, tables can be examined that list the minimum values of correlation coefficients required for statistical significance for different sample sizes and significance levels. The critical values of Pearson's r are listed in Table 15.3. In that table you can notice that as the sample size (N) increases, the critical value of r required to reject the null hypothesis decreases. As noted above, that's because sampling error decreases as sample size increases. Sampling error is more likely to explain our finding a strong correlation with a tiny sample than with a large sample.

Earlier in this chapter we saw that in our hypothetical evaluation the Pearson's r was -0.550 for the correlation between amount of change in trauma symptoms and the number of therapy sessions that the client's therapist had to cancel. Let's examine Table 15.3 to see if that negative (inverse) correlation would be statistically significant in a real study with the same sample size ($N = 50$) as in our hypothetical study. There is no row for an N of 50, so we have to go to the row with the next highest N, which would be 52. There we can see that our r of -0.550 exceeds every value in the row. Therefore, it would be statistically significant for every level of significance listed in the table's column headings. Notice that we ignore the minus sign when we compare our negative 0.550 to the positive values listed in the table. Remember, the plus or minus sign only signifies whether the two variables co-vary in the same or opposite directions; it does not bear on the strength of the relationship or its statistical significance.

SOME CAUTIONS TO REMEMBER ABOUT CORRELATION

There are four cautions to keep in mind when you calculate, report, or read about correlations. Let's look at each one briefly before concluding this chapter.

Table 15.3 Critical Values of r

	LEVEL OF SIGNIFICANCE FOR A ONE-TAILED TEST				
	0.05	0.025	0.01	0.005	0.0005
	LEVEL OF SIGNIFICANCE FOR A TWO-TAILED TEST				
N	0.10	0.05	0.02	0.01	0.001
5	0.8054	0.8783	0.9343	0.9587	0.9912
6	0.7293	0.8114	0.8822	0.9172	0.9741
7	0.6694	0.7545	0.8329	0.8745	0.9507
8	0.6215	0.7067	0.7887	0.8343	0.9249
9	0.5822	0.6664	0.7498	0.7977	0.8982
10	0.5494	0.6319	0.7155	0.7646	0.8721
11	0.5214	0.6021	0.6851	0.7348	0.8471
12	0.4973	0.5760	0.6581	0.7079	0.8233
13	0.4762	0.5529	0.6339	0.6835	0.8010
14	0.4575	0.5324	0.6120	0.6614	0.7800
15	0.4409	0.5139	0.5923	0.6411	0.7603
16	0.4259	0.4973	0.5742	0.6226	0.7420
17	0.4124	0.4821	0.5577	0.6055	0.7246
18	0.4000	0.4683	0.5425	0.5897	0.7084
19	0.3887	0.4555	0.5285	0.5751	0.6932
20	0.3783	0.4438	0.5155	0.5614	0.6787
21	0.3687	0.4329	0.5034	0.5487	0.6652
22	0.3598	0.4227	0.4921	0.5368	0.6524
27	0.3233	0.3809	0.4451	0.4869	0.5974
32	0.2960	0.3494	0.4093	0.4487	0.5541
37	0.2746	0.3246	0.3810	0.4182	0.5189
42	0.2573	0.3044	0.3578	0.3932	0.4896
47	0.2428	0.2875	0.3384	0.3721	0.4648
52	0.2306	0.2732	0.3218	0.3541	0.4433
62	0.2108	0.2500	0.2948	0.3248	0.4078
72	0.1954	0.2319	0.2737	0.3017	0.3799
82	0.1829	0.2172	0.2565	0.2830	0.3568
92	0.1726	0.2050	0.2422	0.2673	0.3375
102	0.1638	0.1946	0.2301	0.2540	0.3211

Source: From Table VII of R. A. Fisher and F. Yates, *Statistical Tables for Biological, Agricultural, and Medical Research*, published by Longman Group, Ltd., London (previously published by Oliver and Boyd, Ltd., Edinburgh) and by permission of the authors and publishers.

Linearity and Other Assumptions

Sometimes evaluators choose the wrong type of correlation to calculate, and when they do, their results can be misleading. Perhaps the most common mistake is to calculate the parametric correlation, Pearson's r, when its assumptions are not met in the data. For example, Pearson's r requires data at the interval or ratio levels of measurement. If there is little variability in either variable, as is the case with many nominal- or ordinal-level variables, Pearson's r will understate the degree of association. Pearson's r also requires data that are reasonably linear in the scatterplot. As mentioned earlier, marked curvilinearity will produce misleadingly low Pearson's r's 0. Finally, the data should be *homoscedastic*, which means that the degrees of variance in the two variables being correlated are similar. If one variable has much more variance than the other, the data are called *heteroscedastic*, and the Pearson's r will be misleading. Fortunately, however, when these assumptions are not met, we usually have an alternative way to measure correlation. For example, when data are at nominal or ordinal levels of measurement, we might be able to use one of the non-parametric approaches to correlation discussed in this chapter. With curvilinear data, we might opt to calculate different correlation coefficients for different levels of one of the variables.

Handling Outliers

Earlier in this text we discussed how outlying cases with extreme values can complicate the interpretation of central tendency and influence whether to use a t-Test or a median test when comparing group averages. Outliers can exert similar influences on the calculation and interpretation of correlation coefficients. Consider, for example, the outlier depicted in the lower right-hand corner of the scatterplot in Figure 15.9. Notice how it is an extreme exception to the overall consistent pattern of the two variables moving together in the same direction. As such, it would exert an inordinate influence on the correlation coefficient, lowering it considerably in a way that misrepresents the stronger correlation between the two variables for almost all the cases.

Should the outlier in Figure 15.9 be eliminated from the calculation of r? Because this is such an

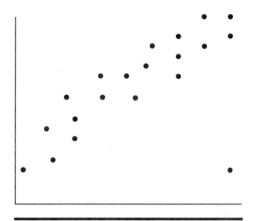

Figure 15.9 Scatterplot Illustrating the Influence of an Outlier on a Strong Correlation

extreme example, it probably should be eliminated. But in many studies the correct decision is less obvious. Moreover, when the decision about several outliers is a close call, researchers might be tempted to choose the option that best supports their hypothesis, thus biasing the analysis. In those situations, the best solution usually is to calculate and report two correlation coefficients, one in which the outliers are included and one in which they are excluded. The scatterplot can also be reported, enabling readers to judge for themselves which of the two analyses seems more appropriate.

Can a Correlation Ever be too Strong?

Suppose in our hypothetical evaluation we found a perfect -1.0 correlation between the number of days that youths receive a serious incident report and the number of days they do not. It would be silly to examine or report that correlation because it would have to be perfect by definition. There are not really two variables in the correlation; both "variables" are really just opposite categories of the same variable.

But some studies measure the same variable in different ways that are less obvious than in the above example. Suppose we were conducting an exploratory study looking for variables that might explain the quality of the therapist-client relationship. Suppose further that the scale we used to measure the quality of the relationship consisted of items pertaining primarily to the clients' perceptions of how warm, accepting, and understanding their therapists are. Next suppose that one of the variables we are exploring to help explain quality of relationship is the degree of therapist empathy. Finally, suppose we measure therapist empathy via a self-report scale in which therapists respond to vignettes of client statements and are scored higher on empathy to the extent that their responses reflect warmth, acceptance, and understanding. If our findings indicate a 0.92 correlation between scores on the therapist empathy scale and scores on the therapist-client relationship scale, have we really learned much of anything new or valuable in trying to explain the quality of the therapist-client relationship? Probably not. All we would have found is that therapists whose self-report scores are higher in regard to empathy also are perceived to be more empathic by their clients. That finding might have considerable value if our aim is to validate either of the two instruments we used. But since both instruments essentially measure the same thing from two different sources, one does not really help *explain* the other.

In contrast, suppose we found a 0.50 correlation between therapist score on a cultural competence scale and score on the therapist-client relationship scale. Assuming that the cultural competence scale was not measuring empathy, that 0.50 correlation would give us a more useful potential factor that might partially help explain quality of therapist-client relationship than our 0.92 correlation between two scales measuring virtually the same thing. I am not implying that therapist empathy is not an important variable in trying to understand the quality of the therapist-client relationship. It may be the most important variable! But if we measure the quality of the therapist-client relationship with a scale that essentially just measures empathy, then we learn nothing new from finding that it is correlated with another scale that also measures empathy.

Unless the aim of our study is to assess the reliability or validity of a measure, then we should exercise caution in interpreting correlation coefficients that are near perfect. Such correlations might merely indicate that we have inadvertently measured the same variable in two different ways. However, when our aim is to assess reliability or validity, then near-perfect correlations can be quite useful. When assessing the reliability of a unidimensional scale, for example, we want the correlations between sub-scores of different halves of the scale (as represented by coefficient alpha, discussed in this text's appendix) to be very high, with 0.90 or above being ideal. That's because each item is supposed to measure a different aspect of the same variable. Likewise, a very high correlation between two scales that purport to measure the same variable supports the validity of each scale.

Finally, suppose two items on the same scale have a near-perfect correlation in a preliminary analysis to see which items to keep and which to delete in finalizing (and shortening) the scale. Suppose one item asks clients whether they agree or disagree that their therapist makes them feel accepted. Suppose another item asks them whether they agree or disagree that their therapist accepts them for who they are. A 0.90 or higher correlation between the two items would indicate that since they both may be measuring the same indicator of relationship quality, the scale can be shortened by deleting one of the items. Alternatively, the decision could be made to keep both items as a reliability check on each other. The latter course of action, however, may be unnecessary, since overall measures of internal consistency reliability, such as coefficient alpha, serve the same purpose without lengthening the scale with redundant items.

Correlation Does Not Prove Causation

No matter how strongly correlated an independent and dependent variable may be, the correlation does not tell us whether the independent variable is the cause of the dependent variable. Research methods texts, for example, point out that although correlation is a necessary condition for inferring causality, it is only one of three criteria required to infer causality (Rubin & Babbie, 2005). Another is time sequence. If substance-abusing adolescents have worse relationships with their parents than other adolescents, did the relationship problem contribute to the development of substance abuse, or did the substance abuse cause the relationship to deteriorate? The correlation alone, without knowing which variable changed first, won't tell us the answer. Knowing that the two variables are correlated is *consistent* with the hypothesis that one causes the other, but it does not *verify* that hypothesis. In fact, a third variable, such as negative peer influences, might be causing both problems.

Countless other examples of the difference between correlation and causality could be cited. Some are rather silly, such as the correlation between the number of storks in a geographical area and that area's birth rate. That correlation has nothing to do with storks delivering babies. It merely means that there are more and bigger zoos in areas with larger populations and thus higher birth rates.

This caution about correlation and causality applies to all types of correlations, not just those involving Pearson's r, Spearman's rho, or Kendall's tau-b. It also applies to hypotheses tested with t-Tests, ANOVA, chi-square, or many other statistics. Regardless of how impressive our statistical analysis may be, and no matter how strong the relationships we find, our research design must show which variable came first and must control for other threats to internal validity (such as history, maturation, and so on) before we can infer causality from our statistical findings. For example, if a t-Test finds that clients who complete substance abuse treatment have better outcomes than those who drop out early in treatment, that finding may have more to do with client motivation to change than with treatment effects, since the two groups (completers versus dropouts) are not really comparable.

Main Points

• The term *correlation* refers to the degree to which the values of two variables vary together in a consistent fashion.

• Two variables have a positive correlation when they move in the same direction. As the values of one increase, the values of the other tend to increase; or as the values of one decrease, the values of the other tend to decrease.

• Variables are negatively (inversely) correlated if when one goes up, the other goes down. That is, they co-vary together but in opposite directions.

• Correlation coefficients between variables at the ordinal, interval, or ratio level of measurement can range from -1.0 to $+1.0$. The plus or minus sign in front of the correlation coefficient indicates whether the correlation is positive or negative (inverse); it does not indicate the strength of the correlation.

• A graphical representation of the degree of correlation between two ordinal-, interval-, or ratio-level variables is called a *scatterplot*.

• Linear relationships (linear correlations), or the lack thereof, can be accurately depicted with a straight line. Sometimes, however, the direction or degree of a correlation (relationship) changes at different levels of each variable. Such relationships are portrayed by a curved line and are therefore called curvilinear relationships or curvilinear correlations.

• Curvilinear correlations complicate the interpretation of correlation coefficients because the positive and negative directions can cancel each other out, resulting in an overall correlation coefficient near 0. If the scatterplot depicts a curvilinear correlation, it would be inaccurate to just report the overall correlation coefficient. It might be more appropriate to calculate separate coefficients for different levels of the independent variable.

• Either a parametric or a nonparametric formula is used in calculating the correlation coefficient. Nonparametric formulas apply when one or both variables are at the nominal or ordinal level of measurement or are not distributed normally within the population. A parametric formula can be used when both variables are at the interval or ratio level of measurement and are distributed normally within the population.

• The most commonly used formula is a parametric one called the Pearson's product-moment correlation coefficient. It is usually referred to more briefly as Pearson's r or simply as r. The Pearson's r correlation coefficient can range from the perfect correlation of -1.0 to the perfect correlation of $+1.0$, with 0 representing no correlation.

• The two most commonly used nonparametric formulas for calculating correlation coefficients with variables that are at the ordinal level of measurement, or with interval- or ratio-level data that are not distributed normally, are Spearman's rho and Kendall's tau-b. They both produce correlation coefficients ranging from -1.0 to $+1.0$ that have the same meaning as Pearson's r. Instead of using the actual variable values in their calculations, however, these two nonparametric formulas require that we first rank-order the values for each of the two variables being correlated and then plug the ranks into the formula instead of the raw values. When there are many ties in the rank ordering, Kendall's tau-*b* is the more appropriate of the two nonparametric formulas. Otherwise, Spearman's rho is commonly used.

• When comparing the means of two or more categories of a nominal variable, we can use the *eta* statistic to depict the strength of the relationship. Eta is interpreted like the above correlation coefficients and can range from a zero correlation to a perfect correlation of 1.0. The main difference is that because one variable in eta is nominal, negative (inverse) correlations are not applicable since only the other variable can be high or low. Thus, eta contains only positive values.

• When both variables are nominal, two commonly used measures of correlation are the phi coefficient (Φ) and Cramer's *V*. Phi is used when both nominal variables have only two categories (i.e., they are each dichotomous), and thus form a 2-by-2 table.

• It is necessary to test the significance of correlation coefficients. Even when there is no relationship between two variables in a population, studies will typically find some minuscule correlation between them just due to sampling error. Likewise, studies with very small samples might find strong correlations due to sampling error.

• Testing the statistical significance of correlation coefficients involves the same logic as testing the statistical significance of differences between group means or proportions. Whereas the null hypothesis in the latter tests states that there is no real difference between groups in the population and that any observed difference in our sample is due to sampling error, the null hypothesis with correlation coefficients states that there is no real correlation in the population (i.e., $r = 0.00$) and that any observed correlation in our sample is due to sampling error. Just as in other tests of significance, sampling error when testing the statistical significance of correlation coefficients involves the use of theoretical sampling distributions with an assumed mean correlation of 0.

• Because sampling error decreases as sample size increases, sampling error is more likely to explain our finding a strong correlation with a tiny sample than with a large sample.

• Pearson's *r* requires data at the interval or ratio levels of measurement, that are reasonably linear in the scatterplot, and that are *homoscedastic,* which means that the degrees of variance in the two variables being correlated are similar. If one variable has much more variance than the other, the data are called *heteroscedastic,* and the Pearson's *r* will be misleading.

• Outliers can influence the calculation and interpretation of correlation coefficients. When the decision about several outliers is a close call, the best solution usually is to calculate and report two correlation coefficients, one in which the outliers are included and one in which they are excluded. The scatterplot can also be reported, enabling readers to judge for themselves which of the two analyses seems more appropriate.

• We should exercise caution in interpreting correlation coefficients that are near perfect. Such correlations might merely indicate that we have inadvertently measured the same variable in two different ways.

• No matter how strongly correlated an independent and dependent variable may be, the correlation does not tell us whether the independent variable is the cause of the dependent variable.

Review Questions and Exercises

1. For each of the following interpretations of correlation results in fictional studies, indicate whether you agree with the interpretation and explain why. If you do not agree with the interpretation, explain why not and explain how you would interpret the results.

a. A survey of 100 nursing home residents finds a $+0.35$ correlation between number of recreational and social activities attended and physical well-being. It also finds a -0.50 correlation between number of recreational and social activities attended and level of depression. Because the first correlation has a plus sign and the second a minus sign, the administrator conducting the survey concludes that the correlation between number of recreational and social activities attended and physical well-being is the stronger, and more important correlation. She cites its 0.001 significance as another indication that it is a very strong correlation.

b. A practitioner reading the above survey results concludes that the findings indicate the need to provide more recreational and social activities and to devote more resources into encouraging attendance, since increased attendance appears to enhance physical well-being.

c. Another nursing home administrator assesses the quality of care provided by each direct care staff member and finds a zero correlation between length of time employed at the nursing home and quality of care. In light of that correlation and the scatterplot in Figure 15.10, he concludes that length of time a staff member is employed at the nursing home is not related to quality of care.

d. A nationwide survey of 1000 foster parents finds a +0.10 correlation between their degree of religiosity and the quality of their relationship with the child placed in their care. The correlation is significant at the 0.01 level, so the researchers conclude that foster parents who are more religious are much more likely than their less religious counterparts to have a good relationship with the child placed in their care. The study recommends using religiosity as an important screening criterion for selecting foster parents.

e. A school social worker tests the hypothesis that troubled students who attend more sessions of the

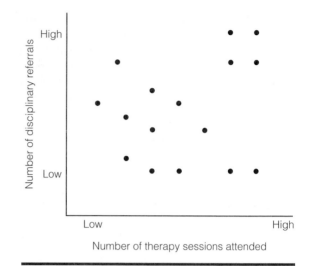

Figure 15.11   Fictional Scatterplot for Question 1.e.

therapy he invented will have fewer disciplinary referrals than those who attend fewer sessions. The correlation coefficient he finds is lower than he had hoped and expected to find, so he examines his scatterplot, which appears in Figure 15.11. Each point in the scatterplot represents one of the 16 students in his study. Then he decides to delete from his correlation analysis the four students in the upper right hand corner of the scatterplot, on the grounds that they are outliers. After deleting them, he re-computes the correlation coefficient and finds it much more to his liking and expectations. In writing his research report, the latter correlation (after deleting the outliers) is the one he reports.

f. Radio talk show host Russ Farwright cites a study showing a 0.93 correlation between the length of time states allow unemployed single mothers to receive welfare benefits and the length of time unemployed single mothers in the state receive welfare benefits. He therefore concludes that allowing unemployed mothers to stay on welfare longer fosters economic dependency. In response to a later study that shows a 0.60 correlation between the length of time states allow unemployed single mothers to receive welfare benefits and the emotional and physical well-being of their children, he argues that because the 0.60

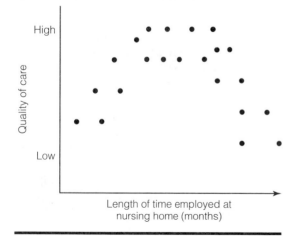

Figure 15.10   Fictional Scatterplot for Question 1.c.

correlation is lower than the 0.93 correlation, the earlier study has the more important finding.

2. A study compares the re-arrest rates for prisoners who voluntarily attend a faith-based prison rehabilitation program and prisoners who choose not to attend. The results are displayed in the 2-by-2 table below. The chi-square for these results is 8.0, and it is statistically significant ($p < 0.01$). Using the formula presented in this chapter, calculate and interpret phi for the results. Do these results imply that the faith-based program is effective in preventing re-arrest? Why or why not?

REARRESTED?	FAITH-BASED PRISON REHABILITATION PROGRAM PARTICIPANTS	NON-PARTICIPANTS
Yes	40	60
	40.0%	60.0%
No	60	40
	60.0%	40.0%

3. A chi-square value of 20.0 for a 3-by-4 table is significant at the 0.01 level in a study with an N of 100. Using the formula presented in this chapter, calculate and interpret Cramer's V for those results.

4. What two correlation coefficients would you consider using when testing the hypothesis that

client satisfaction rating (excellent, good, fair, or poor) is related to client motivation to change (high, medium, or low)? What type would you not use? Why not?

5. In developing a scale to measure parental attitudes toward child rearing, you find a 0.95 correlation between the two preliminary items that appear below. Your preliminary scale is rather lengthy, and you hope to shorten it. What would you do in light of the 0.95 correlation between these two items? Why?

Item 3: Spare the rod, spoil the child

Strongly Agree   Agree   Disagree   Strongly Disagree

Item 26: A child will be spoiled if not spanked after misbehaving

Strongly Agree   Agree   Disagree   Strongly Disagree

InfoTrac Exercise

1. Read the following letter to the editor and describe how it illustrates that correlation does not prove causation. Can you think of another example of this caveat? If so, identify it and briefly explain.

Secker, P. J. (2003). Causation or correlation? *First Things: A Monthly Journal of Religion and Public Life, 133,* 16–17.

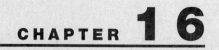

Interpreting the Strength and Importance of Relationships

INTRODUCTION

We have seen in previous chapters that trivial relationships can be statistically significant in studies with very large sample sizes. Likewise, studies with small sample sizes may not find statistical significance when examining relationships that might in reality be important. Thus, we have seen the need to exercise caution when interpreting the term *significance*. "Statistically significant" does not necessarily mean strong or important, and relationships that are strong or important are not always statistically significant.

In discussing correlational measures, Chapter 15 provided ways to augment findings on statistical significance with measures of relationship strength. We saw that 0 is the lowest possible correlation coefficient, signifying no relationship whatsoever. We also saw that plus or minus 1.0 is the strongest possible correlation coefficient, signifying a perfect relationship. Chapter 15 also briefly mentioned some correlation coefficents that are commonly deemed to be strong, moderate, or weak. In this chapter we'll begin by examining some criteria for depicting correlation coefficients as weak, moderate, or strong.

COEFFICIENT OF DETERMINATION

We know that the closer a correlation coefficient is to plus or minus 1.0, the stronger the relationship between two variables. But what is the basis for calling one correlation, by itself, strong, moderate or weak? One criterion commonly used in portraying the strength of a particular correlation coefficient is to square it. When we square the correlation coefficient (by multiplying it by itself), we get a smaller coefficient, called the **coefficient of determination**. The **coefficient of determination**, whose symbol is r^2, tells us *what proportion of variance in the dependent variable is explained by the independent variable*. Thus, if $r = 0.6$, then $r^2 = 0.36$, which means that 36% of the variation in the dependent variable has been explained. The other 64% of the variation is unaccounted for. Perhaps some other variables that we could study might account for part of that remaining variation. If $r = 0.3$, then $r^2 = 0.09$, which means that 9% of the variation in the dependent variable has been explained, and 91% is unaccounted for.

Thus, although 0.60 is twice as high as 0.30, it is four times as strong in terms of the amount of dependent variable variation it accounts for (0.36 is four times 0.09). Likewise, if $r = 0.9$, then $r^2 = 0.81$, which means that 81% of the variation in the dependent variable has been explained, and only 19% is unaccounted for. Thus, although 0.90 is three times as high as 0.30, it is nine times as strong in terms of the amount of dependent variable variation it accounts for (0.81 is nine times 0.09).

To clarify the meaning of coefficients of determination, imagine we are trying to understand why some youths in our hypothetical residential treatment center have more serious behavioral incident reports than others, as illustrated in Figure 16.1. For the first pair of overlapping circles in Figure 16.1 (labeled a), suppose one independent variable we consider is the extent to which the youths have a conduct disorder, as measured by a scale we'll call the Conduct Disorder Checklist. Suppose further that the scale lists a variety of serious undesirable behaviors and asks the cottage parent to indicate how often the child exhibits each serious undesirable behavior. Each youth's relative score on the scale should correspond rather closely with the relative number of serious behavioral incident reports they receive, since the scale essentially is just assessing conduct disorder in terms of the frequency of the same types of behavior reflected by the serious incident reports. Thus, the correlation between the two variables might be near-perfect, such as 0.90, with 81% of the variance in each variable being shared with the other variable. Although the 0.90 correlation would be very strong, it might not help us understand why some youths in our hypothetical residential treatment center have more serious behavioral incident reports than others, because both variables are essentially measuring the same thing.

For the second pair of overlapping circles in Figure 16.1 (labeled b), suppose the independent variable is the extent to which the youths had been abused before being admitted to our center. If the correlation between extent of prior abuse and number of serious behavioral incidents is 0.60, then 36% of the variation in the number of serious behavioral incidents is accounted for by the extent of prior abuse. By looking at this correlation alone, we wouldn't know what accounts for the other 64% of the variation in the number of serious behavioral incidents reported. The list of possible

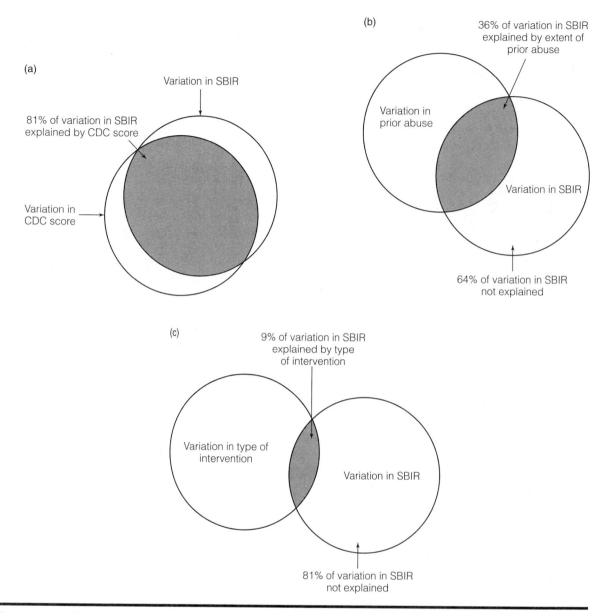

Figure 16.1 Illustration of Three Hypothetical Coefficients of Determination for Variables Correlated with Number of Serious Behavioral Incident Reports (**a**) 0.90 Correlation (0.81 Coefficient of Determination) Between Score on Conduct Disorder Checklist (CDC) and Number of Serious Behavioral Incident Reports (SBIR); (**b**) 0.60 Correlation (0.36 Coefficient of Determination) Between Extent of Prior Abuse and Number of Serious Behavioral Incident Reports (SBIR); (**c**) 0.30 Correlation (0.09 Coefficient of Determination) Between Type of Intervention Group and Number of Serious Behavioral Incident Reports (SBIR)

factors that could be influencing the remaining variation would be extensive. It might include various biological factors, such as the extent to which the youth has an attention deficit hyperactivity disorder or a neurological condition affecting the ability to control one's impulses. It might include vari-

ous factors in the youth's prior social environment, such as peer influences, role models, influences on self-esteem, performance in school, poverty, substance abuse, family disruptions, inadequate supervision or affection from parents, and many others. It might also include some psychological factors, such as intelligence, depression, bipolar disorder, or pre-morbid schizophrenia.

Considering the extensiveness of the list of other possible influences casts a different light on the fact that 64% of the variation in our dependent variable is unaccounted for by our independent variable. The fact that our independent variable accounts for as much as 36% of the variation might seem more impressive when we consider how many factors can influence the variables that practitioners deal with. In light of that consideration, explaining 36% of the variation in a variable becomes much more impressive than, say, scoring 36% on a statistics test!

For the third pair of overlapping circles in Figure 16.1 (labeled c), suppose the independent variable is whether the youth received a particular intervention at our center whose effectiveness we are evaluating. (Because that variable would be nominal, this third correlation coefficient would be nonparametric, but it can be squared and interpreted in the same manner as the parametric correlations discussed above.) If the correlation between type of intervention and number of serious behavioral incidents is 0.30, then 9% of the variation in the number of serious behavioral incidents is accounted for by whether the youth received the intervention.

At first glance 9% may seem trivial, suggesting that the intervention was not very effective even if the 0.30 correlation was statistically significant. Again, however, that 9% becomes more impressive in light of two other considerations. First, with so many biological, psychological, and social forces influencing the problems that practitioners deal with—forces that are largely beyond the control of any type of intervention—having an intervention account for 9% of the variation in a problem is not too shabby.

Second, the coefficient of determination can be a misleadingly low depiction of an intervention's effectiveness. To illustrate how misleading it can be, consider the hypothetical results of an evaluation of an intervention as displayed in Table 16.1. If you plug those results into the formula for calculating phi, you will find that phi equals 0.28, slightly less than the 0.30 correlation for the intervention in part c of Figure 16.1. Squaring 0.28, we get 0.078, again less than the 0.09 coefficient of determination in part c of Figure 16.1. But if we examine the proportions in Table 16.1 (which would be statistically significant in a chi-square analysis at the 0.01 level),

Table 16.1 Illustration of Results of an Evaluation of a Hypothetical Intervention with a Phi of 0.28 ($p < 0.01$) and a Coefficient of Determination of 0.078

	NUMBER OF CLIENTS PER TREATMENT GROUP	
OUTCOME	EXPERIMENTAL (RECEIVED INTERVENTION)	CONTROL (DID NOT RECEIVE INTERVENTION)
Success	64	36
Failure	36	64

we see that 64% of the clients receiving the evaluated intervention had successful outcomes, whereas only 36% of those not receiving it had successful outcomes. For most human service interventions—for example, efforts to prevent school dropout, recidivism by abusive parents or spouses, and so on—making that much of a difference would be considered quite meaningful.

Although it can be misinterpreted, the coefficient of determination is a helpful statistic. It clarifies the meaning of the correlation coefficient, and it is commonly mentioned in reports of research studies. So it is important that you know what it means. Understanding what it means, however, also implies the need to exercise caution in its interpretation. It is commonly misinterpreted by some who seem to think it is akin to a score on an exam. I have encountered professors, for example, who have deemed correlation coefficients as high as 0.30 (with a 0.09 coefficient of determination) as weak. As illustrated in Table 16.1, that interpretation is not applicable to practice evaluation. In fact, as we will see shortly, interventions that have been evaluated and found to be effective—that is, interventions that are considered at least somewhat evidence-based—tend to explain on average about 9% of the variation in the dependent variables they seek to influence!

EFFECT SIZE

Another measure of the strength of a relationship is *effect size*. If that term sounds familiar to you, it's because we examined the most prominent type of effect size statistic back in Chapter 8. That effect size (ES) statistic, you may recall, is based on the *z*-score concept and is calculated as follows:

$$ES = \frac{|(\text{Experimental Group Mean}) - (\text{Control Group Mean})|}{\text{Control Group Standard Deviation}}$$

You are most likely to encounter the above effect size statistic when you read reports of experimental or quasi-experimental evaluations of the effectiveness of interventions in which group means are compared. It is called Cohen's *d*. Sometimes it is referred to as Cohen's *d*, instead of effect size. Some statisticians prefer putting the pooled standard deviation of both groups in the denominator instead of just the control group's standard deviation. When that alternative formula is used, the ES is called the Δ index or just plain Δ. Both formulas usually produce similar ES results.

However, all of the types of correlation coefficients that we have been discussing, as well as the coefficient of determination, are also sometimes called *effect size* statistics. The term *effect size,* then, is synonymous with the term *strength of relationship*. All effect-size statistics, including correlation coefficients or coefficients of determination, enable us to compare the effects of different interventions across studies using different types of outcome measures.

Whereas the Δ or Cohen's *d* ES statistic portrays relationship strength in standard deviation units, correlation approaches to effect size portray relationship strength in terms of a proportion between 0 and 1, or between 0 and 100% of variation explained. Suppose a study sets out to evaluate the effectiveness of Intervention A using a chi-square analysis with nominal variables and finds that Intervention A increases the proportion of youths whose good behavior earns them off-campus privileges from 40% to 60%, with a phi of 0.20 (and a coefficient of determination of 0.04). Suppose another study evaluates Intervention B for the same target population but uses a ratio-level dependent variable and reports its results in terms of the Δ or Cohen's *d* ES statistic. Let's say that Δ or Cohen's *d* = 0.60. How can we compare the meaning of the two effect size statistics in terms of relationship magnitude? In other words, how can we determine which intervention had the stronger effects?

We can answer the above questions by finding the eta statistic for Intervention B's effect size. You may recall from Chapter 15 that eta is a correlation statistic, derived from an ANOVA when the independent variable is nominal and the dependent variable is interval or ratio. You may also recall that eta can be squared and interpreted like other correlations. Thus, if the eta for the Intervention B results is 0.30 (with a coefficient of determination of 0.09), we would conclude that Intervention B had stronger effects than Intervention A, because Intervention A's correlation effect size (phi) was lower at 0.20 (with a coefficient of determination of 0.04).

But how do we find eta? If we conducted the two studies ourselves, or had access to the Intervention B evaluation data, we could obtain it via SPSS, as discussed in Chapter 15. If we did not have access to the Intervention B evaluation data, and only knew its results from a published report, we might find eta by using the following formula:

$$eta = \frac{df_b F}{df_b F + df_w}$$

The numerator in the above formula represents the degrees of freedom between groups times the *F* ratio. The denominator adds the within-groups degrees of freedom to the product in the numerator. Suppose the report of the Intervention B evaluation indicates an *F* ratio of 6.0, with 2 degrees of freedom between groups and 28 degrees of freedom within groups. The numerator would be $2 \times 6 = 12$, and the denominator would be $12 + 28 = 40$. Twelve divided by 40 equals 0.30; thus, eta would be 0.30.

But what if the report of Intervention B's evaluation fails to supply important details such as the *F* ratio or the degrees of freedom? All reports using ANOVA *should* supply such details, but alas, not all do. You might still be able to compare the relative strengths of the two different effect sizes. For example, as will be discussed shortly, we know from meta-analytical literature reviews that the mean effect size reported in evaluations of human service interventions with statistically significant findings is approximately 0.60 when Δ or Cohen's *d* is reported and 0.30 when eta is reported. Thus, if one study reports a Cohen's *d* of 0.60 and another study reports an eta of 0.50, we would know that the latter study's effect size was stronger than the former study's because an eta of 0.50 is well above the mean correlation effect size of 0.30 and thus has stronger than average effects, whereas the former study's d of 0.60 is right at the average for that statistic.

HOW STRONG IS "STRONG"?

When we compare the effect sizes of two or more studies, we can tell whether one effect size is stronger than another. More commonly, however, we conduct or read one study and have to interpret the strength of its effect size without comparing it to any other particular study. What criteria do we then use to decide whether the effect size is weak, moderate, or strong?

How we characterize the strength of an effect size depends in part on how many independent variables we are examining in trying to explain a dependent variable. In Chapter 17 and Appendix D we'll be discussing multivariate analyses. Multivariate analyses may involve assessing how well an entire set of multiple independent variables correlates with one dependent variable. Suppose, for example, one study hypothesizes that a set of 20 independent variables will predict the number of serious behavior incidents among youths and finds that the overall correlation for all 20 variables as a whole with the dependent variable is 0.30. Suppose another study finds that one variable alone has the same 0.30 correlation with that dependent variable. Because a large set of independent variables is involved in the first study, its 0.30 correlation might be deemed relatively weak. Because only one independent variable is involved in the second study, its 0.30 correlation would not be deemed weak. The criteria that we'll be examining in this chapter pertain to bivariate relationships only. That is, they pertain to relationships involving only one independent variable and one dependent variable. If you happen to see other texts or professors using different criteria from the ones in this chapter, chances are those criteria apply to multivariate relationships involving multiple independent variables.

As noted earlier, interpreting effect sizes based on correlation coefficients is unlike interpreting reliability coefficients or scores on exams. Some interventions can have quite valuable effects with correlations of 0.20 or 0.30, even though their coefficients of determination indicate that they are explaining only 4% or 9% of the variation in the dependent variable. For example, if an intervention with parents referred for child abuse reduces recidivism from 60% to 40%, phi would equal only 0.20 despite the fact that the intervention produces a 33% reduction in recidivism (the 20% drop is one-third of 60%).

Fortunately, statisticians have developed standards for interpreting the strength of effect sizes. One esteemed statistician, Jacob Cohen, advocated criteria based on various effect sizes found in studies. According to Cohen (1988), effect sizes should be deemed strong when the correlation is approximately 0.50 or more (or Δ or Cohen's d is approximately 0.80 or more). They should be deemed moderate (or medium) when the correlation coefficient is approximately 0.30 (or Δ or Cohen's d is approximately 0.30). They should be deemed weak when the correlation coefficient is approximately 0.10 or less (or when Δ or Cohen's d is approximately 0.20 or less). Other statisticians have developed similar standards based on calculating the mean effect size and the standard deviation of hundreds of published studies. In light of their rather consistent findings and the fact that their standards are similar to Cohen's guidelines, Table 16.2 displays *approximate* criteria that can be used to describe effect sizes as strong, moderate, or weak. I emphasize the word *approximate* because these are merely rough guidelines.

SUBSTANTIVE (PRACTICAL) SIGNIFICANCE

The various effect size statistics have great value that extends beyond statistical significance to help us interpret whether particular relationships found in one study are strong, moderate, or weak relative to the relationships found in other studies. If two interventions are assessed in the same way, and one yields a stronger effect size than the other, then the effect size statistic can indicate which intervention is more effective. But different studies usually assess different interventions in different ways, and consequently differences in effect sizes might not automatically indicate which intervention is more effective or valuable.

Suppose two different studies evaluate the effectiveness of two different interventions with parents referred for child abuse. One study finds that Intervention A has a moderate Δ of 0.60 (or a moderate

Table 16.2   Approximate Criteria for Interpreting the Strength of Effect Sizes of Bivariate Relationships

	VALUES PER EFFECT SIZE STATISTIC		
STRENGTH	Δ OR COHEN'S *d*	CORRELATION COEFFICIENT	COEFFICIENT OF DETERMINATION
Strong	0.80 or more	0.50 or more	0.25 or more
Moderate to Strong	0.70	0.40	0.16
Moderate	0.45 to 0.65	0.25 to 0.35	0.06 to 0.12
Weak to Moderate	0.40	0.20	0.04
Weak	0.20 or less	0.10 or less	0.01 or less

correlation coefficient of 0.30) in preventing further abuse. The other study finds that Intervention B has a strong Δ of 0.80 (or a strong correlation coefficient of 0.50) in improving scores on a test measuring parent knowledge of proper child disciplinary techniques. If you were starting a new program to intervene with parents referred for child abuse, which of the two interventions would you select for your program (assuming you could afford only one)?

Without demeaning the potential value of Intervention B, chances are you would select Intervention A. Despite its lower effect size, you might prefer an intervention that has been found to prevent actual abuse with a moderate ES over one that has a strong ES in terms of knowing the correct answers on a test, but is of unknown effectiveness in preventing actual abuse.

Thus, effect size statistics, by themselves, do not reveal the meaningfulness or practical importance of research findings. When we ask about the practical value or importance of a relationship—that is, how meaningful it is to clients, significant others, society, or practitioners concerned about a problem—we are inquiring as to the **substantive significance** of that relationship. Because the practical value of a finding is an important issue in considering substantive significance, the terms *substantive significance* and **practical significance** are often used interchangeably. (In fact, one of my Microsoft Word software definitions of "substantive" is as an adjective signifying "with practical importance.")

Here's another example of how statistical significance and a strong effect size do not necessarily

imply substantive (or practical) significance. Suppose an experiment with a large sample is conducted to evaluate an intervention to help extremely obese people lose weight. The participants in the experimental and control groups are at risk for serious health problems due to their obesity. The experimental group participants lose an average of 3 pounds after receiving the intervention. The control group participants lose, on average, no weight during the entire study period, and their standard deviation is 1 pound. Cohen's *d* would equal 3 (3 minus 0 divided by 1). With an adequate sample size, a very strong Cohen's *d* of 3 would be statistically significant at a very low level of significance. Also, the Cohen's *d* of 3 means that the average experimental group participant lost more weight than 99% of the control group participants. But losing only 3 pounds would have virtually no substantive significance for the extremely obese participants, society, or anyone else concerned about the health implications of their obesity. Losing 3 pounds would not have a meaningful impact on their quality of life or their risk of life-threatening health problems.

Likewise, if an intervention for spouse abusers lowered the number of times they abused their spouse from twice a month to once a month, regardless of statistical significance and no matter how strong the effect size, we might be far from satisfied with the substantive significance of the intervention. Unfortunately, however, there are no universally accepted standards—statistical or otherwise—that we can use to assess substantive significance in the way we can calculate statistical significance. Ultimately, the substantive significance of any statistical finding depends on idiosyncratic value judgments about the meaningfulness of the finding and its practical value to clients, significant others, society, or practitioners concerned about a problem to which that finding pertains. Those value judgments might consider any number of intangibles, such as whether the benefits of revising services or policies based on the implications of the finding outweigh the costs of the revisions, whether the variables assessed in the finding are really important, whether the finding adds much to what is already known, and whether previous studies have already had other findings with more important implications. For example, if previous studies have consistently shown that Intervention A prevents recidivism among 95% of spouse abusers who receive it, and a new study shows that a Intervention B prevents recidivism among 80% of service recipients, then some may judge the latter finding to have very limited substantive significance since its effect size is less than Intervention A's effect size.

CLINICAL SIGNIFICANCE

When referring to the substantive significance of studies evaluating the effectiveness of *clinical* interventions, the term *clinical significance* is usually used instead of the term *substantive significance*. These terms are largely synonymous, but the literature on clinical significance includes some distinctive concepts and measurement approaches.

Clinical significance refers not only to the meaningfulness and practical value of the overall findings of a study—in terms of an intervention's ES, for example. It also refers to the meaningfulness and practical value of the benefits of an intervention for *each individual* recipient of the evaluated intervention.

Suppose an evaluation of an intervention for spouse abusers finds that one-third of the recipients in the experimental group did not change at all, one-third reduced the frequency of abuse by only a trivial amount, and one-third never again perpetrated any abuse. Because of the impact of the latter one-third, a statistically significant and very large mean difference might be found between an experimental group and a control group in which no improvements occurred. While the overall effect size might be deemed *substantively significant,* the

intervention would be deemed *clinically significant* only for the one-third of recipients who never recidivated.

Thus, researchers and practitioners concerned about clinical significance will not be satisfied with just knowing the overall ES and judging its meaningfulness—they will want to know how many *individual* clients in each group experienced clinically significant improvements. In fact, they might want to conduct a test of statistical significance to find the probability that sampling error might account for the difference in the proportion of clients in each group experiencing clinically significant improvements.

Three statistical approaches have been proposed—primarily in clinical psychology journals—for measuring clinical significance among individual clients. Each statistical approach is controversial and is arguably of limited relevance to many practitioners, especially those working with clients with severe and persistent disorders. One approach emphasizes something called *statistically reliable change*. Different statistical methods have been developed using this approach, each of which applies a formula separately to every client to assess whether their amount of change from pretest to posttest can be attributed to measurement error. One problem with this approach is that many studies do not use pretests. For example, this approach would be inapplicable to evaluating whether an intervention prevents recidivism among spouse abusers. Another problem is that this approach does not guarantee that the type or amount of change will be meaningful to clients or anyone else. Even if we have pretest and posttest scores regarding spouse abuse, for example, if the degree of measurement error is very small then a reduction in abusive incidents from four times a month to three times a month could be statistically reliable according to a statistically reliable change formula without really being clinically significant to anyone. That is, the formula would only enable us to eliminate measurement error as the explanation for a trivial amount of change. It would not necessarily depict the meaningfulness or practical value of that change.

Moreover, even if the amount of change is large, this approach does not ensure that the dependent variable being measured adequately reflects the problem that clients or others really care about.

If substance-abusing parents referred for child abuse receive a parent education intervention and then show a large and statistically reliable increase in correct answers on a child-rearing exam, skeptics might still doubt the clinical significance of that finding as to whether it really reflects any meaningful change in abusive behavior by parents in stressful situations or under the influence of drugs or alcohol.

A second statistical approach to clinical significance emphasizes *recovery* and the use of *normative comparisons*. One way to use this approach is to conduct diagnostic interviews before and after treatment and to see whether clients who meet the criteria for a particular disorder before treatment no longer meet those criteria after treatment. Another way is to compare client scores on a measurement instrument to existing norms for that instrument. This approach requires the use of instruments that have had norms established for populations with and without a particular disorder or at different levels of that disorder. The idea would be to see if clients whose pretest scores were not far from the mean of the clinical population (those with the disorder) had posttest scores that were closer to the mean of the normal population than the mean of the clinical population. For example, suppose previous large-scale studies have established that the mean on a depression scale is 50 for people in treatment for depression, with a standard deviation of 10, while the mean and standard deviation of people not in treatment for depression are 20 and 5. Clients who score 40 at pretest are only one standard deviation below the clinical mean but four standard deviations above the normal mean. But if their scores drop to 25 at posttest, they would be only one standard deviation above the normal mean but 2.5 standard deviations below the clinical mean. Their improvement would therefore be deemed clinically significant because they moved from having a high probability of being in the clinical distribution and a low probability of being in the normal distribution to the reverse—that is, having a high probability of being in the normal distribution and a low probability of being in the clinical distribution.

One problem with this approach is that many measures of treatment outcome have not had norms established that enable such comparisons. Another problem is that many clients with severe or chronic impairments can make improvements that are meaningful to themselves and others without having to become free of the impairment or "normal." Practitioners can help clients with severe and persistent mental or physical disabilities make meaningful improvements in their quality of life without having them recover from their disability completely. Likewise, helping people who are so severely depressed that they cannot function become moderately depressed and able to perform chores of daily living may have immense value even if their depression scores remain in the clinical range. Thus, if a scale has norms for different levels of depression, then showing that treatment moved people from the severe range to the moderate or mild range might be a more reasonable way to use a normative approach to clinical significance than to require that they be free of depression in order for the improvement to be clinically significant. But even that less stringent approach may not apply to helping people whose disorder remains severe, but who are helped to improve their quality of life while coping with their severe disorder. For example, helping someone suffering from schizophrenia keep a job, avoid homelessness, and stay out of the hospital might have great clinical significance even if the severity of the schizophrenia is not reduced.

A third statistical approach to clinical significance combines the above two approaches. Thus, it is even more stringent than either of the above approaches because it requires statistically reliable change from pretest to posttest as well as movement from a clinical distribution to a normal distribution. In combining the above two approaches, it combines their problems and has even less applicability to most clinical evaluations.

In contrast to the above statistical approaches is the perspective that clinical significance is a subjective phenomenon that depends on the nature of the problem being treated, the goals of treatment, and who is judging the clinical significance. Suppose a therapist believes that the reason a husband is emotionally abusive to his wife is his low self-esteem. Suppose that as a result of therapy, the husband feels more positive about himself despite the fact that he is no less abusive to his wife. The husband may feel that the treatment was clinically significant. The therapist may feel the same way, especially if clinical significance is judged statistically in terms of pretest to posttest improvements on a self-esteem scale. His wife, however, would probably disagree. Because the level of emotional abuse has not changed, his wife—as well as society—would probably deem the treatment effects to be clinically insignificant.

Despite the elusive nature of clinical significance and substantive significance, it is important that you address these issues when discussing the results of your evaluation. Although you may have to recognize that people might disagree about whether your results are clinically or substantively significant, it is better to discuss the different perspectives than to avoid the issue altogether and perhaps imply that because your findings are statistically significant or involve moderate to large effect sizes they are automatically of great value and meaningfulness from a practical standpoint. You might even want to apply one of the statistical approaches to clinical significance in your analysis and interpretation of your data. Despite the problems inherent in those approaches, if they are applicable to your outcome measure then reporting them will help readers who prefer a statistical approach to judge the clinical significance of your findings from their standpoint. Moreover, if you can use one of the statistical approaches, but do not, readers who value those approaches may view your study more skeptically. By the same token, if you do not use one of the statistical approaches, you should probably explain why you didn't. That way, at least, readers will see that you understand those approaches and did not just omit them as an oversight or because you don't know about them. On the other hand, if you do use one of the statistical approaches, you should point out its limitations and discuss alternative subjective perspectives on the clinical significance of your findings.

The foregoing recommendations are even more important if you are writing a research proposal for funding. Among those rating your proposal might be some reviewers who are particular keen on measuring clinical significance statistically. It won't hurt to include a statistical approach in your proposal, accompanied perhaps by an explanation of its limitations and the need to consider clinical significance from alternative perspectives as well. Additional statistical information on each of the above three approaches to clinical significance is provided in an online appendix, titled *Assessing Clinical Significance Statistically*. You can find that appendix by going to this book's Wadsworth web site at <http://www.wadsworth.com/helping_profs/>.

STATISTICAL POWER ANALYSIS

Some studies have sample sizes that are so small that researchers have little likelihood of being able to refute sampling error even with effect sizes that most would agree are substantively or clinically significant. For example, we might agree that reducing recidivism among spouse abusers by 20% is clinically significant, but with a sample of only 10 clients it is very unlikely that we would attain statistically significant results even if our intervention would reduce recidivism by 20% if provided to the population of spouse abusers.

If we fail to rule out sampling error—that is, if our findings are not statistically significant—when we are evaluating an intervention that really is effective, then we have committed a Type II error. And if the true effects of the intervention that we have evaluated are of a magnitude that would be substantively or clinically significant, then we have committed a particularly unfortunate Type II error.

In Chapter 11 we saw that researchers reduce the probability of making a Type II error by increasing their sample size. However, we have not yet discussed how they can assess their degree of risk of making a Type II error. We have saved that assessment for this chapter because it requires an understanding of measuring and interpreting the strength of relationships.

A statistical significance test only assesses the probability of committing a Type I error—of incorrectly rejecting a null hypothesis that is true. Assessing the probability of committing a Type II error is called **statistical power analysis.** The statistical power of a study is its probability of correctly rejecting a null hypothesis that is false and thus avoiding a Type II error. Conversely, the probability of committing a Type II error is 1 minus statistical power. Thus, if statistical power equals 0.90, then the probability of committing a Type II error is 0.10. Likewise, if the probability of committing a Type II error is 0.20, then the statistical power is 0.80.

A study's statistical power will be influenced by its sample size, the effect size it assumes in the population for the hypothesis it tests, the significance level selected, and various other methodological factors, such as the reliability of its measurement instruments and strength of its research design. The formulas used in calculating a study's statistical power are too complex for an introductory statistics text like this. You can find those formulas in a book titled *Statistical Power Analysis for the Behavioral Sciences* by Jacob Cohen (1988). Also in that book you can find tables that enable you to identify a study's statistical power rather simply without performing calculations. Cohen constructed different tables for different statistical significance tests. The tables show different levels of statistical power for different levels of significance, different sample sizes, and different effect sizes.

Based on the figures in Cohen's tables, Table 16.3 displays the power of testing the significance of correlation coefficients at the 0.05 and 0.10 levels of significance for small, moderate, and large effect sizes. The statistical power levels in Cohen's tables for other types of significance tests are similar to those in Table 16.3. Therefore, you can use Table 16.3 to plan a research study even if your significance test does not involve correlation coefficients. However, for greater precision, I recommend using Cohen's book and tables.

When using a statistical power analysis table to plan a research study, we first choose a significance level. Next we estimate the effect size that we assume to exist in the population between our independent and dependent variables. For example, the columns in Table 16.3 are for small ($r = 0.10$; $r^2 = 0.01$), moderate ($r = 0.30$; $r^2 = 0.09$), and large ($r = 0.50$; $r^2 = 0.25$) effect sizes. (You can find the power for other effect sizes in Cohen's book.)

Students often ask, "What basis is there for assuming an effect size in the population before we conduct our study and obtain our findings?" While there is no way to know the true effect size before collecting our data, there are some bases for making reasonable assumptions. One basis is to suppose that the intervention we want to evaluate has a moderate effect size. We might use Cohen's standard of a Δ or Cohen's d of 0.5 or a correlation coefficient of about 0.30 for our assumed moderate effect size. On the other hand, we might want to assume a weaker effect size, especially if even a weak effect size would have substantive or clinical significance. Perhaps the best alternative is to find in the table the statistical power for a variety of

effect sizes, so that we know how likely we are to attain statistically significant findings for each.

Another question often asked is as follows: "How do statistical power analyses indicate in advance the probability of committing a Type II error when it is impossible to know in advance whether the null hypothesis is false or true?" This question is based on the incorrect notion that if our statistical power is low and we fail to reject the null hypothesis, then the null hypothesis must have been false and we must have been wrong in not rejecting it. But our statistical power says nothing about the actual truth or falsity of the null hypothesis; it only tells us the probability that we will reject the null hypothesis if it really happens to be false. Thus, when conducting a statistical power analysis in planning a study, we suppose that the null hypothesis really is false and that the relationship we are testing really has a particular effect size. Then we ascertain the probability that we will avoid making a Type II error *based on those assumptions*.

To illustrate how to use statistical power tables, let's assume a moderate effect size with a Pearson's r of 0.30 ($r^2 = 0.09$). In Table 16.3 we would locate one of the columns for that effect size. In that column we can find the statistical power for that effect size at different levels of sample size. If we imagine a decimal point before each figure in that column, that figure (i.e., the statistical power) tells us the probability of correctly rejecting a false null hypothesis for the different sample sizes that are listed in the "Sample Size" column.

If you scan down the column, you can see how statistical power—that is, the probability of correctly rejecting a false null hypothesis—increases as sample size increases. For example, if our sample size is only 20 cases and our significance level is 0.05, then our probability of correctly rejecting a false null hypothesis (our statistical power) is only 0.25. Thus, we would have a probability of 1.00 minus 0.25, or 0.75, of incorrectly accepting a false null hypothesis and thus committing a Type II error. But if our sample size is 100 cases, then our power would be 0.86 and our probability of committing a Type II error would be only 0.14. Cohen recommends 0.20 as the maximum acceptable probability of committing a Type II error. Accordingly, he recommends 0.80 as the minimum acceptable level of statistical power. These standards have become generally accepted in the social sciences.

Table 16.3 Power of Test of Significance of Correlation Coefficient by Level of Significance, Effect Size, and Sample Size[a]

	0.05 SIGNIFICANCE LEVEL			0.10 SIGNIFICANCE LEVEL[b]			
	EFFECT SIZE			EFFECT SIZE			
	SMALL	MODERATE	LARGE	SMALL	MODERATE	LARGE	
SAMPLE SIZE[a]	$r = 0.10$ $r^2 = 0.01$	$r = 0.30$ $r^2 = 0.09$	$r = 0.50$ $r^2 = 0.25$	$r = 0.10$ $r^2 = 0.01$	$r = 0.30$ $r^2 = 0.09$	$r = 0.50$ $r^2 = 0.25$	SAMPLE SIZE[a]
10	06	13	33	11	22	46	10
20	07	25	64	13	37	75	20
30	08	37	83	15	50	90	30
40	09	48	92	16	60	96	40
50	11	57	97	18	69	98	50
60	12	65	99	20	76	99	60
70	13	72	*	22	82	*	70
80	14	78		23	86		80
90	16	83		25	90		90
100	17	86		27	92		100
200	29	99		41	*		200
300	41	*		54			300
400	52			64			400
500	61			72			500
600	69			79			600
700	76			84			700
800	81			88			800
900	85			91			900
1000	89			94			1000

[a] The figures in this table are approximately the same as for tables on chi-square test (with a 2-by-2 table) and *t*-tests. For *t*-tests, the number of cases in each group, added together, would approximate the sample size in this table.

[b] The figures at each level of significance are for a two-tailed test; however, the power figures at the 0.10 level approximate the power of one-tailed tests at the 0.05 level.

*Power values below this point exceed 0.995.

The figures for this table were derived from tables in Jacob Cohen, *Statistical Power Analysis for the Behavioral Sciences*, 2nd ed., New York: Lawrence Erlbaum Associates, Inc. 1988.

By using a statistical power table, you can select a sample size that will provide you with the level of statistical power (and the level of risk of a Type II error) that you desire. In many clinical evaluation studies it is impossible to obtain a sample large enough to attain statistical power of 0.80 with a 0.05 significance level. When that happens, it is reasonable to increase your statistical power by raising your significance level to 0.10. Suppose we are able to obtain the participation of only 60 clients in an outcome evaluation of an intervention's effectiveness. Consulting Table 16.3, we can see that by increasing our significance level from 0.05 to 0.10 and assuming a moderate effect size, we would increase our statistical power from 0.65 to 0.76 and thus reduce our Type II error probability from 0.35 to 0.24. Although our statistical power would still fall short of Cohen's recommended minimum, it comes very close to that minimum with a 0.10 significance level.

Although we should do all we can to increase our sample size and statistical power, in practice settings it is often impossible to meet Cohen's standard. If evaluations of practice effectiveness were not done unless Cohen's statistical power standard had been met, there would be far fewer evaluations of practice or programs. Many would agree that it is usually better to conduct an evaluation with less than 0.80 power than to conduct no evaluation. Perhaps the effect size will be larger than moderate, and we will learn that an intervention has statistically significant and clinically significant effects in a study with less than ideal power.

But even when our findings are not statistically significant, if our effect size is large enough our findings may be useful. On the one hand, we cannot call an effect size clinically significant if we cannot rule out sampling error as a very implausible explanation for that finding. But if our study's sample size is small and our statistical power therefore low, and if the effect size we actually find is at a level that would have been clinically significant and statistically significant in a study with more power, then our high risk of a Type II error implies the need to evaluate the intervention further. Future studies, especially those with more power than ours, may find that the intervention we evaluated has clinically significant effects. Some even believe that clinical outcome evaluations with low statistical power should eschew statistical significance testing and instead merely report effect sizes as descriptive statistics, rather than attempt to rule out sampling error with too much risk of a Type II error. If future studies consistently replicate a meaningful effect size, those replications can serve to rule out sampling error.

Although statistical power analyses are commonly conducted in planning a study to determine the needed sample size, they also can be conducted as part of the data analysis in a completed study that failed to obtain statistically significant results.

In the latter case, the effect size in the findings, rather than an assumed effect size, can be used in assessing power. Readers can be informed of the Type II error probability associated with that effect size. If the effect size is meaningful and statistical power is low, then the evaluated intervention should not be dismissed as simply ineffective, particularly if it is being applied to a problem for which there are no known evidence-based interventions.

Main Points

• "Statistically significant" does not necessarily mean strong or important, and relationships that are strong or important are not always statistically significant.

• The coefficient of determination, symbolized by r^2, tells us what proportion of variance in the dependent variable is explained by the independent variable.

• The term *effect size* is synonymous with the term *strength of relationship*. All effect-size statistics, including correlation coefficients or coefficients of determination, enable us to compare the effects of different interventions across studies using different types of outcome measures. Whereas the Δ or Cohen's *d* effect size statistic portrays relationship strength in standard deviation units, correlation approaches to effect size portray relationship strength in terms of a proportion between 0 and 1, or between 0 and 100% of variation explained.

• A formula can be used to obtain eta in studies that report Δ or Cohen's *d*. This enables us to compare the relative effect sizes of studies using different effect size statistics.

• Statisticians have developed standards for interpreting the strength of effect sizes. Effect sizes can be deemed strong when the correlation is approximately 0.50 or more (or Δ or Cohen's *d* is approximately 0.80 or more). They can be deemed moderate (or medium) when the correlation coefficient is approximately 0.30 (or Δ or Cohen's *d* is approximately 0.50). They can be deemed weak when the correlation coefficient is approximately 0.10 or less (or Δ or Cohen's *d* is approximately 0.20 or less).

• Differences in effect sizes might not automatically indicate which intervention is more effective or valuable.

• When we ask about the practical value or importance of a relationship—that is, how meaningful it is to clients, significant others, society, or practitioners concerned about a problem—we are inquiring as to the substantive significance of that relationship.

• When referring to the substantive (or practical) significance of studies evaluating the effectiveness of *clinical* interventions, the term *clinical significance* is usually used instead of the term *substantive significance*. These terms are largely synonymous, but the literature on clinical significance includes some distinctive concepts and measurement approaches.

• Clinical significance refers not only to the meaningfulness and practical value of the overall findings of a study; it also refers to the meaningfulness and practical value of the benefits of an intervention for *each individual* recipient of the evaluated intervention.

• Three statistical approaches have been proposed for measuring clinical significance among individual clients. Each approach is controversial and is arguably of limited relevance to many practitioners. Nevertheless, if you are writing a research proposal for funding, among those rating your proposal might be some reviewers who are particular keen on measuring clinical significance statistically. Therefore, it won't hurt to include a statistical approach in your proposal, accompanied perhaps by an explanation of its limitations and the need to consider clinical significance from alternative perspectives as well.

• Some studies have sample sizes that are so small that researchers have little likelihood of being able to refute sampling error even with effect sizes that most would agree are substantively or clinically significant.

• Assessing the probability of committing a Type II error is called *statistical power analysis*. The statistical power of a study is its probability of correctly rejecting a null hypothesis that is false and thus avoiding a Type II error. Conversely, the probability of committing a Type II error is 1 minus statistical power. Thus, if statistical power equals 0.90, then the probability of committing a Type II error is 0.10. Likewise, if the probability of committing a Type II error is 0.20, then the statistical power is 0.80.

• A study's statistical power will be influenced by its sample size, the effect size it assumes in the population for the hypothesis it tests, the significance level selected, and various other methodological factors, such as the reliability of its measurement instruments and strength of its research design.

• Although statistical power analyses are commonly conducted in planning a study to determine the needed sample size, they also can be conducted as part of the data analysis in a completed study that failed to obtain statistically significant results. In the latter case, the effect size in the findings, rather than an assumed effect size, can be used in assessing power. Readers can be informed of the Type II error probability associated with that effect size. If the effect size is meaningful and power is low, then the evaluated intervention should not be dismissed as simply ineffective, particularly if it is being applied to a problem for which there are no known evidence-based interventions.

Review Questions and Exercises

1. A study is conducted evaluating motivational Intervention A, which aims to motivate substance-abusing adolescents to complete a 12-session treatment program. It finds that of the 100 youths receiving motivational Intervention A, the mean number of sessions attended is 4, with only 10 youths completing the treatment program and the other 90 dropping out in less than 6 sessions. The control group, which did not receive the motivational intervention, attended from 0 to 4 sessions, with a mean of 2 and a standard deviation of 0.5. The results are statistically significant ($p < 0.001$).

a. Calculate the study's Cohen's *d*.

b. Is that *d* considered strong, moderate, or weak? Why?

c. Would you consider the effects of Intervention A to be clinically significant? Why or why not?

2. A study is conducted evaluating motivational Intervention B, which also aims to motivate substance-abusing adolescents to complete the same 12-session treatment program. It finds that of the 100 youths receiving motivational Intervention B, the mean number of sessions attended is 5, with 30 youths completing the treatment program and the other 70 dropping out in less than 6 sessions. The control group, which did not receive the motivational intervention, attended from 0 to 8 sessions, with a mean of 4 and a standard deviation of 1.0. The results are statistically significant ($p < 0.05$).

a. Calculate the study's Cohen's d.

b. Is that d considered strong, moderate, or weak? Why?

c. Would you consider the effects of Intervention B to be clinically significant? Why or why not?

3. In light of the results of the above two studies, which of the two interventions, Intervention A or Intervention B, would you consider to be more clinically significant? Why or why not?

4. Another study evaluates the effectiveness of the above treatment program for the youths in the experimental group who complete all 12 sessions. It finds that 80% of those youths self-report that they abstained from any further substance abuse, while 20% self-report that they continued to abuse substances. In the control group, 20% of the youths self-report that they abstained from any further substance abuse, while 80% self-report that they continued to abuse substances. The results are statistically significant ($p < 0.001$), with a nonparametric correlation coefficient (phi) of 0.60. Would you consider the results to be clinically significant? Why or why not?

5. An alternative treatment program for substance-abusing youths is evaluated in terms of re-arrest rates for substance abuse. It finds that 20% of the youths in the experimental group are re-arrested after completing the treatment, as compared to 40% of the youths in the control group. The results are statistically significant ($p < 0.05$), with a nonparametric correlation coefficient (phi) of 0.20.

a. Would you consider the results to be clinically significant? Why or why not?

b. Which of the two treatment programs—the one in number 4 above, or the alternative one in number 5—would you consider to have had a more clinically significant effect? Why or why not?

6. The effectiveness of an intervention to prevent substance abuse is evaluated with a sample size of 30 participants. The dependent variable is a valid measure of future substance abuse. Its results show

that a Δ of 0.5 is *not* statistically significant at the selected 0.05 level of significance. The effectiveness of another intervention to prevent substance abuse is evaluated with a sample size of 1000 participants. The dependent variable is a self-report measure of substance abuse. Its results show that a Δ of 0.2 is statistically significant at the selected 0.05 level of significance.

a. What is the statistical power of each study? (In using Table 16.3 to answer this question, disregard the correlation headings in that table. Instead, just refer to the words *small, moderate,* and *large* because Δ is a z-score statistic, not a correlation.)

b. What is the Type II error probability of each study?

c. In light of statistical power and substantive (practical) significance considerations, what do the results of these two studies imply for practice and future research?

InfoTrac Exercises

1. After reading the following article, briefly discuss something in it that you learned and think is helpful to know as an evidence-based practitioner:

Trusty, J., Thompson, B., & Petrocelli, J. V. (2004). Practical guide for reporting effect size in quantitative research in the Journal of Counseling and Development. *Journal of Counseling and Development, 82*(1), 107–110.

2. Briefly discuss how the findings in Table 2 in the article below illustrate the relationship between effect size and statistical power. (The term *post hoc* in the table means that the statistical power analysis was conducted after the study was completed and the effect sizes were calculated.)

Hinkelman, L., & Granello, D. H. (2003). Biological sex, adherence to traditional gender roles, and attitudes toward persons with mental illness: An exploratory investigation. *Journal of Mental Health Counseling, 25*(4), 259–270.

3. For the article below, calculate the Δ (effect size) for each of the three statistically significant t-Test findings, using the data in the "Difference" columns of Table 2. Do you agree with how the authors implicitly interpreted the clinical (or substantive) significance of these three findings and drew implications for practice? Briefly state why or why not.

Roberts, C. S., Piper, L., Denny, J., & Cuddeback, G. (1997). A support group intervention to facilitate young adults' adjustment to cancer. *Health and Social Work, 22*(2), 133–141.

Regression Analysis

INTRODUCTION

In the previous two chapters we looked at correlation as a measure of the direction and strength of the relationship between two variables. We saw the various uses of correlations in research and evaluation and in guiding evidence-based practice. In this chapter we'll examine another important way in which the correlation concepts we've been discussing can guide practice: by helping us make relatively accurate and useful predictions.

You may realize that we've already alluded to prediction in the previous chapters. For example, we saw that when two interval- or ratio-level variables are correlated, it means that knowing whether an individual is low, medium, or high on one variable improves the accuracy with which we can predict whether he or she is low, medium, or high on the other variable. We also saw that with a perfect ($+1.0$ or -1.0) correlation, knowing the value of one variable enables us to predict with perfect accuracy the value of the other variable. And with no correlation, knowing one variable's value offers no help whatsoever in predicting the other variable's value.

When we want to predict specific future values for use in practice, we use **regression analysis.** Regression analysis is a form of correlation analysis that employs an equation enabling us to predict the value of one variable based on the value of another variable. For example, suppose you are the clinical coordinator in a residential treatment center like the one in the hypothetical evaluation we've returned to throughout this text. Suppose you would like to be able to identify with a reasonable degree of accuracy those new admissions who are going to have more serious behavioral incidents than other new admissions during their stay at your center. Being able to predict this will be useful in making clinical decisions about the cottage in which a new admission will live, which therapist to assign, whether to assign the new admission to a particular intervention modality geared for the most or the least disturbed youths, and so on.

Suppose you find a fairly strong correlation between the score on a trauma symptom scale upon admission and the number of serious behavioral incidents later reported during the youth's stay at the center. You could conduct a regression analysis that will identify how many serious behavioral incidents you can predict for future new admissions based on

their scale scores upon admission. Based on those predictions, you could decide what cottage, therapist, intervention, and so on are most appropriate for the new admission.

THE REGRESSION EQUATION

As noted above, we use a regression equation to predict one variable's values based on another variable's values. To do so, however, our data must meet the assumptions discussed in Chapter 15 regarding Pearson's r. Thus, our data must be at the interval or ratio level of measurement, reasonably linear in the scatterplot, and homoscedastic (which means that the degrees of variance in the two variables being correlated are similar). Of course, it's also necessary that the two variables in question be correlated. By definition, an absence of correlation means that knowing one variable's value is of no help in predicting the other variable's value.

If our data meet the above assumptions, we can apply the following **regression equation:**

$$Y' = a + bX$$

where Y' = the value of variable Y predicted from a known particular X value

   a = the point where the regression line intersects the y-axis

   b = the slope of the regression line, determined by the amount of change in Y for each amount of change in X

   X = the value of the X variable used to predict Y'

We use the symbol Y' in the above equation instead of just Y to signify that we are dealing with a *predicted* value and not an actual one. The equation provides our best basis for predicting the Y value, but it does not guarantee that the prediction will be precise in every case. It's our best prediction because the equation attempts to average the various distances on the y-axis for each value along the x-axis. That is, it enables us to draw a line where the sum of squared distances (or deviations) of the actual data points from the line will be minimized. That's why the regression equation is also called the *least-squares regression equation.*

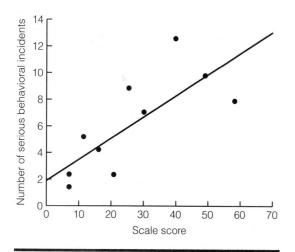

Figure 17.1   Scatterplot with Regression Line for Predicting Number of Serious Behavioral Incidents Based on Trauma Symptoms Scale Scores for Ten Clients

For example, suppose we want to predict the number of future serious behavioral incidents in a residential treatment center based on scores on a trauma symptoms scale completed by clients upon admission. The box "Applying the Least-Squares Regression Equation to Data for Ten Fictional Clients" shows how that would be done. Figure 17.1 displays the regression line on a scatterplot based on the results of the calculations. Notice that the line comes close to the data points but does not hit most of them. Notice also how the line attempts to balance the y-axis value distances above and below the line.

To predict a specific new admission's future number of serious behavioral incidents, we would plug his or her trauma scale score into the formula as the X value after the slope. That is, it would be the X value in that part of the equation that reads bX. But before we could draw the regression line and thus find where the predicted Y′ value is for that new admission on the regression line, we have to calculate the a and the b in the equation. The a in the equation tells us where the regression line starts along the y-axis. That is, it shows us where the regression line intersects the vertical y-axis line, which is where we'd begin to draw the regression line. The b in the equation shows us the slope we would use as we draw the line moving from our starting point along the y-axis to the right as the line moves higher and lower above the various x-axis values.

For example, if we are dealing with a positive correlation, the b value will tell us how steep the increases should be in the line as it moves higher and higher while going to the right. If we are dealing with a negative (inverse) correlation, the b value will indicate how steeply the line should descend as it moves lower and lower while going to the right. With our example of predicting the future number of serious behavioral incidents based on a trauma symptoms scale score at admission, we'll assume that there is a positive correlation, with higher scale scores predicting more incidents.

Let's suppose our next new admission, Sam, scores 10 on the scale. To predict Sam's number of future incidents we multiply that score, 10, times the b value (0.16) that we find when we apply the equation for ascertaining the slope, as illustrated in the box, "Applying the Least-Squares Regression Equation to Data for Ten Fictional Clients." Next we add that product to the starting point (a) on the y-axis. Thus, we multiply 10 times 0.16 and get 1.6 and then add the 1.6 product to the a value (1.9) as illustrated in the box. This would give us 3.5 for Sam's predicted number of serious behavioral incidents. Likewise (as shown in the box), if new client Jill's scale score is 50, then her predicted number of serious behavior incidents is $1.9 + (50)(0.16) = 1.9 + 8.0 = 9.9$.

Let's now re-examine Figure 17.1. If we find Sam's score of 10 on the x-axis and then look above it, we can see that the point on the regression line directly above it corresponds to a value of 3.5 on the y-axis. Likewise, if we find Jill's score of 50 on the x-axis and then look above it, we can see that the point on the regression line directly above it corresponds to a value of 9.9 on the y-axis. This illustrates how the regression line predicts the Y′ values for each known X value.

Most of these predictions will not turn out to be precisely accurate. For example, it is impossible for one client to get precisely 3.5 incidents or 9.9 incidents. A single client can only get a whole number, perhaps somewhere near 3 or 4 incidents for the 3.5 prediction or near 10 incidents for the 9.9 prediction. However, if you got these two predicted scores for Sam and Jill, they will tell you approximately how many incidents it is reasonable to expect from each of them, and this information can be used in clinical planning. You might not, for example, want to place all the new clients with predictions like Jill's in the same cottage. On the other hand, maybe your clinical strategy is to have one cottage for youths with the least incidents, one with the most, and one in the middle. If so, you'd want to assign Sam and Jill to cabins where other youths have been predicted to have a similar number of incidents. Either way, this regression information would help you decide where to place each new client.

Most statistical software programs (like SPSS) can do all of the regression calculations that we have discussed for you. To see how to use SPSS for this purpose, examine the section headed "Using SPSS to Obtain a Regression Line and Calculate the Regression Equation (Chapter 17)" in Appendix G.

Nevertheless, going through all of these steps manually (as we have just done) may help you better comprehend the meaning of the results you get from your software program as well as how those results can be applied to practice decisions. But remember, if the correlation between X and Y is very weak (near 0.0), using regression will be of little or no value to your decision making. The great degree of dispersion of Y values for every X value would render your predictions so inaccurate that they would be useless.

More on the Meaning of Slope

As mentioned above, the regression coefficient (b) refers to the slope of the regression line, determined by the amount of change in a dependent variable (Y) for each amount of change in a predictor variable (X). The term *slope* in regression analysis is analogous to the slope (or steepness) of a hill. A higher b value signifies a steeper hill. Likewise, the X value is analogous to horizontal distance, and the Y value is analogous to the amount of rise or fall in altitude with each unit of horizontal distance.

Imagine, for example, that you are climbing up a very steep hill. One step might take you 20 inches forward and 12 inches higher. The b value, or *slope,* would mean that for every change of 20 inches horizontally (X), you increase 12 inches in altitude (Y). In other words, for every inch of change in X you change 0.60 inches in Y (12 equals 0.60 times 20). If you were walking down the same hill, you'd have the same b value, or *slope,* but because you are descending the b value is preceded by a minus sign, signifying that for every increase of horizontal distance there is a decrease in altitude.

Applying the Least-Squares Regression Equation to Data for Ten Fictional Clients

The following steps are necessary before we can calculate the least-squares regression line manually:

1. List all the pairs of values for two variables for each case in the sample.

2. Sum the values separately for each variable.

3. Square each X value for each case.

4. Multiply each pair of values for each case.

5. Sum the product of the two values multiplied in Step 4.

6. Sum the squares (from Step 3) for the first (X) variable.

7. Plug the sums obtained in the above steps into the following formula to find b, which is

the slope of the regression line:

$$b = \frac{N \Sigma XY - (\Sigma X)(\Sigma Y)}{N \Sigma X^2 - (\Sigma X)^2}$$

where

ΣX is the sum of the values for the first variable (X)

ΣY is the sum of the values for the second variable (Y)

ΣXY is the sum of the products from multiplying each X value by each Y value

ΣX^2 is the sum of the squares of each X value

8. Find the mean of the Y values and the mean of the X values, and plug those means into the following formula to find a (the y-intercept, where the regression line intersects the y-axis):

$$a = \bar{Y} - b\bar{X}$$

where

$\bar{Y}$ = the mean of the Y values

$\bar{X}$ = the mean of the Y values

$b\bar{X}$ = the slope (b) times the mean of the X values

To illustrate how to apply the above formula, suppose we have an N of 10 clients, with data in the chart below. Variable X values are clients' scores on a trauma symptoms scale upon their admission to a residential treatment center. Variable Y values are their numbers of subsequent serious behavioral incidents during their stay at the center. The column headed X^2 lists the square of each scale score. The column headed Y^2 lists the square of each value for number of serious behavioral incidents. The column headed XY lists the products from multipling each X value by each Y value.

Plugging the above sums for our N of 10 into the above least-squares regression formula,

we get the following value for the slope (b):

$$b = \frac{(10)(2103) - (263)(61)}{(10)(10,039) - (263)^2}$$

$$= \frac{21,030 - 16,043}{100,390 - 69,169}$$

$$= \frac{4987}{31,221}$$

$$= 0.16$$

Thus, the slope is 0.16, meaning that for every increase of 1 point in scale scores there is a 0.16 increase in the number of serious behavioral incidents. Next we find a by plugging in the means of the X column and the Y column into the formula for a. Because we have 10 cases, the means will be $263/10 = 26.3$ for X and $61/10 = 6.1$ for Y. Thus,

$$a = 6.1 - [(0.16)(26.3)]$$

$$= 6.1 - 4.2$$

$$= 1.9$$

Therefore, we will start drawing our regression line at 1.9 on the vertical y-axis. Now that we have our values for a and b, we can also predict

Client	Trauma Symptoms Scale Score X	Number of Serious Behavioral Incidents Y	X^2	XY
A	5	2	25	0
B	8	1	64	8
C	10	5	100	20
D	15	4	225	45
E	20	2	400	100
F	25	9	625	200
G	30	7	900	300
H	40	13	1600	440
I	50	10	2500	1000
J	60	8	3600	1320
SUMS	$\Sigma X = 263$	$\Sigma Y = 61$	$\Sigma X^2 = 10,039$	$\Sigma XY = 2103$

a Y' value for any new client's X score, using the formula for Y':

$$Y' = a + bX$$

Thus, if new client Sam's scale score is 10, his predicted number of serious behavioral incidents is $1.9 + (10)(0.16) = 1.9 + 1.6 = 3.5$.

If new client Jill's scale score is 50, then her number of serious behavior incidents is $1.9 + (50)(0.16) = 1.9 + 8.0 = 9.9$.

Fortunately, most statistical software programs (like SPSS) can do all of the above calculations for you!

Thus, the *slope*, or b value, is related to the correlation coefficient. If r is near 0, it's like walking in Wichita, Kansas, or Lubbock, Texas. You are in the flatlands, and no matter how far you walk, you perceive virtually no change in altitude. In other words, there is virtually no correlation between horizontal distance (X) and altitude (Y). If, on the other hand, r is $+1.0$, it's like climbing a pyramid. Each step forward is accompanied by the same increase in altitude. (If r is -1.0, it's like descending from the top of the pyramid.)

Although the slope (b) will equal zero when r equals zero, it does not follow that the slope will be plus or minus 1.0 every time r is plus or minus 1.0. The perfect $(1.0)r$ means that each unit of distance forward is accompanied by a consistent unit of distance in altitude. For example, r would be $+1.0$ if for every 20 inches forward you rose 8 inches in altitude, just as it would be $+1.0$ if for every 20 inches forward you rose 12 inches in altitude. The two slopes would be 0.40 (8/20) and 0.60 (12/20) respectively, but the r would be $+1.0$ each time because there would be no deviations in how much you rose in altitude for the same unit of change horizontally.

Additional Illustrations of the Utility of Regression Analysis in Evidence-Based Practice

So far we have considered the utility of regression analysis in evidence-based practice only in terms of our hypothetical illustration involving a residential treatment center. Perhaps you are skeptical as to how useful regression analysis might be to you in your practice, especially if you work in a setting other than a residential treatment center for troubled youths. So let's look at some additional applications of regression analysis to evidence-based practice.

Suppose you work in a child welfare agency and are concerned about how often foster care placements don't work out and children consequently get shuffled from placement to placement. Such shuffling might be severely detrimental to children's ability to form close attachments to people and might exacerbate any emotional or behavioral problems they had to begin with.

Suppose you have a scale that measures the ability of prospective foster parents to cope with and handle provocative and acting-out behavior. Suppose further that a study has been done showing a high correlation between foster parents' scale scores and the length of time children remain in placement with them. Suppose a regression analysis finds that the predicted number of months that children with severe emotional or behavioral problems will remain in a particular placement is 0.20 plus $0.50X$. In other words, in the regression equation $Y' = a + bX$, a equals 0.20 and b equals a slope of 0.50 (meaning that for every increase of one point in the scale score there is an increase of one-half month in the placement duration).

You could administer the scale to each prospective foster parent to help you decide whether they would make good foster parents for children with severe emotional or behavioral problems. Suppose Mr. Smith gets a score of 80 on your scale. You could predict that the duration of a placement with him will be approximately 40.20 months, or more than 3 years. That's because $0.20 + (0.50)(80) = 0.20 + 40 = 40.20$.

Suppose Ms. Jones scores only a 10 on your scale. You could predict that the duration of a placement with her will be approximately 5.20 months. That's because $0.20 + (0.50)(10) = 0.20 + 5 = 5.20$. Comparing Mr. Smith's predicted placement duration with that of Ms. Jones would tell you that

Mr. Smith appears to be a much more appropriate foster parent with whom to place a child who has severe emotional or behavioral problems.

In addition to comparing various sets of parent scores, you could develop a cutoff point for considering a prospective foster parent as a suitable placement for children with severe emotional or behavioral problems. For example, suppose you decide that the minimal acceptable foster placement duration is 1 year, or 12 months. In order to get a predicted placement duration of at least 12 months, a prospective foster parent would have to score approximately 24 on your scale. That's because $0.20 + (0.50)(24) = 12.20$. Thus, with a minimal acceptable placement duration of 12 months, you could establish 24 as the cutoff point for scale scores in deciding whether or not to consider a prospective foster parent as a suitable placement for children with severe emotional or behavioral problems. Of course, if you have more foster parent applicants than youths to be placed, you won't have to accept everyone with a score of 24 or more. You could select those with the highest scale scores and put those with lower scores that are above the 24 cutoff point on a waiting list.

Let's consider one more example. Suppose you are an administrator or clinical coordinator in an inpatient facility for substance abusers or for people suffering from severe and persistent brain disorders. You have to decide when patients are ready for discharge, and if ready, what type of community living arrangements they'll need. Suppose a discharge readiness inventory has been developed that accurately predicts how long discharged patients are likely to live independently in the community without relapsing.

Suppose a regression analysis predicts that the number of days before relapse is $1 + 10X$. Thus, if Bob scores only a 2 on your inventory, you could predict that he'll probably relapse within approximately 21 days after discharge to independent living arrangements (such as his own apartment). You might therefore decide that he is not yet ready to be discharged, and if you are legally forced to discharge him, you would probably try to place him in a community halfway house offering close supervision and support. In contrast, suppose Sue scores 150 on your inventory. You'd predict that she has a good chance to last 1501 days (more than 4 years) without relapsing, and thus decide that she can be discharged to her own apartment.

MULTIPLE CORRELATION

Our discussion of correlation and regression so far has been at the bivariate level. That is, it has been limited to analyses involving only two variables. Phenomena of concern to evidence-based practitioners, however, almost always involve more than two variables. For example, in Chapter 16 we noted that the average effective intervention in the human services explains about 9% of the variation in the dependent variable. That means that other factors account for the remaining 91%.

Along the same lines, in Chapter 15 we noted that unless the aim of our study is to assess the reliability or validity of a measure, then we should exercise caution in interpreting correlation coefficients that are near perfect. Such correlations might merely indicate that we have inadvertently measured the same variable in two different ways. Implicit in that caution is the notion that variables in evidence-based practice and evaluation are almost never explained or caused completely by just one other variable. Instead, multiple variables are almost always involved in a complete explanation of the variance in another (dependent) variable.

If you think of some common foci of human service interventions, it's hard to imagine any that are caused by just one variable. Regardless of whether you focus on strengths that clinical practitioners attempt to build or problems that they attempt to alleviate, you probably won't be able to imagine any that are explained by a single variable.

Take child abuse or neglect, for example. Does that have only one cause? Of course not. Factors that would impinge on the effectiveness of an intervention with parents referred for abuse or neglect might include the parents' psychopathology, their substance abuse involvement, how their own parents treated them as children, socioeconomic stress, marital conflict, the availability of support systems, the number of past incidents of abuse, the child's personality, the parents' child-rearing knowledge and skills, and so on. If you've studied child abuse and neglect, you may think of any number of additional variables that I haven't mentioned.

What about something positive, like the self-esteem of adolescents? Will only one factor—such as your intervention—influence the extent to which self-esteem improves? What about parental influences, teacher influences, peer influences, hormonal influences, and so on? For another positive, what about the mood of frail, elderly nursing home residents? Will your efforts to elevate their mood be the sole influence on their spirits? What about how often they are visited by loved ones? What about the quality of their relationships with those who visit them? How about the way they are treated by direct care staff, some of whom might be very warm and supportive while others might be unfriendly or even abusive? What about biological factors, such as their worsening physical deterioration that might vary from resident to resident in the degree to which they are becoming increasingly unable to get around or take care of their own bodily functions?

In fact, when textbooks or professors mention the person-in-environment perspective, they are implicitly acknowledging that practitioners are concerned with things that have multiple causes. That is, the person-in-environment perspective takes into account biological, psychological, familial, peer, economic, and other environmental and societal forces that interact in the explanation of the problems that practitioners confront and that influence how effectively practitioners intervene with those problems.

Consequently, the most useful efforts in evidence-based practice and evaluation will be those that don't restrict their focus to a single explanation or predictor, but instead take multiple factors into account. When conducting correlation or regression analyses, this means incorporating multiple independent variables into the equation instead of just one. When we do so, we are engaging in **multiple regression analysis** or **multiple correlation analysis.**

Multiple regression analysis and multiple correlation analysis are interrelated and are forms of *multivariate analysis*. The previous chapters of this book have focused on univariate analysis or bivariate analysis. We considered univariate analysis when we were discussing statistics used to describe the distribution or central tendency of a single variable. We dealt with bivariate forms of analysis when we examined inferential statistics for testing the significance of or the strength of relationships between two variables. In contrast, multivariate analysis looks simultaneously at the interrelationships of three or more variables.

Multiple regression analysis and multiple correlation analysis are not the only forms of multivariate analysis. Appendix D of this text summarizes other forms. But because they are perhaps the most common forms of multivariate analysis that you are likely to encounter, and because they are extensions of bivariate correlation and regression analysis, we'll consider them in some detail now. We will not, however, delve into their formulae and calculations to the same extent as with bivariate regression and correlation. Doing so would go way beyond the scope of this introductory text. For example, multiple regression equations cannot be portrayed graphically with straight lines. Instead, they represent planes in multi-dimensional space. Don't worry about what that means; even statisticians struggle with understanding and explaining that concept.

But we can conceptualize the meaning and utility of multiple regression and multiple correlation results without getting into the complexities involved in the formulae and graphs associated with them, Although you might find the ensuing discussion somewhat challenging, I think you'll see how you can interpret multiple regression and multiple correlation in guiding your practice and how you can use it in practice evaluation. If you'd like to utilize SPSS to do the calculations for these procedures, you can examine the section of Appendix G headed, "Using SPSS for Multiple Regression and Multiple Correlation (Chapter 17)."

Multiple and Partial Correlation

Before discussing multiple regression analysis, let's begin with the concept of *multiple and partial correlation*. **Multiple correlation** refers to the degree of correlation between a group of independent variables and a dependent variable. For example, if we want to explain or predict why some youths in our residential treatment center have greater numbers of serious behavioral incidents than others, we probably would not limit our consideration exclusively to their trauma symptoms. We might also consider how many prior incidents of abuse they experienced, their age, their ethnicity, whether they have an attention deficit hyperactivity disorder (ADHD), what cottage they are in, the attributes of their cottage parents or therapists, their intellectual capabilities and school performance, peer influences, what happens when relatives visit them or when they go home on a weekend pass, and a host of other factors.

To keep things manageable, let's just assume that we limit our study to three independent variables: trauma symptom scale score, age, and the number of prior incidents of abuse they experienced. Suppose we conduct a series of bivariate analyses looking at the correlation that each of these variables has with the dependent variable, *number of serious behavioral incidents*. Let's further assume that we obtain three statistically significant bivariate correlation coefficients, as follows: $r = 0.70$ for trauma symptom scale score, $r = 0.40$ for age, and $r = 0.70$ for number of prior incidents of abuse.

As you may recall from our discussion of coefficients of determination in Chapter 16, by squaring r we find the proportion of variation in the dependent variable that is attributable to variation in the independent variable. I suggest that you take a moment now to calculate the coefficient of determination for each of the three r's above. Next, I suggest that you sum the three coefficients of determination.

The three squares you should have summed are 0.49 (the square of the 0.70 for trauma symptom scale score), 0.16 (the square of 0.40 for age), and 0.49 (the square of 0.70 for number of prior abuse incidents). Your sum therefore should be 1.14. Does that strike you as strange? It should. Why? Because in adding up the proportions of variation in the dependent variable attributable to each independent variable, your sum exceeded 1.0. That means that these three variables would be explaining more than 100% of the variation in the dependent variable (114% to be exact). But that's impossible. Once we explain 100% of the variation, we've explained all of it. There's none left to explain. What the heck is going on here?

The sum exceeded 100% because in adding the three bivariate correlations, we failed to account for the overlap among our independent variables. That is, we failed to account for the correlations they had with each other. We cannot, therefore, find the correlation between a set of independent variables and a dependent variable merely by adding up the bivariate correlations that each has with the dependent variable. This concept is illustrated with overlapping circles in Figure 17.2.

In Figure 17.2, each circle represents the variation of a different variable. The middle circle represents the variation in the dependent variable, number of serious behavioral incidents. That's the variation we are attempting to explain with our three independent variables. The other circles represent the variation in each of the three independent variables. The extent of overlap between those circles represents the amount of shared variance, or the amount of variance in one variable attributable to another variable.

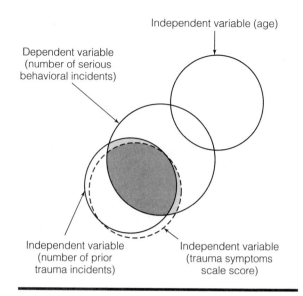

Figure 17.2 Illustration of Multiple Correlation Between a Set of Three Independent Variables with a Dependent Variable, with Multicollinearity

Off the bat, you can probably recognize that less than 100% of the middle circle—the one representing the variation in our dependent variable—is overlapping with the three other circles. Thus, we see that the three independent variables really are not explaining 114%—or even 100%—of the variation in our dependent variable. That's because there is so much shared variation between two of the independent variables: trauma symptoms scale score and number of prior trauma incidents. Notice the very large degree of overlap between the circles for those two variables. They are so strongly correlated themselves that the two of them together add very little to what either one alone accounts for in the dependent variable variation.

Notice also that although age accounts for less variation in the dependent variable, it does not overlap with the other independent variables. Therefore, its 0.16 coefficient of determination need not be reduced. Instead, it can be added to the variation explained by the other two independent variables. Let's assume that the other two independent variables combined account for 51% of the area of the dependent variable circle. In other words, so much of their 0.70 bivariate correlations with the dependent variable is taken up by their own mutual correlation that only 2% more is explained by the two variables combined. Said another way, most of their separate 0.49 coefficients of determination are eaten up by the overlap between the two independent variables themselves, and only a small additional portion (approximately 1% per variable) of the dependent variable variance gets explained by the combined set of the two variables above and beyond what either one of them alone explained.

(I am not suggesting that in reality these are the correlations we would find in a real study. Their strengths and degrees of overlap might be quite different. Perhaps the two 0.70 correlations would be much lower and overlap less. Perhaps each would overlap with age. I have rigged these figures to make the concepts we are discussing easier to visualize and comprehend. I hope you can visualize how the degree of dependent variable variation explained by a set of independent variables is reduced to the extent that there is shared variation among the independent variables. That is, I hope you can see how the shared variation accounts for why a multiple correlation involving a set of independent variables can actually be much less than the sum of the separate bivariate correlations.)

The large overlap between trauma symptoms scale score and number of prior trauma incidents in Figure 17.2 also illustrates something called *multicollinearity*—a problem in multiple correlation and multiple regression analysis that occurs when two or more independent variables in the analysis are so highly correlated that the analysis gets distorted. We'll return to this problem shortly.

Partial *r*

Partial correlation coefficients can be calculated to find the portion of correlation between two variables that is not shared with other variables. (You can use SPSS to do the calculations.) We can refer to a partial correlation coefficient as **partial *r*.** For example, in Figure 17.2 the partial *r* for trauma symptom scale score is about 0.10, and the partial *r* for number of prior incidents of abuse is also about 0.10. We know that because above we noted that each of these two variables uniquely added 1% beyond their three-way shared variation with the dependent variable. Because the coefficient of determination is the square of *r*, then the square root of the coefficient of determination is *r*. Thus, if each of these variables uniquely accounts for 0.01 of the dependent variable variation, then 0.01 represents

the square of the partial *r*, or partial r^2. The square root of 0.01 is 0.10; therefore the partial *r* is 0.10.

Said another way, when considering either the trauma symptom scale score variable or the number of prior trauma incidents variable, only 0.10 of the bivariate correlation of 0.70 is that part which is unique when assessed in a multivariate analysis. The other 0.60 is attributable to the overlap between the two independent variables. And all but 1% of the bivariate coefficient of determination is shared with the other independent variable when assessed in a multivariate analysis.

Multicollinearity

Above I noted that the problem of **multicollinearity** is present when independent variables are this strongly correlated in a multiple correlation or multiple regression analysis. Let's consider how the multicollinearity in this hypothetical illustration would distort our findings. Above we saw that the partial *r* for each of the two variables with multicollinearity is only 0.10. Likewise each had a partial r^2 of only 0.01. Because the age variable in Figure 17.2 does not overlap with the other two independent variables, its partial *r* and partial r^2 would be the same as its bivariate *r* and r^2, which would be 0.40 and 0.16.

Thus, if we considered only the partial *r* and the partial r^2 for each variable, and did not take *multicollinearity* into account, we would conclude that age was a stronger predictor of the dependent variable than trauma symptom scale score or number of prior trauma incidents, because age accounted for 16% of the dependent variable variance, whereas the other two variables each accounted for only 1%. This would be misleading because the reason the other two variables have such low partial *r*'s is that they are both measuring essentially the same thing in two different ways. We can see in Figure 17.2 that the impact of trauma is a stronger predictor of the dependent variable than the impact of age, but when two variables are entered in the equation that overlap so much that they are largely measuring the same factor, they'll both take up nearly the same amount of explanatory space and therefore cancel each other out in terms of each of their unique shared variance with the dependent variable.

How much correlation between independent variables is too much? That is, how much must there be for multicollinearity to be considered a problem? Some say it is a problem when independent variables are correlated at about 0.60 or higher. Some put the threshold at 0.80, and some say 0.90. The decision as to the cutoff point actually is up to the person conducting the analysis. Your statistical software program will let you specify the threshold you'd like, and it also has a built-in default option. It will alert you as to whether multicollinearity is a problem in your analysis either in terms of the default threshold or the alternative cutoff point you select.

When variables have too much multicollinearity, you should not include them all in your multiple correlation or multiple regression analysis. Instead, you should combine their values into a single variable, or—if their correlations are at about 0.90 or higher—you might just eliminate one of the two variables, since they are both essentially measuring the same thing.

One way you could combine variables into a single variable is to create a factor score using another multivariate procedure called *factor analysis*. (Appendix D of this text provides a conceptual introduction to factor analysis and identifies some advanced texts on the topic.) Another option to combine variables is by creating an index in which the value of each variable will be weighted and then combined into one overarching index score. (Indexing is discussed in most basic research methods texts, such as Rubin & Babbie, 2005.)

Multiple *R*

A multiple correlation coefficient can be calculated to find the degree to which an entire set of independent variables, as a whole, correlates with a dependent variable. We can refer to the multiple correlation coefficient as **Multiple *R*** or just **R.** We can square R to find the total amount of variation in the dependent variable explained by the entire set of independent variables. Likewise, if we know R^2, we can find R by obtaining the square root of R^2. In Figure 17.2, if we add the amount of variation explained by all three variables we get 67%. That's because age accounted for 16% of the variation, and the trauma symptom scale score variable combined with the number of prior incidents of abuse variable together accounted for 51% of the variation. Thus, since 16% plus 51% equals 67%, we know that Multiple R^2 equals 0.67. The square root of 0.67 is 0.82; therefore Multiple R is 0.82.

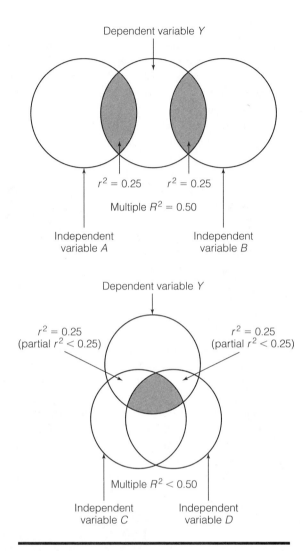

Figure 17.3 Illustration of Multiple Correlations Involving Independent Variables that Do and Do Not Correlate with Each Other

For another pictorial illustration of multiple correlation—one in which multicollinearity is not a problem—we can examine Figure 17.3. In the top diagram, we see that two uncorrelated independent variables (A and B) each account for 25% of the variation in dependent variable Y. Because they are not correlated with each other, the two independent variables together account for 50% of the variation in Y. (That is, their Multiple R^2 is 0.50.) In the bottom diagram, we see that two correlated independent variables (C and D) each have the same bivariate correlation with Y as did variables A and B, but because they are correlated, their overlapping portion of the explanatory space reduces their Multiple R^2 to less than 0.50.

MULTIPLE REGRESSION

Earlier in this chapter we saw how regression analysis employs an equation enabling us to predict the value of a dependent variable based on the value of an independent variable. **Multiple regression analysis** enables us to predict the value of a dependent variable based on the values of a set of at least two independent variables. Sometimes the term *predictor variables* is used instead of the term *independent variables* when discussing multiple regression analysis. That's because multiple regression analysis is often used to identify which variables in a larger set of variables are the best predictors of another variable instead of being used to test a specific hypothesis about the set of variables.

When the term *predictor variables* is used instead of *independent variables*, the term *criterion variable* might be used instead of *dependent variable*. To keep things less complicated, we'll stick with the terms *independent* and *dependent* when discussing the variables in multiple regression analysis. But if you see others using the terms *predictor* and *criterion*, understand that they are referring to the same things you are reading in this chapter. Let's leave semantics now and examine the multiple regression equation.

Multiple Regression Equation

Earlier we saw that the bivariate regression equation is $Y' = a + bX$. We saw that Y' is the value of variable Y predicted from a known particular X value, and that it is estimated by multiplying the slope of the regression line b times X and then adding a constant value a, which is the beginning point where the regression line intersects the y-axis. The multiple regression equation extends the bivariate regression formula by adding more independent variables after bX. Each additional variable is multiplied by its own slope, and thus the multiple regression equation is as follows:

$$Y' = a + b_1X_1 + b_2X_2 + {''}{>}\cdots + b_kX_k$$

The subscripts in the above formula refer to the order in which variables enter the equation. Thus, X_1 is the first variable, X_2 is the second, and X_k is the last. Likewise b_1 is the first slope, b_2 is the second, and so on.

Let's apply the above formula to an example discussed earlier in this chapter. Suppose you work in a child welfare agency and are concerned about how often foster care placements don't work out and children consequently get shuffled from placement to placement. Suppose instead of only one scale for prospective foster parents to complete, you have three scales. One measures their child-rearing knowledge and skills. Let's call that Scale 1. A second scale (Scale 2) measures their anger control, and a third (Scale 3) measures their self-esteem. You conduct a study in which you perform a multiple regression analysis using the three scales as your three independent variables and duration of foster care placement (in days) as your dependent variable. Your results might look like this:

$$Y' = 5 + 3(\text{Scale 1 score}) + 2(\text{Scale 2 score}) + 0.50(\text{Scale 3 score})$$

Suppose a parent scored 80 on Scale 1, 60 on Scale 2, and 70 on Scale 3. You would predict the duration of foster care placement with that parent to be as follows:

$$\begin{aligned}
\text{Predicted duration} \\
\text{(in days)} &= 5 + 3(80) + 2(60) + 0.50(70) \\
&= 5 + 240 + 120 + 35 \\
&= 400 \text{ days}
\end{aligned}$$

Standardized Beta

In addition to finding the b values (slopes) for each variable in the multiple regression equation, multiple regression analysis calculates a statistic for each variable called the **standardized beta,** or the **beta weight.** The symbol for this statistic is β (the Greek letter *beta*). The larger the β, the greater influence a variable has in explaining the variation in the dependent variable when other variables are controlled.

You may be wondering why β is used instead of the slope statistic, b. That's because b is influenced by the way a variable is measured. For example, suppose one independent variable is a scale with scores that can be as high as 100. Suppose another independent variable is how many children a parent has. Suppose the b for the scale is 2, and the b for number of children is 4. Which of those two independent variables would have more influence on the dependent variable? Would it be number of children, because its *b* was higher? Suppose a parent scores 50 on the scale and has 3 children. Multiplying the *b* of 2 times their scale score of 50 would add 100 to their predicted *Y'* value, whereas multiplying the *b* of 4 times their 3 children would add 12 to their predicted *Y'* value. Thus the higher *b* actually has less of an impact on the predicted score because of the difference in scale between the two independent variables.

To make the different variables more comparable, their values are standardized by converting them to *z*-scores. (Recall our discussion of *z*-scores in Chapter 8.) The resulting β statistics then can be compared to determine the relative importance of each independent variable in explaining the variation in the dependent variable.

Perhaps you are a visual learner. If so, it might help to examine Figure 17.4. There we see three overlapping circles for three independent variables, *A*, *B*, and *C*. We also see the overlap of each with the dependent variable, *Y*. Notice that the portion of variable *Y* that overlaps with variable A alone is

greater than the portion that overlaps with variable *B* alone. Notice also that variable *C* has the least amount of unique overlap with variable *Y*. Thus, variable *A* would have the highest β, variable *B* would have the second highest β, and variable *C* would have the lowest β.

Alternative Methods for Including Variables in Multiple Regression

Depending on the purpose of a multiple regression analysis, three main alternative methods exist for the order in which independent (predictor) variables are entered into the analysis. In one method called the **all-possible-subsets method,** all of the independent variables are entered *simultaneously*. Using this method, your statistical software program considers all possible combinations and orders of variables in the equation and chooses the one that most accurately predicts the dependent variable. An alternative method called the **hierarchical method** is used when you have hypothesized in advance which variables, or which sets of variables, are more influential than others in predicting the dependent variable. A third method called the **stepwise method** is used when you have a large number of possible independent variables that you want to explore, and you want your software to find a smaller set of these variables to use in predicting the dependent variable, eliminating other variables that add only an insignificant or trivial amount of explained variation in the dependent variable beyond the smaller set.

The stepwise method itself can be implemented in alternative ways. Using the **forward stepwise method,** the independent variable with the strongest *bivariate* correlation with the dependent variable is entered first. The second variable to be introduced into the equation is the one that has the greatest *partial* correlation with the dependent variable after partialing out the effects of the first variable. The remaining variables are entered according to how much additional variation they explain in the dependent variable after partialing out the effects of the variables already entered. This process ends when the remaining variables would add only an insignificant or trivial amount of explained variation.

Using the **backward stepwise method,** all the variables are entered into the equation first. Then the variable with the smallest partial correlation is

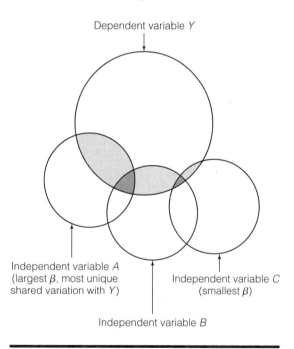

Independent variable *A*
(largest β, most unique shared variation with *Y*)

Independent variable *C*
(smallest β)

Independent variable *B*

Figure 17.4   Illustration of Three Independent Variables (*A*, *B*, and *C*) with Different Beta Weights (β) in Accounting for the Variance in Dependent Variable *Y*

removed from the batch and the equation is computed again. This identifies the next variable to be eliminated from the equation based on its partial correlation. This process is repeated until the only variables left in the equation are those that add a significant or meaningful amount of explained variation in the dependent variable.

To illustrate these alternative methods, let's suppose you are an administrator or clinical coordinator in a child guidance center. Each child treated at your center receives a global assessment score of his or her emotional and social functioning at the start of treatment and again at the end of treatment. You want to improve your ability to identify those variables which best predict the amount of improvement in scores. Your hope is to identify variables that can be used in treatment planning. For example, is it the treatment modality—such as play therapy, family therapy, group therapy, or perhaps some combination of modalities—that best predicts improvement? What about therapist characteristics, such as level or type of educational degree, whether they are of the same gender or ethnicity as the child, years of experience, specialized training, and so on? What about child factors? What's the child's diagnosis? Is ADHD involved? How about ethnicity, intelligence, age, prior traumas, medical conditions, school performance, hobbies, social and athletic activities, and so on? How about family factors, such as age of parents, their level of education and socioeconomic status, whether both parents are present, marital conflict or violence, sibling factors, substance abuse by parents or siblings, presence of extended family members, emotional disorders among family members, and so on? The foregoing factors don't exhaust all the possible variables that you might consider, but you get the idea: it could be a very long list of potential predictors.

Let's suppose that your agency has a comprehensive intake procedure and that all of the foregoing factors, as well as others, have been included in your agency's computerized database. We'll also need to assume that the database has this information on a very large number of clients. Let's assume that it includes all clients who have entered your program dating back several years or more. (You'll need a large sample size to conduct a multiple regression analysis on such an extensive list of variables.)

If you don't have any firm reason to expect certain variables to be the strongest predictors of improvement, and you want to come up with a shorter list of the most important predictors, you'd probably opt to conduct a stepwise regression. Although you might get different results depending on whether you use a forward or backward stepwise inclusion method, the difference will probably be negligible.

Using the stepwise method, you can come up with a shorter list of variables that will be manageable in clinical planning. For example, suppose the results of your analysis are as displayed in Table 17.1. That

Table 17.1   Results of an Imaginary Stepwise Multiple Regression Analysis Using the Forward Entry Method for an Imaginary Study Predicting Improvement in Functioning

VARIABLES	UNSTANDARDIZED B	STANDARDIZED β	p	R	R^2	R^2 CHANGE
Combination of individual, group, play and family therapy	0.30	0.42	0.001	0.40	0.16	0.16
Extent of prior traumas	−0.20	−0.30	0.001	0.50	0.25	0.09
Extent of marital conflict or violence	−15	−0.25	0.001	0.56	0.31	0.06
Extent of therapist training in the treatment of trauma	0.10	0.15	0.01	0.58	0.34	0.03
Therapist and client share the same gender and ethnicity	0.07	0.10	0.03	0.60	0.36	0.02

table shows that whether the child received a combination of individual, group, play, and family therapy is the strongest predictor (with the largest β) and explains 16% of the variation in improvement. After it come extent of prior traumas (explaining an additional 9%); extent of marital conflict or violence (explaining another 6%); extent of therapist training in the treatment of trauma (explaining another 3%); and whether therapist and client share the same gender and ethnicity (explaining another 2%). No other variable adds a significant amount of explained variation in improvement.

Table 17.1 also shows that by adding the above percentages, we see that those five variables explain 36% of the variation. Variables that were excluded from the table are not significant predictors. Thus, your Multiple R^2 would be 0.36, and your Multiple R would be the square root of that, or 0.60. Not too shabby! You might use your results in seeking additional funding that would enable your agency to provide a more comprehensive battery of treatments to more clients and to obtain specialized training for your staff in dealing with trauma and marital conflict. You might also try—whenever feasible—to assign therapists to a case who have the same ethnicity and gender as the child. Keep in mind, however, that correlation does not imply causation. Your multiple regression results, therefore, don't guarantee that your efforts will lead to improvement in client outcomes. But they do provide an evidentiary basis for at least trying these efforts out (and perhaps testing them using an experimental or quasi-experimental design).

So far we've applied the stepwise method to this practice example. What about the hierarchical method? You'd use the hierarchical method if, instead of wanting to shorten the long list of potential predictors in an exploratory fashion, you had a hypothesis as to which individual factor or factors were most important. Suppose you hypothesized that whether the child received a combination of individual, group, play and family therapy was the most important factor. However, you recognized the possibility that perhaps some of the other variables influenced whether the child received a combination of individual, group, play and family therapy. Thus, you'd want to enter those variables in the equation first, and then see how much more variation in improvement is explained when the variable—whether the child received a combination of individual, group, play, and family therapy—is added to the equation. If it adds a significant and meaningful amount of variance, your hypothesis will be supported, and you might recommend providing a combination of individual, group, play, and family therapy when clinically appropriate.

Instead of entering each individual variable separately in each step, you could enter combinations of them in blocks, such as a block of family factors, a block of child factors, a block of therapist characteristics, and so on. Let's assume that you want to see how much of the variation in improvement is explained by child factors after controlling for family factors, therapist characteristics after controlling for family and child factors, and whether the child received a combination of individual, group, play, and family therapy after controlling for all of the above blocks of variables.

Table 17.2 displays imaginary results of such a hierarchical regression. It shows that even after

Table 17.2   Results of a Hierarchical Multiple Regression Analysis for an Imaginary Study Predicting Improvement in Functioning

VARIABLES	UNSTANDARDIZED B	STANDARDIZED β	p	R	R^2	R^2 CHANGE
Family factors	−0.30	−0.40	0.001	0.40	0.16	0.16
Child factors	−0.28	−0.38	0.001	0.50	0.25	0.09
Therapist characteristics	0.15	0.25	0.01	0.53	0.28	0.03
Combination of individual, group, play, and family therapy	0.25	0.35	0.001	0.60	0.36	0.08

controlling for all other variables, whether the child received a combination of individual, group, play, and family therapy is statistically significant and explains 8% of the variation in improvement. You may be wondering why it explained more (16%) using the forward stepwise method. That's because the forward stepwise method enters first the variable with the strongest bivariate correlation with the dependent variable, and thus nothing else gets partialed out before calculating its R square. In the hierarchical method, however, we force the variable we are most interested in to be entered last, after everything we want to control for has been partialed out. Thus, explaining 8% of the variation after various blocks of control variables have been partialed out can be viewed as more impressive than explaining 16% with nothing else partialed out first.

You may also be wondering why some variables (or blocks of variables) in Tables 17.1 and 17.2 have minus signs in the first two columns. The minus signs simply signify negative correlations. For example, greater amounts of family violence, prior traumas, and so on would be associated with smaller amounts of improvement.

If you read various research articles reporting the results of multiple regression and multiple correlation analyses, you'll soon see that the structure of the tables reporting such results varies considerably from article to article. It's hard to find two articles with multiple regression tables that include exactly the same columns. Therefore, rather than display the results of an actual article, Table 17.1 and Table 17.2 display the important things to understand in such tables. Most tables that you'll find won't look exactly like these tables or contain all of the elements that I've put into these tables, but if you know how to interpret the contents of Tables 17.1 and 17.2 you shouldn't have much trouble understanding the various multiple correlation or multiple regression tables you'll encounter in research articles.

Assumptions of Multiple Regression Analysis

As you may recall, bivariate regression requires the same assumptions as bivariate correlation. The data must be at the interval or ratio level of measurement, reasonably linear in the scatterplot, and homoscedastic (which means that the degrees of variance in the two variables being correlated are similar). These assumptions change somewhat in multiple regression and multiple correlation. The data must still be reasonably linear and homoscedastic. The dependent variable must be at the interval or ratio level of measurement. But not all independent variables need be at that level.

Nominal and ordinal variables can be converted into "dummy" variables for entry into the equation. To convert them, you would recode them into dichotomous categories using 0 and 1. (If you were using SPSS to do this, you would use the *Transform* and *Recode* commands in SPSS, as discussed in the Chapter 3 section of Appendix G.) For example, if your codes for gender are 1 for male and 2 for female, you could change the 2 for female to a 0. (Alternatively, you could change the 1 for male to 0 and the 2 for female to 1.) If your nominal variable has more than two categories, you would convert them into a set of dichotomous variables. For example, suppose you had four categories of ethnicity, as follows: 1-Caucasian, 2-African American, 3-Hispanic, and 4-Other. One dummy variable would be coded 1 for Caucasian and 0 for everything else. Another dummy variable would be coded 1 for African American and 0 for everything else. A third dummy variable would be coded 1 for Hispanic and 0 for everything else. (No dummy variable would be created for Other, because multiple regression analysis requires using one less dummy variable than the original number of categories.)

Finally, as discussed above, the degree of multicollinearity among independent variables must not be excessive. You can check for multicollinearity by examining the various correlations among your independent variables, to see if any have extremely high correlations. Likewise, you can examine scatterplots to detect problems in linearity (such as curvilinear relationships). As mentioned earlier, however, your software program will warn you when you have too much multicollinearity or when your data are violating other assumptions.

As we conclude our examination of multiple correlation and regression, you may have noticed that we did not delve into their formulae and calculations to the same extent as we did with bivariate regression and correlation. In case you'd like to dig more deeply into the more mathematical content, information can be found in advanced texts on this topic (Hair, Anderson, Tatham, & Black, 1998; Kachigan, 1991; Mertler & Vannatta, 2005; Stevens, 2002).

You may also recall my mentioning that multiple regression analysis and multiple correlation analysis are not the only forms of multivariate analysis. Appendix D of this text summarizes other forms. I hope this chapter has whetted your appetite for examining that appendix, which offers a conceptually oriented glimpse into some other prominent forms of multivariate analysis without delving into their formulae and calculations.

Main Points

- Regression analysis is a form of correlation analysis that employs an equation enabling us to predict the value of one variable based on the value of another variable.

- The regression equation is as follows: $Y' = a + bX$. In this equation, Y' = the value of variable Y predicted from a known particular X value; a is the point where the regression line intersects the y-axis; b is the slope of the regression line, determined by the amount of change in Y for each amount of change in X, and X is the value of the X variable used to predict Y'.

- The regression equation, also called the *least-squares regression equation*, enables us to draw a line where the sum of squared distances (or deviations) of the actual data points from the line will be minimized.

- Most statistical software programs (such as SPSS) can do all of the regression calculations for you.

- If the correlation between X and Y is very weak (near 0.0), using regression will be of little or no value to your decision making. The great degree of dispersion of Y values for every X value would render your predictions so inaccurate that they would be useless.

- In contrast to bivariate analysis, multivariate analysis looks simultaneously at the interrelationships of three or more variables.

- Multiple correlation refers to the degree of correlation between a group of independent variables and a dependent variable.

- We cannot find the correlation between a set of independent variables and a dependent variable merely by adding up the bivariate correlations that each has with the dependent variable. First we must see whether there is overlap among the independent variables in sharing the explained variation of the dependent variable. The multiple correlation will be the sum of each variable's unique amount of shared variance with the dependent variable plus the amount of shared variance.

- A partial correlation coefficient can be calculated to find the portion of correlation between two variables that is not shared with other variables. The partial correlation coefficient is called *partial r*. We can square the partial r to find the proportion of dependent variable variation uniquely attributable to the independent variable, when the effects of other variables are partialed out.

- *Multicollinearity* can distort the findings of a multiple correlation or multiple regression analysis. Multicollinearity is present when independent variables are highly correlated.

- When variables have too much multicollinearity, you should not include them all in your multiple correlation or multiple regression analysis. Instead, you should combine their values into a single variable, or—if their correlations are at about 0.90 or higher—you might just eliminate one of the two variables, since they are both essentially measuring the same thing.

- A multiple correlation coefficient can be calculated to find the degree to which an entire set of independent variables, as a whole, correlates with a dependent variable. We can refer to the multiple correlation coefficient as Multiple R or just R. As with partial r, we can square R to find the total amount of variation in the dependent variable explained by the entire set of independent variables.

- Multiple regression analysis enables us to predict the value of a dependent variable based on the values of a set of at least two independent variables.

- The multiple regression equation extends the bivariate regression formula by adding more independent variables after bX. Each additional variable is multiplied by its own slope, and thus the multiple regression equation is as follows: $Y' = a + b_1X_1 + b_2X_2 + \cdots + b_kX_k$.

• In addition to finding the b values (slopes) for each variable in the multiple regression equation, multiple regression analysis calculates a statistic for each variable called the standardized beta, or the beta weight. The symbol for this statistic is β (the Greek letter *beta*). The larger the β, the greater influence a variable has in explaining the variation in the dependent variable when other variables are controlled.

• Three main alternative methods exist for the order in which independent (predictor) variables are entered into the analysis. The all-possible-subsets method enters all of the independent variables simultaneously. The hierarchical method is used when you have hypothesized in advance which variables, or which sets of variables, are more influential than others in predicting the dependent variable. The stepwise method is used when you have a large number of possible independent variables that you want to explore, and you want your software to find a smaller set of these variables to use in predicting the dependent variable, eliminating other variables that add only an insignificant or trivial amount of explained variation in the dependent variable beyond the smaller set.

• The forward stepwise method enters the independent variable with the strongest bivariate correlation with the dependent variable first. The second variable to be introduced into the equation is the one that has the greatest partial correlation with the dependent variable after partialing out the effects of the first variable. The remaining variables are entered according to how much additional variation they explain in the dependent variable after partialing out the effects of the variables already entered. This process ends when the remaining variables would add only an insignificant or trivial amount of explained variation.

• The backward stepwise method enters all the variables into the equation first. Then the variable with the smallest partial correlation is removed from the batch and the equation is computed again. This identifies the next variable to be eliminated from the equation based on its partial correlation. This process is repeated until the only variables left in the equation are those that add a significant or meaningful amount of explained variation in the dependent variable.

• In multiple regression and multiple correlation the data must lack multicollinearity and be reasonably linear and homoscedastic. The dependent variable must be at the interval or ratio level of measurement. But not all independent variables need be at that level. Nominal and ordinal variables can be converted into "dummy" variables for entry into the equation.

Review Questions and Exercises

1. Your agency provides a 10-session intervention for parents of teens who abuse alcohol or drugs. However, attendance at the sessions by parents is poor. Your agency's client intake records have information from the parents on how many times they got high from alcohol or drugs in the 30 days before intake. You'd like to predict attendance by parents of future admissions, so you conduct a bivariate regression analysis on the data in Table 17.3. (These data are limited to 10 clients to simplify the calculations.) The parent of the next teen admitted to your program got high 5 times in the 30 days prior to intake. Using the bivariate regression formula $Y' = a + bX$, how many session absences would you predict that parent to have?

2. In your analysis of your data on all 1000 teens served by your agency, you find a bivariate correlation of 0.60 between number of times parents were high and number of session absences. You also find a correlation of 0.40 between scale score measuring degree of parent-child conflict and number of session absences. The coefficients of determination for the two correlations are 0.36 and 0.16, respectively. Would you therefore conclude that the two variables combined necessarily explain 52% of the variation in the dependent variable? Explain your answer. To illustrate the logic of your answer, draw three circles representing the overlap in variation among the three variables.

3. A multiple correlation analysis finds that the partial r^2 for the above variables is 0.10 for number of times high and 0.05 for degree of parent-child conflict. Does that mean that the Multiple R^2 is 0.15? Explain your answer. To illustrate the logic of your answer, draw three circles representing the overlap in variation in among the three variables.

4. You want to redo the above analysis, this time adding to the equation a scale score measuring the

Table 17.3 Data for Review Question 1

PARENT	NUMBER OF TIMES HIGH X	NUMBER OF SESSION ABSENCES Y	X^2	XY
A	1	2	1	2
B	8	5	64	40
C	7	6	49	42
D	1	1	1	3
E	0	0	0	0
F	0	0	0	0
G	6	4	36	24
H	4	3	16	12
I	3	2	9	6
J	2	1	4	2
SUMS	$\Sigma X = 32$	$\Sigma Y = 24$	$\Sigma X^2 = 180$	$\Sigma XY = 131$

quality of the parent-child relationship. First you check the bivariate correlations among the variables and find that quality of the parent-child relationship has a 0.90 correlation with degree of parent-child conflict. What do you do in light of this correlation?

5. A multiple regression analysis is conducted with the aim of predicting how many times the teens in your outpatient substance abuse program will get high during the first six months after treatment completion. It finds that $a = 1$. It also finds that $b_1 = 1$ for number of close friends who are chronic substance abusers, $b_2 = 0.10$ for degree of parent-child conflict, and $b_3 = 0.5$ for number of session absences by parents. Pete's values on these variables are 2 for number of close friends who are chronic substance abusers, 30 for degree of parent-child conflict, and 4 for number of session absences by parents. Using the multiple regression equation $Y' = a + b_1 X_1 + b_2 X_2 + \cdots + b_k X_k$, how many times would you predict that Pete will get high during the first 90 days after he completes treatment?

6. The standardized betas (the beta weights, or β statistics) for the above three variables are as follows: $\beta = 0.42$ for number of close friends who are

chronic substance abusers, $\beta = 0.24$ for degree of parent-child conflict, and $\beta = 0.16$ for number of session absences by parents. Given these results, how would you rank the relative strength of each of the three independent variables in explaining the dependent variable? Explain your answer.

7. You wonder whether the number of close friends who are chronic substance abusers might be influenced by the degree of parent-child conflict, previous involvement in athletics, and several other variables. You want to see how strongly it predicts amount of substance abuse after the other variables are controlled—that is, after the shared variation between the other variables and amount of substance abuse have been partialed out. What method would you use for ordering the variables in your multiple regression equation? Explain your answer.

8. Your agency has data on a very large number of variables that you think conceivably might predict amount of substance abuse. But you have no strong basis for supposing that some are more important than any others. You'd like to find the best set of a small number of predictors. What method would you use for ordering the variables in your multiple regression equation? Explain your answer.

InfoTrac Exercises

1. Read the following article and then respond to items a and b below.

Zhang, N., & Dixon, D. N. (2003). Acculturation and attitudes of Asian international students toward seeking psychological help. *Journal of Multicultural Counseling and Development, 31*(3), 205–222.

a. Briefly explain why the authors tested for multicollinearity.

b. Briefly explain why the authors used the hierarchical method for including variables in the multiple regression analysis.

CHAPTER 18

Applications to Single-System Evaluation Designs

INTRODUCTION

An important area of evidence-based practice involves the use of single-system designs by practitioners to evaluate their own practice effectiveness. These designs commonly involve a sample size of only one case, such as one individual client or one family. Sometimes they'll involve several cases, but even then the data analysis is conducted differently from studies using other designs. That's because the focus is on patterns of change within each case over time, not on aggregated data across many cases.

In other types of research and evaluation designs, such as surveys and group experiments and quasi-experiments, descriptive and inferential statistics are used in reference to data sets containing columns for different variables and rows for different people (or other elements) in a sample or a population. Even when the data involve whether people change over time, the focus is on comparing means or proportions involving many different cases. And usually there are no more than a few time points involved, such as a pretest and a posttest and perhaps one or more follow-up tests.

In contrast, with single-system evaluation designs the emphasis is on obtaining observations at many more time points, resulting in a larger set of measures of how one variable changes across many time points for one case. For example, a practitioner may obtain data on how many temper tantrums a child has each day for 10 days prior to implementing a cognitive-behavioral intervention and then 10 days after the intervention is introduced. The data set then would consist of 20 numbers, 10 numbers for how many tantrums occur on each of the 10 baseline days (prior to intervention), and 10 numbers for how many tantrums occur on each of the 10 days after the intervention commences.

Despite their differences from other forms of research and evaluation, many of the statistical concepts and procedures discussed throughout this text in reference to other types of designs can also be applied to single-system designs. The purpose of this chapter, therefore, is to cover the most feasible and commonly used ways that practitioners can apply these statistical concepts and procedures when they use single-system designs to evaluate their own practice.

VISUAL ANALYSIS

This chapter assumes that the reader has learned about single-system designs, as discussed in various texts (Rubin & Babbie, 2005; Bloom, Fischer, & Orme, 2003). Thus, we won't go over the logic of the designs or the research methods used to collect data in them. Instead, we'll limit our focus to the *statistical* analysis of single-system design data. That said, however, it should be noted that perhaps the most useful way to analyze single-system design data is not with tests of statistical significance, but rather through a *visual* analysis of the graphs depicting whether the level or trend in the chronologically plotted data during intervention differs in a *visually* significant way from the level or trend during baseline. You can learn about *visual significance* from the texts mentioned above. But even if your analysis stays at the visual level, you will be applying concepts about line graphs that we discussed in Chapter 4. For example, the line graph in Figure 18.1 depicts a visually significant change from baseline to intervention in the number of temper tantrums.

EFFECT SIZE

Even if we remain at the level of visual significance and don't ask whether the differences between the

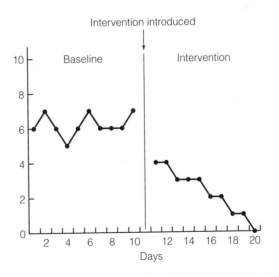

Figure 18.1 A Line Graph Depicting a Visually Significant Change from Baseline to Intervention in Number of Temper Tantrums

set of baseline data and intervention data are statistically significant, we would want to apply some descriptive statistics discussed earlier in this text. For example, we would want to express the change in the level of temper tantrums in terms of the mean or median (as discussed in Chapter 5). This would help us begin to consider the clinical significance of the visually significant findings. Thus, we might say that before intervention (during baseline) the mean number of tantrums per day was 5, as compared to a mean of only 2.6 after intervention.

Better yet, we should calculate the effect size (as discussed in Chapters 8 and 16). Doing so involves calculating the standard deviation (as discussed in Chapter 6) of the baseline data and then dividing that into the difference between the baseline and intervention mean. When we are calculating an effect size involving single-system design data, the baseline data are treated like a control group and the intervention data are treated like an experimental group. When we have a relatively small number of baseline observations, it is better to use the pooled standard deviation across both phases than just the standard deviation for the baseline phase (Bloom, Fischer, & Orme, 2003). Let's suppose that our standard deviation is 1.2. With a baseline mean of 5 and an intervention mean of 2.6, our effect size would be as follows:

$$\frac{2.6 - 5.0}{1.2} = \frac{-2.4}{1.2} = -2.0 \longrightarrow +2.0$$

As discussed in Chapter 8, we would change the minus sign to a plus sign because our dependent variable (temper tantrums) is undesirable. Thus, we want the intervention mean to be lower than the baseline mean. Also as discussed in Chapters 8 and 16, an effect size of 2.0 is considered to be quite strong and means that the average data point during intervention is two standard deviations away from the baseline mean. Knowing this, we might be inclined to deem our intervention clinically significant (although we would want to take other factors into consideration regarding clinical significance, as discussed in Chapter 16).

STATISTICAL SIGNIFICANCE

Several procedures discussed earlier in this text can be applied to single-system data to assess the probability that chance accounts for differences in the data patterns between baseline and intervention phases. Just as with other types of research designs, which procedure to use is influenced by the level of measurement of our outcome variable, the way the data are distributed, and how many data points we have. (The number of data points in a single-system design is analogous to sample size in other designs.)

t-Test

For example, under certain conditions we could conduct a t-Test (see Chapter 12 and Appendix G) to see whether there is a statistically significant difference between the baseline and intervention means. In the t-Test calculations, the intervention data would be treated like experimental group data, and the baseline data would be treated like control group data. Of course, one of the conditions required for calculating a t-Test is that the outcome variable be at the interval or ratio level of measurement. If it were at the nominal level—such as whether or not something happened at all each day (yes or no)—then means and standard deviations could not be calculated in a meaningful way. It's also desirable to have at least 6 observations per phase (more would be better) when applying a t-Test (Bloom, Fischer, & Orme, 2003).

Another consideration involves how the data are distributed. The data in each phase should be distributed normally (see Chapter 7). Violation of this assumption is particularly problematic when we have a small number of data points. Also, the data should not be autocorrelated. Single-system design data are autocorrelated if they are not independent of each other; that is, when we can predict the value of one data point knowing the value of other data points in the series. We'll return to the problem of autocorrelation in more detail soon, since the t-Test is not the only statistical procedure that it can affect.

Two-Standard-Deviation Procedure

Busy practitioners who want a simpler alternative to the t-Test for outcome data at the interval or ratio level of measurement can use the **two-standard-deviation procedure**. This procedure basically just involves calculating an effect size, using the standard deviation of the baseline data as the denominator (as described above). If the effect size is at least 2.0, then the difference between the two means (in the numerator) can be deemed statistically significant. The rationale for this approach is that if we assume that the baseline represents the sampling distribution of the null hypothesis, which would be a normal curve, then values falling 2 standard deviations away from the baseline mean are located in the critical region containing less than 5% (0.05) of the normal curve values. Thus, chance (sampling error) can be seen as having less than a 0.05 probability of explaining an intervention mean that is at least two standard deviations away from the baseline mean.

You may recall that earlier chapters discussed the possibility of getting statistically significant findings with effect sizes that are much smaller than 2.0. But single-system evaluation designs employed by clinical practitioners rarely have enough data points (i.e., a large enough sample size) to attain a sufficient level of statistical power with lower effect sizes. The two-standard-deviation procedure should be viewed merely as a rough rule-of-thumb method to give practitioners an approximate sense of whether it is reasonable to rule out chance as a plausible explanation for their findings. One problem with it is that some clinically significant and very effective interventions have effect sizes that are much less than 2.0. If your findings have clear visual significance, and if the difference between your baseline and intervention data attains an effect size that appears to have clear clinical significance from a subjective clinical standpoint, you risk a particularly unfortunate Type II error if you deem the tested intervention ineffective merely because the effect size did not reach 2.0. Of course, the same caveat applies to the *t*-Test as well as all other significance tests with single-system evaluations with insufficient data points to attain a reasonable level of statistical power (at 0.80 or above, as discussed in Chapter 16).

X-Moving Range-Three-Standard-Deviation Method

An alternative method for analyzing interval or ratio single-system data—one with even less power than the two-standard-deviation procedure—is recommended by Bloom, Fischer, and Orme (2003). They call this method the **X-Moving Range-Chart (X-mR-chart)** or the **three-standard-deviation band** approach. To simplify things, let's just use the term *X-mR-chart*.

The X-mR-chart method has less statistical power than the two-standard-deviation approach because it uses a more stringent critical region of at least three standard deviations away from the baseline mean for statistical significance, where the probability of a Type I error is only 0.0027. The advantage of the X-mR-chart approach, however, is that it calculates the baseline standard deviation in a way that attempts to smooth out unstable, fluctuating baseline patterns. Bloom and his associates also say that this moving range approach for calculating the standard deviation, combined with the more stringent significance level, enables the X-mR-chart approach to be less vulnerable to the problem of autocorrelation and to identify a statistically significant difference involving just one data point. In addition to determining change *between* phases, it also can detect whether a data point *within* any phase is significantly different from other data points within the same phase. The latter advantage has particular relevance to practitioners because an abrupt change within a phase can signal the need to modify an intervention or to search for the cause of the change.

To use the X-mR-chart, we first calculate the mean of the data points in the referent phase and then calculate the moving-range standard deviation. If any data point falls three or more such standard deviations away from the mean, it is considered statistically significant at the 0.0027 level. The steps for calculating the X-mR-chart standard deviation are displayed in the box titled "Steps for Calculating the X-mR-Chart." Notice that the last three data points of intervention are in the statistically significant desired zone. However, the *mean* of the 10 data points during intervention (26/10 = 2.6) falls short of the significant zone because it is less than three standard deviations better than the baseline mean of 5. Yet it is more than two standard deviations ($5 - 2 \times 1.125 = 2.75$) better than it. This illustrates the different results we would get depending on which approach we use and whether our criterion for significance uses the intervention mean or just one or more intervention data points.

Autocorrelation

All three of the above methods can yield distorted results if there is a significant amount of **autocorrelation** in the data. As mentioned earlier, single-system design data are autocorrelated if we can

Steps for Calculating the X-mR-Chart

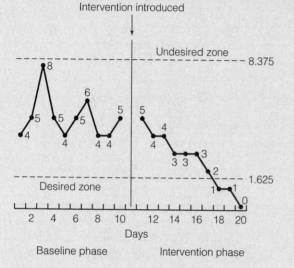

Figure 18.2 Graph of an Imaginary Client's Number of Temper Tantrums Before and After Intervention

The steps below are based on data in Figure 18.2, which displays a graph of an imaginary client's number of temper tantrums.

Step 1 Calculate the baseline mean:

$$\frac{4 + 5 + 8 + 5 + 4 + 5 + 6 + 4 + 4 + 5}{10}$$

$$= \frac{50}{10} = 5$$

Step 2 Calculate and then sum the ranges of each pair of adjacent data points, ignoring any minus signs. (There will be one less pair than the number of data points.)

$$4 - 5 = 1$$
$$5 - 8 = 3$$
$$8 - 5 = 3$$
$$5 - 4 = 1$$
$$4 - 5 = 1$$
$$5 - 6 = 1$$
$$6 - 4 = 2$$
$$4 - 4 = 0$$
$$\underline{4 - 5 = 1}$$
$$\text{Sum} = 13$$

Step 3 Calculate the mean range by dividing the sum of the ranges by the number of data points minus 1.

$$13/9 = 1.444$$

Step 4 The standard deviation will be the mean range divided by a correction factor of 1.128.

$$1.444/1.28 = 1.125$$

Step 5 Multiply the standard deviation by 3.

$$3 \times 1.125 = 3.375$$

Step 6 Draw band lines on your graph three standard deviation above the mean and three standard deviations below the mean. Any data points above and below those band lines will be considered statistically significant either in the desired or undesired direction, depending on whether the data refer to something you'd like to increase (i.e., positive behaviors) or decrease (i.e., antisocial behaviors).

predict the value of one data point knowing the value of other data points in the series. Autocorrelated data therefore are also called *serially dependent*.

To illustrate autocorrelation, suppose a client seeks your help in his effort to stop smoking. To construct a baseline, you ask him if he can recall how many cigarettes he has smoked each day for the last seven days. "Let's see," he says. "For the past six days, I kept a count each time I lit up. I smoked 8 cigarettes yesterday (Sunday), 10 on Saturday, 12 on Friday, 14 on Thursday, 16 on Wednesday, and 18 on Tuesday. But I'll have to think hard to remember how many I smoked last Monday. Hold on while I try to remember."

As you wait for him to recall the number, you're probably expecting him to say that he smoked a whole pack of 20 cigarettes that day. That's because he has been reducing the number smoked by 2 cigarettes each day. Knowing that the series going backward in time is 8 10 12 14 16 18, the most reasonable number to predict is 20. Likewise, if you showed your colleague the first five numbers and asked her to predict the sixth, she'd predict 18 and would be correct because the serial dependency of the data enables us to predict any data point in the series if we know where it fits in chronologically with the rest of the points whose values we do know.

In contrast, consider the following chronological series of data that are not autocorrelated: 5 4 6 6 5 6 5 7. Block out any number in the series and see if you can detect a pattern that enables you to predict the missing number. You might make a correct guess, but it would just be dumb luck because there is no pattern that would enable different people to predict with consistent accuracy any of the blocked-out numbers.

Some serial data are autocorrelated in ways that are not visually obvious. Consequently, statistical procedures are available to test whether a set of data is autocorrelated. Bloom, Fischer, and Orme (2003) show how to test statistically for autocorrelation. However, procedures to detect and transform autocorrelated data require a lot more data points than are feasible for most clinical practitioners.

Pronounced Trends

One of the ways in which single-system design data can be autocorrelated is when there is a pronounced

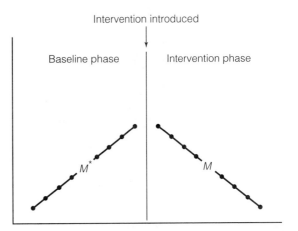

$*M$ = approximate level of mean in each phase.

Figure 18.3 A Graph of Temper Tantrums with Pronounced Reversing Trends That Illustrate the Inapplicability of Analyzing Statistical Significance Based on Means and Standard Deviation

increasing or decreasing trend in the data. This is particularly problematic if the trend occurs during baseline. Imagine, for example, a problem that gets progressively worse during baseline and then reverses direction during intervention, as displayed in Figure 18.3. The means of the baseline and intervention phases would be essentially identical despite the fact that the intervention may have effectively reversed a deteriorating problem. It would be inappropriate to use any of the three foregoing statistical significance approaches with such sloped data, since each of them only looks for changes in the *level* of the data points, not the change in the direction or slope of the trends.

A similar problem occurs when the baseline trend continues to increase or decrease at roughly the same rate during intervention. For example, the graph in Figure 18.4 lacks visual significance because the ongoing change process during baseline merely continues during intervention. The intervention does not appear to have accelerated it or to have had any effect on it. Yet the *level* of the intervention mean would be lower than the baseline mean and possibly statistically significant (in a misleading way). In a situation like this, an analysis of visual significance can be more meaningful and less misleading than an analysis of statistical significance.

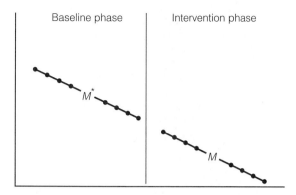

*M = approximate level of mean in each phase.

Figure 18.4   A Graph of Temper Tantrums with a Pronounced Trend During Baseline That Continues During Intervention to Illustrate a Situation Where Statistical Significance Can Be Misleading and Visual Analysis Would Be Preferable

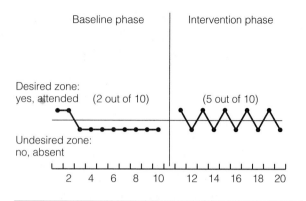

Figure 18.5   A Proportion-Frequency Graph of Weekly Treatment Sessions Attended

Proportion-Frequency Procedure

The foregoing procedures all require interval- or ratio-level data. When our data are dichotomous, such as in a "yes/no" format, we can use the **proportion-frequency procedure.** Instead of calculating means and standard deviations, which are inapplicable with dichotomous data, we draw a horizontal line to divide the yes zone from the no zone on a graph, and then plot each data point as either a yes or a no.

Suppose we are evaluating a motivational interviewing intervention that aims to engage and retain a client in a substance abuse outpatient treatment group. Figure 18.5 displays how the proportion-frequency graph would look for an imaginary client. At the start of baseline, the client attended only the first two weekly treatment sessions, and then never returned. Thus, his proportion of data points in the desired zone during baseline was 0.20 (two out of ten). During the intervention period, however, he attended alternating weekly treatment sessions, for a total of 5 sessions attended.

After constructing our dichotomous graph, we examine a binomial distribution table, as displayed in Table 18.1, to see if the difference in proportions is statistically significant. First we look down the left column under "Proportion of Data Points in the Desired Zone During Baseline." In that column we locate the row that corresponds to the referent proportion in our graph, which is 0.20. Next, we look across that row until it intersects with the column for the total number of data points in the intervention period, including those in the undesired as well as the desired zone. For our graph, that would be the column headed "10," since our client attended 5 sessions and missed 5 sessions for a total of 10 data points.

The number we see where the 0.20 row intersects with the 10 column is a 5. That means we need 5 data points in the desired zone during intervention for the difference in proportions to be statistically significant at the 0.05 level. Since we had that many in the desired zone, we can deem the difference to be statistically significant. With one less intervention data point in the desired zone, the difference would not have been statistically significant.

This example also reminds us of the important difference between statistical and clinical significance. Suppose the group treatment intervention is effective only when clients attend all 10 sessions, or perhaps 9 of the 10. Motivating the client to attend sessions on alternating weeks—for a total of five sessions—would not be clinically significant despite its statistical significance.

Thus, as we reach the end of this book, we should be reminded of the limits of statistical significance. An absence of statistical significance does not necessarily imply an ineffective intervention. It could be the result of a Type II error, especially when our statistical power is low due to a small sample size in a group evaluation or a small number of data points in a single-system evaluation. And a presence of statistical significance does not necessarily imply a practically meaningful intervention. As we've seen, some results can be statistically significant while lacking substantive (or clinical) significance.

Moreover, statistical significance pertains only to ruling out chance, or sampling error, as a plausible explanation for findings. It offers no basis whatsoever for ruling out other alternative explanations stemming from design flaws or measurement bias. And in the case of single-system designs, even with a sound design and sound measurement, a clear lack of visual significance renders statistical significance irrelevant. For example, if an improving trend in baseline merely continues unabated through the intervention phase, then the cause of the improvement—such as maturation, the passage of time, or a pre-existing and ongoing self-change process—is something other than the intervention. This is so no matter how much better the intervention mean is as compared to the baseline mean, and no matter how impressive the statistical significance level may be. Although this entire book has sought to help you understand the value of statistics and to help you utilize them, you should never become so enamored of statistics that you let them camouflage design and measurement flaws or distract you from alternative explanations for study findings.

Main Points

- Perhaps the most useful way to analyze single-system design data is not with tests of statistical significance, but rather through a *visual* analysis of the graphs depicting whether the level or trend in the chronologically plotted data during intervention differs in a *visually* significant way from the level or trend during baseline.

- When calculating an effect size involving single-system design data, the baseline data are treated like a control group and the intervention data are treated like an experimental group.

- Just as with other types of research designs, which statistical significance procedure to use with single-system design data is influenced by the level of measurement of our outcome variable, the way the data are distributed, and how many data points we have.

- In the t-Test calculations, the intervention data would be treated like experimental group data, and the baseline data would be treated like control group data.

- A simpler alternative to the t-Test for outcome data at the interval or ratio level of measurement is the two-standard-deviation procedure. This procedure basically just involves calculating an effect size using the standard deviation of the baseline data as the denominator. If the effect size is at least 2.0, then the difference between the two means (in the numerator) can be deemed statistically significant.

- The X-mR-chart method has less statistical power than the two-standard-deviation approach because it uses a more stringent critical region of at least three standard deviations away from the baseline mean for statistical significance, where the probability of a Type I error is only 0.0027. The advantage of the X-mR-chart approach, however, is that it calculates the baseline standard deviation in a way that attempts to smooth out unstable, fluctuating baseline patterns.

- The X-mR-chart approach can identify a statistically significant difference involving just one data point. In addition to determining change *between* phases, it also can detect whether a data point *within* any phase is significantly different from other data points within the same phase. The latter advantage has particular relevance to practitioners because an abrupt change within a phase can signal the need to modify an intervention or to search for the cause of the change.

- Single-system design data are autocorrelated if we can predict the value of one data point knowing the value of other data points in the series. Statistical significance tests can yield distorted results if there is a significant amount of autocorrelation in the data.

- When there are pronounced increasing or decreasing trends in the data, an analysis of visual significance can be more meaningful and less misleading than an analysis of statistical significance.

Table 18.1 Table of Significant Values at the 0.05 Level for the Proportion-Frequency Procedure

Brief Instructions: This table shows the *number* of observations of a specified type (e.g., desired behaviors) during the *intervention period* that are necessary to represent a significant increase at the 0.05 level of statistical significance as compared to the *proportion* of like observations during the *baseline period*. The steps in using the table are as follows:

1. Identify the proportion of observations in the desired zone in the baseline in the left-hand column (divide number of specified baseline events by *total number of baseline events*). Use "conservative rule" as needed.

2. Identify the total number of observations in the intervention period in the top row of table. Use "conservative rule" as needed.

3. Compare the total number of specified observations in the intervention period with the number at the intersection of the correct column and row. If the observed number is equal or greater than the number at the intersection then the comparison is statistically significant at the 0.05 level.

TOTAL NUMBER OF DATA POINTS IN THE INTERVENTION PERIOD

PROPORTION OF DATA POINTS IN THE DESIRED ZONE DURING BASELINE	4	6	8	10	12	14	16	18	20	24	28	32	36	40	44	48	52	56	60	64	68	72	76	80	84	88	92	96	100
.05	2	2	3	3	3	3	3	4	4	4	4	5	5	5	5	6	6	6	7	7	8	8	8	8	9	9	9	10	10
.10	3	3	3	4	4	4	5	5	5	6	7	7	8	8	9	9	10	10	11	12	12	13	13	14	14	15	15	16	16
1/8	3	3	4	4	5	5	5	6	6	7	8	8	9	10	10	11	12	12	13	14	14	15	15	16	17	17	18	19	19
.15	3	3	4	4	5	5	6	6	7	8	8	9	10	11	12	12	13	14	15	15	16	17	18	18	19	20	21	21	22
1/6	3	4	4	5	5	6	6	7	7	8	9	10	11	12	12	13	14	15	16	17	18	18	19	20	21	22	22	23	24
.20	3	4	5	5	6	6	7	8	8	9	10	11	12	13	14	15	16	17	18	19	20	21	22	23	24	25	26	27	28
.25	4	4	5	6	7	7	8	9	9	11	12	13	14	16	17	18	19	20	22	23	24	25	26	27	29	30	31	32	33
.30	4	5	6	6	7	8	9	10	10	12	13	15	16	18	19	21	22	24	25	26	28	29	30	32	33	35	36	37	39
1/3	4	5	6	7	8	9	9	10	11	13	15	16	18	19	21	22	24	26	27	29	30	32	33	35	36	38	39	41	42
.35	4	5	6	7	8	9	10	11	12	13	15	17	18	20	22	23	25	27	28	30	31	33	35	36	38	39	41	42	44
3/8	4	5	6	7	8	9	10	11	12	14	16	18	19	21	23	25	26	28	30	31	33	35	36	38	40	42	43	45	47
.40	4	5	6	8	9	10	11	12	13	15	16	18	20	22	24	26	28	29	31	33	35	37	38	40	42	44	46	47	49

TOTAL NUMBER OF DATA POINTS IN THE INTERVENTION PERIOD

PROPORTION OF DATA POINTS IN THE DESIRED ZONE DURING BASELINE

BASELINE	4	6	8	10	12	14	16	18	20	24	28	32	36	40	44	48	52	56	60	64	68	72	76	80	84	88	92	96	100
.45	4	6	7	8	9	10	11	13	14	16	18	20	22	24	26	28	30	32	34	36	38	40	42	44	46	48	50	52	54
.50	—	6	7	9	10	11	12	13	15	17	19	22	24	26	28	31	33	35	37	40	42	44	46	48	51	53	55	57	59
.55	—	6	8	9	10	12	13	14	16	18	21	23	26	28	31	33	35	38	40	43	45	48	50	52	55	57	59	62	64
.60	—	6	8	9	11	12	14	15	17	19	22	25	27	30	33	35	38	41	43	46	48	51	54	56	59	61	64	66	69
5/8	—	—	8	10	11	13	14	16	17	20	23	25	28	31	34	36	39	42	45	47	50	53	55	58	61	63	66	69	71
.65	—	—	8	10	11	13	14	16	17	20	23	26	29	32	35	38	40	43	46	49	52	54	57	60	63	65	68	71	74
2/3	—	—	8	10	12	13	15	16	18	21	24	27	30	32	35	38	41	44	47	50	53	55	58	61	64	67	70	72	75
.70	—	—	—	10	12	13	15	17	18	21	24	28	31	34	37	40	43	46	49	52	55	58	61	64	67	70	73	75	78
.75	—	—	—	—	12	14	16	17	19	22	26	29	32	35	39	42	45	48	51	55	58	61	64	67	70	74	77	80	83
.80	—	—	—	—	—	14	16	18	20	23	27	30	34	37	40	44	47	51	54	57	61	64	67	71	74	77	81	84	87
5/6	—	—	—	—	—	—	—	18	20	24	27	31	34	38	42	45	49	52	56	59	63	66	69	73	76	80	83	87	90
.85	—	—	—	—	—	—	—	—	20	24	28	31	34	38	42	46	49	53	56	60	63	67	70	74	78	81	85	88	92
7/8	—	—	—	—	—	—	—	—	—	24	28	32	36	39	43	47	50	54	57	61	65	68	72	76	79	83	86	90	94
.90	—	—	—	—	—	—	—	—	—	—	—	32	36	40	44	47	51	54	58	62	66	69	73	77	80	84	88	91	95
.95	—	—	—	—	—	—	—	—	—	—	—	—	—	—	—	—	52	56	60	64	68	72	76	79	83	87	91	95	99

*Tables of the Cumulative Binomial Probability Distribution—By the staff of the Harvard Computational Laboratory, Harvard University Press, 1955. This table constructed under the direction of Dr. James Norton, Jr., Indiana University—Purdue University at Indianapolis, 1973.

(This table is reproduced by permission of the author and the publisher from the *Paradox of Helping:Introduction to the Philosophy of Scientific Practice* by Martin Bloom [Boston: Pearson Education, 1975].)

• When our data are dichotomous, such as in a "yes/no" format, we can use the proportion-frequency procedure. Instead of calculating means and standard deviations, we draw a horizontal line to divide the yes zone from the no zone on a graph, and then plot each data point as either a yes or a no. After constructing our dichotomous graph, we examine a binomial distribution table as displayed in Table 18.1, to see if the difference in proportions is statistically significant.

• Statistical significance pertains only to ruling out chance, or sampling error, as a plausible explanation for findings. It offers no basis whatsoever for ruling out other alternative explanations stemming from design flaws or measurement bias. In the case of single-system designs, even with a sound design and sound measurement, a clear lack of visual significance renders statistical significance irrelevant.

• You should never become so enamored of statistics that you let them camouflage design and measurement flaws or distract you from alternative explanations for study findings.

Review Questions and Exercises

1. For each of the following data sets pertaining to daily verbal spouse abuse incidents, assess the statistical significance twice: once with the two standard deviation approach and once with the X-moving range-three-standard-deviation method. Interpret your results and discuss which method seems more reasonable to use for each data set. Also discuss the clinical significance of the degree of improvement.

BASELINE

Set 1: 6 3 2 6 9 3 6 9 9 7
Set 2: 3 6 5 2 5 4 5 6 5 4
Set 3: 8 7 8 9 7 5 8 7 4 7

INTERVENTION

6 5 4 3 2 2 2 2 2 2
1 1 1 1 1 1 1 1 1 1
1 2 2 3 3 4 5 6 7 7

2. For each of the following data sets pertaining to whether or not any abuse occurred on a given day, use the proportion-frequency procedure to assess statistical significance. Interpret your results and discuss their clinical significance. (Y = yes; N = no)

BASELINE

Set 1: Y Y N Y Y N Y Y N Y
Set 2: Y Y Y Y N Y Y N N N

INTERVENTION

N Y N Y N Y N Y N Y
N N N N N N N N Y Y

3. Which of the following baseline data sets appear to have the most and the least autocorrelation? Explain your answer.

BASELINE

Set 1:	1	3	3	5	5	7	7	8	9	8
Set 2:	1	8	1	8	1	8	1	8	1	8
Set 3:	4	3	2	4	4	4	3	4	2	4

4. Assuming that the following results are statistically significant using the X-moving range-three-standard-deviation method, how would you interpret the effectiveness of the intervention, which aims to decrease the number of days per week that a high school student smokes marijuana?

BASELINE	INTERVENTION
7 7 7 6 6 6 5 5 5 4	4 4 3 3 3 2 2 2 1 0

InfoTrac Exercises

1. Read the article below and discuss how at least one of its conclusions is relevant to evidence-based practitioners.

Parker, R. I., Brossart, D. F., Vannest, K. J., Long, J. R., De-Alba, R. G., Baugh, F. G., & Sullivan, J. R. (2005). Effect sizes in single case research: How large is large? *School Psychology Review, 34*(1), 116–132.

2. Examine the graphs in Figure 1 of the article below. Do you agree with the authors' interpretation of visual significance, especially in light of the number of baseline data points? Do you agree with the authors' emphasis on the statistical significance of the data in these graphs? Briefly explain your answers.

March, J. S., Amaya-Jackson, L., Murray, M. C., & Schulte, A. (1998). Cognitive-behavioral psychotherapy for children and adolescents with post-traumatic stress disorder after a single-incident stressor. *Journal of the American Academy of Child and Adolescent Psychiatry, 37*(6), 585–593.

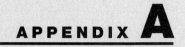

Review of Key Research Methodology Concepts and Terms

INTRODUCTION

In order to understand statistics, it helps if you are familiar with the concepts and terminology associated with research methods. The purpose of this appendix is to review—in summary fashion—those concepts and terms. Let's begin by recognizing that the statistical material in this text, as well as the concepts and terms to be reviewed in this appendix, are associated with what is called *quantitative research methods*. **Quantitative methods** typically are used when studies aim to develop precise, objective, and generalizable findings. These studies rely on *quantitative analysis;* that is, they involve numbers and statistics. Statistics also may be included in studies that primarily employ **qualitative methods;** however, qualitative studies put less emphasis on precise and generalizable statistics than on more flexible observational and interview procedures that produce narratives that attempt to probe in a more subjective fashion into deeper, non-numerical underlying meanings and patterns.

This appendix is not meant as a substitute for a research methods course. You may need to take such a course to fully comprehend the concepts and terms covered in this appendix. If you haven't yet studied research methods, you may wish that this appendix would go into more depth about some of the concepts and terms. To go into them in depth, however, would require an entire research methods text. In case you happen to have a copy of the fifth edition of the research methods text by Rubin and Babbie (2005), I'll note the chapter numbers of that text that provide in-depth coverage of the material in this appendix.

Although you may not fully comprehend everything in this appendix, I hope that at least it will make it easier for you to handle the statistical material in the main body of this text. If you have already studied research methods, I hope this appendix will serve as useful refresher regarding the research concepts and terms that are used when discussing statistics.

THE RESEARCH PROCESS

As discussed in Chapter 4 of the Rubin and Babbie text, at any point in the research process investigators may encounter problems or new insights that prompt them to return to an earlier phase in the process. Nevertheless, it is helpful to think of the research process as going through the following sequential phases. The first phase involves **problem formulation.** In this phase, we recognize the need for more knowledge about some issue. We pose a research question and then progressively sharpen it to increase its specificity and value to our professional knowledge base. We also encounter and try to resolve potential obstacles to the feasibility of the research. At the end of this phase, after a thorough literature review, we finalize the purpose and conceptual elements of the research.

In the second phase, we *design the study.* This involves decisions about sampling, measurement, data collection procedures, logical arrangements, and so on. The third phase involves *data collection.* That is followed by the **data processing** phase, which typically involves preparing and entering our data for computer analysis. Then comes **data analysis,** when we click on computer prompts to obtain appropriate statistical analyses. Next, we *interpret the findings.* Our computer output won't do this for us. There is usually more than one way to interpret statistical findings. Rival interpretations must be considered and discussed along with the study's methodological limitations. Conclusions may or may not be rather tentative, and typically will include implications for policy, practice, theory, and/or future research. The final phase involves *writing the research report,* although this phase really (ideally!) should be implemented incrementally as we go along through each of the prior phases. The report typically includes an *introduction* section that provides a background to the study and its value, a *methodology* section that delineates in precise terms the decisions made in the study design phase, a *results* section that merely reports statistical data without drawing conclusions, and a *discussion* section that covers what was mentioned above regarding interpreting the findings.

CONCEPTUAL ELEMENTS OF QUANTITATIVE RESEARCH STUDIES

The conceptual elements of research studies are discussed in Chapter 5 of Rubin and Babbie (2005). A **hypothesis** is a tentative statement about a presumed relationship between *concepts.* For example, a hypothesis might predict that changes in one concept will be accompanied by changes in another concept. As discussed in Chapter 1 of this text, the concepts in a hypothesis statement are represented by variables. They are called *variables* because hypotheses postulate that they *vary* together. Consequently, a variable must be capable of varying. That requires that it comprise more than one attribute or value category. **Attributes,** or **value categories,** are the concepts that make up a variable. The attributes, or value categories, of *gender*, for example, are *male* or *female*.

Independent variables are those that are postulated to *explain or cause something*. **Dependent variables** are the ones *being explained or caused*. For example, a hypothesis might predict that one particular intervention will be more effective than another in reducing level of substance abuse. The foregoing hypothesis consists of two variables: (1) type of intervention—the independent variable; and (2) level of substance abuse—the dependent variable.

Some multivariate studies, such as multiple regression analysis and logistic regression, use the term **predictor variable** instead of the term *independent variable*. Those studies usually are trying to discover which variables among a large set of possible predictors turn out to be the best predictors of a dependent variable or how well a set of predictor variables as a whole predicts a dependent variable.

Multivariate studies also may include what some call **control variables, mediating variables,** and **intervening variables.** Rather than worry about the precise distinctions among these types of variables, the main thing you need to know for the purposes of this text is that these variables are studied to see whether and how they shed light on or perhaps even explain away relationships we observe between our independent and dependent variables.

For example, suppose cancer patients who receive more social work services pass away sooner than those who receive fewer social work services. Were the social work services harmful? Quite unlikely indeed! Instead, we'd expect that the difference almost surely can be explained away by the fact that patients who are already terminally ill (and their families) will need more services than those whose illnesses are not terminal. Thus, we'd want to include in our study as a *control* variable whether or not the patient's illness was diagnosed as terminal *before* receiving social work services.

To illustrate an *intervening* or *mediating* variable, suppose we think that the reason why substance abusers who receive a motivational intervention have better clinical outcomes than non-recipients is not because of the motivational intervention alone, but rather because the intervention motivates them to seek and complete more intensive treatment. Thus, the motivational intervention might work through an intervening variable that chronologically comes between (mediates) it and the dependent variable.

Research studies test hypotheses by conducting *observations* based on the way they operationally define their variables. **Operational definitions** specify precisely what observations will determine which attribute or value category applies to a particular variable for a particular research participant. Thus, we might operationally define level of substance abuse in terms of the results of a urinalysis or the number of arrests for substance abuse. Operational definitions, in other words, help determine how variables will be measured.

KEY MEASUREMENT CONCEPTS

Key measurement concepts are discussed in Chapter 6 of Rubin and Babbie (2005). Variables can be measured in terms of *frequencies*, such as head counts, or they can be measured metrically, such as in terms of magnitude or duration. As discussed in Chapter 1 of this text, measurements of frequencies are at the *nominal level* of measurement. They count the number (frequency) of cases in non-metric, qualitative value categories, such as the number of men and women, the percentage of cases in various categories of ethnicity, and so on. **Metric measurements,** on the other hand, can be at the ordinal, interval, or ratio level. At the *ordinal level,* we know only whether one case has more or less of something than another case, but we don't know how much more. For example, we have an ordinal measure if we know that the horse Seabiscuit won the race and Mr. Ed came in second, but we don't know by how much. Likewise, if clients say they are very satisfied with Service A, but only slightly satisfied with Service B, then we have an ordinal measure because we don't know the precise difference in degree of satisfaction. At the *interval level,* in contrast, we know that the differences between different levels of a variable have the same meanings. Thus, the difference between an IQ score of 95 and 100 is considered to be of the same magnitude as the difference between 100 and 105. Variables at the *ratio level* of measurement have the same attribute as interval measures, but in addition have a true zero point. Thus, a person can have no arrests, one arrest, two arrests, and so on. Because there is a true zero point, we know that the person with 4 arrests has been arrested exactly twice as many times as the person with 2 arrests.

Measures at any level should be both *reliable* and *valid*. Measures have **reliability** when they are consistent. If you ask most people their gender on several different occasions, you'll probably get the same answer every time. Thus, your information about gender would be reliable. Measures have **validity** when they truly and accurately measure what they intend to measure. Thus, asking about gender will probably result in information that is not only reliable, but also valid. However, suppose a probation officer asks probationers how many crimes they committed since their last contact. The probation officer would probably get a reliable (i.e., consistent) reply of "none" from all of them regardless of whether that answer was true or not. Thus, the information would be reliable, but not valid. The reason for the lack of validity would have to do with *measurement bias*.

Measurements can be conducted in various ways. One way is by **direct observation.** Cottage parents can directly observe and count, for example, how many fights a child gets into each week in a residential treatment facility. Another way is through **self-reports.** Thus, children can be asked in interviews how often they get into fights, have nightmares, and so on. Or they can be asked the same things in paper-and-pencil self-report *questionnaires* or *scales*. A third option is by examining *available records*. For example, we can examine school records regarding grades, disciplinary referrals, absences, and so on. Regardless of which measurement approach we use, we should try to make sure that our approach is as *unbiased* and *objective* as possible, and we should assess its reliability and validity. One way to try to minimize bias is by using **unobtrusive** measurement procedures. That means conducting observations in such a way that those who are being observed are unlikely to notice or be affected by the observation. Examining school records, for example, is an example of unobtrusive measurement. Having the therapist sit in on a classroom session would be an example of **obtrusive** observation. A related concept here is the principle of **triangulation,** which means using more than one measurement approach and seeing if they obtain similar results.

KEY SAMPLING CONCEPTS

Key sampling concepts are discussed in Chapter 8 of Rubin and Babbie (2005). For studies that attempt to *generalize* to a population, the ideal sample will be *representative* of that population. The safest way to obtain a representative sample is by using *probability sampling* methods. That means selecting your sample by means of *random numbers* so that every element in the larger population has an equal chance of being selected for your sample. By using *random sampling,* you ensure that your biases, limited knowledge about a population, or errors in judgment cannot influence which elements get selected for inclusion in your study and which do not. There are several ways to obtain a probability (i.e., random) sample, but for the purposes of this book the key issue to remember is that whether or not yours is a probability sample will influence your choice of statistical procedures.

Evaluation researchers often have difficulty obtaining probability samples, due to the settings in which human services are provided or the nature of their target populations. Consequently, many evaluation studies have to use the less desired, but often useful, technique of **non-probability sampling.** For example, studies evaluating the effectiveness of human service programs or interventions often have to rely on convenience, or availability, samples. Typically we cannot randomly select who our service recipients will be; we must instead rely on who happens to be available as clients when we conduct our studies.

KEY CONCEPTS IN DESIGNS FOR EVALUATING PROGRAMS AND PRACTICE

The prime issue when we evaluate our effectiveness is determining whether our programs or practice are the true causes of any client outcomes we observe. Determining this involves three overarching criteria. First, clients who receive the interventions being evaluated should have better outcomes than clients who don't receive those interventions. Second, the improvement in client outcome should occur after, not before, we intervene. Third, we need to rule out plausible alternative explanations for the improvement.

One of the prominent plausible alternative explanations we seek to rule out is **history,** which refers to other events that may coincide with our intervention and cause the improvement. Thus, if we are evaluating an intervention to reduce antisocial behavior by a boy in a residential treatment center, and while we are still delivering that intervention the boy gets transferred from one cottage where he had personality conflicts to a different cottage where he fit in better, we would not know if the improvement in his behavior was caused by our intervention or by the cottage transfer.

Another prominent plausible alternative explanation is **maturation,** or the **passage of time.** Thus, if we are evaluating our play therapy intervention for a recently traumatized child, and the child's trauma symptoms were less severe 6 months later, we would want to know whether our intervention or the mere passage of time caused the improvement.

A third prominent alternative plausible explanation involves **selection biases,** which pertain to possible differences between the clients who receive the interventions we are evaluating and clients to whom we are comparing them—differences that render the two groups of clients incomparable. Thus, if we compare substance-abusing teens who voluntarily agree to use our services to substance-abusing teens who refuse to use our services, we would not know whether any better outcomes for the teens we treated were caused by our treatment or by the fact that they were more motivated to change to begin with and perhaps already engaged in a change process before engaging our services.

There are additional possible alternative plausible explanations that you can examine in a research text, but those mentioned above will suffice for our purposes in this statistics text. Our evaluation design has something called **internal validity** to the extent that our evaluation design enables us to logically rule out the plausibility of these alternative explanations. The more internal validity we have, the more confidence we have that our intervention, and not something else, is the cause of the outcomes we observe.

There are three overarching types of designs that are used when we seek to evaluate our programs or practice in ways that are internally valid. These are experimental designs, quasi-experimental designs, and single-system designs. **Experimental designs** involve randomly assigning clients to different groups and then providing the intervention we seek to evaluate to one or more groups whose outcomes will be compared to one or more groups that receive no intervention or a different form of intervention. The group that receives the intervention being evaluated is usually called the **experimental group.** The other group is usually called the **control group.** The foregoing concepts regarding internal validity and experimental designs are discussed in Chapter 10 of Rubin and Babbie (2005).

Chapter 11 of Rubin and Babbie discusses **quasi-experimental designs,** which are used when random assignment is not feasible. When we use quasi-experimental designs, we either try to find existing groups that appear to be comparable and then provide the tested intervention to one of the groups, or we use multiple measurements before and after intervention to try to rule out the influences of history or the passage of time. **Single-system designs** (discussed in Chapter 12 of Rubin and Babbie) also involve the use of multiple measurements before and after intervention to try to rule out history or the passage of time. They are a form of quasi-experimental designs that receive special attention in evidence-based practice because practitioners can use them to evaluate their own practice effectiveness with individual client systems.

Sometimes feasibility constraints keep us from using any of the above designs, and we are forced to use designs that have less internal validity (as discussed in Chapters 10 and 11 of Rubin and Babbie). Among these designs are *pre-experimental designs, cross-sectional designs* and *case control designs.* The value of these designs can be strengthened by using multivariate statistical procedures that are discussed in Chapter 13, Chapter 17, and Appendix D of this text.

In closing this appendix, I should reiterate that it has not reviewed all the concepts that are covered in a research methods course. It has reviewed only those terms and concepts that I think you'll need to be familiar with as you read this book. I hope it helps!

Review of Some Math Basics

INTRODUCTION

When I first started teaching research and statistics, I was surprised to discover that many of my students had forgotten such basics as how to calculate a percentage or what happens to the minus sign when you square a negative number. If you are one of these students, you have lots of company, and this appendix is intended for you. This review will not be comprehensive. Instead, it will just cover selected areas that are most pertinent to the material in this text and those which, based on my experience, give students the most trouble. Let's begin with positive (+) and negative (−) signs.

POSITIVE AND NEGATIVE SIGNS

Suppose you ask clients to rate their satisfaction with your agency's services, and you assign numbers to their ratings as follows:

$+2$ Very Satisfied

$+1$ Satisfied

0 Neither Satisfied Nor Dissatisfied

$+1$ Dissatisfied

$+2$ Very Dissatisfied

Addition

When adding signed numbers, if the signs are the same, then you add the numbers and keep the same sign. Thus, we would have the following sums for two pairs of clients:

$+2 + 1 = +3$

$-2 - 1 = -3$

If the signs are different, then the sum is the difference between the numbers, as follows:

$+2 - 1 = +1$

$+1 - 2 = -1$

The minus sign in the sum −1 above means that the negative number is greater than the positive number. Likewise, if we add more than two numbers, and the negative ones add up to a number greater than the sum of the positive ones, then the sign of the sum will be negative, as follows:

$+1 + 3 + 1 - 2 - 2 - 2 = -1$

(The positives add up to +5 and the negatives add up to −6.)

Subtraction

When subtracting signed numbers, first change the sign of the number being subtracted and then add the numbers. Thus, we would have the following for three pairs of clients:

Subtracting $+1$ from $+2 = 2 - (+1) = 1$

Subtracting $+2$ from $+1 = 1 - (+2) = -1$

Subtracting -1 from $+2 = 2 - (-1) = 3$

Perhaps the idea that turning a minus into a plus with subtraction seems odd to you. If so, imagine that 4 clients responded with +2 (Very Satisfied), and one responded with −2 (Very Dissatisfied). The sum of the five ratings would be 6, as follows:

$+2 + 2 + 2 + 2 - 2 = 6$

However, suppose we learn that the −2 rating came from a questionnaire in a survey from an earlier year that mistakenly got included in the current pile of questionnaires. We therefore decide to exclude (subtract) it from our current data analysis. What would that do to our sum of 6? We'd subtract the −2 from it. Because subtracting a minus means changing it to a plus, our sum would become 6 + (+2) = 8, which is the sum we would have had without the −2 in the five ratings above.

Here's another example. Suppose your agency took in $10,000 in a fundraising event, but owes the hotel $1000 for providing the room and food for the event. Thus, your agency ends up with an additional $9000 in funds. But what if the hotel manager wants to support your agency's mission and therefore calls you and says the hotel will forgive (take away) the $1000 you owe it. Subtracting that debt (a negative $1000) adds $1000 to the funds you end up with, which become $10,000.

Multiplication

If the signs of numbers being multiplied are the same, then the product will be positive. If the signs are different, then the product will be negative. Thus, if two clients both give a rating of +2, then our total is 2 clients times +2, or +4. If they both give a −2, then we get 2 clients times −2 = −4. Suppose a pair of −2 ratings had to be excluded from the analysis. In getting rid of both −2 ratings, we would actually be increasing our total by 4. Thus, −2 clients times −2 = +4.

You should also be reminded of the following two multiplication symbols:

X

( )

For example, 2 × 2 means 2 multiplied by 2. The same applies to (2)(2). But what about (2)(2 + 1)? Before multiplying, we have to perform the operations inside the parentheses. Thus, (2)(2 + 1) becomes (2)(3) = 6. Notice how that differs from (2 × 2) + 1, which would come to 5.

Division

As with multiplication, if the signs of numbers being involved are the same, then the dividend will be positive. If the signs are different, then the dividend will be negative. Thus if we have a sum of 10 in the ratings of 5 clients, and we divide the sum by the number of clients, we get +2 per client. Likewise, if our sum is −10, then we get −10 divided by +5, which equals −2 per client.

What if we wanted to know how many negative 2's there are in −10? Negative ten divided by negative 2 would become a positive 5, because there are 5 negative 2's in a sum of −10.

Symbols used for division, using the sum of 10 divided by 5, are as follows:

10 ÷ 5

10/5

$$\frac{10}{5}$$

As with multiplication, division requires performing the operations within parentheses first. Thus,

$$10/(2 + 3) = 10/5 = 2$$

Notice how the above answer is different from (10÷2) + 3, which would be 5 + 3 = 8.

PROPORTIONS AND PERCENTAGES

A proportion represents how much of one value is in another value. For example, suppose we bake two pumpkin pies on Thanksgiving and cut each into four equally sized pieces. If you eat one of the pieces of the first pie to come out of the oven, you will have consumed one-fourth of one pie. To turn that fraction into a proportion, we divide your one piece by four pieces. One divided by 4 equals 0.25. To turn this into a percentage, we multiply by 100. Thus, you ate 25% of the first pie. Considering all 8 pieces in both pies, you will have consumed 1/8 = 0.125 of the total amount of pumpkin pie. Multiplying that by 100, we get 12.5%. To turn a percentage back into a proportion, we divide by 100; thus, 12.5 (percent) divided by 100 equals 0.125.

Calculating Increases or Decreases in Terms of Proportions or Percentages

When calculating increases or decreases in terms of percentages, we should always divide the amount of change by the number being increased or decreased. For example, an increase from 1 to 2 is a 100% increase, not a 50% increase. That is, the increase of 1 is 100% of the original number (1). Calling it a 50% increase because 1 is half of 2 would be incorrect. But a decrease from 2 to 1 is a 50% decrease, because the number 2 fell by half of its original amount.

Suppose there are 100 incidents of child abuse in a county in 2004, followed by 90 such incidents in 2005. The difference of 10 incidents represents a drop of 10/100, or 0.10 (10%), from 2004 to 2005. Thus the 90 incidents in 2005 comprise 90% (0.90) of the incidents in 2004.

Suppose in 2006 the number goes back up to 100. In terms of a proportion or percentage, the latter increase would *not* be 0.10 (10%), because the increase of 10 is based on the 90 incidents in 2005. Thus, it would be an increase of 10/90, or 0.11 (11%). Thus, the 100 incidents in 2006 represent 111% of the incidents in 2005. If the number were to double in 2007, from 100 to 200, that would be a 100% increase, and the 2007 number would be 200% of the 2006 number.

Adding and Subtracting Proportions

When adding and subtracting proportions, we must keep the decimal points in a straight line. Thus, if you eat 0.25 pumpkin pies and I eat 1.333 pumpkin pies (Oink!), we add our amounts as follows:

$$\begin{array}{r} 0.250 \\ +1.333 \\ \hline 1.583 \end{array} \text{ pies}$$

How many more pies did I eat than you? See below:

$$\begin{array}{r} 1.333 \\ -0.250 \\ \hline 1.083 \quad \text{pies} \end{array}$$

Multiplying Proportions and Percentages

When multiplying proportions, after we multiply all the numbers, we position the decimal point in the product so that it is to the left of the total number of digits to the right of the decimal points in the two proportions being multiplied. Thus, suppose that 10% (0.10) of the number of incidents of abuse in our country occurred in our large state, and that 33.3% (0.333) of the incidents in our state occurred in our city. To find the proportion of nationwide incidents that occurred in our city based on this information we would get the following:

$$\begin{array}{r} 0.333 \\ \times \quad 0.10 \\ \hline 0.03330 \end{array}$$

[Notice we had to add a zero between the decimal point and the first digit (3) in the product in order to get 5 digits to the right of the decimal point in the product. We had to do this because there are five digits to the right of the two decimal points in the two proportions being multiplied.]

If we are multiplying percentages, we simply change them to proportions first, then multiply the proportions, and then multiply the product by 100 to convert it back to a percentage. Thus 50% × 50% = 0.50 × 0.50 = 0.25 = 25%. If we are multiplying a percentage by a number that is not a percentage, then we simply convert the percentage to a proportion and multiply. Nothing else is needed. Thus, 50% of 100 is 0.50 × 100 = 50.

Dividing Proportions

When dividing proportions, we have to get rid of the decimal point in the denominator by moving it to the right so that the number becomes whole. Then we have to move the decimal point in the numerator to the right past the same number of digits. Thus, dividing 0.75 by 1.5 would be as follows:

$$0.75/1.5 = 7.5/15 = 0.50$$

SQUARES AND SQUARE ROOTS

Whenever a number or an expression in parentheses is followed by a raised 2 immediately above and to the right of it, it means we should square the number or expression. For example 5^2 means we should square 5. Squaring a number means multiplying it by itself. Thus, $5^2 = 5 \times 5 = 25$. Likewise, the expression $(2 + 5)^2$ means we should add 2 plus 5 first, and then square. Thus $(2 + 5)^2 = 7^2 = 49$, while $2 + 5^2 = 2 + 25 = 27$.

The same rules apply if we are dealing in algebraic letter symbols, such as X and Y. Thus, XY^2 calls for squaring Y and then multiplying it by X, whereas $(XY)^2$ calls for multiplying X times Y first, and then squaring the product. Thus, if $X = 5$ and $Y = 4$, $XY^2 = 5 \times 4^2 = 5 \times 16 = 80$, and $(XY)^2 = (5 \times 4)^2 = 20^2 = 400$.

The raised number is called the exponent. An exponent of 2 calls for squaring, an exponent of 3 calls for cubing, and so on. Cubing simply means multiplying the square by the original number; or said another way, including the original number three times in the equation, such as $4 \times 4 \times 4 = 64$ (which is 4^3). An exponent of 1 is sort of unnecessary; it simply means the number remains unchanged. Thus, $4^1 = 4$.

A negative number squared means that the sign changes, as discussed earlier regarding multiplying two negative numbers. Thus, $-4^2 = +16$. However, cubing a negative number results in a negative number, as follows:

$$-4^3 = (-4)(-4)(-4) = +16(-4) = -64$$

When a number or expression appears under a radical sign ($\sqrt{}$), it calls for taking the square root of that number or expression. The square root is the original number before it was squared (multiplied by itself). Thus, $\sqrt{16} = 4$. Suppose $X = 3$ and $Y = 6$. Then

$$\sqrt{X + Y} = \sqrt{3 + 6} = \sqrt{9} = 3$$

Likewise,

$$\sqrt{XY} = \sqrt{3 \times 6} = \sqrt{18} = 4.24$$

Statistical Symbols

This appendix lists and explains some statistical symbols that appear in this text and were not explained in the previous appendix that reviewed some math basics. Beside each symbol is its meaning. If you are perplexed when you encounter any of these symbols in this text, referring to this appendix might help. These are not the only potentially perplexing symbols found in this text. However, those that require a lengthier explanation are explained when they are introduced in the text.

SYMBOL	MEANING	EXAMPLE
>	Greater than	$5 > 3$
<	Less than	$3 < 5$
X or Y	Scores	$X = 10$ means there is a score of 10 on variable X
		$Y = 5$ means there is a score of 5 on variable Y
N	Sample size	Number of values for a variable in the data set
Σ	Sum	ΣX is the sum of all scores on variable X.
μ	Population mean	If the population of $N = 40{,}000$ social work students in the United States buys a total of $\Sigma X = 80{,}000$ practice methods textbooks, then the mean number of textbooks purchased for the population $[\Sigma X/N]$ is $80{,}000/40{,}000 = 2$ practice methods textbooks.
$\bar{X}$	Sample mean	If the sample of 20 social work students in my statistics class buys a total of 20 statistics textbooks, then the sample mean is $20/20 = 1$ statistics textbook. (Can you guess which one?)
r	Correlation coefficient	There is a strong correlation between height and weight.
p	Probability	The probability of heads on a coin toss is $p = 0.50$.

APPENDIX **D**

Additional Multivariate Procedures: A Conceptual Overview

Introduction

Discriminant Analysis

Logistic Regression

Event History Analysis (Survival Analysis)

Path Analysis

Factor Analysis

INTRODUCTION

Chapter 13 introduced the concept of multivariate analysis with a discussion of ANCOVA, two-way ANOVA, and MANOVA. Chapter 17 returned to that concept in connection with multiple correlation and multiple regression analysis. As promised at the end of each of those chapters, this appendix offers a conceptually oriented glimpse into several additional prominent forms of multivariate analysis. It does so without delving into their formulae and calculations. Although this appendix won't prepare you to use these multivariate procedures independently in your own research and evaluation, it will attempt to help you understand the meaning and practical utility of findings that others report based on these procedures. It might also help you to understand better the advice you may get from statistical consultants who assist you in your research and evaluation efforts. Perhaps it might even whet your appetite for learning more about how to use these procedures yourself. Let's begin with a multivariate procedure akin to multiple regression analysis but designed for use when our dependent variable is at the nominal level of measurement.

DISCRIMINANT ANALYSIS

You may recall that multiple regression analysis requires a dependent variable at the interval or ratio level of measurement. Very often in practice research and evaluation, however, our dependent variable is at the nominal level of measurement, such as measuring whether clients relapse, recidivate, drop out and so on. Discriminant analysis can examine a group of independent variables at the interval or ratio level of measurement and—as multiple regression analysis does with an interval- or ratio-level dependent variable—identify which of those variables most accurately predict a nominal-level dependent variable. The nominal-level dependent variables in discriminant analysis are often dichotomous (i.e., having only two categories, such as relapse versus non-relapse, and so on). Discriminant analysis also can be used with nominal-level dependent variables having more than two categories, such as when we want to examine factors that predict which one of three or more treatment options or living arrangements to which a client is to be assigned.

Discriminant analysis employs a concept similar to the regression equation, called the **discriminant function.** The discriminant function uses weighted values of predictor variables to assign a person to one of the qualitative categories of the nominal-level dependent variable. Thus, whereas the regression equation will use weighted values to predict a person's score on an interval- or ratio-level dependent variable, discriminant analysis will do so to predict whether a person will drop out or not drop out, get rearrested or not, and so on. The discriminant function equation will add up the products of the weights of each variable times a person's score on each variable and produce a composite score (like Y' in the regression equation) that is used to predict which group a person is likely to be in. It also produces a *cutoff score* for each possible dependent variable category. A person's discriminant function score is compared to the cutoff score to predict the category in which he or she will fall. For example, if the cutoff score for predicting dropping out is 21 or more, and a client's weighted values on the set of predictor variables add up to 21 or more, that client will be predicted to drop out. If these values add up to 20 or less, the client will be predicted to be among the group that does not drop out.

Just as regression analysis uses a least squares approach to come up with an equation that will most accurately predict a quantitative value, discriminant analysis derives variable weights that minimize the number of errors in classifying people into one nominal category or another. Also like regression analysis, discriminant analysis offers the option to use stepwise procedures to reduce a large number of possible predictor variables to a smaller list of variables that excludes those variables that do not significantly reduce the number of classification errors produced by the equation.

Discriminant function analysis also will produce a summary statistic akin to the R^2 in multiple correlation. Often that statistic will be called either *Wilks' Lambda, Mahaloanobis D^2,* or *Rao's V.* You need not study the mathematical and statistical details of each to know that whichever of these statistics you may encounter, their purpose is essentially the same—to depict the strength of the discriminant function in accurately predicting the nominal-level dependent variable and to provide a summary statistic that can be tested for statistical significance to

Table D.1 A Confusion Matrix with Imaginary Data on Predicted Versus Actual Foster Care Placement Successes and Failures for 400 Placements

ACTUAL OUTCOME OF FOSTER CARE PLACEMENT	PREDICTED OUTCOME OF FOSTER CARE PLACEMENT		TOTALS
	SUCCESS	FAILURE	
Success	180 (90% correct)	40 (errors)	220
Failure	20 (errors)	160 (80% correct)	180
Totals	200 (100%)	200 (100%)	400

rule out chance in explaining the number of correct classifications.

To assess the number of errors produced by the discriminant function equation, discriminant analysis uses something usually called a *confusion matrix*, such as the one illustrated in Table D.1. The matrix displays the number of people predicted to be in a particular group and whether in reality they actually are in that group. Thus, the confusion matrix shows the proportion of correct and incorrect predictions produced by the discriminant function equation.

I've concocted simplified hypothetical data in Table D.1 to illustrate the use of a confusion matrix in an imaginary study that attempts to identify predictors of whether a foster placement will be successful or not (based on weighted values assigned to various predictor variables associated with the child, the foster parents, and so on). Looking down the columns of the matrix, we see that 180 (90%) of the 200 placements that were predicted to be successes actually were successes and that 160 (80%) of the 200 placements predicted to be failures actually were failed placements. Overall, then, 340 of the 400 predictions were correct, for an accuracy rate of 85%.

Results like these would be of great value in helping practitioners in child welfare settings make decisions about prospective foster placements. The

results of discriminant analysis also will provide squared standardized beta weights for each predictor variable that—as in regression analysis—depict the relative strength of each variable in predicting the dependent variable.

Although the potential utility of discriminant analysis may be evident, there are two caveats about it that you should remember. One is that when our data are at the interval or ratio level of measurement, regression analysis is usually preferable to reducing those data to a nominal level for the purpose of conducting a discriminant analysis. That's because we lose precision and statistical power when we collapse data into broader categories. A second caveat is that the results of any regression analysis should be *cross-validated* with a separate sample. Replication is important in all research studies, and it is particularly important in discriminant analysis because—for complex statistical reasons—the discriminant equation typically produces more correct classifications with its original sample than with a fresh sample.

LOGISTIC REGRESSION

As noted above, discriminant analysis requires independent variables that are quantitative, not nominal. But many multivariate analyses examine nominal-level independent variables in relation to a nominal-level dependent variable. When we have a nominal-level dependent variable and not all of our independent variables are at the interval or ratio level (as required in discriminant analysis), an extension of multiple regression analysis and of discriminant analysis can be used, called **logistic regression.** A logistic regression analysis will produce an equation that predicts the probability of a given category on the dependent variable in light of the values of each independent variable. That probability is called an **odds ratio.** The odds ratio indicates how much more likely certain independent variable categories are than other categories to have a given category of the dependent variable.

For example, Hodge, Cardenas, and Montoya (2001) conducted a logistic regression analysis to assess the influence of religious participation and spirituality as predictors of never using alcohol, marijuana, or hard drugs among teens living in a rural part of New Mexico. Because prior studies showed that gender and age are strong predictors of substance abuse among teens, the researchers controlled for these variables in a hierarchical form of logistic regression (analogous to hierarchical multiple regression). As discussed in Chapter 17, a hierarchical analysis enters variables in a regression equation according to which variables whose effects you want to have partialed out first before other variables are entered.

Three separate logistical regression analyses were performed: one for alcohol, one for marijuana, and one for hard drugs. Table D.2 displays a slightly simplified version of their results for never having used hard drugs. One column (B) shows the unstandardized regression coefficient for each predictor variable. Another shows the *Wald* statistic (a multivariate form of *chi-square*), which is used to test statistical significance in logistic regression (with the significant values asterisked). The final column displays the odds ratio for each predictor variable. Higher odds ratios signify a greater likelihood of *never* using hard drugs.

Odds ratios above 1.0 mean that having a higher value on the independent variable increases the probability of a specific category of the dependent variable. Odds ratios below 1.0 signify the opposite— that is, a lower likelihood of being in that category of the dependent variable at higher levels of the independent variable. For example, in Table D.2 we see a statistically significant odds ratio of 1.90 for spirituality. That means that with each unit increase in the amount of spirituality, the teens were 1.90 times more likely to *never* use hard drugs. (Said another way, this odds ratio means that teens who are less spiritually oriented are more likely to ever use hard drugs and teens who are more spiritually oriented are less likely to ever use them.)

As to religious participation, the absence of an asterisk beside the *Wald* statistic shows that it was *not* a statistically significant predictor of the dependent variable. However, the control variable, gender, was a significant predictor. Its statistically significant odds ratio of 2.18 means that females (who were coded higher than males) were 2.18 times more likely than males to never use hard drugs.

The other control variable, age, also was a significant predictor. But its odds ratio of 0.80 is less than 1.0, which means that teens in the older age category are less likely than those in the younger category to *never* use hard drugs. In precise terms,

Table D.2 Results of a Logistic Regression Analysis Displaying the Odds Ratios for Gender, Age, Spirituality, and Religious Participation in Predicting Teens Never Using Hard Drugs ($N = 414$)[1]

PREDICTOR	B	WALD	ODDS RATIO
Gender (male coded 0; female coded 1)	0.78	7.65**	2.18
Age	−0.23	5.89*	0.80
Spirituality	0.64	5.90*	1.90
Religious participation	−0.26	2.94	0.78

1. This table is adapted from a larger table in Hodge, Cardenas, & Montoya (2001).
*$p < 0.05$
**$p < 0.01$

the 0.80 odds ratio means that for each unit increase in age the probably of *never* using hard drugs is multiplied by 0.80, which signifies a 20% decrease ($1.00 - 0.80 = 0.20$) in the probability of *never* using hard drugs. (The double negative in the study can be confusing. Said another way, this odds ratio means that older teens are more likely to ever use hard drugs and younger teens are less likely to ever use them.)

Based on their findings about spirituality in connection with use of hard drugs (and a similar finding regarding religious participation and alcohol use) the authors suggested that programs attempting to prevent substance abuse among similar groups of teens might improve their effectiveness if they integrate spirituality and religious participation into their efforts. They also recommended research on the effectiveness of interventions incorporating these considerations in trying to prevent teen substance abuse.

EVENT HISTORY ANALYSIS (SURVIVAL ANALYSIS)

The foregoing multivariate procedures are not designed to take into account the way variables change over time. For example, suppose we want to study variables that influence the effectiveness of an intervention that aims to prevent out-of-home placements of children in families at high risk for abuse or neglect. The variables influencing the need for out-of-home placements during the intervention period or very soon after it might be very different from the variables influencing the need for out-of-home placements among families that avoided the need for one or more years after intervention. Moreover, our study won't last indefinitely. Perhaps it will end in three years or in five years. If we use length of time without an out-of-home placement as the dependent variable, we will have underestimated the length of time for those families that have not had such a placement by the end of the study period.

A relatively new statistical procedure, called **event history analysis,** extends the ideas of multiple regression analysis and logistic regression to overcome these difficulties. Because it can handle these problems, its use in practice research is increasing. Event history analysis is also called **survival analysis,** because it commonly is used in studies of variables that predict the avoidance of an undesirable event such as rearrest, out-of-home placement, or death (in medical studies).

A key concept in event history analysis is **censoring.** Censoring refers to cases for which the dependent variable value is unknown for a specified period. For example, suppose we conduct a two-year study of an intervention that attempts to shorten the time lag between the termination of parental rights and adoption finalization. Those children who have not yet been adopted by the end of the two-year period will have been censored because we will not know by the end of the study how long it will take them to get adopted. Festinger and Pratt (2002) report such a study—one in which a large proportion of control group cases were censored because they had not yet been adopted by the end of the study.

To handle the problem of censoring as well as potential changes over time in the influence of various predictor variables, event history analysis will break down the analysis of the influence of the various variables into different time periods. For example, the variable most predictive of the time lag until adoption during the first year of a study might be whether or not the children are in the intervention group or the control group. During the second year, however, perhaps other factors are more influential, such as attributes of the children or of the adoptive parents.

For each time period, event history analysis includes only those cases that have not yet had the event in question happen during a prior time period. For example, the children adopted during year one would not be included in the analysis during year two of variables influencing the time lag until adoption. Only the cases that had not yet been adopted during the first time period analysis would be included. Thus, event history analysis can tell us the probability that individuals still at risk for an event during a particular time period will have that event during that period.

Suppose a prospective adoptive parent is single during year one, but married during year two. That parent's value for the marital status variable during the year two analysis will be different from the value during the year one analysis. However, if the child gets adopted during year one, then that parent (and child) will not be part of the year two analysis.

There are various forms of event history analysis, as well as various types of statistics that are reported in differing studies using this approach. Those statistics go beyond the scope of this text [for more information, see Allison (1984)].

One of the less complicated ways that the results of event history analysis can be reported is in the form of survival curves. Kirk and Griffith (2004) report several such curves in an evaluation of the effectiveness of intensive family preservation services (IFPS) in preventing out-of-home placements of children in abusive or neglectful families. Figure D.1 displays one of their survival curves—one that doesn't control for family risk factors. It shows that early during intervention the IFPS cases had lower out-of-home placement rates than non-IFPS cases. However, from 330 days onward there was little or no difference between the two rates. Figure D.2 shows another of the Kirk and Griffith survival curves, this one controlling for family risk factors. It shows that when family risk factors are controlled, the IFPS cases had lower out-of-home placement rates than non-IFPS cases throughout the follow-up period.

PATH ANALYSIS

Some studies extend regression analysis to see if the various beta-weights fit a causal model hypothesized by the researcher. A diagram using circles and arrows is developed to depict the causal order of the variables. The circles represent variables, and the arrows show which variables are presumed to

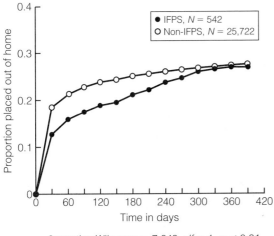

6 months: Wilcoxon = 7.649, $df = 1$, $p < 0.01$
12 months: Wilcoxon = 1.693, $df = 1$, ns

SOURCE: From R. S. Kirk and D. P. Griffith (2004). "Intensive family preservation services: Demonstrating placement prevention using event history analysis" *Social Work Research,* vol. 28, no. 1, p.9. Copyright © 2004, National Association of Social Workers, Inc., Social Work Research.

Figure D.1   Cumulative Risk of Placement for IFPS and Non-IFPS Cases in North Carolina

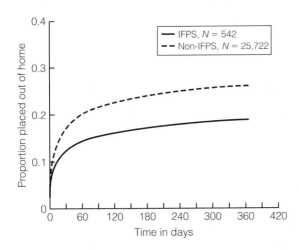

SOURCE: From R. S. Kirk and D. P. Griffith (2004). "Intensive family preservation services: Demonstrating placement prevention using event history analysis" *Social Work Research,* vol. 28, no. 1, p.13. Copyright © 2004, National Association of Social Workers, Inc., Social Work Research.

Figure D.2   Adjusted Cumulative Risk of Placement for IFPS and Non-IFPS Cases in North Carolina from the Cox Proportional Hazards Regression Model

have direct effects and indirect effects on other variables. When indirect effects are involved, there are *intermediary variables* between the independent and dependent variable. Those intermediary variables, called *endogenous variables*, are presumed to be affected by one variable and then in turn to affect the dependent variable. The arrows connecting the variables are called *paths*, and the overall diagram is called a *path model*. Thus, the term for this extension of regression analysis is **path analysis.** A more complex form of path analysis is called **structural equation modeling.**

We'll keep things manageable here by just focusing on the conceptual meaning and utility of path analysis. This focus is intended to help you understand studies that use path analysis or structural equation modeling. A full treatment of these approaches requires a complete text (such as Kline, 1998).

With the above caveat in mind, let's examine a simplified hypothetical illustration of how path analysis works. Suppose we want to evaluate the effectiveness of a pre-discharge, inpatient, psychoeducational intervention for hospitalized people with the dual diagnosis of schizophrenia and chemical dependency (substance abuse). The ultimate aim of our intervention is to prevent rehospitalization after discharge. The intervention is designed to accomplish this ultimate aim through the following two intermediary aims: (1) to increase knowledge of the particularly harmful effects substance abuse has on people suffering from schizophrenia, such as the toxic interactions drugs and alcohol have with antipsychotic medications, so people will be less inclined to abuse substances after discharge; and (2) to motivate clients to comply with their aftercare treatment plan (such as taking anti-psychotic medications and keeping appointments with their case manager).

If we conduct a randomized experiment that compares recipients of our intervention with a control group that only receives routine care before discharge, we might postulate that recipients of our intervention will have longer stays in the community before rehospitalization than routine care recipients. We might also postulate that outcome will be best among those recipients with lower amounts of substance abuse after discharge and who comply the most with their aftercare treatment plan. Thus, our causal model might look like the one depicted in Figure D.3.

Notice that in Figure D.3 there are no lines leading to our independent variable: *type of intervention.* That's because we assigned clients randomly

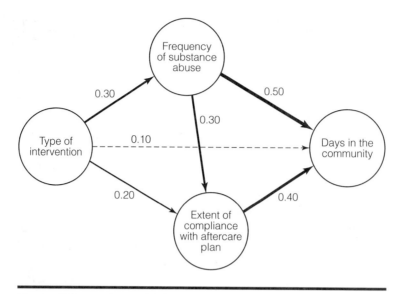

Figure D.3   Path Model for an Imaginary Randomized Evaluation of a Pre-Discharge Psychoeducational Intervention for Hospitalized People Dually Diagnosed with Schizophrenia and Chemical Dependency

to the two treatment conditions. Thus, our model does not postulate any other variable causing which intervention a client receives. (If clients could self-select which intervention to use, then other variables—such as prior level of functioning or level of motivation to change—might influence type of intervention and therefore have arrows pointing toward it.) In path analysis, variables that have no arrows pointing toward them are called *exogenous* variables. At the opposite end, the dependent variable (which in our study is days in the community) has only incoming arrows. And, as mentioned above, intermediary (or intervening) variables that have both incoming and outgoing arrows are called *endogenous* variables. Thus, our two intermediary treatment aims are our endogenous variables and have both incoming and outgoing arrows.

The numbers next to each arrow are the *beta weights* (standardized regression coefficients) that reflect the relative strength of the partial correlation between the two connected variables after controlling for the other variables. In path analysis, these beta weights can also be called *path coefficients*, or *path weights*.

The arrow going directly from the independent/ exogenous variable to the dependent variable represents the *direct effects* of the independent variable on the dependent variable. In Figure D.3, the direct effect of the hypothetical intervention on days in the community would be 0.10.

When two or more variables are connected by arrows before leading to the dependent variable, the value of their path is the product of their path coefficients. That value depicts the *indirect effects* of the independent variable on the dependent variable. In Figure D.3, the arrows going from type of intervention through frequency of substance abuse and then to days in the community would have an indirect effect product of $(0.30)(0.50) = 0.15$. Likewise, the arrows going from type of intervention through extent of aftercare treatment compliance and then to days in the community would have an indirect effect product of $(0.20)(0.40) = 0.08$. The path with three arrows going from type of intervention through frequency of substance abuse, to extent of aftercare treatment compliance and then to days in the community would have an indirect effect product of $(0.30)(0.30)(0.40) = 0.036$.

The indirect effect products can be summed to find the total indirect effect of the independent variable on the dependent variable. Thus, $0.15 + 0.08 + 0.036 = 0.266$ means that the total indirect effects of the intervention on days in the community in our imaginary study is 0.266. This value can be added to the direct effect of 0.10 to find the *total effect* of the independent variable on the dependent variable, which would be 0.10 + 0.266 = 0.366. By considering the various direct and indirect effects along with the visual diagram of the overall causal model, we can say that the intervention's effects on days in the community in our imaginary study are primarily indirect and rely largely on the intervention's effectiveness in decreasing the frequency of substance abuse, which in turn influences days in community as well as extent of compliance with aftercare treatment, with the latter variable also influencing days in the community.

Before we leave path analysis, a caveat should be mentioned. Just as correlation does not imply causation, path analysis does not confirm causation. All path analysis does is help us to see whether multivariate correlation data fit the causal model that is hypothesized in advance of the data analysis. The software program does not develop the model; the researcher does. The data analysis then merely calculates the path coefficients that apply to the model. If the data fit the model, then the causal model is supported but not confirmed. This is analogous to the issue of causation in bivariate correlation analysis. A correlation between two variables offers evidence that one variable *may* indeed cause the other, but it does not rule out alternative explanations. Likewise, when the results of a path analysis fit a hypothesized causal model, we merely have evidence that is consistent with one model and may show which of several possible models best fits the evidence, but the results do not rule out alternative causal models that were not included in the analysis.

FACTOR ANALYSIS

The final multivariate technique that we'll examine in this appendix is **factor analysis.** This procedure is commonly found in studies on the development, use, and validity of measurement scales. When factor analysis is used in studies of measurement scales, the general idea is to see which clusters of items correlate more strongly with each other than with other items. Suppose we have developed a scale to measure posttraumatic stress. One cluster of items might refer to somatic symptoms, such as headaches, stomachaches, sleeplessness, and lethargy. Another cluster might refer to nightmares, flashbacks, and intrusive thoughts. A third cluster

might refer to feelings of depression and anxiety. A fourth cluster might refer to irritability, fighting, arguing, and having an explosive temper.

We may not know in advance whether our scale has different factors and, if so, what they are. An *exploratory factor analysis* will examine the way items are correlating with one another and will help us to see how many factors we have and what the items in each factor seem to have in common. Based on our perceptions of what is common among the items, we give the factor a name. For example, we may give the name "somatic symptoms" to the factor including those items asking about headaches, stomachaches, sleeplessness, and lethargy.

An alternative form of factor analysis is called *confirmatory factor analysis.* With confirmatory factor analysis, we specify in advance the number and type of factors we think we are measuring in our scale and then conduct the factor analysis to see whether the scale really is measuring the constructs we think it measures. Used the latter way, factor analysis assesses a scale's factorial validity or construct validity.

The factors identified in a factor analysis of a measurement scale have another use. Each factor can comprise a subscale of the overall scale, and the items on each subscale can be summed to get a subscale score. A specific subscale can be used in future studies dealing with its relevant factor only. For example, suppose our posttraumatic stress scale for children is lengthy, containing more than 100 items, and that a practitioner wants to use it in an evaluation of a cognitive-behavioral intervention to help children reduce externalizing antisocial behaviors such as losing their temper, fighting, and so on. If the entire scale is too lengthy for these children, the practitioner might just use the subscale containing items for that externalizing factor.

Several advanced statistical concepts that go beyond the scope of this text are involved in determining the number of factors that are identified in a factor analysis and how things get calculated. To learn more about those concepts, you can examine the books mentioned near the end of Chapter 17 (Hair, Anderson, Tatham, & Black, 1998; Kachigan, 1991; Mertler & Vannatta, 2005; Stevens, 2002). As a reader of articles reporting factor analysis findings, the main thing you need to know involves the practical meaning of such findings. In particular, you should know how to interpret the factor loadings in tables that report factor structures. Each row in such tables represents a variable. Each column represents a factor that has been identified in the factor analysis. Each cell displays the factor loading for a particular variable on a particular factor. A factor loading can be interpreted as the correlation between the variable and the factor. Typically, every variable in a factor analysis will have some loading on every factor. Most variables, however, will load more highly on one factor than on the other factors. The variables that have their highest loadings on the same factor are considered to comprise that factor. Other variables that have their highest loadings on another factor are considered to comprise that other factor.

To illustrate how to interpret a factor analysis, Table D.3 displays some of the results that I've extracted and adapted from a study I co-authored (Greenwald & Rubin, 1999). Each row in the table is an item on a self-report scale designed to assess the severity of posttraumatic symptoms in children. For each item, children indicated how much it fit their behavior during the past week. Three factor columns are in the table. Items loading highest on the first factor cover symptoms such as feelings of self-blame and being different. Notice how the first four items in the table load the highest on that factor. (Each item's highest loading is shown in bold, large font.) The second column represents a somatic

Table D.3   Partial Results from a Factor Analysis of a Self-Report Scale Assessing Severity of Posttraumatic Symptoms in Children*

	FACTORS		
ITEM	1 FEELINGS OF SELF-BLAME AND BEING DIFFERENT	2 SOMATIC SYMPTOMS	3 AVOIDANCE AND INTRUSIVE THOUGHTS
I feel strange or different from other kids.	**0.731**	0.275	0.288
I feel like there is something wrong with me.	**0.694**	0.445	0.266
I feel like it is my fault when bad things happen.	**0.692**	0.484	0.394
I am a jinx or a bad luck charm.	**0.739**	0.254	0.144
I get headaches.	0.251	**0.786**	0.235
I get stomachaches.	0.251	**0.803**	0.279
I feel sick or have pains.	0.329	**0.739**	0.304
I feel tired or have low energy.	0.347	**0.692**	0.305
I try to forget about bad things that have happened.	0.240	0.367	**0.789**
I do special things to make sure nothing bad happens.	0.260	0.107	**0.672**
I avoid reminders of bad things that have happened.	0.107	0.330	**0.731**
I am on the lookout for bad things that might happen.	0.459	0.307	**0.639**

*The data in this table are adapted from Greenwald & Rubin (1999). To simplify things for pedagogical purposes, not all of the items on the actual scale are included above.

factor. The second four items in the table load highest on that factor. The third column represents a factor dealing with avoidance and intrusive thoughts. The final four items in the table load highest on that factor.

One way to think about the results illustrated in Table D.3 is to consider each factor as a subscale that contains the four items that load highest on it and to consider each of those four items' loadings on that subscale as their correlation with the overall subscale. The square of each factor loading indicates the percentage of variance in a particular item that is explained by the factor it loads on. Thus, if we square the first item, whose loading is 0.731 on the first factor, we find that 53.4% of the variance on that item is explained by factor 1.

Factor analysis also may be used in studies that—due to an insufficient sample size—need to combine variables into factors so as to reduce a larger set of theoretically relevant variables into a smaller set of factors. Suppose we are studying the effectiveness of a small program that intervenes with parents referred for child abuse and neglect. Let's assume that there is a great deal of variation in treatment outcome and that in light of that variation we want to conduct a multiple regression analysis (or perhaps a logistic regression analysis) to identify those variables that most strongly predict treatment outcome. Finally, let's suppose that the list of variables we have available in our agency records and that we wish to include as potential predictors in our analysis is quite lengthy. The more variables we include in our analysis, the less statistical power we have. (Statistical power was discussed in Chapter 16.) Therefore, to increase our statistical power we need to reduce the number of independent variables to be included. But suppose every variable seems equally important to include. One way to resolve this dilemma would be to run a factor analysis on our independent variables.

Suppose three of the variables—income, educational level, and occupational status—all load very highly on one factor. Let's call that factor socioeconomic status (SES). Using statistical software, we could obtain one factor score per client that combines the three variables into one variable, SES. Or, the factor loadings might be so high that we could assume that the three variables are essentially all measuring the same thing and are therefore redundant. Thus, we could choose just one of them—income, perhaps—and eliminate the other two from the analysis. If we find other variables that are loading in a similar fashion on other factors, we could pare them down into one variable just as we did with SES.

A similar use of factor analysis applies when we want to run a multiple regression analysis but have too much multicollinearity (as was discussed in Chapter 17). A factor analysis can identify those sets of correlated variables that can be collapsed into factors that do not correlate with other factors. The factors then can be entered into the multiple regression analysis, and we would no longer have a multicollinearity problem.

Additional Nonparametric Statistics

Introduction

Comparing Two or More Independent Groups with Nominal-Level Data

Comparing Two or More Independent Groups with Severely Skewed Ordinal-, Interval-, or Ratio-Level Data

Comparing Two Related Groups with Nominal-Level Data

Comparing Two Related Groups with Ordinal-Level Data

Comparing Two Independent Groups with Ordinal-Level Data

Comparing More Than Two Independent Groups with Ordinal-Level Data

Correlation with Skewed Interval or Ratio Data or Between Two Ordinal Variables

INTRODUCTION

This appendix introduces some nonparametric statistics that were not covered in the main part of this text and explains when to use each. The nonparametric procedure most commonly used in practice evaluation—chi-square—was covered in Chapter 14. In this appendix we'll see when to use that procedure, too, but we won't delve very much into most of the calculations of the others. You'll need statistical software for that and perhaps some more math-oriented texts (Heiman, 2000; Siegel, 1956). However, two examples will be provided to illustrate briefly how rank-ordered data are used in some of the formulas.

In Chapter 14 we saw that parametric statistics require that at least one variable be at the interval or ratio level of measurement so that *parameters* such as means and standard deviations can be calculated. We also saw that these parameters are assumed to be distributed normally in the population and that groups being compared are independent of each other and randomly assigned or selected. Although parametric statistics are sometimes used even when one or more of their assumptions cannot be met, it's often necessary to use nonparametric statistics that do not require all of the parametric assumptions. The most common reason to use nonparametric procedures is when our variables are at the nominal or ordinal level of measurement. Nonparametric procedures also may be used with interval- or ratio-level variables that are not normally distributed.

Which nonparametric procedure to use will depend upon the level of measurement of our variables, the size of our sample, how many groups we are comparing, and whether those groups are independent or related. You may recall from our discussion of the paired-samples *t*-Test (a parametric statistic) in Chapter 12 that groups are considered to be related when they can influence each other's values on the variables being compared. For example, if we are evaluating whether a family therapy intervention influenced husbands and wives differently, we have related groups because the husbands and wives can influence each other's values on the variable being measured. Likewise, we have related groups if we are assessing changes over time within one group. A person's posttest score, for example, is likely to be related to his or her pretest score.

With the above ideas in mind, let's look at some nonparametric statistics and describe when to use each. There are others, but these are the ones you are most likely to encounter in your own research or in utilizing the research of others.

COMPARING TWO OR MORE INDEPENDENT GROUPS WITH NOMINAL-LEVEL DATA

As discussed in Chapter 14, the chi-square test is appropriate when we are comparing the frequencies of two or more independent groups. When our sample size is small, however, we may need to alter the formula. A correction for continuity is used whenever our cross tabulation table has only two rows and two columns and has any expected frequencies less than 10. The Fisher's Exact Test is used whenever any cells in our 2-by-2 cross-tabulation table have an expected count of less than 5.

COMPARING TWO OR MORE INDEPENDENT GROUPS WITH SEVERELY SKEWED ORDINAL-, INTERVAL-, OR RATIO-LEVEL DATA

Also as discussed in Chapter 14, the chi-square formula can be used instead of a *t*-Test when we have a severely skewed dependent variable that is at the ordinal, interval, or ratio level of measurement. In this instance, it is called the *median test* because it compares the proportions above and below the overall median in two groups.

COMPARING TWO RELATED GROUPS WITH NOMINAL-LEVEL DATA

Another adaptation of chi-square, called *McNemar's test*, applies when comparing pretest to posttest change within one group on a nominal variable. We would use this test, for example, if we wanted to see whether an intervention changed whether battered spouses or partners lived with or apart from their batterers. Likewise, we would use it to see whether an intervention changed the eligibility for certain privileges (yes or no) of clients in a residential treatment center.

COMPARING TWO RELATED GROUPS WITH ORDINAL-LEVEL DATA

Similar to the *McNemar's test*, the **sign test** applies when comparing pretest to posttest change within one group on an ordinal variable. (The pretest group of data and the posttest group of data, though coming from the same sample, would be considered two related groups.) We would use this test, for example, if we wanted to see whether an intervention changed the responses of battered spouses or partners to an ordinal scale about the likelihood that they will remain living with their batterers or move out. Suppose the scale response categories are very likely, somewhat likely, somewhat unlikely, and very unlikely. The sign test would count the number of clients whose self-reported likelihood of leaving the batterer increased from pretest to posttest.

Another procedure applicable with two related groups with ordinal-level data is the **Wilcoxin matched-pairs test.** Similar to the sign test, as well as the paired-samples *t*-Test, this procedure—which might also be called the **Wilcoxin signed-ranks test** or the **Wilcoxin *T* test**, compares the differences between groups according to rank-ordered values. For example, suppose our scale for victims of battering contains three ordinal-level items that get summed to a possible total score ranging from 3 to 12. If seven clients had the pretest and posttest scores displayed in Table E.1, this procedure would assess the likelihood that chance could account for the sums of the positive and negative rank-ordered differences. In assigning the ranks in the difference column, the plus or minus sign is ignored. Thus, a client who had a

−10, would have a higher rank than another client with a +8. The signs are used to separate the ranked differences into the plus and minus columns to the right. The plus column ranks and the minus column ranks then get summed. The smaller of the two sums is the Wilcoxin *T* value, and that value is compared to a table showing what value is needed for statistical significance for a particular significance level and sample size. The smaller of the two sums in Table E.1 is 3(1 + 2 in the minus column). Examining a table of critical Wilcoxin *T* values, we would find that sum to be statistically significant in a one-tailed test at the 0.05 level for our sample size of seven.

COMPARING TWO INDEPENDENT GROUPS WITH ORDINAL-LEVEL DATA

One of the most commonly used nonparametric statistics is the **Mann-Whitney *U* test.** It provides an alternative to the *t*-Test when our dependent variable is at the ordinal level. It also can be used with interval- or ratio-level data as well, when those data are not distributed normally (as the *t*-Test requires). Rather than comparing the means of two groups, the Mann-Whitney *U* test converts the raw scores of the total sample into ranks. Then it sums the ranks for each of the two groups and subtracts each sum using the formula displayed in the box titled "Formula and Illustration of Data for the Mann-Whitney *U* Test." The smaller of the two *U*'s is then compared to a table of critical *U* values to determine whether the difference in ranks between the two groups is statistically significant.

Table E.1 Illustration of Data for the Wilcoxin Test for Two Related Groups

CLIENT	PRETEST SCORE	POSTTEST SCORE	DIFFERENCE	RANK OF + DIFFERENCES	RANK OF − DIFFERENCES
A	3	10	+7	6	
B	5	11	+6	5	
C	8	7	−1		1
D	4	12	+8	7	
E	6	10	+4	3	
F	9	7	−2		2
G	4	9	+5	4	

Formula and Illustration of Data for the Mann-Whitney U Test

Formula:

$$U_1 = (n_1)(n_2) + \frac{n_1(n_1 + 1)}{2} - \Sigma R_1$$

$$U_2 = (n_1)(n_2) + \frac{n_2(n_2 + 1)}{2} - \Sigma R_2$$

where n_1 and n_2 are the sample sizes of each group

ΣR_1 and ΣR_2 are the sum of the ranks in each group

$$U_1 = (5)(5) + \frac{5(5 + 1)}{2} - 17 = 23.0$$

$$U_2 = (5)(5) + \frac{5(5 + 1)}{2} - 38 = 2.0^*$$

Illustrative Data:

Experimental Group		Control Group	
Raw Score	Ranked Score	Raw Score	Ranked Score
8	6	12	10
3	1	10	8
7	5	9	7
5	3	6	4
4	2	11	9
	$\Sigma R_1 = 17$		$\Sigma R_2 = 38$
	$n_1 = 5$		$n_2 = 5$

*Looking up the lower U value in a table of critical U values, we find that $U = 2.0$ is statistically significant at the 0.05 level.

COMPARING MORE THAN TWO INDEPENDENT GROUPS WITH ORDINAL-LEVEL DATA

Just as the Mann-Whitney U test uses sums of ranks as an alternative to the t-Test, the **Kruskall-Wallis H test** uses sums of ranks as an alternative to a one-way analysis of variance when more than two groups are being compared using ordinal data or skewed interval- or ratio-level data.

CORRELATION WITH SKEWED INTERVAL OR RATIO DATA OR BETWEEN TWO ORDINAL VARIABLES

As mentioned in Chapter 15, there are two commonly used nonparametric formulas for calculating correlation coefficients with variables that are at the ordinal level of measurement or with interval- or ratio-level data that are not distributed normally. The two nonparametric correlations are **Spearman's rho** and **Kendall's tau-b**. Each correlation coefficient can range from -1.0 to $+1.0$. Each has the same meaning as Pearson's r. As with some of the above nonparametric procedures, these two formulas use rank-ordered values for each of the two variables being correlated instead of the raw values. When there are many ties in the rank ordering, Kendall's tau-b is the more appropriate of the two nonparametric formulas. Otherwise, Spearman's rho is commonly used. The box on page 256 shows how to calculate Spearman's *rho*.

How to Calculate Spearman's Rho

Some cognitive-behavioral interventions with abused clients involve trying to change negative self-statements about the abusive incident (such as "I am bad" or "It was my fault") into positive ones (such as "I am good" or "I was not to blame"). Suppose we want to assess the correlation between the degree to which clients believe a positive self-statement and the extent of distress they feel when recalling the abusive incident. Let's say we predict a negative correlation: the stronger the belief in the positive cognition, the less distress in recalling the incident. Suppose each variable is assessed with an ordinal scale. For the cognition, the clients provide a rating from 1 (they do not believe the positive cognition to be true at all) to 10 (they are convinced that it is true). For the degree of distress, they provide a

rating from 1 (no distress whatsoever) to 10 (worst possible amount of distress imaginable). Data that support our hypothesis, along with the Spearman's rho calculations, appear below.

$$\text{Formula:} \quad r_s = 1 - \frac{6(\Sigma D^2)}{N(N^2 - 1)}$$

where
r_s = Spearman's rho
ΣD^2 = Sum of the squared differences between ranks
N = Number of cases

Plugging the data into the formula, we get

$$r_s = 1 - \frac{6(286)}{10(100 - 1)} = 1 - \frac{1716}{990}$$

$$= 1 - 1.73 = -0.73$$

Client	Cognition Rank	Distress Rank	Difference Between Ranks	Squared Diffrence
A	1	10	9	81
B	2	7	5	15
C	3	6	3	9
D	4	5	1	1
E	5	9	4	16
F	6	8	2	4
G	7	3	4	16
H	8	4	4	16
I	9	2	7	49
J	10	1	9	81
				Sum = 286

The minus sign in front of our correlation does not mean it is weak; it just signifies an inverse relationship, as we predicted. To see if this correlation is statistically significant, we would look it up in the same table as is used for the significance of the parametric Pearson's r statistic, as displayed in Table 15.3 of Chapter 15. There we would see that for a sample size of 10, we need an r of 0.5494 for a one-tailed test and an r of 0.6319 for a two-tailed test. Our r of −0.73 (ignore the minus sign) exceeds both of those figures and is thus statistically significant. Moreover, it is a strong correlation in light of the guidelines discussed in Chapter 16 for interpreting relationship magnitude.

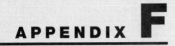
Hypothetical Data Set for SPSS

The data set in this appendix (also available online at <http://humanservices.wadsworth.com/rubin_statistics>) contains 14 variables (in the columns) for each of 50 fictional clients (in the rows) for the hypothetical evaluation in a residential treatment center used throughout this test to illustrate various statistical concepts and the use of SPSS. The codebook for the data set precedes the data set.

VARIABLE NUMBER	SPSS ACRONYM	CODEBOOK VARIABLE LABEL	CODES-CATEGORIES			
1	gender	Gender	1-Male	2-Female		
2	ethnic	Ethnicity	1-Caucasian	2-African American	3-Hispanic	4-Other
3	age	Age	Enter raw number			
4	trauma	Number of traumas experienced	Enter raw number			
5	group	Treatment group	1-New Treatment	2-Routine Treatment		
6	sbi	Number of serious behavioral incidents	Enter raw number			
7	campus	Earned off-campus privileges?	1-Yes	2-No		
8	cottage	cottage	1= Cottage A	2= Cottage B	3 = Cottage C	
9	postsum	Posttest score on Trauma Symptoms Scale	Enter actual score			
10	presum	Pretest score on Trauma Symptoms Scale	Enter actual score			

(continued)

VARIABLE NUMBER	SPSS ACRONYM	CODEBOOK VARIABLE LABEL	CODES-CATEGORIES	
11	change	Change score on Trauma Symptoms Scale from pretest to posttest	Enter actual score	
12	campus2	Earned off-campus privileges post-treatment?	1-Yes	2-No
13	qual	Quality of therapist-client relationship	Enter scale score	
14	cancel	Number of canceled therapy sessions	Enter raw number	

DATA SET:

VAR 1	VAR2	VAR3	VAR 4	VAR 5	VAR 6	VAR 7	VAR 8	VAR 9	VAR 10	VAR 11	VAR 12	VAR 13	VAR 14
1.00	1.00	7.00	1.00	1.00	0.00	1.00	1.00	13.00	53.00	40.00	1.00	10.00	0.00
2.00	1.00	12.00	1.00	1.00	0.00	1.00	1.00	12.00	43.00	31.00	1.00	10.00	1.00
1.00	3.00	9.00	1.00	1.00	1.00	1.00	1.00	19.00	33.00	14.00	1.00	10.00	4.00
1.00	2.00	8.00	3.00	1.00	8.00	2.00	3.00	14.00	43.00	29.00	1.00	9.00	4.00
2.00	2.00	10.00	1.00	1.00	1.00	1.00	2.00	11.00	52.00	41.00	1.00	7.00	1.00
2.00	3.00	9.00	1.00	1.00	2.00	1.00	2.00	18.00	43.00	25.00	1.00	10.00	4.00
2.00	1.00	10.00	1.00	1.00	0.00	1.00	1.00	15.00	53.00	38.00	1.00	10.00	3.00
2.00	2.00	14.00	9.00	1.00	21.00	2.00	3.00	12.00	43.00	31.00	1.00	10.00	0.00
2.00	3.00	9.00	1.00	1.00	0.00	1.00	1.00	19.00	33.00	14.00	1.00	7.00	1.00
2.00	4.00	13.00	2.00	1.00	3.00	1.00	1.00	12.00	43.00	31.00	2.00	7.00	0.00
2.00	1.00	15.00	1.00	1.00	0.00	1.00	2.00	15.00	57.00	42.00	1.00	10.00	1.00
2.00	2.00	12.00	2.00	1.00	3.00	1.00	2.00	20.00	43.00	23.00	2.00	8.00	3.00
2.00	3.00	9.00	8.00	1.00	19.00	2.00	3.00	13.00	53.00	40.00	1.00	7.00	1.00
1.00	2.00	11.00	1.00	1.00	2.00	1.00	2.00	17.00	43.00	26.00	1.00	7.00	4.00
2.00	1.00	8.00	10.00	1.00	22.00	2.00	3.00	20.00	33.00	13.00	2.00	8.00	5.00

DATA SET:

VAR 1	VAR2	VAR3	VAR 4	VAR 5	VAR 6	VAR 7	VAR 8	VAR 9	VAR 10	VAR 11	VAR 12	VAR 13	VAR 14
1.00	1.00	13.00	9.00	1.00	20.00	2.00	3.00	15.00	43.00	28.00	1.00	7.00	5.00
2.00	2.00	11.00	1.00	1.00	0.00	1.00	2.00	13.00	57.00	44.00	1.00	8.00	0.00
1.00	3.00	12.00	6.00	1.00	11.00	2.00	3.00	19.00	43.00	24.00	1.00	7.00	6.00
2.00	1.00	13.00	1.00	1.00	1.00	1.00	1.00	12.00	54.00	42.00	1.00	6.00	1.00
1.00	1.00	10.00	1.00	1.00	1.00	1.00	2.00	15.00	43.00	28.00	1.00	6.00	5.00
2.00	1.00	10.00	1.00	1.00	2.00	1.00	2.00	22.00	27.00	5.00	1.00	5.00	5.00
1.00	2.00	10.00	1.00	1.00	2.00	1.00	1.00	13.00	41.00	28.00	1.00	8.00	1.00
2.00	1.00	11.00	6.00	1.00	18.00	2.00	3.00	11.00	57.00	46.00	1.00	8.00	1.00
1.00	2.00	15.00	4.00	1.00	7.00	2.00	3.00	19.00	43.00	24.00	1.00	10.00	2.00
2.00	3.00	9.00	3.00	1.00	6.00	2.00	3.00	11.00	53.00	42.00	1.00	7.00	1.00
2.00	2.00	10.00	2.00	2.00	3.00	1.00	2.00	21.00	43.00	22.00	1.00	6.00	2.00
1.00	2.00	8.00	2.00	2.00	3.00	1.00	1.00	29.00	33.00	4.00	1.00	2.00	6.00
2.00	3.00	11.00	2.00	2.00	4.00	1.00	1.00	20.00	37.00	17.00	2.00	6.00	5.00
1.00	1.00	12.00	3.00	2.00	5.00	2.00	3.00	22.00	57.00	35.00	1.00	10.00	2.00
2.00	1.00	7.00	3.00	2.00	6.00	2.00	3.00	28.00	45.00	17.00	1.00	4.00	3.00
1.00	3.00	13.00	3.00	2.00	6.00	2.00	1.00	22.00	53.00	31.00	1.00	7.00	5.00
1.00	1.00	11.00	2.00	2.00	4.00	1.00	2.00	23.00	41.00	18.00	1.00	7.00	4.00
1.00	2.00	9.00	2.00	2.00	5.00	2.00	2.00	27.00	33.00	6.00	2.00	4.00	5.00
1.00	3.00	9.00	2.00	2.00	5.00	1.00	1.00	22.00	43.00	21.00	1.00	4.00	3.00
1.00	4.00	11.00	2.00	2.00	3.00	1.00	2.00	20.00	49.00	29.00	1.00	6.00	3.00
1.00	1.00	11.00	3.00	2.00	6.00	2.00	3.00	28.00	43.00	15.00	1.00	4.00	4.00
1.00	2.00	10.00	4.00	2.00	8.00	2.00	1.00	21.00	53.00	32.00	2.00	7.00	3.00
1.00	3.00	14.00	2.00	2.00	5.00	2.00	2.00	22.00	46.00	24.00	1.00	10.00	2.00
2.00	1.00	10.00	2.00	2.00	5.00	2.00	3.00	26.00	31.00	5.00	2.00	3.00	2.00
1.00	3.00	13.00	3.00	2.00	7.00	2.00	1.00	23.00	43.00	20.00	2.00	8.00	2.00
1.00	1.00	10.00	2.00	2.00	3.00	1.00	2.00	24.00	57.00	33.00	1.00	9.00	3.00
2.00	2.00	11.00	2.00	2.00	4.00	1.00	2.00	26.00	43.00	17.00	1.00	6.00	4.00
1.00	3.00	12.00	2.00	2.00	5.00	2.00	1.00	22.00	53.00	31.00	2.00	6.00	4.00
2.00	1.00	13.00	2.00	2.00	5.00	2.00	2.00	20.00	42.00	22.00	2.00	7.00	4.00
1.00	1.00	10.00	2.00	2.00	6.00	2.00	3.00	28.00	32.00	4.00	2.00	3.00	5.00
2.00	1.00	10.00	2.00	2.00	5.00	2.00	1.00	24.00	43.00	19.00	2.00	4.00	4.00
1.00	2.00	14.00	3.00	2.00	7.00	2.00	3.00	23.00	57.00	34.00	2.00	5.00	3.00
2.00	1.00	11.00	2.00	2.00	5.00	2.00	3.00	29.00	43.00	14.00	2.00	6.00	2.00
1.00	2.00	13.00	3.00	2.00	6.00	2.00	1.00	20.00	53.00	33.00	2.00	10.00	2.00
2.00	3.00	9.00	2.00	2.00	4.00	1.00	2.00	21.00	32.00	11.00	1.00	6.00	1.00

SPSS Instructions and Exercises

INTRODUCTION

This appendix will show how to use SPSS to perform statistical procedures discussed in various chapters of this book. Each section of this appendix is cross-referenced to the chapter that discussed the specified procedure. Chapters that did not discuss procedures applicable to SPSS will not be cross-referenced in this appendix. Also provided in this appendix are exercises that might enhance your learning of this material. If you do not have access to SPSS, but have access to alternative statistical software, you can complete the exercises using the alternative software. [Helpful guides for alternatives to SPSS include Albright, Winston, & Zappe (1999), Brightman (1990), and Cherry (2003). Also, the *StatPages.net* web site at <http://members.aol.com/johnp71/javastat.html__#Power> provides links to various Internet sites where you can plug in data and obtain various statistical calculations. Some of the sites are free.]

If you do have access to SPSS, don't worry about which SPSS version you are using. The material in this appendix covers basics that apply to the newer as well as older versions of SPSS.

GETTING STARTED (SEE CHAPTER 2)

When you first open SPSS software, a dialog box will appear asking what you would like to do. The menu will give you several options. If you are new to SPSS, it is a good idea to begin by clicking on the first option: **Run the tutorial.** Then click **OK.** This option will familiarize you with some SPSS basics.

When you are ready to enter your data for analysis, you can choose from other options on the same first menu that gave you the *Run the tutorial* option. Right under that option, for example, is the option **Type in data.** You would click on this option (and then **OK**), if you wanted to enter your own data directly into a blank SPSS data spreadsheet, called a *Data View* window, which will appear after you click *OK*. The **Data View** window is one of two windows that can appear on the **Data Editor** screen, as displayed in Figure G.1. (The other is the **Variable View** window, which we will examine shortly. At the bottom left of the Data Editor screen are prompts that you can click to see either the Data View window or the Variable view window.)

The columns in the Data View window are for your variables. The rows are for your cases. Thus,

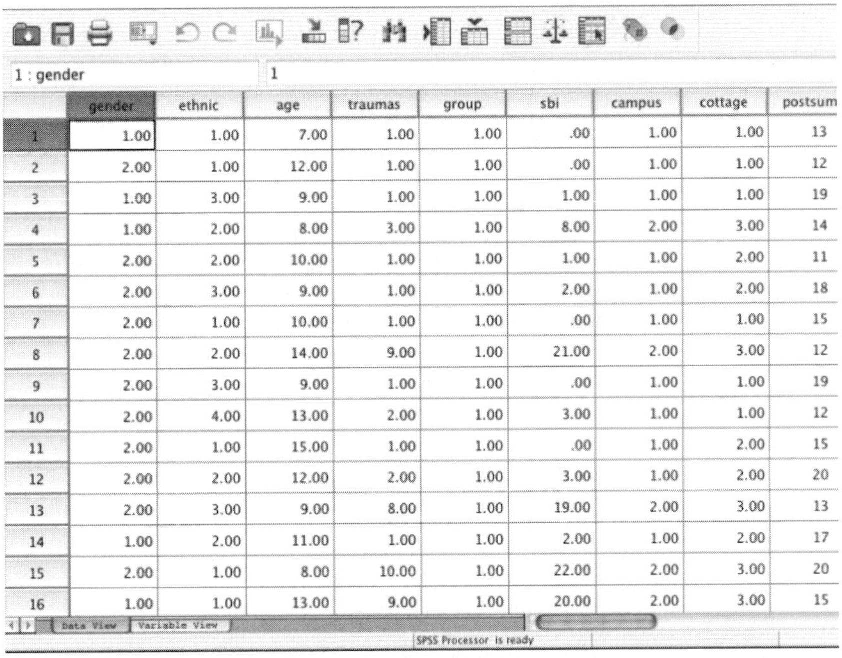

	gender	ethnic	age	traumas	group	sbi	campus	cottage	postsum
1	1.00	1.00	7.00	1.00	1.00	.00	1.00	1.00	13
2	2.00	1.00	12.00	1.00	1.00	.00	1.00	1.00	12
3	1.00	3.00	9.00	1.00	1.00	1.00	1.00	1.00	19
4	1.00	2.00	8.00	3.00	1.00	8.00	2.00	3.00	14
5	2.00	2.00	10.00	1.00	1.00	1.00	1.00	2.00	11
6	2.00	3.00	9.00	1.00	1.00	2.00	1.00	2.00	18
7	2.00	1.00	10.00	1.00	1.00	.00	1.00	1.00	15
8	2.00	2.00	14.00	9.00	1.00	21.00	2.00	3.00	12
9	2.00	3.00	9.00	1.00	1.00	.00	1.00	1.00	19
10	2.00	4.00	13.00	2.00	1.00	3.00	1.00	1.00	12
11	2.00	1.00	15.00	1.00	1.00	.00	1.00	2.00	15
12	2.00	2.00	12.00	2.00	1.00	3.00	1.00	2.00	20
13	2.00	3.00	9.00	8.00	1.00	19.00	2.00	3.00	13
14	1.00	2.00	11.00	1.00	1.00	2.00	1.00	2.00	17
15	2.00	1.00	8.00	10.00	1.00	22.00	2.00	3.00	20
16	1.00	1.00	13.00	9.00	1.00	20.00	2.00	3.00	15

Figure G.1   SPSS Data View Window

if the first variable for the first case is coded 1, you will click on the first cell in the first row and hit the number *one* on your keyboard. Hitting the tab key will move you to the next cell in that row, where you can enter the code for your next variable.

Alternatively, you may already have a data file saved on your computer—perhaps using different software, such as Excel. To transpose those data into the SPSS Data View window, you would click on **Open an existing data source** (and then **OK**) in the first SPSS dialog box. Doing so will spare you the redundant work of re-entering all your data from scratch manually into the SPSS Data View window. After you click on *OK*, you will have to find and open the existing data file in your computer. The data in your saved data file will then appear in the SPSS Data View window.

Either before or after you enter your data in the Data View window, you will need to insert information about your variables in the **Variable View** window. The Variable View window is displayed in Figure G.2. Each row in that window is for a different variable. In the first column (**Name**) you enter the SPSS name for that variable. Be sure to enter the variable names from row to row in the same order as they are listed in your codebook. The names atop each column in the Data View window will be in the same order as they appear in the rows of the Variable View window.

SPSS requires that each variable name must start with a letter, not contain a blank space, and be no more than eight characters in length. If you'll refer back to the codebook in Figure 2.1 in Chapter 2, you'll see that the variable *ethnicity* was given the SPSS variable name *ethn*. That's because the word *ethnicity* contains more than eight characters. For the same reason, shorter SPSS variable names were given to country of origin, practitioner degree, and reason for dropping out. Notice also that the SPSS name for *country of origin* is *cofo*, and not *c of o*. That's because SPSS won't allow blank spaces in the variable names.

You probably won't have to do anything with most of the other columns in the Variable View window. SPSS will enter default values for each of them. The **Label** column, however, is one you probably will want to complete, especially if you have variables that had to receive an abbreviated SPSS name (of eight characters or less) in the **Name** column. In the Label column you can enter the full variable name, which will appear in your data analysis results. That can expedite reading your results—especially if your data file contains a long list of variables—since you won't have to keep referring back to your codebook to find out what variable is signified by each abbreviated SPSS name.

For example, suppose your study has separate variables for the age of clients, their spouse's age, and

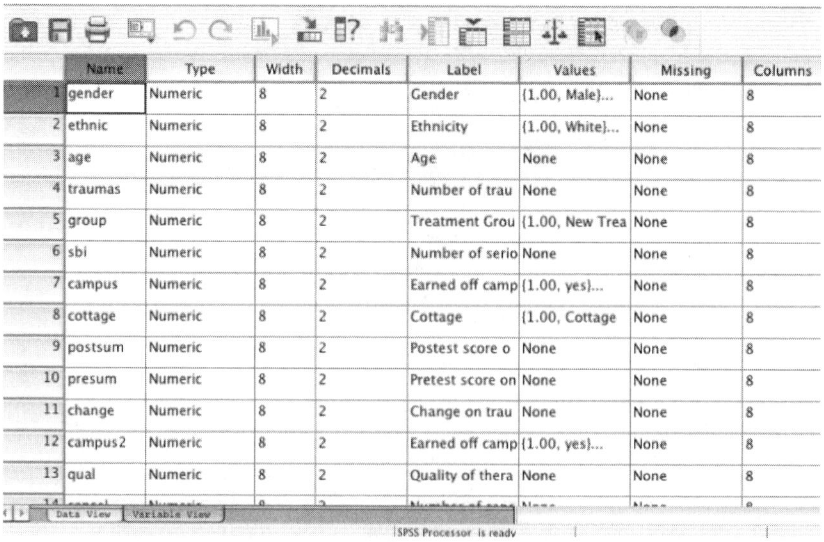

	Name	Type	Width	Decimals	Label	Values	Missing	Columns
1	gender	Numeric	8	2	Gender	{1.00, Male}...	None	8
2	ethnic	Numeric	8	2	Ethnicity	{1.00, White}...	None	8
3	age	Numeric	8	2	Age	None	None	8
4	traumas	Numeric	8	2	Number of trau	None	None	8
5	group	Numeric	8	2	Treatment Grou	{1.00, New Trea	None	8
6	sbi	Numeric	8	2	Number of serio	None	None	8
7	campus	Numeric	8	2	Earned off camp	{1.00, yes}...	None	8
8	cottage	Numeric	8	2	Cottage	{1.00, Cottage	None	8
9	postsum	Numeric	8	2	Postest score o	None	None	8
10	presum	Numeric	8	2	Pretest score on	None	None	8
11	change	Numeric	8	2	Change on trau	None	None	8
12	campus2	Numeric	8	2	Earned off camp	{1.00, yes}...	None	8
13	qual	Numeric	8	2	Quality of thera	None	None	8

Figure G.2 SPSS Variable View Window

the age of each of their children. You might use similar abbreviations for each of these variables, such as agecli, agespou, agechil1, agechil2, and so forth. Entering the full label for these variables will save time and prevent confusion when you are examining your data analyses involving such variables.

For similar reasons, you'll probably want to complete the **Values** column for some or all variables. Consider the *reason for dropping out* variable in the codebook in Figure 2.1 of Chapter 2, for example. Imagine how cumbersome it will be to read and interpret your data analysis if all you see in that analysis for the various reasons are their code numbers. You'd have to keep referring back to your codebook to see what each code represents. In the Values column, however, you can enter each code and its corresponding label. Thus, by entering the codes and their values for the *reason for dropping out* variable, instead of just seeing how many respondents got a code 4 for that variable, you would see in your analysis how many respondents dropped out because of problems in the practitioner-client relationship.

To assign value labels for each code for a particular variable, click on the cell in the **Values** column for the row containing the variable whose codes you want to label. A **Value Labels** dialog window will then appear. It will let you enter a code in the **Value** box and a label for that code in **Value Label** box. You must then click **Add** after each entry. Click **OK** after you have done this for each label, and you will return to the Variable View window.

You need not enter values for every variable. For example, with ratio-level variables such as age or number of children, you do not need to enter value labels to know that 24 for the variable *age* means 24 years old or that 2 for the variable *children* means 2 children. But what if you use the code 0 to indicate that age was not reported (as in the codebook in Figure 2.1 of Chapter 2)? You'd want to enter that zero in the next column, **Missing**. That way, when you ask SPSS to calculate the average age of your clients, it will know not to include any cases with zeros for that variable in the calculation.

Although we've considered the Data View window before the Variable View window, you'll probably want to complete the Variable View window before manually entering your data in the Data View window. That way, as you enter your data

across each column, you'll see the SPSS variable name atop each column. If you are erroneously entering a code 5 for the variable *ethnicity* in the column for *gender,* for example, you might instantly recognize the error and save work later on in data cleaning.

When you've completed the Variable View window and entered all your data in the Data View window, be sure to save your SPSS data file for future use. In fact, you shouldn't wait until you've completed all the data entry work to save this file. Computers often freeze no matter what type of software may be in use, and I've found that mine has a particular proclivity to freeze when I'm using SPSS. So, just as you should do when writing a long document using any word processing program, be sure to save your SPSS file incrementally as you work on it so that if your computer freezes, you won't lose the work you've already completed.

SPSS Exercise on Getting Started

1. If you have access to SPSS, complete a Variable View window for the codebook displayed in Figure 2.1 of Chapter 2. Then, in your Data View window, enter the data for the first three cases in the data file in Figure 2.1. Write down any problems you encounter and discuss them with your instructor.

USING SPSS TO CREATE FREQUENCY DISTRIBUTIONS (CHAPTER 3)

After entering your data into SPSS (as discussed in the preceding section), click on the **ANALYZE** button in the menu atop the SPSS screen. Then click on **DESCRIPTIVE STATISTICS** and then select **FREQUENCIES**, as displayed in Figure G.3. A new screen will show a list of all of your variables. As displayed in Figure G.4, next highlight each variable for which you want a frequency distribution by clicking on it and then clicking the right-pointing triangular arrow. This will move the variable labels from the left-hand to the right-hand column. Next click the OK button and soon all the frequency distribution tables you requested will be displayed in a new window called OUTPUT.

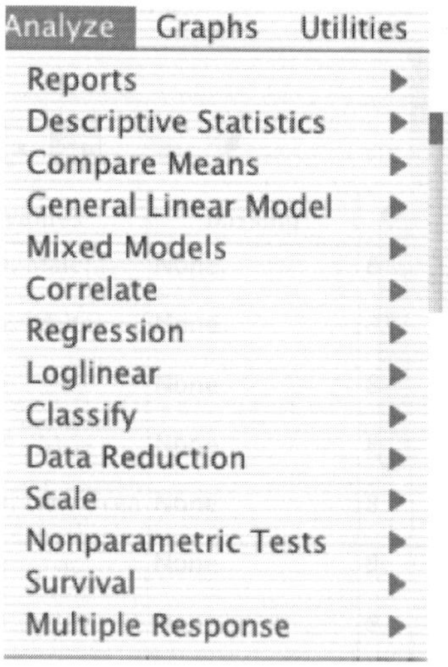

Figure G.3 Using SPSS ANALYZE Menu to Obtain Frequencies

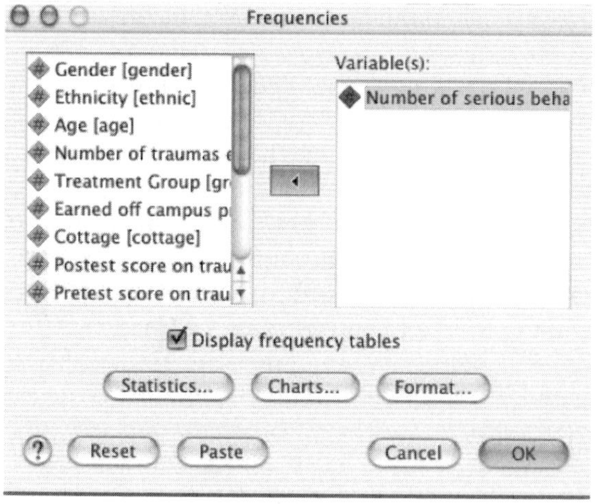

Figure G.4 SPSS Frequencies Screen

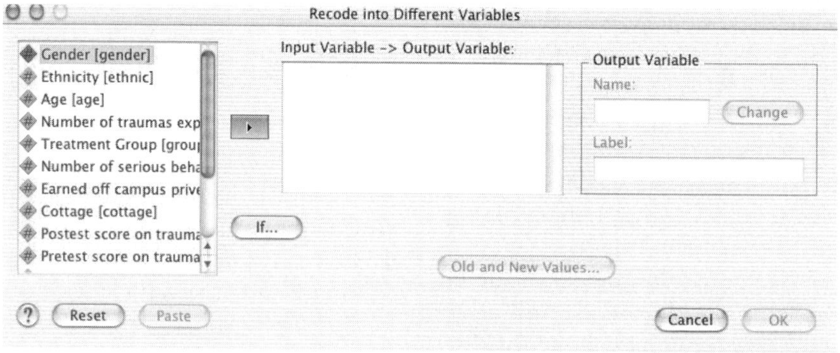

Figure G.5 SPSS Dialog Box for Recoding into a Different Variable

USING SPSS TO CREATE GROUPED FREQUENCY DISTRIBUTIONS (CHAPTER 3)

Using **SPSS** to create a grouped frequency distribution involves one extra step before following the same procedure (mentioned above) for creating ungrouped frequency distributions. That extra step involves recoding the variable you want to collapse into a new variable with combined code categories.

To begin the SPSS recoding process you must be working on the **Data View** window. First, click on the **Transform** menu at the top of the screen and then move your pointer down to the **Recode** button. A choice will then appear, giving you two options: (1) replace the existing codes with the new

ones in the existing column of data for the variable being transformed, and thus lose the existing data; or (2) create a new variable with the recoded grouped data that will appear in a currently empty data column to the right of your current data, thus preserving the column with your original data for the variable being recoded.

The safe thing to do in a situation like this is to choose the second option because you may need to return to the ungrouped original data for certain analyses. Once you click on that (second) option, a dialog box will appear showing you a list of all of your variables, as displayed in Figure G.5. Next, highlight the variable that you want to recode by clicking on it. Then click the right-pointing triangular arrow to move that variable to the center frame.

Next, in the space headed *Output Variable Name,* type in an abbreviated name for the new, recoded, grouped variable you are creating, and then click **CHANGE.** (SPSS requires a maximum of 8 characters for the Name.)

Under that, in the space headed *Label,* you can type in the entire variable label. Thus, you might type in *Age Recoded* as the variable label after having typed in an abbreviation for it, such as agerecod, in the space under Name. Next, click the button labeled **Old and New Values.** Another dialog box will then appear with prompts for typing in the old values for the variable you are changing and the new values with which you are replacing the old ones. To recode the age variable into grouped categories, for example, you would first click on the button for **Range under Old Value,** and then enter 7 through 8. Then you would move over to the righthand side under *New Value,* click on **Value,** and enter a 1 (representing our new code for 7-8). Then click on the **Add** button and repeat the process for each additional recode category you wish to add. When you've completed the process for each new category, click on **CONTINUE** and then click on **OK.**

One additional step will make it easier to read any tables you create that contain the recoded variable. That step involves giving word labels to your newly created numerical codes. For example, instead of just seeing the code 1 on any tables you create, you could give code 1 the label *Ages 7-8.* To do that, you need to return to the **Data View** window and scroll to the right until you find the column for your recoded, new variable, abbreviated *agerecod.* Then double-click on *agerecod* at the top of the column. A **Variable View** window will then open with prompts enabling you to type in labels for your new codes. After you do that for each new code, click **Continue,** and then **OK.**

Now you are ready to go through the same steps as you did for creating the original, ungrouped frequency distribution table. That is, you would click on the **ANALYZE** button in the menu atop the SPSS screen. Then click on **DESCRIPTIVE STATISTICS** and then select **FREQUENCIES.** A new screen will display a list of all of your variables. Next, highlight the new variable *agerecod* by clicking on it and then clicking the right-pointing triangular arrow. This will move *agerecod* from the left-hand to the right-hand column. Next click the **OK** button, and

then the grouped frequency distribution table for *agerecod* will be displayed in a new window called **OUTPUT.**

SPSS Exercises on Frequency Distributions (Chapter 3)

1. Enter the raw data from Appendix F into the SPSS Data View window. Then create a frequency distribution for each variable in the data file, including absolute, relative, and cumulative frequencies. **Be sure to save the SPSS data file you create so you can use it in additional exercises throughout this text.** Compare your SPSS output for the variables *ethnicity* and *number of serious behavioral incidents* to the tables on those variables that appeared in Chapter 3 to see if they match. If they do not, check for errors or discuss any discrepancies with your instructor.

2. Using the same data file, create a grouped frequency distribution for the variable *age.* Compare your grouped frequency distribution to those of several of your classmates. Discuss any differences in how you combined categories and which approach (if any) seems most reasonable.

USING SPSS TO CREATE GRAPHS (CHAPTER 4)

One way to create a bar graph using SPSS is to start by clicking on **GRAPHS** in the menu atop your SPSS screen, as displayed in Figure G.6. Then click on **BAR** and then click on **DEFINE.** A new screen will show a list of your variables. Highlight the variable for your bar graph and then click the right-pointing triangular arrow. This will move the variable label you highlighted into the **CATEGORY AXIS** space. Next click the **OK** button and soon all the bar graph will be displayed in your **OUTPUT** window. Another way to create the bar graph is by using the same steps discussed earlier for creating a frequency distribution and then clicking on **CHARTS** when the **FREQUENCIES** menu appears. You can then select the type of chart you prefer and then click the **OK** button.

Suppose you want to create another form of graph that is discussed in Chapter 4 (such as pie

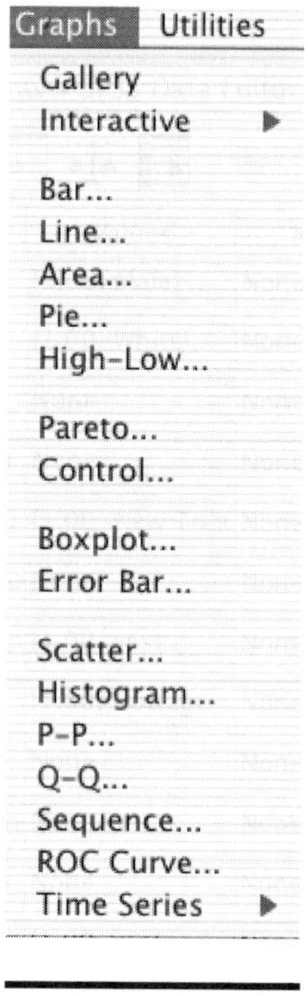

Graphs	Utilities
Gallery	
Interactive	▶
Bar...	
Line...	
Area...	
Pie...	
High–Low...	
Pareto...	
Control...	
Boxplot...	
Error Bar...	
Scatter...	
Histogram...	
P–P...	
Q–Q...	
Sequence...	
ROC Curve...	
Time Series	▶

Figure G.6 SPSS GRAPHS Menu

graphs, histograms, and so on). You can do so by following the same steps as above, but instead of clicking on **BAR,** you would click on the other type of graph you prefer. (If you want a frequency polygon, you'll need to click on **LINE.**)

SPSS Exercises on Graphs and Charts (Chapter 4)

1. Using the raw data file that you saved from Appendix F, create a bar graph and pie chart for each nominal-level variable in the file.

2. Using the raw data file that you saved from Appendix F, create a histogram and frequency polygon for the variable *age*.

USING SPSS TO CALCULATE MEASURES OF CENTRAL TENDENCY (CHAPTER 5)

Earlier, in reference to Chapter 3, we examined how to create frequency distributions using SPSS. You can obtain measures of central tendency by following most of the same steps. First you click on the **ANALYZE** button in the menu atop your SPSS screen. Then click on **DESCRIPTIVE STATISTICS** and select **FREQUENCIES.** A new screen will show you a list of all of your variables. Next, you highlight each variable for which you want a frequency distribution by clicking on it and then clicking the right-pointing triangular arrow. This will move the variable labels from the left-hand to the right-hand column. So far, we've followed the steps for creating distributions. The next step, however, will get you measures of central tendency. Before you click the **OK** button, click the **STATISTICS** button. A new screen will appear that lists all the measures of central tendency discussed in Chapter 5. You can click on the box beside each one you want, and a check mark will then appear in that box. After you've checked all the measures you want, click the **CONTINUE** button. That will return you to the previous screen. On that screen, click **OK** and soon all the measures you requested will be displayed in a new window called **OUTPUT.**

SPSS Exercise on Central Tendency (Chapter 5)

1. Using the raw data file that you saved from Appendix F, calculate the mean, median, and mode for the variables *age* and *number of serious behavioral incidents*.

USING SPSS TO CALCULATE MEASURES OF DISPERSION (CHAPTER 6)

Above, in reference to Chapter 5, we examined how to calculate measures of central tendency using SPSS. We can obtain measures of dispersion by following most of the same steps. First click on the **ANALYZE** button in the menu atop your SPSS screen. Then click on **DESCRIPTIVE STATISTICS** and select **FREQUENCIES.** A new screen will show a list of all of your variables. Next, highlight each variable for which you want a frequency distribution by clicking on it and then clicking the right-pointing triangular arrow. This will move the variable labels from the left-hand to the right-hand column. So far, you've followed the steps for creating distributions. Your next step, however, will get you measures of central tendency and dispersion. Before you click on the **OK** button, click on the **STATISTICS** button. A new screen will appear that lists all the measures of central tendency and dispersion that were discussed in Chapter 6 and Chapter 5. You can click on the box beside each measure you want, and a check mark will then appear in that box. After you've checked all the measures you want, click on the **CONTINUE** button. That will return you to the previous screen. On that screen, click **OK** and soon all the measures you requested will be displayed in a new window called **OUTPUT**.

SPSS Exercise on Calculating Measures of Dispersion (Chapter 6)

1. Use SPSS to calculate the range, interquartile range, variance and standard deviation of the variables age and number of serious behavior incidents for the data you've saved from Appendix F.

USING SPSS TO CALCULATE MEASURES OF KURTOSIS AND SKEWNESS (CHAPTER 7)

Above, in reference to Chapters 5 and 6, we examined how to obtain measures of central tendency and dispersion. Those same steps can obtain measures of skewness and kurtosis. First, you click on the **ANALYZE** button in the menu at the top of the SPSS screen. Then click on **DESCRIPTIVE STATISTICS**. After that, you could select **FREQUENCIES** or **DESCRIPTIVES**. A new screen will show a list of all of your variables. Next, highlight each variable for which you want measures of kurtosis or skewness by clicking on it and then clicking the right-pointing triangular arrow. This will move the variable labels from the left-hand to the right-hand column. If you've selected **FREQUENCIES**, your next step would be to click the **STATISTICS** button. A new screen will appear that lists all the measures of central tendency and dispersion that you might want. You can click on the box beside each one you want, such as **SKEWNESS** and **KURTOSIS**, and a check mark will then appear in those boxes. Then click the **CONTINUE** button. That will return you

to the previous screen. On that screen, click **OK** and soon all the measures you requested will be displayed in a new window called **OUTPUT**.

If you've selected **DESCRIPTIVES** instead of **FREQUENCIES**, click on the **OPTIONS** button, and another screen appears letting you click on boxes to check the statistics you want, such as **SKEWNESS** and **KURTOSIS**. When you select **SKEWNESS** and **KURTOSIS**, SPSS automatically also provides statistics on the standard error of skewness and on the standard error of kurtosis. You can divide the skewness statistic by the standard error of skewness. You can also divide the kurtosis statistic by the standard error of kurtosis. If either ratio is greater than $+2.0$ or less than -2.0 (e.g., -2.50), then you may not be able to use some inferential statistics (to be discussed in later chapters) that can be used only with normally distributed data.)

SPSS Exercise on Calculating Measures of Kurtosis and Skewness (Chapter 7)

1. Using the raw data file that you saved from Appendix F for our hypothetical evaluation, calculate measures of skewness and kurtosis for the variables *age* and *number of serious behavioral incidents*.

USING SPSS TO CALCULATE *z*-SCORES (CHAPTER 8)

To calculate *z*-scores for a particular interval- or ratio-level variable, first click on the **ANALYZE** button in the menu at the top of your SPSS screen. Then click on **DESCRIPTIVE STATISTICS**. After that, click on **DESCRIPTIVES**. A new screen will show a list of all of your variables. Next, highlight each variable for which you want to calculate *z*-scores by clicking on it and then clicking the right-pointing triangular arrow. This will move the variable labels from the left-hand to the right-hand column. The next step is to check (by clicking on) the box in the bottom left corner labeled **SAVE STANDARDIZED VALUES AS VARIABLES**. Then click **OK**. Next you will see some descriptive statistics listed in your **OUTPUT** window. But you won't see any *z*-scores. Instead of listing the z scores in your **OUTPUT** window, SPSS creates a new variable in a column to the right of your existing variables in the **DATA VIEW** window for every variable that you requested z-scores on. At the top of the new column of data will be the existing SPSS acronym for each variable preceded by the letter z. Thus, if your SPSS acronym (which must be no more than 8 characters) for the variable *serious behavioral incidents was sbi*, and you requested z-scores for that variable, a new column would appear to the right of your data window with the heading zsbi. You could then request any other statistic you might want on that new, z-score variable.

SPSS Exercise to Calculate z-Scores (Chapter 8)

1. Using the raw data file that you saved from Appendix F for our hypothetical evaluation, calculate the z-scores for the variables *age* and *number of serious behavioral incidents*.

USING SPSS TO CALCULATE t–TESTS (CHAPTER 12)

Once your data are entered in the **DATA** window, you can instruct SPSS to conduct a variety of statistical tests by clicking on the **ANALYZE** button in the menu button atop your **SPSS** screen. Then click

on **COMPARE MEANS**. A new screen will present several buttons offering different ways to test for the statistical significance of differences between or among means. Among the choices are three types of t-Tests:

(1) **INDEPENDENT-SAMPLES t-TEST;**

(2) **PAIRED SAMPLES t-TEST;** and

(3) **ONE-SAMPLE t-TEST.**

When to choose each of these types of t-Tests is discussed in this chapter. If you want an independent-samples t-Test, click on the **INDEPENDENT-SAMPLES t-TEST** button. A new screen will then appear listing all of your variables in a box on the left, as displayed in Figure G.7. Then highlight by clicking on the variable that you want to be your dependent variable in the t-Test. Then click on the arrow pointing to the rectangle where you enter your dependent variable, which SPSS will call the **TEST** variable. That is the interval- or ratio-level variable whose means will be calculated.

Next, highlight by clicking on the variable that you want to be your independent variable in the t-Test. Then click the arrow pointing to the rectangle where you enter your independent variable, which SPSS will call the **GROUPING** variable. That is the nominal, dichotomous variable consisting of

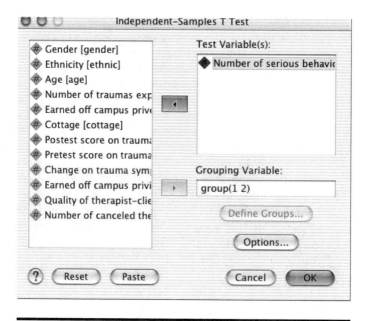

Figure G.7 SPSS Screen for INDEPENDENT-SAMPLES t-TEST

the two groups whose means you want to compare. SPSS will then prompt you with a couple of question marks to define your two groups. After you click on that prompt, enter the code for each group. For example, if the codes entered in your data spreadsheet are 1 for Group 1 and 2 for Group 2, you would enter a 1 and a 2 when prompted to define your groups. Then click on **CONTINUE** and then on **OK**. The results of your *t*-Test will appear almost immediately in your **OUTPUT** window.

If you want a paired-samples *t*-Test, click on the **PAIRED-SAMPLES *t*-TEST** button after clicking on **COMPARE MEANS**. Then click on the two variables whose means you want to compare and then click on the arrow. After you click on **CONTINUE**, your paired-samples *t*-Test results will appear in the **OUTPUT** window. If you want a one-sample *t*-TEST, click on the **ONE-SAMPLE *t*-TEST** button after clicking on **COMPARE MEANS**. Then click on the variable whose mean you want to compare to a population value and then click on the arrow. In the box labeled **TEST VALUE**, enter the known population value to which you are comparing your sample mean. Again, the final step is to click on OK to obtain your results in the **OUTPUT** window.

SPSS *t*-Test Exercises

1. Using the data you've saved from Appendix F, run an independent samples *t*-Test to find out in our hypothetical evaluation if males and females differ in mean number of serious behavioral incidents. Interpret the results.

2. Using the data you've saved from Appendix F, run a one-sample *t*-Test to find out if the overall sample of 50 cases in our hypothetical evaluation had better or worse posttest scores on our trauma symptoms scale than the national mean score on the same scale for youths graduating from comparable residential treatment centers. Assume that the national mean is 25. Interpret the results.

USING THE COMPUTE PROCEDURE IN SPSS TO CREATE CHANGE SCORES (CHAPTER 12)

To create a new variable that consists of the difference between a pretest score and a posttest score, first click on the **TRANSFORM** button in the menu button atop your **SPSS** screen. Then click on the **COMPUTE** command that will appear under the **TRANSFORM** menu. A dialog screen will appear, as displayed in Figure G.8. In the upper left corner a small box labeled **TARGET VARIABLE** allows you to enter the SPSS name for the change score variable you want to create. It must be no more than 8 characters long, so a name like *change* would work as the new variable name. After typing the word *change* in that small box, move to the lengthier box to its right and enter the variables that

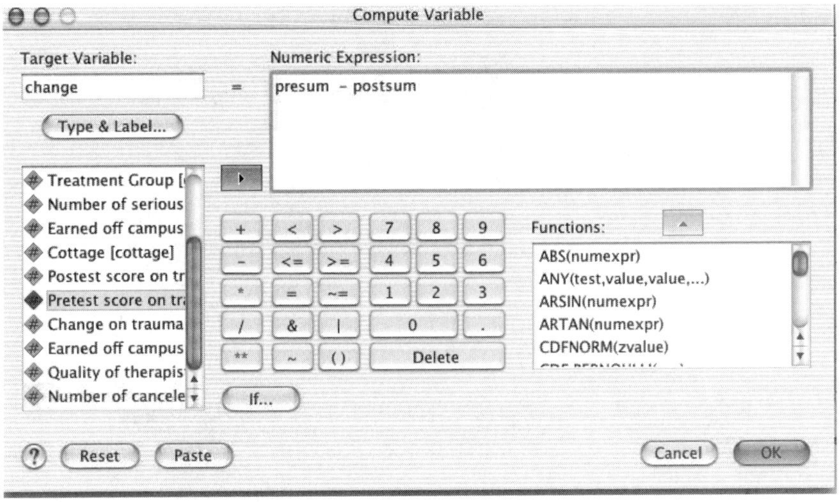

Figure G.8   SPSS Dialog Screen for Computing a New Variable

will be involved in creating the target variable. You must enter them as a numeric expression, showing which variable gets added to which, subtracted from which, multiplied from which, and so on. To do this, first click on one variable listed in the box to the left and then on the arrow to move it to the **NUMERIC EXPRESSION** box. To create a change score in our hypothetical evaluation, for example, you would first move the pretest score variable (**PRESUM**) into the **NUMERIC EXPRESSION** box. Next, click on one of the arithmetic functions from the keypad in the dialog box. Since the new variable that you want to change is the difference between pretest and posttest scores, click on the *minus* (−) function. A minus sign will then appear in the **NUMERIC EXPRESSION** box after the **PRESUM** variable. Next, click on the next variable involved in creating the change score. In our hypothetical study that would be the posttest score (**POSTSUM**). Now click on the arrow to move into the **NUMERIC EXPRESSION** box, where it will appear after the minus sign. Since the change score involves only those two variables, your numeric expression is complete. Next, click on **OK**, and a new variable called *change* will appear in a new column on your data screen. That new variable will be the difference between the pretest and posttest score for each of our 50 cases. You are now ready to conduct an independent-samples t-Test, using the new variable *change* as the **TEST VARIABLE.**

USING SPSS TO CONDUCT A ONE-WAY ANOVA (CHAPTER 13)

Once your data are entered in the **DATA** window, click on the **ANALYZE** button in the menu button atop your **SPSS** screen. Then click on **COMPARE MEANS.** A smaller screen will then appear to the right, where you click on **ONE-WAY ANOVA.** A dialog screen will then appear, as displayed in Figure G.9, in which you click on your dependent variable (for example, number of serious behavioral incidents) and then click on the arrow to move it to the **DEPENDENT LIST** box. Then click on our independent variable (for example, cottage) and click on the arrow to move it into the **FACTOR** box. Next, click on the **POST HOC** button at the bottom of the dialog screen and click on the post hoc procedure you desire (such as the Bonferroni procedure, the Scheffe method, or the Tukey procedure). After you click on the post hoc test you want, click on **CONTINUE** and then **OK** to run your analysis.

SPSS Exercise for a One-Way Anova

1. Using the data you've saved from Appendix F, conduct an ANOVA to find out if there are statistically significant differences in the number of serious behavioral incidents between Caucasian,

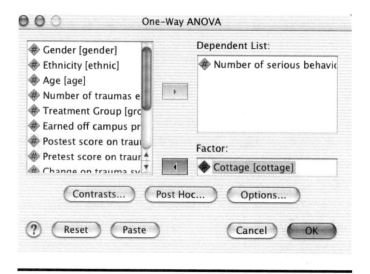

Figure G.9 SPSS Dialog Screen for One-Way ANOVA

African American, and Hispanic youths in our hypothetical evaluation. Interpret the results.

USING SPSS TO CONDUCT AN ANCOVA (CHAPTER 13)

Once your data are entered in the **DATA** window, click on the **ANALYZE** button in the menu button atop your **SPSS** screen. Then click on **GENERAL LINEAR MODEL** and then on **UNIVARIATE**. A dialog screen will then appear, as displayed in Figure G.10, in which you click on your dependent variable (for example, **POSTSUM**) and then the arrow to move it to the **DEPENDENT VARIABLE** box. Then click on your independent variable (for example, **GROUP**) and then the arrow to move it into the **FIXED FACTOR(S)** box. Next, click on the variable you will use as a covariate (for exam-

ple, **PRESUM**) and then the arrow to move it into the **COVARIATE(S)** box. Then click on the **OPTIONS** box. A dialog screen will appear enabling you to request means for each group being compared by checking the box next to the button **DESCRIPTIVE** under the **DISPLAY** section. Then click on **CONTINUE** to return to the main dialog screen. There you can click on the **POST HOC** button to be given several post hoc test multiple comparison options to choose from. After clicking on the desired post hoc test click on **CONTINUE** and then **OK** to run your analysis.

SPSS Exercise for ANCOVA

1. With the data you've saved from Appendix F, and using pretest score as the covariate and posttest score as the dependent variable, run an ANCOVA to find out if males and females differ in regard to

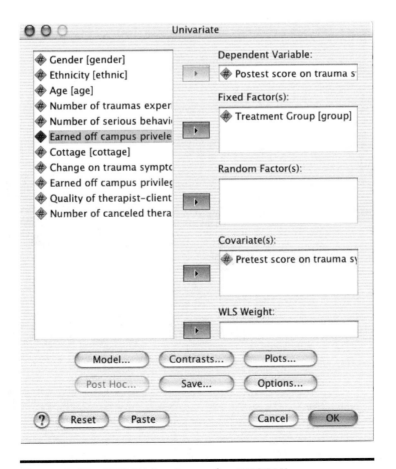

Figure G.10 SPSS Dialog Screen for ANCOVA

how much improvement they made on our trauma symptoms scale from pretest to posttest. Interpret the results and compare them to the results you got in SPSS *t*-Test Exercise 1 (page 269).

USING SPSS TO CONDUCT A TWO-FACTOR ANOVA (CHAPTER 13)

You can use SPSS to conduct a two-factor ANOVA by following the same initial steps as described above with ANCOVA. Instead of moving just one independent variable into the **FIXED FACTOR(S)** box, however, you move two independent variables there. (You can move a third independent variable there if you want a three-factor ANOVA, four for a four-factor ANOVA, and so on.) The rest of the steps are the same as with ANCOVA, except that you skip entering any covariate.

USING SPSS TO CALCULATE CHI-SQUARE (CHAPTER 14)

Once your data are entered in the **DATA** window, you can instruct SPSS to conduct a chi-square test by first clicking on **ANALYZE** in the top menu and then clicking on **DESCRIPTIVE STATISTICS** and **CROSSTABS**. A new dialog screen, as displayed in Figure G.11, will present a box on the left listing all of your variables. Click on each of the two variables in your analysis and then the arrow, moving one variable to the **ROW(S)** box and one to the **COLUMN(S)** box. At the bottom of the screen are three buttons. Click on the **STATISTICS** button to see a list of statistics that you can request. Check the **CHI-SQUARE** box to request the chi-square test. After making your requests regarding **STATISTICS**, click on **CONTINUE**, which will bring you back to the main **CROSSTABS** screen. Then, by clicking on the **CELLS**

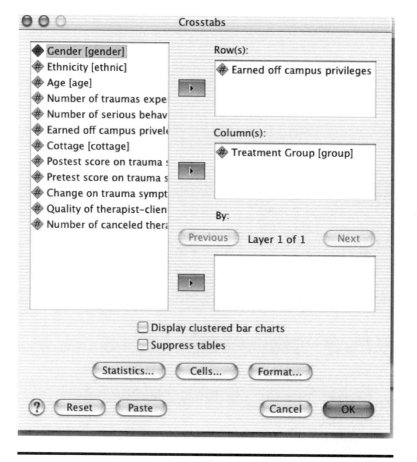

Figure G.11 SPSS CROSSTABS Dialog Screen (Used for Calculating Chi-Square)

button, you can view the expected frequency in each cell (along with the observed frequency) of your cross-tabulation table. You can also indicate whether you want percentages to be calculated by rows or columns. (Remember to percentage according to the categories of the independent variable. Thus, if you place the independent variable in the **COLUMN(S)** box, request percentages by columns.) After making your requests regarding **STATISTICS**, click on **CONTINUE** to return to the main **CROSSTABS** screen. Now click on **OK** to obtain the output displayed in Tables 14.1 and 14.2 in Chapter 14.

If you want to use SPSS to conduct a median test, which is based on the chi-square formula, you have three options. One is to click on **ANALYZE** and then on **NONPARAMETRIC TESTS** and then **K INDEPENDENT SAMPLES**. A dialogue box will then appear, allowing you to move your independent variable into the **TEST VARIABLES LIST** box and your dependent variable into the **GROUPING VARIABLE** box. (In our hypothetical evaluation the independent variable would be *group* and the dependent variable would be *SBI*.) Next, click on **DEFINE RANGE** and then enter the code values (usually 1 and 2) for the two categories of your independent variable (i.e., the two groups whose medians you wish to compare). Then check the small box next to **MEDIAN** at the bottom of the screen and click on **OK**. Notice that in this chi-square analysis, your dependent variable is at the interval or ratio level—not nominal as in regular chi-square analyses. SPSS will calculate the median (rounding off to a whole number) and collapse the dependent variable into two ordinal categories—above and below the median. Then it will give results based on the chi-square formula, treating the two dependent variable categories as if they were nominal and lumping the cases with the rounded-off median value in with the cases below the median.

If the number of cases falling at the rounded-off median is relatively large, you might want to choose the second median test option. That would be to exclude from the median test the cases falling at the rounded-off median. You would do that before requesting the median test by clicking on **DATA** in the top menu and then on **SELECT CASES**. Then click on the button beside *"If condition is satisfied"* and click on the **IF** button. Next, move the variable of concern into the right-hand box and click on the symbol for not equal ($\sim=$) and then enter the me-

dian value. Then click on **CONTINUE** and then **OK**. That returns you to the **DATA** window, and you then follow the steps in the foregoing paragraph for requesting the median test.

The third option would be to use the regular chi-square procedure (as described in the first paragraph in this section) after recoding your dependent variable into the two categories above or below the exact median. For example, if your exact median before rounding off is 4.61 you would recode your ratio data into two (dichotomous) categories: (1) the scores that fall above the 4.61 median; and (2) the scores that fall below the 4.61 median. You would do this before requesting your chi-square analysis and do so by using the **RECODE** command. First, click on **TRANSFORM** in the top menu bar. Then click on **RECODE** and then **INTO DIFFERENT VARIABLES**. (If you clicked on **INTO SAME VARIABLE**, your ratio data would be replaced with your recoded dichotomous data, and thus you would no longer have the ratio data. By clicking on **INTO DIFFERENT VARIABLES**, you create a new variable with the dichotomous data, while keeping the original ratio data.) In the dialogue box that appears, transfer the dependent variable that you want to recode into the middle box. Then give the recoded variable a name that is different from its original one by typing the new name in the **OUTPUT VARIABLE** box headed **NAME**. Then click on **OLD AND NEW VALUES**. A new dialog box will appear. Then click the button under **OLD VALUE** for the range from the lowest value through 4. Then click on **VALUE** under **NEW VALUE**, and type in a 1. That will be the new code for all values under the median of 4.61. Then click on **ADD**. Repeat that procedure for the range from 5 through highest, typing in a 2 as the code for all values above the median. Then click **CONTINUE** and then **OK**. That will return you to the **DATA** window where you now can request the regular chi-square procedure as described in the first paragraph in this box.

If you want to use SPSS to conduct a **goodness-of-fit test,** which is also based on the chi-square formula, click on **ANALYZE** and then on **NONPARAMETRIC TESTS** and then on **CHI-SQUARE**. A dialog screen will then appear, allowing you to transfer the variable you want to test into the **TEST VARIABLES LIST** box. Then click on the button next to **VALUES** in the **EXPECTED VALUES** box. Then enter the expected frequencies (that you know in advance) for each cell, and then click on **ADD** after entering each expected value. Then click **OK** to get your goodness-of-fit test output (as displayed in Table 14.5).

SPSS Exercises for Chapter 14

1. Using the data you've saved from Appendix F, use SPSS to conduct chi-square tests to see whether the two treatment groups in our hypothetical evaluation have significantly different proportions of each gender and of each ethnic group. Interpret the results.

2. Use SPSS to conduct a Fisher's exact test for the following data set. Then interpret your results.

CLIENT NAME	GROUP	RE-ARRESTED?
Al	experimental	no
Bob	experimental	no
Donna	experimental	no
Eve	experimental	no
Jan	experimental	no
Kim	experimental	no
Larry	experimental	yes
Mel	experimental	yes
Nat	control	yes
Oprah	control	yes
Pat	control	yes
Ron	control	yes
Sam	control	yes
Ty	control	yes
Val	control	yes
Zelda	control	no

3. Use SPSS to conduct a goodness-of-fit test to see if the sample of 16 cases above is representative of the relevant population with respect to re-arrest rate. Assume that the re-arrest rate for the population is 0.40 (40%). Interpret your results.

4. Use SPSS to conduct a median test for the above data set, but using the variable below, *number of arrests*, instead of the above *yes/no* variable. Then interpret your results.

CLIENT NAME	GROUP	NUMBER OF ARRESTS
Al	experimental	1
Bob	experimental	1
Donna	experimental	1
Eve	experimental	1
Jan	experimental	1
Kim	experimental	1
Larry	experimental	2
Mel	experimental	2
Nat	control	3
Oprah	control	3
Pat	control	3
Ron	control	3
Sam	control	3
Ty	control	3
Val	control	3
Zelda	control	1

USING SPSS TO CALCULATE CORRELATION COEFFICIENTS AND SCATTERPLOTS (CHAPTER 15)

After your data are entered in the **DATA** window, you can instruct **SPSS** to calculate correlation coefficients between two variables by first clicking on **ANALYZE** in the top menu. Next, drag the cursor down and click on **CORRELATE** and then on **BIVARIATE**. A dialog screen will appear listing all of your variables in a box to the right, as displayed in Figure G.12. You can click on as many variables as you want to correlate with each other and then on the arrow to move each variable to the box on the right. Each variable that you insert in the right-hand box will be correlated separately with each other variable in that box. Underneath the box you next click in the small square beside each correlation coefficient you'd like to have calculated. There are three options: **Pearson's *r*, Kendall's tau-*b*,** and **Spearman's rho.** You can check all three if you like. Below that box are buttons to click to request either a **two-tailed** or **one-tailed test of significance** for each correlation coefficient that you've requested. Then click on **CONTINUE** and then **OK,** and every correlation that you've requested, along with its *p*-value, will appear in your output screen.

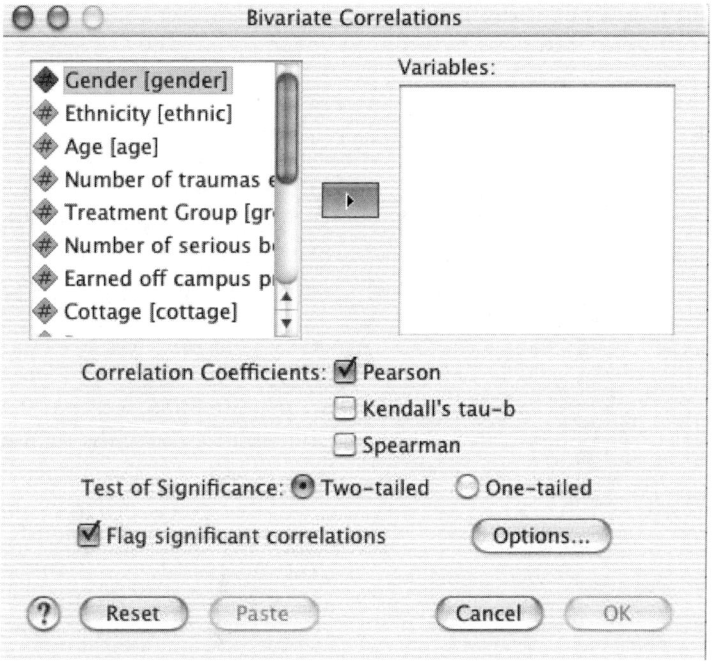

Figure G.12   SPSS Dialog Screen for Bivariate Correlations

To obtain a scatterplot that graphically represents the correlations you've requested, you have to go back to the top menu bar and click on **GRAPHS.** Then you click on **SCATTER.** A **SCATTERPLOT** dialog screen will then appear, displaying four types of scatterplots (scattergrams) to choose from. You'll probably want to choose the one labeled **SIMPLE,** so click on that box and then on **DEFINE.** Another dialog screen will then appear allowing you to click on the two variables for which you want a scatterplot. Move one into the **Y AXIS** box and one into the **X AXIS** box. Then click on **OK,** and your scatterplot will appear in your output screen.

Eta

To obtain the eta statistic, all you have to do is click on **ANALYZE** in the top menu, then on **COMPARE MEANS,** then on **MEANS,** and then, after clicking on the variables involved, click on **OPTIONS.** The options dialog box will allow you to check a box beside **ANOVA TABLE AND ETA,** which, after you click **CONTINUE** and then **OK,** will give you an

ANOVA analysis along with the eta statistic. (You can do this even if your significance test is a t-Test with a nominal independent variable that is dichotomous. That is because ANOVA is identical to the t-Test with dichotomous independent variables. Thus, eta has the same meaning regardless of whether you use a t-Test or ANOVA for significance testing.)

Phi or Cramer's *V*

Using **SPSS,** all that is required to obtain phi or Cramer's *V* is checking the box beside **PHI AND CRAMER'S V** when you request the chi-square statistic. The prompt includes Cramer's *V* along with phi because Cramer's *V* is the correlation coefficient to use when at least one of the two nominal variables you are examining has more than two categories.

SPSS Exercises for Correlation and Scatterplots (Chapter 15)

1. Using the data you saved from Appendix F, use SPSS to find Pearson's *r* for the relationship between age and serious behavioral incidents in our hypothetical evaluation in a residential treatment center. Also obtain a scatterplot. Interpret the data you obtain.

2. Enter the following data into an SPSS data file.

CLIENT #	GROUP	RE-ARRESTED?	NUMBER OF PRIOR ARRESTS
1	experimental	no	0
2	experimental	no	0
3	experimental	no	0
4	experimental	no	0
5	experimental	no	1
6	experimental	no	1
7	experimental	yes	1
8	experimental	yes	2
9	experimental	yes	2
10	experimental	no	1
11	experimental	yes	3
12	experimental	no	0
13	experimental	yes	4
14	experimental	no	1
15	experimental	no	1
16	control	no	0
17	control	no	0
18	control	no	0
19	control	no	1
20	control	yes	5
21	control	no	1
22	control	yes	2
23	control	yes	3
24	control	yes	3
25	control	yes	4
26	control	yes	3
27	control	yes	2
28	control	yes	1
29	control	yes	2
30	control	yes	4

a. Use SPSS to obtain phi for the association between group and whether re-arrested. Interpret your results.

b. Use SPSS to obtain eta for the relationship between whether re-arrested and the number of prior arrests. Interpret your results.

USING SPSS TO OBTAIN A REGRESSION LINE AND CALCULATE THE REGRESSION EQUATION (CHAPTER 17)

Once your data are entered in the **DATA** window, click on the **ANALYZE** button in the menu button atop your **SPSS** screen. Then click on **REGRESSION** and then (to the right of that) **LINEAR.** A dialog screen will then appear in which you click on your dependent variable and then the arrow to move it to the **DEPENDENT** box. Then click on your independent variable and then the arrow to move it into the **INDEPENDENT(S)** box. Next, click on **OK** to run the analysis.

SPSS Exercise for a Bivariate Regression Analysis

1. Using the data you've saved from Appendix F, conduct a regression analysis for the variables age and *serious behavioral incidents* in our hypothetical evaluation in a residential treatment center. Interpret the results.

USING SPSS FOR MULTIPLE REGRESSION AND MULTIPLE CORRELATION (CHAPTER 17)

Once your data are entered in the **DATA** window, click on the **ANALYZE** button in the menu button atop your **SPSS** screen. Then click on **REGRESSION** and then (to the right of that) **LINEAR.** A dialog screen will then appear, as displayed in Figure G.13, in which you click on your dependent variable and then the arrow to move it to the **DEPENDENT** box. Then click on each independent variable you want to include and then the arrow to move each into the **INDEPENDENT(S)** box. The next step is to choose your method of entry. To use the all-possible-subsets method (which enters all of the independent variables simultaneously), you would choose **ENTER** in the **METHOD** box. To

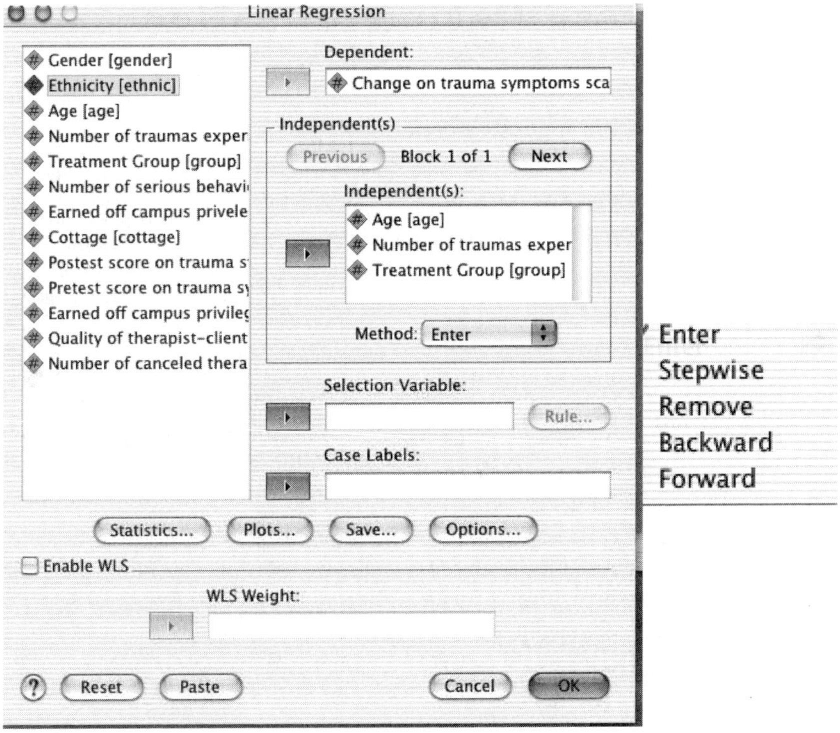

Figure G.13   SPSS Dialog Screen for Multiple Regression

use the stepwise method, you would choose **STEP-WISE** in that box. To use the hierarchical method, you would choose **ENTER** in that box, but you'd also have to use a different approach to selecting independent variables. Your first step would be to enter each independent variable to be analyzed (without controlling for other variables) in the **INDEPENDENT(S)** box (as above). Next you would click on the **NEXT** button above that box. That will permit you to enter a second block of variables that you want to have analyzed after the first block is entered and controlled. You would then click on **NEXT** and repeat the process for each block of independent variables in the order you want them entered into the multiple regression equation. Finally, click on **OK** to run your analysis.

SPSS Exercise on Multiple Regression (Chapter 17)

1. Using the data you've saved from Appendix F, conduct a multiple regression analysis to see which variables are the strongest predictors of how much improvement was made on the trauma symptoms scale from pretest to posttest. (Thus, you would enter the SPSS variable *change* in the dependent variable box.) For your independent variables, choose *age, group* (treatment group) and *qual* (quality of therapist-client relationship). Use the all-possible-subsets method (which enters all of the independent variables simultaneously) by choosing **ENTER** in the **METHOD** box. Interpret the results.

Answers to Selected Review Questions

Chapter 1

1. Although the average might be above the poverty line, many residents may still be poor; the presence of some very affluent households in the community could be the reason the average is so high.

2. Some reasons for studying statistics that you might include are (a) to be able to understand articles that evaluate practice effectiveness; (b) to protect yourself from being misled by others who misinterpret statistics or who attempt to mislead with them; (c) to deal with statistics in needs assessment surveys; (d) to be a more effective advocate for improving social policies by being able to marshal statistics in support of your position; (e) to know how to interpret data appropriately when you evaluate your own practice effectiveness and to communicate your findings to others in a clear and credible manner; and (f) to be a more evidence-based, compassionate, and ethical practitioner because you are able to do the foregoing things.

3. a. Type of intervention is nominal. Precise number of sessions attended is ratio. Level of motivation is ordinal.

   b. By combining the precise numbers into grouped ranges, you could transform the variable from the ratio to the ordinal level. By collapsing the numbers into yes/no regarding ever attending you could transform it into the nominal level.

Chapter 2

1. One way to construct the codebook would be as shown in the table below.

COLUMN	VARIABLE	SPSS VARIABLE NAME	CODES-CATEGORIES
1	Case Number	ID	Enter actual number atop questionnaire
2	Treatment Group	group	1 = Experimental
			2 = Control
3	Gender	gender	1 = Female
			2 = Male
4	Age	age	Enter actual number
			00 = not answered
5	No. of Children	child	Enter actual number
			99 = not answered
6	SES	ses	1 = low
			2 = medium
			3 = high
			0 = not answered
7	Abuse?	abuse	1 = yes
			2 = no
			0 = not answered

2. If your codebook matches the one above, then the following answer would be correct:

12228321

21124212

32100211

41227422

3. Treatment group, gender, or abuse: Any number over 2 or preceded by a minus sign.

Age: Any number well over 100 or preceded by a minus sign.

No. of children: Any number well over 20 or preceded by a minus sign.

SES: Any number over 3 or preceded by a minus sign.

4. Because *treatment group* is nominal, it doesn't matter which category gets which code number, but because *SES* is ordinal, the middle category (medium) should get the middle code number.

5. One acceptable scheme would be as follows:

1 = boring (includes responses such as boring, yawn)

2 = irrelevant (includes responses such as irrelevant to practice, not useful, why do I have to study something I'll never use)

3 = useful (includes responses such as more useful than most students think)

4 = too difficult (includes responses such as too difficult, scary, math formulas are too complicated)

Chapter 3

1. a.

MAIN SUBSTANCE ABUSED	FREQUENCY	PROPORTION	PERCENT
alcohol	8	0.27	27
marijuana	10	0.33	33
cocaine	6	0.20	20
heroin	4	0.13	13
other	2	0.07	7
Total	30	1.00	100

1.b.

AGE	FREQUENCY	CUMULATIVE FREQUENCY	PROPORTION	PERCENT	CUMULATIVE PERCENT
12	3	3	0.10	10	10
13	3	6	0.10	10	20
14	8	14	0.27	27	47
15	7	21	0.23	23	70
16	5	26	0.17	17	87
17	4	30	0.13	13	100
Total		30	1.0	100	

1.c.

NUMBER OF TREATMENT SESSIONS ATTENDED	FREQUENCY	CUMULATIVE FREQUENCY	PROPORTION	PERCENT	CUMULATIVE PERCENT
0	1	1	0.03	3	3
1	1	2	0.03	3	6
2	1	3	0.03	3	10
3	1	4	0.03	3	13
4	2	6	0.07	7	20
5	4	10	0.13	13	33
6	2	12	0.07	7	40
7	3	15	0.10	10	50
8	6	21	0.20	20	70
9	4	25	0.13	13	83
10	3	28	0.10	10	93
11	1	29	0.03	3	96
12	1	30	0.03	3	100*
Total	30		1.00		100

*The cumulative percentage comes to 100 because of rounding off percentages to only two decimal points.

1.d.

NUMBER OF TREATMENT SESSIONS ATTENDED	FREQUENCY	CUMULATIVE FREQUENCY	PROPORTION	PERCENT	CUMULATIVE PERCENT
0–3	4	4	0.13	13	13
4–6	8	12	0.27	27	40
7–9	13	25	0.43	43	83
10–12	5	30	0.17	17	100
Total	30		1.00	100	

2. Advise not to make the claim because percentages can be misleading when based on a small number of cases, such as "doubling" the percentage with just one more case.

Chapter 4

1. a. Marijuana was the most frequently reported main substance abused, Alcohol was the next most frequently reported main substance, followed by cocaine, heroin, and then other substances.

Main substance abused

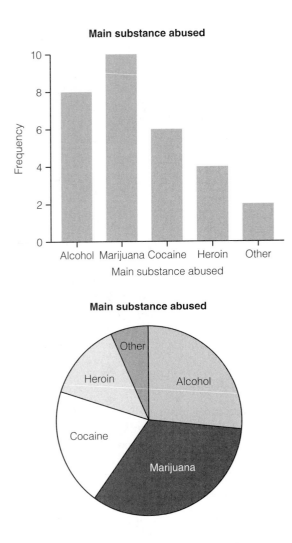

b. Half (15) of the participants were either 14 or 15 years old. Nine were 16 or 17 years old, while six were 12 or 13. There were more 14-year-olds in this sample than any other age. Fifteen-year-olds composed the next most frequent age group. There were fewer 12- and 13-year-olds than members of other age groups.

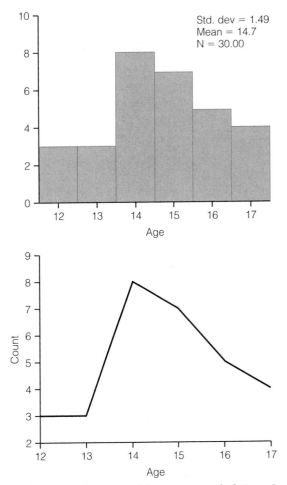

c. Thirteen of the participants attended 7 to 9 sessions, while only one participant did not attend any sessions. Five participants completed 10 to 12 of the sessions. The majority of participants attended at least 7 treatment sessions.

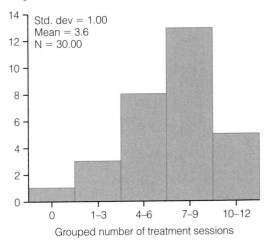

2. a.

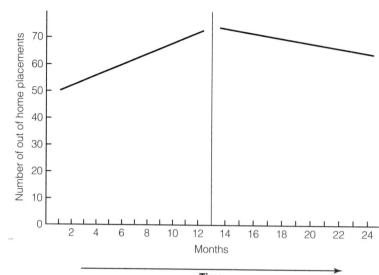

b.

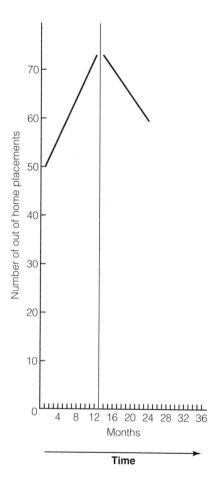

Chapter 5

1. a. Program 1: mean = 6, median = 6, mode = 6; Program 2: mean = 5, median = 5, mode = 0 and 10

2. The mean might be influenced by extreme values. Because the income of some very affluent residents might be inflating the mean, we need to look for outliers and perhaps calculate a trimmed mean. We also should consider the median and the mode.

Chapter 6

1. a. Program 1: range = 7 (or 3 to 9), interquartile range = 5–7, variance = 3.27, standard deviation = 1.8; Program 2: range = 11 (or 0 to 10), interquartile range = 1–9, variance = 21.09, standard deviation = 4.48.

b. Program 2 had more dispersion.

2. Range = 0–9 (or 10), interquartile range = 2–6, variance = 9.64, standard deviation = 3.1

Chapter 7

1. a. Distribution B

b. Distribution C

c. Distribution A

d. **1.** Distribution C

2. Distribution B
3. Distribution A

Chapter 8

1. a. $z = 1.0$, percentile $= 84.13$
   b. $z = 2.0$, percentile $= 97.72$
   c. $z = 3.0$, percentile $= 99.87$
   d. $z = -1.0$, percentile $= 15.87$
   e. $z = -2.0$, percentile $= 2.28$
   f. $z = -3.0$, percentile $= 0.13$
   g. $z = 0.0$, percentile $= 50.00$

2. *Adams: $z = 0.33$, percentile $= 62.93$

   Doe: $z = -1.67$; percentile $= 4.75$

   *Jones: $z = 1.17$, percentile $= 87.90$

   *Smith: $z = 1.83$, percentile $= 96.64$

   Woods: $z = -2.17$, percentile $= 1.50$

   * Families with asterisks are most in need of further intervention. Doe and Woods families are least in need.

3. a. Home A: $+3.0$; Home B: $+2.0$
   b. Home A: 99.87; Home B: 97.72
   c. Home A
   d. A good argument can be made for Home B, because its dependent variable (abuse) might be more important than job satisfaction.

Chapter 9

1. a. Because it doesn't take sampling error into account. You need to calculate a confidence interval and a confidence level for the population instead of equating your sample statistic with the population parameter.
   b. Inferential statistics provide a basis for generalizing to the population and estimating a confidence interval for a population parameter, whereas descriptive statistics only describe the sample, which in this case is only 100 out of 2000.
   c. Standard error of the mean, confidence interval, confidence level

2. 95%: 6.604 to 6.996

   99%: 6.542 to 7.058

There is a 95% probability that the population mean satisfaction level is between 6.604 and 6.996. There is a 99% probability that it is between 6.542 and 7.058.

3. Yes, because the standard error would be reduced by the increase in sample size. Instead of 0.10, it would become 0.05.

4. a. 95%: 0.2373 to 0.3627

      99%: 0.2174 to 0.3826

   b. Disagree because 0.35 is within the 95% confidence interval for the 0.30 sample statistic. Therefore, we cannot be 95% confident that the population mean and sample mean are different.

Chapter 10

1. a. There is no difference in dropout rates among the population of recipients of Intervention A and Intervention B. Or: Any difference in dropout rates among the recipients of Intervention A and Intervention B is due to sampling error.
   b. 0
   c. The case for a one-tailed test is that (a) you have more chance of getting significance in the predicted direction; (b) it is hard to get significance with a small sample; and (c) you have a directional hypothesis.
   d. The case for a two-tailed test is that (a) you can get significant results if the intervention effects are in the opposite of the predicted direction; and (b) it's not as hard to get significance with a large sample.

2. a. Because the possibility of harmful effects seems serious and real, you might opt for a two-tailed test. But the tradeoff is that with such a small sample, it will be hard to get statistical significance.
   b. You might want to report the p-value, instead of just calling it not significant, and alert readers to the implications of the small sample size. Further research with larger samples should evaluate this approach, and in the meantime readers should not interpret the lack of significance of your results as implying that the null hypothesis has been confirmed and that the intervention is ineffective.

c. They do not prove such a thing, especially not at the 0.05 level, since by including both tails, the 0.05 is doubled to 0.10. But perhaps more research with a larger sample will show that the routine approach is more effective.

3. No. It only means that chance is not a plausible explanation. Design flaws are not sampling errors, and one way to get significant findings is by having a biased design.

Chapter 11

The review questions in this chapter involve essays. For some of these questions, reasonable people might disagree about the best answers, and the main issue is how well your answer reflects comprehension of the concepts discussed in this chapter. I suggest you discuss your answers with your instructor.

Chapter 12

1. a. paired-samples t-Test
   b. independent-samples t-Test
   c. paired-samples t-Test
   d. one-sample t-Test
   e. one-sample t-Test

2. Bottom row. Do NOT reject null hypothesis because probability of t value (0.07) is greater than 0.05. In not rejecting the null hypothesis, they risk a Type II error.

3. The t-scores would decrease and the probability of sampling error would increase because with a reduction in sample size, the variance increases. And because the variance is in the denominator of

the t-Test formula, an increase in it decreases the t-score.

4. Disagree because there may be important differences in pretest scores between the groups he is comparing. Just because one group has a significant change in a paired-sample t-Test and another group does not in its (separate) paired-sample t-Test, that does not imply a significant difference *between* the groups. He should have compared change scores.

Chapter 13

1. No, because comparing more than two means separately inflates the probability of a Type I error. A post hoc test is needed to compare the three means.

2. We cannot reject the null hypothesis. The difference in posttest scores appears to be a function of pretest differences, not a function of the effectiveness of the new intervention.

3. There is a slight main effect for treatment condition, a larger main effect for gender, and an interaction effect in which Intervention B appears to be more effective for females only, with no difference in effectiveness for males.

4. MANOVA, because more than one dependent variable is involved. Separate ANOVAs for each dependent variable can be conducted only if the MANOVA produces a statistically significant result. This avoids inflating alpha through multiple separate ANOVAs.

Chapter 14

1. See below:

		TREATMENT GROUP	
PARTICIPATION?		RECEIVED INTERVENTION	DID NOT RECEIVE INTERVENTION
Yes	Count	30	20
	Percent	60%	40%
No	Count	20	30
	Percent	40%	60%
TOTAL	Count	50	50
	Percent	100%	100%

2. Yes, because 60% of those who received the intervention participated, versus only 40% of those who did not receive it.

3. No, because no expected values are less than 10.

4. Chi-square = 4.0

5. One degree of freedom

6. $p < 0.05$; yes, statistically significant at the 0.05 level

7. Goodness-of-fit test

8. Fischer's Exact Test

9. a. Median test
   b. Exclude them from the analysis
   c. Chi-square = 10.0, 1 df, $p < 0.01$ (statistically significant at the 0.01 level)

Chapter 15

1. a. Disagree. The plus or minus sign does not signify strength of relationship, only its direction. Also, the significance level does not signify strength of relationship—only the probability for ruling out sampling error as its explanation.

   b. Disagree. Correlation does not imply causality. Perhaps physical well-being in the first place explains ability to attend and thus the degree of participation in activities.

   c. Disagree. A curvilinear relationship exists, and the two different directions are the reason the linear correlation is zero.

   d. Disagree. The 0.10 correlation is weak. Its statistical significance is a function of the large sample size. Also, correlation does not imply causality.

   e. Disagree in light of the fact that the "outliers" comprise one-fourth of his sample and in light of his biases.

   f. Disagree. Correlation does not imply causality, and the fact that one correlation is higher than another does not necessarily mean it is more important when the two correlations don't involve the same two variables.

2. phi = 0.20. There is a modest degree of correlation, in which the re-arrest rate for the participants is lower than for the non-participants. However,

correlation does not imply causality, and therefore—especially in light of the potential selection bias with the lack of random assignment—the results do not bear upon relative effectiveness.

3. Cramer's $V = 0.32$

4. Spearman's rho and Kendall's tau-b. Use Kendall's tau-b because with only three categories per variable there will likely be many tied ranks.

5. Delete one of the items because the 0.95 correlation suggests that they are measuring the same thing in a redundant fashion.

Chapter 16

1. a. $d = 4.0$

   b. Strong; it is far more than 0.80, the approximate threshold for considering d to be strong.

   c. Despite the strong d, some might reasonably answer "no" because 90% of the youths receiving the motivational intervention attended less than half of the 12 sessions. However, others might reasonably disagree, citing the fact that 10 youths receiving Intervention A completed the treatment program, while none in the control group completed it.

2. a. $d = 1.0$

   b. Strong; it is greater than 0.80, the approximate threshold for considering d to be strong.

   c. Despite the strong d, some might reasonably answer "no" because 70% of the youths receiving the motivational intervention attended less than half of the 12 sessions. However, others might reasonably disagree, citing the fact that 30 youths receiving Intervention A completed the treatment program, while none in the control group completed it.

3. One could reasonably favor Intervention B, because although it had a lower effect size, its d was still strong, and it had three times more youths completing the entire program than did Intervention A.

4. A reasonable answer is "Yes," because of the strong phi and the 80% success rate. Moreover, it makes a difference between a 20% versus an 80% success rate regarding a very important, clinically meaningful dependent variable of major import to society and the youths' well being. However, some could reasonably argue that the clinical significance

is hampered by the questionable value of plausibly biased self-report data and the fact that the study examined only the 12 most successful cases in the experimental group.

5. a. Despite the somewhat weak phi, some might reasonably answer "yes" because re-arrest rate is a very important dependent variable, and the intervention appears to cut that rate in half.

   b. A reasonable case can be made for either one, because although the one in number 4 has a much stronger effect size, it has the plausible limitations mentioned above.

6. a. Power is 0.37 for first study and near 1.0 for second study.

   b. 0.63 for first and near 0.00 for second.

   c. Replicate the first study with a larger sample because it had a high risk of a Type II error and might be shown to have a more meaningful ES, especially in light of its valid measure and the potential bias in the self-report measure of the second study.

Chapter 17

1. $Y' = 1.5 + (0.7)(5) = 5.0$

2. No, because they may have a 3-way shared variance with the dependent variable, as in the overlapping three circles in the bottom part of Figure 17.3.

3. No, because the two partials do not include the shared variance portion, as in the portion of the overlapping three circles in the bottom part of Figure 17.3 between the two 0.25 partials.

4. Combine the two variables into one to avoid having excessive multicollinearity.

5. $Y' = 8$

6. Number of close friends is strongest, because it has the largest β. Next comes degree of parent-child conflict with the second highest β, followed by number of session absences by parents with the weakest β.

7. Hierarchical method so that number of close friends gets entered last in the equation, after the effects of the other variables have been partialed out.

8. Stepwise method, because there is basis to predict order. The stepwise method will reduce the number of predictors to those that are significant and strongest.

Chapter 18

1. Set 1: Not significant with two standard deviation procedure or the X-moving range-three-standard-deviation method. There is potential clinical significance, especially if over a longer period the abuse would diminish further. However, some reasonably might argue that there is no clinical significance yet, especially in light of the absence of statistical significance. They might want to see virtually no verbal abuse in order to consider the improvement clinically significant.

Set 2: Significant with two-standard-deviation procedure, but not with the X-moving range-three-standard-deviation method. The former seems more reasonable in light of the clear visual significance and the fact that 3 standard deviations of improvement would require a negative number of abuses, which is impossible. Unless we require total absence of verbal abuse, results could be deemed clinically significant, though this would be a subjective value judgment that not everyone would agree on.

Set 3: Significant with two-standard-deviation procedure. The first data point is in the three-standard-deviation zone using the X-moving range method. But neither approach seems reasonable in light of the pronounced trend in the intervention data, implying a lack of visual and clinical significance, with the target problem progressively worsening back to the point it was at before intervention began.

2. Set 1: Not significant statistically or clinically.

Set 2: Statistically significant, but some could reasonably argue not clinically significant because of the lack of visual significance (improvement predated the intervention) and the fact that the problem reemerges toward the end of the intervention period.

3. Sets 1 and 2 have the most. In set 1, the scores by and large progressively increase. Knowing that a value appears early in the series would lead to a lower predicted value, and vice versa for values appearing later. In set 2, the consistent alternation of 1 and 8 enable us to predict a 1 or 8 accurately by

knowing whether the previous number was a 1 or an 8. Set 3 has the least. Knowing the preceding number does not enable us to predict accurately what the next number will be or whether it will be relatively high or relatively low.

4. We cannot infer that the intervention is effective due to the absence of visual significance in light of the pronounced improving trend during baseline which continues at essentially the same rate during intervention.

Glossary

abscissa (*x*-axis) The horizontal line in a graph that typically displays the values of a variable.

absolute frequencies Simple counts of the number of cases per category of a variable.

absolute frequency distribution A table that displays the number of cases in each category of a variable.

all-possible-subsets method One method for multiple regression in which all of the independent variables are entered simultaneously. Using this method, your statistical software program considers all possible combinations and orders of variables in the equation and chooses the one that most accurately predicts the dependent variable.

alpha level (rejection level) The cutoff level (usually 0.05) separating statistically significant findings from nonsignificant findings. Also called **rejection level**. (*See also* **critical region** and **level of significance**.)

analysis of covariance (ANCOVA) A multivariate form of analysis of variance that compares the means of several groups after controlling for the effects of one or more covariates. (*See* **covariate**.) For example, it might examine whether there are significant differences among groups on posttest scores when the effects of the pretest scores are controlled.

analysis of variance (ANOVA) A statistical significance test that compares the means among three or more groups by producing a statistic called the *F*-ratio that reflects the variation among the means of several groups in relation to the variation within the groups.

arithmetic mean The sum of all values divided by the number of values being added together.

attributes (value categories) The concepts that make up a variable. The attributes, or value categories, of *gender*, for example, are *male* or *female*.

autocorrelation A situation that occurs when we can predict the value of one data point in single-system design data if we know the value of other data points in the series. Thus, the data point values are not independent of one another, and results may be distorted.

β (beta). *See* **standardized beta**

backward stepwise method One way to enter variables in a multiple regression analysis. All the variables are entered into the equation first, and then the variable with the smallest partial correlation is removed from the batch and the equation is computed again. This identifies the next variable to be eliminated from the equation based on its partial correlation. This process is repeated until the only variables left in the equation are those that add a significant or meaningful amount of explained variation in the dependent variable. *See also* **forward stepwise method**.

bar graph Diagram depicting frequency distributions, using bars to show the number or percentage of cases for each category of a nominal-level variable. For every category along the *x*-axis there is a bar of equal width. There is an equal distance between each bar, and none of the bars touch. The more cases there are in a particular category, the taller the bar for that category. By looking at the numbers along the *y*-axis that (like a ruler) correspond to the top of each bar, we can see the number and/or percentage of cases for each category.

bell curve. *See* **bell-shaped curve**

bell-shaped curve (or bell curve) Another name for a normal curve based on the fact that the normal distribution is curved in the shape of a bell.

beta weight (or β). *See* **standardized beta**

bimodal distribution A distribution containing two modes.

boxplot A graph that provides a pictorial representation of the median, interquartile range, and range in the distribution of a variable. It can also display outliers.

censoring A key concept in event history analysis. It applies to cases for which the dependent variable is unknown for a specified period. For example, suppose we conduct a two-year study of an intervention that attempts to shorten the time lag between the termination of parental rights and adoption finalization. Those children not yet adopted by the end of the two-year period will have been censored because we will not know by the end of the study how long it will take for them to get adopted.

central limit theorem An assumption that as the size of the sample increases, the theoretical sampling distribution based on that sample size will become increasingly normal in shape, and its mean will become increasingly closer to the population mean.

chance (sampling error) Refers to the possibility that random variation (sampling error) can affect co-variation among variables in sample statistics.

chi-square test of statistical significance The most commonly used nonparametric test, which assesses the probability that sampling error explains the relationships we observe between nominal-level variables displayed in cross-tabulation tables.

clinical significance A term that is essentially synonymous with substantive significance, but which is used when evaluating the effectiveness of clinical interventions. Clinical significance refers not only to the meaningfulness and practical value of the overall findings of a study, but to the benefits of an intervention for each individual recipient of the evaluated intervention.

codebook A document that identifies the location of each variable in a data file and the codes that apply to each attribute for each variable.

coding Converting data to a machine-readable format by assigning a code number or a code letter to each category of a variable.

coefficient of determination The square of the correlation coefficient, whose symbol is r^2. It tells us what proportion of variance in the dependent variable is explained by the independent variable.

concepts Mental images that symbolize ideas, objects, events, behaviors, people, and so on. For example, the concepts *gender, level of client satisfaction,* and *number of arrests* all can serve as variables in research studies.

confidence interval An estimated range of values containing a population parameter.

confidence level The estimated probability that a population parameter lies within a given confidence interval.

control group Those clients who do not receive the intervention being evaluated in an experiment.

control variables (mediating variables or **intervening variables)** Variables included in multivariate analyses to see whether and how they shed light on or perhaps even explain away relationships we observe between our independent and dependent variables.

correction for continuity (*Yate's correction***)** A statistical adjustment used in chi-square tests whenever our cross-tabulation table has only two rows and two columns (i.e., is a 2-by-2 table) and has any expected frequencies less than 10. The correction is needed because the regular chi-square formula produces an inflated chi-square value under those conditions.

correlation The degree to which the values of two variables vary together in a consistent fashion.

correlation coefficient A statistic that depicts the strength of a correlation between two variables that are at the ordinal, interval, or ratio level of measurement. Correlation coefficients can range from -1.0 to $+1.0$. The plus or minus sign indicates whether the correlation is positive or negative (inverse). Having a minus sign does not mean that the correlation is weaker than if it had a plus sign. The minus sign means that the variables are negatively (inversely) related: as one goes up, the other goes down.

covariate An interval- or ratio-level variable (such as a pretest score) that is controlled in an analysis of covariance.

Cramer's *V* A nonparametric correlation statistic used when both variables are nominal and at least one has more than two categories.

critical region The area of the theoretical sampling distribution where our sample statistic needs to fall in order to be deemed statistically significant (that is, too unlikely to be attributable to sampling error).

cross-tabulation tables Tables showing whether and how two or more nominal-level variables are related. They display the frequency and/or percentages of the categories of one variable cross-tabulated with the frequencies and/or percentages of another variable or variables.

cumulative frequencies The sums of absolute or relative frequencies. (The absolute and relative frequencies of cases per category add up as we go from one category to the next in tables displaying cumulative frequencies. These tables typically show each absolute and relative frequency alongside and to the left of each cumulative frequency.)

curvilinear correlation (curvilinear relationship) Correlation in which the direction or degree of the relationship changes at different levels of each variable. Such relationships are portrayed by a curved line.

curvilinear relationship. *See* curvilinear correlation

data analysis A late stage in the research process that typically involves clicking on computer prompts to obtain appropriate statistical analyses, followed by a phase involving the interpretation of those analyses.

data file (or data set) A spreadsheet matrix of rows and columns, with each row representing a particular case (such as a particular respondent in a survey) and each column listing the coded data for that case.

data processing Preparing and entering data for computer analysis.

data set. *See* data file

degrees of freedom The term *degrees of freedom* refers to how many values are *free to vary* in a set of values if we know the summary statistic and the number of values in the set. That is, how many values would we need to know in order to deduce the remaining values?

dependent variables Variables postulated as being explained or caused by independent variables.

descriptive statistics Statistics that organize, summarize, and display the data collected in a particular study without trying to develop inferences beyond the sample or trying to rule out sampling error in hypothesis testing.

direct observation A way to operationally define variables by observing actual behavior.

directional hypothesis A hypothesis that predicts which categories of the independent variable will have higher or lower values on the dependent variable.

discriminant function A statistic calculated in a discriminant analysis that uses weighted values of predictor variables to assign a person to one of the qualitative categories of a nominal-level dependent variable.

effect size A statistic used to depict relationship magnitude, often involving a z-score calculation to compare the difference between two means in standard deviation units.

eta A nonparametric correlation coefficient that can be calculated when one or more variables in a hypothesized relationship is at the nominal level of measurement and the dependent variable is metric. Eta is interpreted like other correlation coefficients, and can range from a zero correlation to a perfect correlation of 1.0.

event history analysis (survival analysis) An extension of multiple regression and logistic regression designed to take into account the way variables change over time.

evidence-based practice Using the best scientific evidence available to guide your practice.

evidence-based practitioners   Those who use scientific evidence to guide their own practice and who conduct or participate in evaluations of their own practice or programs.

experimental designs   Designs for evaluating interventions that involve randomly assigning clients to different groups and then providing the intervention to one or more groups whose outcomes will be compared to one or more groups that receive no intervention or a different form of intervention.

experimental group   Those clients who receive the intervention being evaluated in an experiment.

factor analysis   A multivariate statistical procedure to see which clusters of variables (or items in a measurement scale study) correlate more strongly with each other than with other variables (or items).

factors   (1) The multiple nominal independent variables in a two-factor ANOVA, three-factor ANOVA, and so on; or (2) The dimensions identified in a factor analysis.

F-ratio   A statistic calculated using analysis of variance which compares the variation among the means of several groups in relation to the variation within the groups.

Fisher's Exact Test   A variation of chi-square used whenever any cells in a 2-by-2 cross-tabulation table have an expected count of less than 5.

forward stepwise method   One way of entering variables using the stepwise multiple regression method. The independent variable with the strongest *bivariate* correlation with the dependent variable gets entered first. The second variable to be introduced into the equation is the one that has the greatest partial correlation with the dependent variable after partialing out the effects of the first variable. The remaining variables are entered according to how much additional variation they explain in the dependent variable after partialing out the effects of the variables already entered. This process ends when the remaining variables would add only an insignificant or trivial amount of explained variation. *See also* **backward stepwise method.**

frequencies   Numbers of people, cases, observations, or events. Pertains more to head counts in a particular category than to magnitude.

frequency   A count of the number of cases in a particular category of a variable.

frequency distribution   A list of the number or percentage of cases for each category of a variable.

frequency polygon (line graph)   A graph that uses single points instead of bars to convey the *y*-axis amount for each value along the *x*-axis. Straight lines connect adjacent points, forming a shape that depicts the frequency distribution for the *x*-axis variable.

goodness-of-fit test   An application of chi-square used in connection with a single variable when we know in advance the expected frequencies for the categories of that nominal-level variable. We then test the *goodness of fit* between our observed frequencies and the frequencies that we expect in advance. A common use is when we want to compare our sample proportions to proportions known to exist in the broader population.

grouped frequency distribution   A frequency distribution that involves combining some or all of the categories of a variable into a smaller number of meaningful groupings.

hierarchical method   One method for multiple regression used when we hypothesize in advance which variables, or which sets of variables, are more influential than others in predicting the dependent variable.

histogram   A bar graph for metric data with bars that touch each other.

history   An alternative explanation which refers to other events that may coincide with changes in our independent variable and be the real causes of change in our dependent variable.

hypothesis   A tentative statement about a presumed relationship between concepts.

independent-samples t-Test   A *t*-Test used when we want to compare the means of two independent groups. The term *independent* in this context means that the two groups to be compared are not connected or related to each other. A common way to achieve independent groups is to use random numbers or a coin toss to randomly assign cases to one group or the other.

independent variables   Variables that are postulated to explain or cause something.

inferential statistics   Statistics used to assess the probability of sampling error and that go beyond describing sample data in an effort to make inferences about a population.

interaction effect   Refers to whether the association between an independent variable and dependent variable changes for different categories of another independent variable in a two- (or more) factor ANOVA.

internal validity   The extent to which our evaluation design enables us to logically rule out the plausibility of alternative explanations. The more internal validity we have, the more confidence we have that our intervention, and not something else, is the cause of the outcomes we observe.

interquartile range   The range for the middle 50% of values in a rank-ordered distribution.

interval level of measurement   Measuring variables in such a way that differences between different levels have the same meanings. For example, the difference between an IQ score of 95 and 100 is considered to be of the same magnitude as the difference between 100 and 105.

intervening variables.   *See* **control variables**

inverse correlation.   *See* **negative correlation**

Kendall's tau-b   A commonly used nonparametric formula for calculating correlation coefficients with variables that are at the ordinal level of measurement—or with interval- or ratio-level data that are not distributed normally. It produces correlation coefficients ranging from -1.0 to $+1.0$ that have the same meaning as Pearson's *r*. Instead of using the actual variable values in the calculations, we first rank-order the values for each of the two variables being correlated and then plug the ranks into the formula instead of the raw values. This statistic is preferred over Spearman's rho when there are many ties in the rank ordering.

kurtosis The degree to which a curve is relatively peaked or flat. The degree of kurtosis will depend on the size of a curve's standard deviation relative to the size of its mean and its range.

least-squares regression equation. *See* regression equation

leptokurtic Label for a curve that is tall, narrow, and peaked, with scores clustering relatively close to the mean.

level of measurement Variables may be measured in nominal qualitative categories (such as yes/no), ordinal categories (that depict order but not in precise mathematical terms), or in interval or ratio categories that permit more precise mathematical operations.

level of significance The cutoff point that separates the critical region probability from the rest of the area of the theoretical sampling distribution.

linear correlation (linear relationship) Relationship between two variables that can be accurately depicted on a graph with a straight line.

linear relationship. *See* linear correlation

line graph (frequency polygon) A graph that uses single points instead of bars to convey the *y*-axis amount for each value along the *x*-axis. Straight lines connect each adjacent point, forming a shape that depicts the frequency distribution for the *x*-axis variable.

logistic regression A multivariate procedure used when the dependent variable is at the nominal level of measurement and some of the independent variables are also at the nominal level. It will produce an equation that predicts the probability of a given category on the dependent variable in light of the value of each independent variable.

main effect Refers to whether each particular independent variable in a two- (or more) factor ANOVA has a statistically significant *F*-ratio regarding its association with the dependent variable.

maturation (passage of time) An alternative explanation that refers to developmental changes or passage of time being the real source of change in our dependent variable.

mean The sum all of the values for a variable divided by the number of values summed.

measures of central tendency Statistics that use a single number to summarize data at the ordinal, interval, or ratio level of measurement. Measures of central tendency include the mean, median, and mode.

measures of dispersion Statistics, such as the variance and the standard deviation, that indicate how much variability exists in the distribution for a particular variable.

median The middle value in a ranked distribution of values, calculated by seeing which value has an equal number of cases above and below it.

median test An application of the chi-square formula used when we have a nominal-level dichotomous independent variable and a severely skewed dependent variable that is at the ordinal, interval, or ratio level of measurement.

mediating variables. *See* control variables

mesokurtic Type of curve that is approximately bell-shaped and has a kurtosis value near 0.

metric measurements Measures that at the ordinal, interval, or ratio level.

mode The value that appears most frequently in a distribution of values for a particular variable.

multicollinearity A problem in multiple correlation and multiple regression analysis that occurs when two or more independent variables in the analysis are so highly correlated that the analysis gets distorted.

multiple correlation The degree of correlation between a group of independent variables and a dependent variable.

multiple correlation analysis A multivariate procedure used to calculate the degree of correlation between a group of independent variables and a dependent variable, as well as the partial correlation for each independent variable.

multiple *R* The multiple correlation coefficient that is calculated to find the degree to which an entire set of independent variables, as a whole, correlates with a dependent variable. We can refer to the multiple correlation coefficient as Multiple R or just R. We can square R to find the total amount of variation in the dependent variable explained by the entire set of independent variables.

multiple regression analysis A multivariate procedure that employs an equation enabling us to predict the value of a dependent variable based on the values of a set of at least two independent variables.

multivariate analysis of variance (MANOVA) An analysis of variance involving more than one dependent variable.

negative correlation (inverse correlation) A correlation in which variables co-vary in opposite directions: as one goes up, the other goes down.

negatively skewed distribution A distribution with more values above the mean because the mean is lowered by some extremely low values below it.

nominal level of measurement Classifying a variable according to its qualitative categories, not according to different levels. Gender, for example, would be a variable at the nominal level of measurement.

nominal-level variables Variables that vary only in categories that are qualitative in nature (such as gender).

nondirectional hypothesis A predicted relationship that does not specify which attributes on one variable will have higher or lower values on the other variable.

nonparametric tests Tests of statistical significance that do not require all of the same assumptions as parametric tests, most often used when variables are not at the interval or ratio level of measurement.

non-probability sampling A sampling procedure more vulnerable to bias than probability sampling because it does not involve selecting cases randomly.

normal curve The line graph (frequency polygon) curve depicting the normal distribution in the shape of a bell. Thus, it is often referred to as a bell curve.

normal distribution Symmetrical distribution in which the right and left halves of the curve are mirror images of each other. Consequently, the mean, median and mode in a normal distribution are identical and are located at its center.

null hypothesis Hypothesis that there really is *no* relationship between our hypothesized variables in the population. Even if there is some relationship between the variables in our sample, the null hypothesis postulates that our findings can be attributed to sampling error and that the relationship does not really exist in the population or in a theoretical sense.

obtrusiveness A characteristic of measurement that occurs when observations are conducted in such a way that those who are being observed are likely to notice or be affected by the observation.

odds ratio A logistic regression statistic that indicates how much more likely certain independent variable categories are than other categories to have a given category of the dependent variable.

one-sample *t*-Test A *t*-Test that is used when we want to compare a sample statistic to a population statistic.

one-tailed test of significance A significance test that places the entire critical region at the predicted end of the theoretical sampling distribution. There would be no critical region at the other end.

one-way analysis of variance An analysis of variance involving only one independent variable and one dependent variable.

operational definitions Research definitions that specify precisely what observations will determine what attribute or value category applies to a particular variable for a particular research participant. Thus, we might operationally define level of substance abuse in terms of the results of a urinalysis or the number of arrests for substance abuse.

ordinal level of measurement Classifying a variable according to rank-ordering of its categories by degree, such as high, medium, or low.

ordinal-level variables Variables that are measured in terms of rank order, not in terms of precise amount. For example, degree of satisfaction (very satisfied, moderately satisfied, and so on) would be an ordinal-level variable.

ordinate (*y*-axis) The vertical line in a graph that often displays the number (frequency) or percentage of cases for each value of that variable. It might also display different levels of a second variable, thus showing whether changing levels of categories of the *x*-axis variable move in a consistent fashion with changing levels of the *y*-axis variable.

outliers Very extreme values in a distribution of a variable.

paired-samples *t*-Test A *t*-Test used when the two groups of values that we want to compare are connected or related to each other in some way. The most common use of the paired-samples *t*-Test is when we are assessing changes that take place between two points in time within one group.

parameter A summary statistic describing a given variable for an entire population.

parametric tests Tests of statistical significance that assume that at least one variable in the test has an interval or ratio level of measurement, the tested parameters of those variables are distributed normally in the population, and the groups being compared are independent of each other and have been randomly assigned or selected.

partial *r* The partial correlation coefficient that is calculated to find the portion of correlation between two variables that is not shared with other variables.

passage of time. *See* maturation

path analysis A multivariate statistical procedure that extends regression analysis to see if the various beta-weights fit a causal model hypothesized by the researcher. A diagram using circles and arrows is developed to depict the causal order of the variables. The circles represent variables, and the arrows show which variables are presumed to have direct effects and indirect effects on other variables. A more complex form of path analysis is called *structural equation modeling.*

Pearson's product-moment correlation coefficient, also called Pearson's *r* or *r* The most commonly used parametric formula for calculating a correlation coefficient. It can be used when both variables are at the interval or ratio level of measurement and are distributed normally within the population. It can range from the perfect correlation of -1.0 to the perfect correlation of $+1.0$, with zero representing no correlation.

Pearson's *r*. *See* **Pearson's product-moment correlation coefficient**

percentile A value that incorporates a certain percentage of rank-ordered values in a distribution. For example, the 25th percentile would be that value below which the lowest 25% of the values fall.

phi coefficient (*Φ*) A nonparametric correlation statistic used when both variables are nominal and have only two categories (i.e., they are each dichotomous), and thus form a 2-by-2 table.

pie charts Diagrams that portray frequency distribution data in terms of percentages represented by slices of a pie or sections of a circle.

platykurtic Label that signifies relatively flat curves with scores scattered relatively far from the mean.

point of origin The intersection in the lower left corner of a graph where the vertical and horizontal lines (abscissa and ordinate) meet to form a right angle.

population The entire universe of cases to which we seek to generalize from our sample data.

positive correlation A correlation in which both variables move in the same direction. As the values of one increase, the values of the other tend to increase. Likewise, as the values of one decrease, the values of the other tend to decrease.

positively skewed distribution A distribution in which there are a lot more values below the mean because the mean is being inflated by some extremely high values above the mean.

post hoc test An analysis, employed only after the *F*-ratio in an analysis of variance is significant for the overall data across the multiple groups, to find out which particular comparisons of group means are statistically significant. Post hoc tests tell us which pair or pairs of group means differ significantly from each other.

practical significance. *See* **substantive significance**

predictor variables A term often used instead of *independent variables* when discussing multiple regression analysis, because multiple regression analysis is often used to identify which variables in a larger set of variables are the best predictors of another variable instead of to test a specific hypothesis about the set of variables.

probability The likelihood of a particular outcome occurring, which is equal to the number of ways that particular outcome can occur divided by the total number of all possible outcomes.

probability sampling Selecting a sample randomly so that every element in the larger population has an equal chance of being selected.

problem formulation An early phase in the research process when we recognize the need for more knowledge about some issue, pose a research question and then progressively sharpen it, try to resolve potential obstacles to the feasibility of the research, conduct a literature review, and finalize the purpose and conceptual elements of the research.

proportion-frequency procedure A method for analyzing dichotomous single-system design data. Instead of calculating means and standard deviations, we draw a horizontal line to divide the yes zone from the no zone on a graph, and then plot each data point as either a yes or a no.

***p*-value** The probability that a study's findings are attributable to sampling error.

qualitative methods Research methods that put less emphasis on precise and generalizable statistics than on more flexible observational and interview procedures that produce narratives that attempt to probe in a more subjective fashion into deeper, non-numerical underlying meanings and patterns.

quantitative methods Research methods that typically are used when studies aim to develop precise, objective, and generalizable findings. These studies rely on quantitative analysis; that is, they involve numbers and statistics.

quasi-experimental designs Designs for evaluating interventions used when random assignment is not feasible. When we use quasi-experimental designs, we either try to find existing groups that appear to be comparable and then provide the tested intervention to one of the groups, or we use multiple measurements before and after intervention to try to rule out history or the passage of time.

R. *See* **Multiple *R***

r. *See* **Pearson's product-moment correlation coefficient**

random sampling Selecting a sample using random numbers to ensure that your biases, limited knowledge about a population, or errors in judgment cannot influence which elements get selected for inclusion in your study and which do not.

range The simplest measure of dispersion. It is the total number of possible values between the minimum and maximum values in a distribution

ratio level of measurement Measuring variables in such a way that there is a true zero point and differences between different levels have the same mathematical meanings. Number of arrests would be an example of a variable that could be measured at the ratio level.

regression analysis A form of correlation analysis that employs an equation enabling us to predict the value of one variable based on the value of another variable.

regression equation The equation used in regression analysis to predict the value of one variable based on the value of another variable. Also called **least-squares regression equation.**

rejection level. *See* **critical region, level of significance,** and **alpha level**

relative frequencies The proportions or percentages of cases per category of a variable.

reliability Consistency in measurement.

research hypothesis A tentative and testable prediction about how changes in one (independent) variable are proposed to cause or explain changes in another (dependent) variable.

sample That part of the population from which we have data.

sampling error The possibility that random variation (chance) can affect co-variation among variables in sample statistics.

scattergram. *See* **scatterplot**

scatterplot (scattergram) A graphical representation of the degree of correlation between two ordinal-, interval-, or ratio-level variables, which displays the values of one variable (usually the independent variable) on the horizontal axis (the abscissa) and the values of the other variable on the vertical axis (the ordinate).

selection bias A threat to the internal validity of an evaluation of treatment outcome which pertains to possible differences between the clients who receive the interventions we are evaluating and clients to whom we are comparing them—differences that render the two groups of clients incomparable.

self-reports A way to operationally define variables according to what people say about what they do, think, or feel.

single-system design A form of quasi-experimental design that practitioners can use to evaluate their own practice effectiveness by taking multiple measurements before and after intervention to try to rule out the influence of history or the passage of time.

skewed distribution A distribution in which more values fall on one side of the mean than on the other side of the mean. This imbalance creates a difference between the mean and the median.

Spearman's rho   A commonly used nonparametric formula for calculating correlation coefficients with variables that are at the ordinal level of measurement, or with interval- or ratio-level data that are not distributed normally. It produces a correlation coefficient ranging from -1.0 to $+1.0$ that has the same meaning as Pearson's r. Instead of using the actual variable values in the calculations, we first rank-order the values for each of the two variables being correlated and then plug the ranks into the formula instead of the raw values.

standard deviation   The most commonly cited measure of dispersion that refers to how far the scores in a distribution are deviating from the mean on average. It is the square root of the variance.

standard error.   *See* standard error of the mean

standard error of the mean   The standard deviation of the theoretical sampling distribution, which represents the sampling error involved in estimating the true population mean based on an infinite number of random selections of sample means. The standard error of the mean is usually referred to more simply as the **standard error**. The larger the sample size, the lower the standard deviation of the theoretical sampling distribution (and thus the lower the standard error).

standardized beta (beta weight or β)   A statistic used in multiple regression analysis to depict the relative degree of influence a variable has in explaining the variation in the dependent variable when other variables are controlled. The larger the β, the greater the influence.

statistic   A summary description of a variable in a sample.

statistical power analysis   Assessing the probability of committing a Type II error. The statistical power of a study is its probability of correctly rejecting a null hypothesis that is false and thus avoiding a Type II error. Conversely, the probability of committing a Type II error is 1 minus statistical power.

statistically significant   Description of a finding that allows us to rule out sampling error as a plausible explanation for that finding.

statistical significance   What we have when the probability that the null hypothesis is true is low enough to reject the null hypothesis as a plausible explanation for the relationship observed in a sample.

stepwise method   One method for multiple regression used when we have a large number of possible independent variables that we want to explore, and we want our software to find a smaller set of these variables to use in predicting the dependent variable, eliminating other variables that add only an insignificant or trivial amount of explained variation in the dependent variable beyond the smaller set.

structural equation modeling.   *See* path analysis

substantive significance   The practical value or importance of a relationship—that is, how meaningful it is to clients, significant others, society, or practitioners concerned about a problem.

survival analysis.   *See* Event history analysis

symmetrical   A characteristic of normal distributions, with the right and left halves of the curve being mirror images of each other.

tail   The part of the distribution curve containing the smaller number of extreme values.

theoretical sampling distribution   A normal distribution (depicted in a normal curve) of all possible sample statistics produced by an infinite number of randomly drawn samples from a population. It identifies the probability of obtaining a particular outcome in a sample merely as a result of chance.

three-standard-deviation band approach.   *See* **X-Moving Range-Chart**

triangulation   Using more than one measurement approach and seeing if they obtain similar results.

trimmed mean   A mean that is calculated after trimming off outliers at both the high and low ends of the distribution when those outliers comprise a very small percentage of the distribution (usually 5% or less).

t-Test   A significance test that can be used with an interval- or ratio-level dependent variable and a dichotomous nominal-level independent variable that has only two categories. The most common use of the *t*-Test in evaluating programs and practice is to compare the mean outcome scores of groups assigned to two different treatment conditions.

two-factor ANOVA   An analysis of variance involving two nominal-level independent variables.

two-standard-deviation procedure   A simple approach that practitioners can use to approximate statistical significance (as an alternative to the *t*-Test) for outcome data at the interval or ratio level of measurement. This procedure involves calculating an effect size, using the standard deviation of the baseline data as the denominator. If the effect size is at least 2.0, then the difference between the two means (in the numerator) can be deemed statistically significant.

two-tailed test of significance   A significance test that divides the critical region at both ends of the theoretical sampling distribution.

Type I error   An error that occurs whenever we reject a true null hypothesis. We risk it when we have statistically significant results and therefore reject the null hypothesis. In other words, if our hypothesized relationship does not really exist in a general or theoretical sense, and only appears in our sample data due to sampling error, then the null hypothesis is true. If that is the case, yet a sampling fluke produces a statistically significant result that leads us to reject the null hypothesis, then we are committing a Type I error.

Type II error   An error that occurs when we fail to reject a *false* null hypothesis. Whenever we opt *not* to reject the null hypothesis, we risk making a Type II error.

unobtrusiveness   A characteristic of measurement that occurs when observations are conducted in such a way that those who are being observed are unlikely to notice or be affected by the observation.

validity   Whether a measure truly and accurately measures what it intends to measure.

value categories.   *See* attributes

variables   Concepts that are expected to vary in a research study.

variability The amount of dispersion in the distribution of a particular variable.

variance A measure of dispersion that is the average of the squared deviations from the mean.

variation The extent to which the values in a distribution are clustered near each other or are scattered away from each other.

***x*-axis (abscissa)** The horizontal line in a graph that typically displays the values of a variable.

X-Moving Range-Chart (X-mR-chart or three-standard-deviation band) An alternative to the two-standard-deviation procedure for analyzing single-system design data that calculates the baseline standard deviation in a way that attempts to smooth out unstable, fluctuating baseline patterns. This moving range approach for calculating the standard deviation, combined with the more stringent significance level, is less vulnerable to the problem of autocorrelation. In addition to determining change *between* phases, it also can detect whether a data point *within* any phase is significantly different from other data points within the same phase.

X-mR-chart. *See* X-Moving Range-Chart

***y*-axis (ordinate)** The vertical line in a graph that often displays the number (frequency) or percentage of cases for each value of that variable.   It might also display different levels of a second variable, thus showing whether changing levels of categories of the *x*-axis variable move in a consistent fashion with changing levels of the *y*-axis variable.

Yate's correction. *See* correction for continuity

***z*-score** A statistic that is used to represent how many standard deviation intervals a value falls above or below the mean.

References

Albright, S. C., Winston, W. L., & Zappe, C. (1999). *Data analysis and decision-making with Microsoft Excel*. Pacific Grove, CA: Duxbury Press.

Allison, P. D. (1984) *Event history analysis: Regression for longitudinal data*. Newbury Park, CA:Sage Publications.

Bloom, M., Fischer, J., & Orme, J. G. (2003). *Evaluating practice: Guidelines for the accountable professional* (4th ed.). Boston: Allyn & Bacon.

Brannen, S. E., & Rubin, A. (1996). Comparing the effectiveness of gender-specific and couples groups in a court-mandated spouse abuse treatment program. *Research on Social Work Practice, 6*, 405–424.

Brewer, J. K. (1978). *Everything you always wanted to know about statistics, but didn't know how to ask*. Dubuque, IA: Kendall/Hunt.

Brightman, H. (1999). *Data analysis in plain English with Microsoft Excel*. Pacific Grove, CA: Duxbury Press.

Cherry, A. L., Jr. (2003). Ex*amining global social welfare issues: Using MicroCase*. Pacific Grove, CA: Brooks/Cole–Thomson Learning.

Cohen, J. 1988. *Statistical power analysis for the behavioral sciences* (2nd ed.). New York: Lawrence Erlbaum Associates.

Festinger, T., & Pratt, R. (2002). Speeding adoptions: An evaluation of the effects of judicial continuity. *Social Work Research, 26*(4), 217–224.

Gravetter, F. J., & Wallnau, L. B. (2000). *Statistics for the behavioral sciences*. Belmont, CA: Wadsworth/Thomson Learning.

Greenwald, R., & Rubin, A. (1999). Assessment of posttraumatic symptoms in children: Development and preliminary validation of parent and child scales. *Research on Social Work Practice, 9*(1), 61–75.

Gustavsson, N. S., & MacEachron, A. E. (2001). Perspectives on research-related anxiety among BSW students: An exploratory study. *Journal of Baccalaureate Social Work, 7*(1), 111–119.

Hair, J. F., Jr., Anderson, R. E., Tatham, R. L., & Black, W. C. (1998). *Multivariate data analysis* (5th ed.). Upper Saddle River, NJ: Prentice Hall.

Heiman, G. W. (2000). *Basic statistics for the behavioral sciences*. Boston: Houghton Mifflin.

Hodge, D. R., Cardenas, P., & Montoya, H. (2001). Substance use: Spirituality and religious participation as protective factors among rural youths. *Social Work Research, 25*(3), 153–161.

Irwin, R. M. S. (1995). The identification and treatment of math anxiety among first-year social work graduate students. *Dissertation Abstracts International, A: The Humanities and Social Sciences, 56*(3), 1126-A.

Jacobson, N. S., Follette, W. C., & Revenstorf, D. (1984). Psychotherapy outcome research: Methods for reporting variability and evaluating clinical significance. *Behavior Therapy, 15*, 336–352.

Kachigan, S. K. (1991). *Multivariate statistical analysis: A conceptual introduction* (2nd ed.). New York: Radius Press.

Kirk, R. S., & Griffith, D. P. (2004). Intensive family preservation services: Demonstrating placement prevention using event history analysis. *Social Work Research, 28*(1), 5–15.

Kline, R. B. (1998). *Principles and practice of structural equation modeling*. New York: Guilford Press.

Malgady, R. G., & Colon-Malgady, G. (1991). Comparing the reliability of difference scores and residuals in analysis of covariance. *Educational & Psychological Measurement, 51*(4), 803–807.

Mertler, C. A., & Vannatta, R. A. (2005). *Advanced and multivariate statistical methods: Practical application and interpretation* (3rd ed.). Glendale, CA: Pyrczak Publishing.

NASW (National Association of Social Workers, Inc.). (1999). NASW Code of Ethics.

Ogles, B. M., Lunnen, K. M., and Bonesteel, K. (2001). Clinical significance: History, application, and current practice. *Clinical Psychology Review, 21*(3), 421–446.

Royse, D. (2000). Teaching research online: A process evaluation. *Journal of Teaching in Social Work, 20*(1–2), 145–158.

Rubin, A., & Babbie, E. (2005). *Research methods for social work*. Belmont, CA: Brooks/Cole.

Siegel, S. (1956). *Nonparametric statistics for the behavioral sciences*. New York: McGraw-Hill.

Stevens, J. (2002). *Applied multivariate statistics for the social sciences* (4th ed.). Hillsdale, NJ: Lawrence Erlbaum Associates.

Index

TO THE OWNER OF THIS BOOK:

I hope that you have found *Essential Research Methods for Social Work* useful. So that this book can be improved in a future edition, would you take the time to complete this sheet and return it? Thank you.

School and address:_____

Department:_____

Instructor's name:_____

1. What I like most about this book is:_____

_____

_____

2. What I like least about this book is:

_____

_____

3. My general reaction to this book is:

_____

_____

4. The name of the course in which I used this book is:

_____

5. Were all of the chapters of the book assigned for you to read?_____

   If not, which ones weren't?_____

6. In the space below, or on a separate sheet of paper, please write specific suggestions for improving this book and anything else you'd care to share about your experience in using this book.

_____

_____

_____

_____

FOLD HERE

THOMSON

BROOKS/COLE

BUSINESS REPLY MAIL
FIRST-CLASS MAIL   PERMIT NO. 102   MONTEREY CA

POSTAGE WILL BE PAID BY ADDRESSEE

Attn: *Lisa Gebo, Social Work Editor*

BrooksCole/Thomson Learning
60 Garden Ct Ste 205
Monterey CA 93940-9967

FOLD HERE

OPTIONAL:

Your name:_____ Date: ___

May we quote you, either in promotion for *Essential Research Meth*
or in future publishing ventures?

Yes: _____ No: _____

Sincerely yours,

Allen Rubin and Earl Babbie